The Poetics of Spiritual Instruction

Edinburgh Studies in Classical Islamic History and Culture
Series Editor: Carole Hillenbrand

A particular feature of medieval Islamic civilisation was its wide horizons. The Muslims fell heir not only to the Graeco-Roman world of the Mediterranean, but also to that of the ancient Near East, to the empires of Assyria, Babylon and the Persians; and beyond that, they were in frequent contact with India and China to the east and with black Africa to the south. This intellectual openness can be sensed in many inter-related fields of Muslim thought, and it impacted powerfully on trade and on the networks that made it possible. Books in this series reflect this openness and cover a wide range of topics, periods and geographical areas.

Titles in the series include:

The Body in Arabic Love Poetry: The 'Udhri Tradition
Jokha Alharthi

Arabian Drugs in Early Medieval Mediterranean Medicine
Zohar Amar and Efraim Lev

Towards a History of Libraries in Yemen
Hassan Ansari and Sabine Schmidtke

The Abbasid Caliphate of Cairo, 1261–1517: Out of the Shadows
Mustafa Banister

The Medieval Western Maghrib: Cities, Patronage and Power
Amira K. Bennison

Christian Monastic Life in Early Islam
Bradley Bowman

Keeping the Peace in Premodern Islam: Diplomacy under the Mamluk Sultanate, 1250–1517
Malika Dekkiche

Queens, Concubines and Eunuchs in Medieval Islam
Taef El-Azhari

Islamic Political Thought in the Mamluk Period
Mohamad El Merheb

The Kharijites in Early Islamic Historical Tradition: Heroes and Villains
Hannah-Lena Hagemann

Classical Islam: Collected Essays
Carole Hillenbrand

Islam and the Crusades: Collected Essays
Carole Hillenbrand

The Medieval Turks: Collected Essays
Carole Hillenbrand

Medieval Damascus: Plurality and Diversity in an Arabic Library – The Ashrafiya Library Catalogue
Konrad Hirschler

A Monument to Medieval Syrian Book Culture: The Library of Ibn 'Abd al-Hādī
Konrad Hirschler

The Popularisation of Sufism in Ayyubid and Mamluk Egypt: State and Society, 1173–1325
Nathan Hofer

Defining Anthropomorphism: The Challenge of Islamic Traditionalism
Livnat Holtzman

Making Mongol History: Rashid al-Din and the Jami' al-Tawarikh
Stefan Kamola

Lyrics of Life: Sa'di on Love, Cosmopolitanism and Care of the Self
Fatemeh Keshavarz

Art, Allegory and the Rise of Shiism in Iran, 1487–1565
Chad Kia

The Administration of Justice in Medieval Egypt: From the 7th to the 12th Century
Yaacov Lev

Zoroastrians in Early Islamic History: Accommodation and Memory
Andrew D. Magnusson

A History of Herat: From Chingiz Khan to Tamerlane
Shivan Mahendrarajah

The Queen of Sheba's Gift: A History of the True Balsam of Matarea
Marcus Milwright

Ruling from a Red Canopy: Political Authority in the Medieval Islamic World – From Anatolia to South Asia
Colin P. Mitchell

Islam, Christianity and the Realms of the Miraculous: A Comparative Exploration
Ian Richard Netton

The Poetics of Spiritual Instruction: Farid al-Din 'Attar and Persian Sufi Didacticism
Austin O'Malley

Sacred Place and Sacred Time in the Medieval Islamic Middle East: An Historical Perspective
Daniella Talmon-Heller

Conquered Populations in Early Islam: Non-Arabs, Slaves and the Sons of Slave Mothers
Elizabeth Urban

Owning Books and Preserving Documents in Medieval Jerusalem: The Library of Burhan al-Din
Said Aljoumani and Konrad Hirschler

edinburghuniversitypress.com/series/escihc

The Poetics of Spiritual Instruction

Farid al-Din ʿAttar and Persian Sufi Didacticism

Austin O'Malley

EDINBURGH
University Press

Edinburgh University Press is one of the leading university presses in the UK. We publish academic books and journals in our selected subject areas across the humanities and social sciences, combining cutting-edge scholarship with high editorial and production values to produce academic works of lasting importance. For more information visit our website: edinburghuniversitypress.com

Edinburgh University Press Ltd
The Tun – Holyrood Road
12 (2f) Jackson's Entry
Edinburgh EH8 8PJ

Typeset in 11/15pt EB Garamond by
Cheshire Typesetting Ltd, Cuddington, Cheshire, and
printed and bound in Great Britain

A CIP record for this book is available from the British Library

ISBN 978 1 4744 7511 2 (hardback)
ISBN 978 1 4744 7514 3 (webready PDF)
ISBN 978 1 4744 7513 6 (epub)

Contents

Acknowledgements

This book is the result of nearly a decade of work, from its origins as a dissertation at the University of Chicago through several substantial revisions that led to its current form. A project of this magnitude never belongs just to its ostensible author, and this monograph bears the marks of dozens of friends, former classmates, colleagues, students, teachers and mentors whose intellectual camaraderie I have been privileged to enjoy, especially in these difficult years of the COVID-19 pandemic. Whatever strengths this monograph can claim would not have been possible without their keen insight, criticism and logistical and emotional support. Wherever the book falls short, the error is my own. I offer my deepest gratitude to all of them, and for those whom I have inadvertently omitted, I beg your pardon: Rodrgio Adem, Sabahat Adil, Mahmoud Azaz, Orit Bashkin, Theodore Beers, Anne Betteridge, Kevin Blankenship, Francesca Chubb-Confer, Madeleine Elfenbein, Julie Ellison-Speight, Benjamin Fortna, Carlos Grenier, Ghenwa Hayek, Edmund Hayes, Samuel Hodgkin, Sajedeh Hosseini, Thibaut d'Hubert, Domenico Ingenito, Gianni Izzo, Ahmet Karamustafa, Fatemeh Keshavarz, Paul Losensky, Scott Lucas, Christopher Markiewicz, Louise Marlow, the late Heshmat Moayyad, Nathan Miller, Narges Nematollahi, Alidost Numan, Laurie Pierce, Julia Rubanovich, Myriam Sabbaghi, Rachel Schine, Michael Sells, Fatemeh Shams, Sunil Sharma, Elizabeth Stahmer, Kamran Talattof, Hayedeh Torabi, Saeed Yousef, Alexandra Zirkle.

Special thanks are due to Franklin Lewis, a paragon of both careful scholarship and kind mentorship, who has continued to provide invaluable guidance and support long after his role as chair of my dissertation committee has ended. A number of colleagues have read chapters of this work with a careful eye, including Jane Mikkelson, Nora Jacobsen Ben Hammed, Alexander Jabbari and Yaseen Noorani, and their comments and critiques have been entirely to its benefit. The full manuscript was read in its entirety by Cameron Cross, Alexandra Hoffmann, Michael Pifer and Matthew Miller, who reviewed chapter drafts in development as well. Without them, this work would not exist. This project also received institutional support from the Social and Behavioral Sciences Research Institute at the University of Arizona, and the Provost's Author Support Fund. A section of Chapter 7 is based on a prior publication in *Iranian Studies*, the content of which is used here with the journal's permission.

Finally, I must express my deep debt to my family, including my mother, Linda O'Malley, who has modelled intellectual curiosity and commitment as long as I have known, and especially my beloved partner, Nazafarin Lotfi. I could not have navigated this path without your sound advice, loving care and stimulating intellectual companionship over the past ten years, not only as it pertains to this book, but life in its totality. Nazafarin, thank you for everything.

Note on Transliteration and Style

For the sake of simplicity and accessibility, and in accordance with the series guidelines, transliterations of Persian and Arabic words do not include diacritics. Those who are familiar with Persian or Arabic should still be able to reconstruct names and terms in the original script with little difficulty. Consonants and vowels in Persian names and words are transliterated according to a modified *Encyclopaedia Iranica* system. Arabic titles of Persian works are transliterated as if they were Persian. Transliterations from Arabic texts and the names of individuals who composed primarily in Arabic are based on a modified IJMES system. There are many borderline cases in which it is not immediately obvious if a term or phrase would be more appropriately transliterated according to the Arabic or Persian system. In such cases, I have tended to default to a Persian-style transliteration. Also in accordance with a more Persian style, I have generally omitted the definite article 'al-' when using a *nesba* adjective as a standalone name (i.e. Ghazali, not al-Ghazali), unless I am closely translating from an Arabic text.

Throughout this book, I have chosen to keep 'sufi' lowercased as both a noun and an adjective. Capitalising the term can erroneously imply that sufism is a distinct 'sect' or 'identity', whereas in 'Attar's time it was something much broader: a variegated current of thought and practice that overlapped with other social and intellectual commitments and admitted of various degrees of participation. Also, whenever possible, I have used 'they' and 'theirs' as singular, gender-neutral pronouns rather than defaulting to the male 'he'.

For Franklin Lewis, my *pir* on this way. His final illness prevented him from seeing these pages in their published form, but they bear everywhere the marks of his gentle pedagogy. To acknowledge his influence brings not anxiety, but pride in having been his student, gratitude for his teachings and sadness that he was taken too soon.

Introduction: A Guide for Everyone

My utterances suffice as your leader
for this speech is a spiritual guide (*pir*) on the path for everyone.[1]

So boasts Farid al-Din ʿAttar (d. c. 1221) in the concluding section of his most famous poem, the *Manteq al-tayr* (*Conference of the Birds*). Boasts and self-encomium were expected, conventional elements of the Persian literary tradition, and poets of all stripes would routinely extol the quality of their verses and the unmatched strength of their talent. What makes this particular boast so interesting, however, is that it is articulated in terms that point not only to ʿAttar's skill as an author or the beauty of his compositions, but also to the work's function vis-à-vis its readers. The *Conference of the Birds*, a long didactic poem infused with mystical themes, is here likened to the spiritual guide who shepherds novices along the sufi path. In ʿAttar's time, sufi instruction was increasingly delivered by 'training masters' who would not only teach and lecture but also intimately manage the lives of their followers, prescribing spiritual exercises for the purification of the soul.[2] By personifying the poem as a guide, ʿAttar imparts agency to his text and a ritualistic quality to the textual encounter: through the act of reading, he seems to suggest, the audience is trained, transformed and elevated towards God. And unlike sufi discipleship, which was limited to those who could commit themselves completely to spiritual training for a period of years or even a lifetime, the *Conference of the Birds* is imagined as a 'guide on the path for everyone'. To be sure, this hyperbolic boast should not be taken literally. The guide was a central figure in sufi praxis, and it does not seem likely that ʿAttar was seriously suggesting texts could take the place of personal oral guidance. Nevertheless, this boast would not have been a felicitous form of self-praise if it did not resonate with broader attitudes towards verse, and it shows, at the very least, that it was possible to metaphorically think the work of poetry in such terms.

The *Conference of the Birds* is an example of a 'didactic *masnavi*', one of several explicitly instructive genres in the Persian literary tradition. Most, if not all, poems can be read as providing some form of instruction, but didactic *masnavi*s can be considered didactic in a narrower sense: they are characterised by an explicitly pedagogical stance, frequent direct address and the predominance of the hortatory and imperative moods. Like most didactic *masnavi*s, the *Conference of the Birds* is quite long, coming to nearly 5,000 verses. It contains discourses on a wide range of religious topics studded with illustrative exempla, and it is thereby endowed with an almost encyclopedic quality. As the above-quoted line makes clear, however, readers do not simply extract information from the *Conference of the Birds*. Rather, the text works on them as they work on themselves, and this activity can be metaphorically conceptualised in terms of the non-literary institution of spiritual discipleship. Like a spiritual guide, the text pushes readers in ways that they might not find comfortable or even understand but are ultimately for their own benefit. To consume the *Conference of the Birds*, to accept 'Attar's speech as one's 'spiritual guide on the path', is to submit oneself to its teaching activity and embark on a symbolic act of spiritual wayfaring under its direction.

Since at least the ninth century, sufis had composed occasional verses for sermons and *sama'* ceremonies – especially in the folk quatrain form – and appropriated lines from other poets for use in those settings. These early sufi verses circulated orally and their alleged authorship is often open to question: in most cases, they were not set down in anthologies or hagiographies until a century or more after their putative composition.[3] In the twelfth century, however, more established poets began to expound on sufi themes in the prestige courtly forms of the *qasida*, *masanvi* and *ghazal* (the latter of which was still in the process of crystallisation), and this more extensive poetry was collected into textual *divan*s soon after its authors' deaths or even during their lifetimes. The first 'professional' court poet to experiment with sufi themes in a sustained manner was Sana'i (d. c. 1130), who produced several *masnavi*s and a *divan* of lyric poetry; the latter contains a number of poems that treat religious and sufi themes alongside more conventional specimens of courtly poetry. 'Attar, building on Sana'i's legacy, represents an even more definitive merging of sufi discourse and the Persian literary tradition. Although he does not seem to have composed for a patron, he produced an extensive textual oeuvre that includes a *divan*, an independent collection of quatrains, a prose hagiography and four long didactic *masnavi*s, all of which share a consistently mystical outlook.[4] He is thus a crucial figure in the emergence of an explicitly sufi verse in the early thirteenth century, a moment when, not coincidentally, sufism was well on its way to becoming the dominant mode of piety in Persian-speaking lands and penetrating all levels of society.

Given their encyclopedic nature, accessible language and wide circulation, didactic *masnavi*s like ʿAttar's are an excellent source for understanding the kinds of ideas that comprised this emerging sufi spiritual vernacular. To give but one example, the classic work of ʿAttar studies, Hellmut Ritter's *Ocean of the Soul*, mines the illustrative narratives of the *masnavi*s for their ideational content and thereby seeks to illuminate ʿAttar's particular engagement with the 'world of ideas' of thirteenth-century sufism.[5] A number of other scholars have followed suit, examining the specific theological, metaphysical and ethical positions encoded in his texts from a variety of disciplinary perspectives.[6] Others have focused more on his texts' poetic features including their use of allegory, their common tropes and themes, or their form and structure.[7] But a poem, no matter how eloquent or instructive, is only meaningful when encountered by readers or listeners. Its 'teachings' cannot be so easily separated from its 'teaching activity', and it is the latter that ʿAttar highlights in his boastful characterisation of his text as a spiritual guide. While the teachings of his poems have often been examined, the participatory, rhetorical relationships that they construct with their audiences are frequently taken for granted, as are the ways in which their specific formal features invite readers to consume, respond to and be transformed by the text.[8]

Part of this is due to methodological difficulties: given the nature of our sources, it is difficult to reconstruct exactly how readers consumed, interacted with and responded to poetic texts in the premodern period. Some clues can be found in hagiographies and biographical anthologies, whose anecdotes sometimes contain accounts of reading in literary assemblies or sufi lodges (*khanaqah*s). Such accounts, however, are usually highly stylised and historically suspect, and often tied to very specific contexts. Miscellanies, response poems and other kinds of literary adaptations represent a form of reception and creative reinterpretation, as do marginalia and manuscript production, but they do not really help us understand the psycho-spiritual effects of didacticism or how reading might have functioned as a spiritual practice. Systematic works of poetics and literary theory in Persian and Arabic are not particularly helpful, either. Although the tradition of Perso-Arabic poetics does discuss the power of poetry to emotionally impact readers and even rouse them to action, it focuses primarily on panegyre and love poetry, and single lines are generally the largest unit of analysis.[9] Mystical and didactic poetry, despite its prevalence, was not systematically theorised, and neither was narrative, which was a major component of the didactic mode's instructive work (especially in the genre of the didactic *masnavi*).[10]

Much can be learned, however, by turning to the poems themselves. All poetry depends on its recipients to make meaning, but they are acknowledged in instructional poetry in a much more direct and explicit way than in other poetic modes. Even lyric poetry – which, in John Stuart Mill's famous formulation, is not '*heard*' but '*over*heard' – is uttered for some kind of imagined listener, as Julie Scott Meisami has shown in the case of Hafez (d. c. 1390).[11] In the case of the didactic *masnavi*, with its overtly instructive aims, that imagined listener is only more apparent as the explicit target of the poem's didactic intervention. The poem calls forth an asymmetrical, pedagogical relationship – a sufi guide addressing his disciples, a preacher on the pulpit or a father lecturing his sons – in which the speaker prods his addressee to spiritual action. Vocatives, imperatives and interrogatives are common, as are seemingly pejorative dismissals: 'O you clump of dirt,' writes 'Attar in a characteristic verse, disparaging his addressee, 'Doesn't the desire grip you / that this clump of dirt of yours would become pure soul?'[12] Such lines sound almost exasperated; they are uttered by an authoritative speaker in an attempt to break the recipients' delusions by reminding them of what should be obvious: their bodily materiality and the mortality it implies. The tone is accusatory, but at the same time it offers hope of reform. With proper attention, the dirt of the body can be transformed into pure immortal soul, a transformation that the poem itself seeks to induce through pedagogical action.

This pedagogical relationship between speaker and addressee lies at the heart of didactic poetry, and much of the mode's interest lies in the many variations that this fundamental structure admits. The addressee, of course, is a fiction: it is a function of the text and does not represent any actual reader's experience. In the work of 'Attar and many other didactic poets, however, it does point to a subject position from which readers are invited to consume the poem, even if they will never inhabit it fully. In this sense, 'Attar's addressee comes to represent something like the 'implied reader' as discussed by reader-response theorists such as Wolfgang Iser: it encodes a set of attitudes and presumed reactions to his narratorial persona's speech that the audience is invited to share.[13] Through the imagined social relationship of addressee and speaker, readers are called to adopt the receptive-yet-restive stance of a wayward student who is subjected to repeated pedagogical speech acts calibrated to incite spiritual reform. In this sense, 'Attar's 'implied reader' is by no means an 'ideal' one, at least in terms of their spiritual understanding: they have fallen short religiously and ethically, and his didactic utterances are necessary to rouse them from their ignorance. It is precisely because they have failed to grasp the depth of 'Attar's message that they ought to keep reading.

In addition to guiding reception through the addressee, 'Attar imagines how readers will respond to his works through meta-poetic reflections on his craft, as in the epigraph from the *Conference of Birds* quoted above.[14] He emphasises his poetry's beauty and the freshness of his metaphors, all conventional topics of poetic boasting, but he also draws attention to his verses' power to spiritually transform his audiences. Poetry – and speech more generally – is sometimes likened to medicine in the Persian literary tradition, and 'Attar elaborates on this convention with relish and explicitly ties it to his pen name, 'the pharmacist'. He portrays his poetry as a kind of therapeutic drug; it not only signifies, but heals, elevating its recipients from a state of spiritual sickness to health. He frequently casts the readers' literary encounter with his speech as a performative, ritual activity. His quatrains are thus offered as material for contemplation (*ta'ammol*); his prose hagiography, the *Tazkera*, is a set of daily readings to maintain a sound spiritual state; and a literary encounter with the *Mosibat-nama* is likened to the regimented performance of a forty-day ritual retreat (*chella*). These metaphors are applied to different genres of writing in 'Attar's oeuvre, and they each imply different reading practices and modes of engagement, but they all draw attention to the textual encounter as a participatory, transformative activity by extending sufi ritual practices, with their promise of transformation and purification, into the literary realm. Such meta-poetic metaphors are not objective descriptions of literary practices, of course, but rhetorical strategies meant to guide readers' reactions. They are indicators of how 'Attar hoped his texts would be received, and rhetorical attempts to make it so.

'Attar also reflects on his didactic project in a more indirect fashion through his innovative frame-tale structures. In three of his four *masnavi*s, the homilies and anecdotes common to the genre are not uttered directly by his narratorial persona but are attributed to fictional characters in overarching frame-tales, much like those found in the *Canterbury Tales*, the *Decameron* and *One Thousand and One Nights*. In 'Attar's case, however, these frame-tales encode explicitly didactic speech situations. In the *Conference of the Birds*, a hoopoe, the leader of the birds, exhorts his flock in the manner of a popular preacher, urging them to make the journey towards their king, the Simorgh; in the *Mosibat-nama*, a spiritual guide instructs his disciple and interprets his visionary experiences; and in the *Elahi-nama*, a king discourses with his six sons and steers them towards the spiritual analogues of their earthly desires. These frame narratives embody, in more concrete forms, the speakers and addressees that are only implied in other forms of didactic poetry. The addressee is no longer the implicit, silent target of didactic speech, but a full-fledged fictional character: their responses to their teacher's instruction are now explicitly narrated, as are the results of the latter's teachings. The poet is thus able to perform didactic speech while narratively demonstrating its persuasive power and transformative work: the didactic becomes meta-didactic. Through the stories of the birds in the *Conference of the Birds*, the disciple in the *Mosibat-nama* and the king's sons in the *Elahi-nama*, 'Attar imagines an idealised, fictional reception for his own homiletic utterances.

In these ways, *The Poetics of Spiritual Instruction* explores how 'Attar's *masnavi*s frame their relationship with their audiences, imagine the latter's reactions and engagement with text and idealise their own transformative force; it thereby illuminates the religious function of sufi didactic poetry beyond its ideational content. More specifically, it argues that 'Attar's *masnavi*s attempt to adapt oral pedagogical relationships (e.g. that of master and disciple or preacher and listener) and sufi ritual practices (e.g. the ritual retreat, practices of contemplation) into a textual, literary form, such that the textual encounter becomes a form of spiritual exercise aimed at the purification of the soul. The book seeks to recover the performativity of ʿAttar's didacticism, both in the sense of the text's instructive action on its (imagined) readers, and those (imagined) readers' active use of the text as an intentional activity of spiritual self-shaping.[15] Although its focus remains squarely on ʿAttar and his *masnavi*s in particular, its emphasis on reading as a symbolic form of spiritual wayfaring is applicable to sufi didactic poetry more broadly. Through its analysis of ʿAttar, one of the outstanding practitioners of the tradition, *The Poetics of Spiritual Instruction* demonstrates how the scholarly treatment of didactic poetry can move towards questions of performative function even in cases when external evidence for these poems' reception is scanty or unreliable.

The chapters move progressively deeper into ʿAttar's texts, beginning with his literary and religious context and oeuvre-wide persona before turning to individual *masnavi*s, their frame-tales and the anecdotes embedded therein. Chapter 1 introduces the generic form of the didactic *masnavi* and situates it within the larger tradition of instructive poetry in Persian. The genre is characterised by alternating exhortative homilies and illustrative narratives, and scholarly attention has generally focused on the latter.[16] The homilies, however, are not something extra added onto the narratives, nor can they be dispensed with without doing serious violence to the poem. Building on conventions shared with other didactic genres, the homilies establish an imagined social context that justifies the narration of the accompanying anecdotes as part of a pedagogical relationship. More specifically, the homilies construct imagined didactic relationships of oral guidance between ʿAttar's persona and his addressees, such as that of a preacher on the pulpit haranguing his audience, or a shaykh in a teaching circle instructing his disciples. These rhetorical relationships admit numerous variations across texts, poets and the genres of the didactic mode, but they generally imply a power imbalance between speaker and addressee, a dialectic of pedagogical submission and resistance, and a modular, ad hoc approach to knowledge. Chapter 1 traces the development of this rhetorical relationship between speaker and addressee through various didactic genres, including early Persian wisdom verse (*andarz*) and ascetic poetry in Persian and Arabic (*zohdiyat*), before exploring how those relationships shape the form and function of the didactic *masnavi*, condition the reception of its illustrative narratives and mediate readers' encounters with the poem's teachings.

After exploring the didactic *masnavi* and the didactic mode more generally, Chapter 2 turns to ʿAttar's place in the sufi tradition, including questions of biography, milieu and historical and imagined audiences. ʿAttar was writing in the late twelfth or early thirteenth century as sufism was spreading among new social classes through preaching and saint veneration. Simultaneously, sufi textual production on the Iranian plateau was becoming more Persian, more literary and less bound to scholastic contexts. ʿAttar's poems are exemplary in this regard: although they were appreciated by highly trained shaykhs like Rumi (d. 1273) and Shabestari (d. c. 1340), they were also designed to appeal to variegated audiences with less formal ties to sufism: they are, as he puts it, a 'guide on the path for everyone'. ʿAttar also displays a particular interest in text as a technology of spiritual instruction and practice. He circulated his own works in textual form, which was unusual for a poet of his age, and he compiled the *Mokhtar-nama* for a group of sufi-minded companions who had specifically requested a thematically organised, written collection of quatrains for use as objects of contemplation (*tadabbor*/*ta'ammol*). Through his production of literary, vernacular sufi texts that speak to a wide audience, ʿAttar is a prime example of Persian literary sufism's rising star over the course of the thirteenth century, as Persian-language literary texts became increasingly important vectors for the transmission of sufi culture and sites for the performance of mystical piety.

Chapter 3 focuses on the metaphorical understanding of speech as spiritual medicine, a notion that permeates ʿAttar's poetry and a number of allied philosophical and religious discourses. It is a key part of his persona that is explicitly indexed in his pen name. More than mere ornamentation, this metaphor is critical to a proper understanding of medieval poetics in general and the rhetorical work of ʿAttar's poetry in particular. Spiritual health, for ʿAttar, is not only a question of intellect, but also of sense, affect and even physiology. As a form of medicine, poetry not only carries meaning but affects its readers and listeners on a bodily and emotive level, ontologically transforming them and elevating them towards God. At the same time, like any medicine, the efficacy of these verbal concoctions is dependent on both the manner in which they are consumed, which leads us to questions of reading and recitation practices, and the authority of the prescribing doctor and compounding pharmacist, which brings us to the ethical state of the author. I show how ʿAttar, the druggist of souls, performs his spiritual authority by repeatedly 'taking his own medicine' and thereby demonstrating his freedom from hypocrisy, a rhetorical strategy that he shares with the popular preachers of his day. By following the medicinal metaphor as it unfolds in 'Attar's oeuvre, the chapter seeks to recover an implied sufi poetics whose focus is not limited to the aesthetic characteristics of the text, but extends to the spiritual effects produced in audiences thereby.

Having examined 'Attar's place in the literary tradition, his sufi context and his medicinal poetics, the book then turns to his *masnavi*s, and Chapter 4 focuses on the frame-tale of his most famous work, the *Conference of the Birds*. The frame-tale recounts the homiletic sessions of the hoopoe, the leader of the birds, as he narrates stories and parables to convince his feathered flock to make the journey to the Simorgh, a mythical phoenix-like creature and symbol for God. Frame-tales were frequently used to organise prose story collections in the Perso-Arabic literary tradition, but 'Attar was one of the first to apply allegorical frame-tales to the genre of the didactic *masanvi*.[17] The allegorical meaning of the birds' journey and their encounter with the Simorgh has been much discussed in the literature, but the journey itself is actually only a small part of their story. The vast majority of the poem is devoted not to the birds' travails, but to the homiletic sessions delivered by the hoopoe to prepare them for the quest. The hoopoe mounts a pulpit and exhorts his avian audience in line with contemporary conventions of preaching; the birds respond, question and resist the hoopoe's entreaties before they are ultimately persuaded to set out. Through the frame narrative, the poem concretises the didactic mode's implicit homiletic relationship between speaker and addressee, thematising the dialogical character of spiritual instruction and demonstrating how exhortations and stories successfully guide audiences along the spiritual path. In this way, the poem celebrates the perlocutionary power of speech – including 'Attar's own – to instigate spiritual reform.

Chapter 5 delves deeper into the *Conference of the Birds*' frame-tale and its points of interface with the embedded anecdotes; it explores how the birds' imagined oral homiletic sessions are elided with the readers' textual encounter with the poem as a tool for authorial control. 'Attar was keenly aware of the power of the written word to project his voice to audiences he could not otherwise reach. At the same time, textual communication lacks the shared 'circumambient actuality' of oral discourse in which speaker and audience are present together in the same space, and an absent author cannot monitor or guide his text's reception.[18] Through the frame-tale, however, ʿAttar imagines an oral performance environment within the text, complete with an embodied speaker and reactive recipients. Characters within the frame story and the individual anecdotes become avatars and reception figures, fictive listeners calibrated to guide readers' responses. The self-reflexive potential of the frame-tale is pushed to its limit at the end of the poem, when the birds themselves actually read a manuscript that narrates a scene from the story of Joseph's reunion with his brothers, a story that is allegorically reduplicated in the birds' subsequent reconciliation with the Simorgh. The paradoxical implication of these recursively nested textual encounters is that the *Conference of the Birds*, too, will be re-enacted in the lives of its readers and listeners.

To investigate the function of allegory in more detail, Chapter 6 turns to another *masnavi*, the *Mosibat-nama*, ʿAttar's longest poem and one rife with allegorical mappings. Its frame-tale features a spiritual wayfarer, wracked by existential pain, who visits forty beings from all levels of creation seeking spiritual relief. As has often been pointed out, the wayfarer's course through the cosmos can be understood as a visionary ascent modelled on the Prophet Muhammad's famous journey to heaven. Its structure also recalls the forty-day sufi retreat (*chella*) as well as the stages that populate the spiritual path.[19] By drawing on key passages in the *Mosibat-nama* in conjunction with Avicennian psychology, theories of dream interpretation and normative accounts of sufi praxis, I reconstruct the mystical, Neoplatonic ontological framework under which ʿAttar was operating, and according to which the reading of allegory was not only an act of hermeneutics, but itself a process of ascent – a movement from lower sensible forms to the higher divine realm. The poem is thus offered to the reader as a simulated visionary experience, through which they can not only observe the seeker from a distance, but also accompany him on his journey, synecdochically performing the sufi path in miniature. The chapter examines how the reading process was conceptualised through the notions of ascent, retreat and the spiritual path, and what this can tell us about the ritualistic use of mystical literary texts.

For Chapter 7, I move past the frame-tales and zoom in on the embedded anecdotes that populate ʿAttar's didactic *masnavis*. A number of scholars, most notably Ritter, have examined the thematics of ʿAttar's anecdotes and worked to extract the specific moral points they encode. The basic narrative form of 'Attar's anecdotes, however, has mostly been taken for granted, along with the distinctive mode of disruptive temporality that they enact for readers moving through the text. I show how many (if not quite all) of 'Attar's anecdotes work to establish common-sense religious expectations which are suddenly overturned as they present more radical, more demanding and frequently counter-intuitive interpretations of well-worn religious norms. These narrative reversals are informed by sufism's emphasis on sincerity and its tendency to invert common-sense religious valuations, along with deep rooted notions of conversion and repentance as a sudden, unpredictable event that results in a total life reorientation. By seeding what seem to be reasonable religious hierarchies and understandings only to invert them in the process of redefinition, 'Attar forces readers to reconsider their own spiritual standing while providing an opportunity to break through ossified religiosity and recommit themselves to a life of sufi piety.

In the study of Persian literature, authors and texts have generally found greater purchase as rubrics of analysis than audiences and the reading process, especially when it comes to didactic poetry. Such a focus is understandable given the state of our sources: apart from some stylised accounts in the hagiographic and anecdotal literature, we do not have many external sources that shed light directly on how long didactic poems like 'Attar's *Conference of the Birds* were consumed, who was reading them or how they figured into the latter's religious lives. While explicit accounts of how such poems were read are scarce, *The Poetics of Spiritual Instruction* demonstrates that it is both possible and productive to front questions of audience and consumption by investigating how these texts gesture towards their imagined recipients, structure the reading process and idealise the textual encounter. These are still textual features, of course, and, in 'Attar's case, they tell us more about how he hoped his texts would impact his audiences than how they were experienced by historical readers. But this does not diminish the significance of the endeavour. How the text–audience relationship was idealised in the cultural imaginary is perhaps just as revealing for scholars as how they were 'actually' read. In any case, the two are inextricably linked, conditioning and informing each other even if they cannot be directly equated. This book is based on an investigation of 'Attar's texts, but it highlights how those texts gesture outside of themselves as communicative objects that speak to questions of their own performativity and literary function.

A recipient-centred approach is especially useful when examining sufi didactic poetry, the study of which can easily lapse into a summary of ideational content in which its full spiritual significance will be missed. For ʿAttar and other sufi poets, it is not just the poems' teachings or their eloquent expression that determines the success of the poetic project, but the transformative effects that they produce in readers and listeners thereby, as the model of therapeutic poetry makes clear. ʿAttar was writing at a critical period in the history of sufism, when it was well on its way to becoming the dominant mode of piety across the eastern Islamic world, and he represents a crucial figure in the Persian literary tradition's adaptation of sufi themes and sensibilities. By exploring how ʿAttar's works were imagined to act on their readers and functioned as sites of spiritual exercise, *The Poetics of Spiritual Instruction* shows that the resulting 'literary sufism' was much more than a poetic articulation of sufi discourse: it was a new form of sufi praxis in which variegated audiences were offered a generative opportunity to perform sufi piety in a literary mode.

Notes

1. Farid al-Din ʿAttar, *Manteq al-tayr*, ed. Mohammad Reza Shafiʿi-Kadkani, 2nd ed. (Tehran: Sokhan, 1387 [2008–9]), 439. Shafiʿi-Kadkani's editions are used throughout this monograph. They are not without their problems, however: he consults a wide range of manuscripts and makes a number of editorial interventions, but manuscript variants are not always well documented. The older edition of Sayyed Sadeq Gowharin, which closely tracks one of the oldest manuscripts *Conference of the Birds*, was thus frequently consulted as well.
2. Fritz Meier, 'Khurāsān and the End of Classical Sufism', in *Essays on Islamic Piety*, trans. John O'Kane, ed. Bernd Radtke (Leiden: Brill, 1999). Cf. Laury Silvers-Alario, 'The Teaching Relationship in Early Sufism: A Reassessment of Fritz Meier's Definition of the *Shaykh al-tarbiya* and the *Shaykh al-taʿlīm*', *The Muslim World* 93 (2003): 69–97.
3. On sufi-themed quatrains, see J. T. P. de Bruijn, *Persian Sufi Poetry: An Introduction to the Mystical Use of Classical Persian Poems* (Richmond: Curzon, 1997), 6–28.
4. On Sanaʾi and his place in literary history vis-à-vis ʿAttar, see J. T. P. de Bruijn,

'Comparative Notes on Sanā'ī and 'Aṭṭār', in *Classical Persian Sufism: From Its Origins to Rumi*, ed. Leonard Lewisohn (London: Khaniqahi Nimatullahi Publications, 1993).

5. Hellmut Ritter, *The Ocean of the Soul: Man, the World and God in the Stories of Farīd al-Dīn 'Aṭṭār*, trans. John O'Kane (Leiden: Brill, 2003), 30–3.
6. See, for example, Fritz Meier, 'The Spiritual Man in the Persian Poet 'Aṭṭār', *Papers from the Eranos Yearbooks* 4 (1954): 267–304; Lucian Stone, '"Blessed Perplexity": The Topos of *Ḥayrat* in 'Aṭṭār's *Manṭiq al-Ṭayr*', in *'Aṭṭār and the Persian Sufi Tradition: The Art of Spiritual Flight*, ed. Leonard Lewisohn and Christopher Shackle (London: I. B. Tauris, 2006); Nasrollah Pourjavady, 'Naqd-e falsafi-ye she'r az nazar-e 'Attar va 'Owfi', *Ma'aref* 4, no. 3 (1366 [1987–8]): 3–18; Nasrollah Pourjavady, 'She'r-e hekmat: Nesbat-e she'r va shar' az nazar-e 'Attar', *Ma'aref* 5, no. 2 (1367 [1988]): 3–56; Navid Kermani, *The Terror of God: Attar, Job and the Metaphysical Revolt*, trans. Wieland Hoban (Cambridge: Polity Press, 2011); Taqi Purnamdarian, 'Simorgh va Jebra'il', in *Didar ba simorgh* (Tehran: Pazhuheshgah-e 'Olum-e Ensani va Motala'at-e Farhangi, 1374 [1995–6]); Taqi Purnamdarian, "Attar va resalaha-ye 'erfani-ye Ebn Sina', in *Didar ba simorgh* (Tehran: Pazhuheshgah-e 'Olum-e Ensani va Motala'at-e Farhangi, 1374 [1995–6]); Leonard Lewisohn, 'Sufi Symbolism in the Persian Hermeneutic Tradition: Reconstructing the Pagoda of 'Aṭṭār's Esoteric Poetics', in *'Aṭṭār and the Persian Sufi Tradition: The Art of Spiritual Flight*, ed. Leonard Lewisohn and Christopher Shackle (London: I. B. Tauris, 2006).
7. J. Christoph Bürgel, 'Some Remarks on Forms and Functions of Repetitive Structures in the Epic Poetry of 'Aṭṭār', in *'Aṭṭār and the Persian Sufi Tradition: The Art of Spiritual Flight*, ed. Leonard Lewisohn and Christopher Shackle (London: I. B. Tauris, 2006); Franklin Lewis, 'Sexual Occidentation: The Politics of Conversion, Christian-Love and Boy-Love in 'Aṭṭār', *Iranian Studies* 42, no. 5 (2009): 693–723; Taqi Purnamdarian, 'Negahi be dastan-pardazi-ye 'Attar', in *Didar ba simorgh* (Tehran: Pazhuheshgah-e 'Olum-e Ensani va Motala'at-e Farhangi, 1374 [1995–6]); Dick Davis, 'The Journey as Paradigm: Literal and Metaphorical Travel in 'Aṭṭār's *Manṭiq al-Ṭayr*', *Edebiyat*, n.s., 4 (1993): 173–83; J. A. Boyle, 'The Religious *Mathnavīs* of Farīd al-Dīn 'Aṭṭār', *Iran* 17 (1979): 9–14; J. A. Boyle, 'Popular Literature and Folklore in 'Aṭṭār's *Mathnavīs*', in *Colloquio italo-iraniano sul poeta mistico Fariduddin 'Aṭṭār (Roma, 24–25 Marzo 1977)* (Rome: Accademia Nazionale dei Lincei, 1977).
8. One of the few to have examined the role of the reader in 'Attar is Fatemeh Keshavarz, 'Flight of the Birds: The Poetic Animating the Spiritual in 'Aṭṭār's

Manṭiq al-Ṭayr', in *'Aṭṭār and the Persian Sufi Tradition: The Art of Spiritual Flight*, ed. Leonard Lewisohn and Christopher Shackle (London: I. B. Tauris, 2006). See also Muhammad Isa Waley, 'Didactic Style and Self-criticism in 'Aṭṭār', in *'Aṭṭār and the Persian Sufi Tradition: The Art of Spiritual Flight*, ed. Leonard Lewisohn and Christopher Shackle (London: I. B. Tauris, 2006), 215–17; J. T. P. de Bruijn, 'The Preaching Poet: Three Homiletic Poems by Farīd al-Dīn 'Aṭṭār', *Edebiyat: Journal of Middle Eastern Literatures* 9, no. 1 (1998), 85–8.

9. Justine Landau, 'Naṣīr al-Dīn Ṭūsī and the Poetic Imagination in the Arabic and Persian Philosophical Tradition', in *Metaphor and Imagery in Persian Poetry*, ed. Ali Asghar Seyed-Gohrab (Leiden: Brill, 2012); Lara Harb, *Arabic Poetics: Aesthetic Experience in Classical Arabic Literature* (Cambridge: Cambridge University Press, 2020). See also J. Christoph Bürgel, *The Feather of Simurgh: The "Licit Magic" of the Arts in Medieval Islam* (New York: New York University Press, 1988), 53–88.
10. Geert Jan van Gelder, 'Traditional Literary Theory: The Arabic Background', in *A History of Persian Literature*, ed. Ehsan Yarshater, vol.1, *General Introduction to Persian Literature*, ed. J. T. P. de Bruijn (London: I. B. Tauris, 2009), 124.
11. Julie Scott Meisami, 'The Ghazal as Fiction: Implied Speakers and Implied Audience in Hafiz's Ghazals', in *Intoxication, Earthly and Heavenly: Seven Studies on the Poet Hafiz of Shiraz*, ed. Michael Glünz and J. Christoph Bürgel (New York: Peter Lang, 1991); John Stuart Mill, *Essays on Poetry*, ed. F. Parvin Sharpless (Columbia, SC: University of South Carolina Press, 1976), 12 (emphasis in the original).
12. Farid al-Din 'Attar, *Mosibat-nama*, ed. Mohammad Reza Shafiʿi-Kadkani, 2nd ed. (Tehran: Sokhan, 1388 [2009–10]), 160. Alternate editions of this text include that of Nurani Vesal.
13. Wolfgang Iser, *The Implied Reader: Patterns of Communication in Prose Fiction from Bunyan to Beckett* (Baltimore: Johns Hopkins University Press, 1974).
14. Jerome Clinton and Julie Scott Meisami have shown how productive it can be to investigate such meta-poetic reflections, which they bring to bear on the question of poetic unity: Julie Scott Meisami, *Structure and Meaning in Medieval Arabic and Persian Poetry: Orient Pearls* (London: RoutledgeCurzon, 2003), 15–19; Jerome Clinton, 'Esthetics by Implication: What Metaphors of Craft Tell Us about the "Unity" of the Persian *Qasida*', *Edebiyat* 4, no. 1 (1979): 73–97.
15. The ritual function of panegyric poetry, real or imagined, has been a major focus of scholarship, and the performativity of lyric has also received much attention

in recent years. Didacticism, however, has not been explored in these terms, perhaps because of the frequent – if usually now unspoken – assumption that it is a direct, unpoetic modality more focused on content than form, and that it unnecessarily restricts the interpretive agency of its reader. On the performativity of panegyre and lyric, see Suzanne Pinckney Stetkevych, *The Mantle Odes: Arabic Praise Poems to the Prophet Muhammad* (Bloomington: Indiana University Press, 2010); Suzanne Pinckney Stetkevych, *The Poetics of Islamic Legitimacy: Myth, Gender, and Ceremony in the Classical Arabic Ode* (Bloomington: Indiana University Press, 2002); Domenico Ingenito, *Beholding Beauty: Sa'di of Shiraz and the Aesthetics of Desire in Medieval Persian Poetry* (Leiden: Brill, 2021), 443–523.

16. Ritter quite explicitly brackets the homiletic context of the anecdotes in his analyses, *Ocean of the Soul*, 32–3.
17. The *Rahiq al-tahqiq* is the only extant didactic *masnavi* that predates 'Attar and makes use of the device: Fakhr al-Din Mobarak-Shah Marvrudi, *Rahiq al-tahqiq be enzemam-e ash'ar-e digar-e u,* ed. Nasrollah Pourjavady (Tehran: Markez-e Nashr-e Daneshgahi, 1381 [2002]).
18. The phrase is Walter Ong's: see Walter J. Ong, 'The Writer's Audience Is Always a Fiction', *PMLA* 90, no. 1 (1975), 10.
19. Ritter, *Ocean of the Soul*, 18–20; Kermani, *Terror of God*, 45–7.

1

Situating Wisdom

The didactic *masnavi*s of 'Attar, like those of Sana'i and Nezami (d. 1209) before him, are composed primarily of two distinct forms of discourse: narrative anecdotes and explanatory homilies. The anecdotes are drawn from a host of generic traditions, from stories of the Prophet to Perso-Hellenic romances. They are then embedded in blocks of non-narrative discourse characterised by direct address, a hortatory mood and moralising sententiae. Due to their formal and rhetorical similarity with the discourse of preachers, I refer to these non-narrative sections as 'homiletic', following J. T. P. de Bruijn.[1] The homilies generalise and amplify the stories' moral points and interpret their symbolic meanings, while the stories exemplify and embody the homiletic injunctions in concrete, narrative situations. It is this alternating rhythm of narrative and homily that most obviously characterises the genre of the didactic *masnavi*.

In three of 'Attar's four didactic *masnavi*s, the amount of homiletic material is nearly equal to the amount of narrative. In his *Asrar-nama* and several earlier instances of the genre, it is several times greater. Nevertheless, the narratives have garnered the lion's share of scholarly attention, often in isolation from the homilies that surround them. The most prominent scholarly work on 'Attar, Hellmut Ritter's *Ocean of the Soul*, is devoted almost exclusively to the narratives, and as Ritter himself frankly admits, he interprets the stories 'often in isolation, detached from their context'. He also acknowledges that the meanings he extracts from them do not always correspond to the interpretations that 'Attar himself presents in the corresponding homiletic sections.[2] Other contemporary scholars largely follow suit: Navid Kermani takes the stories themselves as the most fertile material for exploring 'Attar's theodicy and condemnation of God's injustice, as does Claudia Yaghoobi in her investigation of ʿAttar's attitudes towards subalterns, and Dick Davis in his analysis of poetic structure.[3] To be sure, these scholars avail themselves of the poems' homiletic content when appropriate, but their focus is very much on the narratives with the accompanying homiletic sections serving a secondary role in their analyses.

While contemporary scholars have tended to privilege the narratives over the accompanying homilies without passing overt aesthetic judgement on them, early orientalists were quite explicit in their dislike of the same. With all the frankness and confidence of an elite subject of imperial Britain, Edward Browne proclaimed the *Hadiqat al-haqiqa* of Sana'i – a paradigmatic work imitated by generations of later Persian poets and dominated by homiletic content – to be 'one of the dullest books in Persian, seldom rising to the level of Martin Tupper's *Proverbial Philosophy*, filled with fatuous truisms and pointless anecdotes'.[4] This harsh judgement is not levied against Sana'i's poetry in general – Browne goes on to praise his lyric verse – but seems rather to be rooted in a distaste of the *masnavi*'s direct didactic stance. Didactic *masnavi*s attributed to ʿAttar and Jami are likewise condemned as 'dull and monotonous' and dominated by 'paternal advice' that, tellingly, 'does not constitute what we should regard as suitable material for poetry'.[5] Rumi's *Masnavi* receives high praise from Browne, not because of its homiletic content, but in spite of it: although some of its narrative portions are 'sublime and dignified', he is less fond of its 'mystical and theosophical digressions, often of the most abstruse character'.[6]

Such judgements are not just a product of personal taste, but reflect a broader cultural suspicion of overtly instructional verse as inherently unliterary and restrictive, a suspicion that, in its current form, dates back to at least the Romantic period.[7] Poe famously denounced the 'heresy of didacticism', and Shelley declared didactic poetry his 'abhorrence'.[8] Shelley and other Romantics felt that poetry had much to teach, but it should teach, as De Quincey put it, 'as forests teach, as the seas teach, as infancy teaches, viz. by deep impulse, by hieroglyphic suggestion. Their teaching is not direct or explicit, but lurking, implicit, masked in deep incarnations.'[9] To borrow a more modern saw, poetic instruction, in the Romantic view, ought to 'show' rather than 'tell'. These attitudes continue to find purchase in the twentieth and twenty-first centuries: when an author appears to be directly explaining their work – as ʿAttar and other medieval Persian poets often do in the homiletic sections of their *masnavi*s – this is frequently taken as an invitation to partake in the 'intentional fallacy' that the New Critics so successfully denounced, a 'tyrannical' form of authorial control, an ill-advised and ultimately illegitimate attempt to restrict the freedom of the reader (and the scholar) to make meaning.[10]

ʿAttar includes more exempla and longer exempla than his predecessors, and he displays a certain virtuosity in tightly constructed stories, so there is good reason to take his narratives seriously. And the homilies do privilege certain readings while downplaying or obfuscating others. Davis, for example, has argued that the homiletic meanings extracted by ʿAttar do not always sit comfortably with his narratives.[11] Christine van Ruymbeke, in a fascinating discussion of *Anvar-e Sohayli*, shows that authorial interpretations can even be misleading or intentionally dissembling.[12] In such situations, it can be productive to read 'against the grain' and resist the text's self-commentary and self-interpretation. At the same time, generations of readers have valued ʿAttar's interpretive guidance in his homilies and accepted his hermeneutic authority as an author and spiritual guide. As illuminating as it can be to read 'against the grain', this chapter seeks to answer a seemingly simpler question, but one that is profoundly necessary for understanding the significance of didactic sufi texts on their own terms, free from the shadow of Romantic and post-Romantic anxieties: what would it mean to read ʿAttar's poems 'with the grain' of his homiletic commentary? What modes of subjectivity are implied for readers or listeners who accept ʿAttar's interpretations as authoritative? How would this change the nature of the textual encounter?

Didactic verse does not consist of disembodied injunctions, but poetic utterances embedded in imagined social settings that they themselves evoke. Depending on the genre, poet and specific verses under consideration, the setting may be that of a homiletic assembly, a father's paternal conference with his sons or a king's final testament to his subjects. To read didactic poetry 'with the grain' means to grant the speaker his instructive role and, opposite him, to adopt the stance of an attentive student, an inquiring disciple or a grateful recipient of trans-generational wisdom. A host of gendered, rhetorical asymmetries encoded in the poem are thus brought to bear on the reading process, which becomes an imagined social interaction between a student who is potentially resistant but ultimately receptive and a paternal figure who seeks to reform him through speech. In the case of the didactic *masnavi*, the rhetorical relationship constructed in the homilies also provides a communicative context for the narration of the embedded anecdotes and thereby justifies their inclusion. Instead of rejecting direct authorial interpretations as an illegitimate exercise to circumscribe their interpretive freedom, mystically minded readers would have leaned into this relationship and used ʿAttar's guidance as a heuristic starting point for reflection and ethical self-fashioning.

In the pages that follow, I examine how the homiletic sections of ʿAttar's didactic *masnavi*s enact socially situated, imagined rhetorical relationships that condition the textual encounter for those reading 'with the grain'. ʿAttar's rhetorical stance in these poems is not *sui generis*. It is born out of a long tradition of didactic verse in Persian and Arabic that encompasses not only the mystical didactic *masnavi* as it crystallised in the twelfth century, but other genres as well. I thus begin by examining two earlier species of didactic poetry – wisdom verse (*andarz, pand*) and ascetic poetry (*zohdiyat*) – that establish key literary, rhetorical and epistemic conventions that go on to inform the homiletic sections of the didactic *masnavi*. I then examine how the rhetorical relationships evoked in these homiletic sections shape the form, structure and tone of ʿAttar's poems, including the narration of illustrative exempla and their allegedly 'digressive' paratactic arrangement. Most importantly, by investigating these imagined relationships of oral guidance and the manner they are evoked in ʿAttar's didactic *masnavi*s, this chapter shows how readers are called to play the role of a student who willingly – if not always ungrudgingly – submits to their perlocutionary work.

Wise Words, Elegant Expression

In the Persian literary tradition, explicitly instructive verse crosses formal and generic boundaries. It can be found in quatrains, *ghazal*s and *qasida*s; it includes specimens of wisdom verse (*pand/andarz*), ascetic- and homiletic-themed poetry (*zohd*, *mowʿeza*) and the mystical-didactic *masnavi*. For these reasons, didacticism can be more accurately conceptualised as a poetic mode than a specific formal genre of verse, and which consists of a set of associated poetic characteristics, including an explicitly instructive stance, a concern for the social basis of knowledge transmission, conceptual modularity and a pragmatic, heuristic orientation.[13] Several kinds of poems display some or all of these characteristics, albeit in their own particular ways, and on the basis of these family resemblances they can be usefully grouped together under the rubric of didacticism. Moments of didacticism even surface in poems dominated by other poetic modalities, including epics, romances and love poems. The literary history of didacticism, then, is not just a history of a single genre, but of a broader trend in Persian literature.

The didactic mode in Persian is not only broad but deep, reaching back to the emergence of the tradition in the tenth century. Most of the earliest extant New Persian poetry, which exists only in scattered form, consists of concise aphoristic reflections. These treat a wide range of practical moral topics, including the shortness of life, the importance of keeping secrets and the virtue of moderation. Such bon mots for successful living are frequently identified within the verses themselves as a species of wisdom (*hekmat*, *kherad*) or advice (*andarz*, *pand*), terms that were used by later anthologists and prosodists as generic categories. A few verses attributed to the early poet Abu Shakur Balkhi (fl. tenth century), translated below, serve to illustrate the dominant techniques and themes of this early wisdom poetry, in so far as it has been preserved:[14]

When a tree is bitter to its core,
even if you pamper it with sweetness,
it will never give anything but bitter fruit;
you will never taste sweetness from it.[15]

You will find no better teacher
than fate when it sets you before itself.[16]

I have heard a thing is secure
when it has many protectors.
But when it comes to secrets, they are safest
when they have but a single guard.[17]

May wisdom (*kherad*) be forever your guide
May nothing in the world be your companion but wisdom.[18]

When the tree is small, the gardener
can bend it any way he likes,

but when it is grown, he cannot
correct its crookedness.[19]

Don't collect enemies, for even one
is plenty, while friends, even a thousand, are few.[20]

May the army never be led but by an older man;
a youth is still youth, even if he is a master.[21]

I say *my* soul and *my* body –
who am *I*, then, if not my body or my soul?[22]

With resignation, the sage (*kheradmand*) said these words:
'Kiss the hand that you cannot cut.'[23]

These verses, which were preserved in later anthologies and literary works, were all likely extracted from Abu Shakur's *Afarin-nama*; this was one of the first didactic *masnavi*s in New Persian, but it is no longer extant as a complete text. Taken together, in their current form, they present a heterogeneous collection of knowledge artfully arranged into short, pithy utterances. Many are direct imperatives ('Kiss the hand that you cannot cut') or normative observations ('when it comes to secrets, they are safest when they have but a single guard'), but some also take the form of reflective musings ('Who am *I*, then, if not my body or my soul?'). In Abu Shakur's case, a number of verses relate to the proper treatment of enemies, counsellors and army leaders, which might suggest a courtly origin or a 'mirrors for princes' function; nevertheless, like most mirrors, their lessons also speak to the ethics of interpersonal relationships more generally. Although there are clear points of emphasis, the wisdom these lines purport to teach is not systematic. These are modular observations, that, although part of a larger corpus, are linguistically and conceptually self-contained. They do not, in any obvious way, build on one another to produce a systematic, ordered whole. Of course, only scattered lines have been preserved – the connective tissue binding them together has been lost – so their non-hierarchical modularity may be a product of their state of preservation. At the same time, wholly extant didactic *masnavi*s from later periods also display a tendency towards modularity, and one suspects that Abu Shakur's poetry was preserved in scattered fashion precisely because his poems were structured around self-contained observations that could be easily extracted from their surroundings, memorised and deployed in new contexts.

In other words, these verses appear to have functioned much like proverbs, at least in terms of their later reception: pithy, stand-alone utterances that served as ad hoc tools for thought and action. With their rhyme and metre, they would have been easily memorised and kept ready at hand so they could be immediately deployed in discourse to encapsulate attitudes and make sense of a range of situations.[24] For example, Abu Shakur's observation that a supple young tree bends beneath the gardener's hand while a mature tree cannot be straightened could be used to encourage the proper discipline of a child, or to reflect on the futility of teaching an older relative. The lines about a tree with bitter fruit, by contrast, suggest that reform is never possible – no matter how much attention you give the tree, its fruit will always be unpalatable. These two pieces of wisdom might be considered contradictory (one posits a window for reform in youth, the other stresses the impossibility of changing inherent traits), but the purpose was never to create a comprehensive, fully elaborated ethical system. Rather, like proverbs, these verses are a collection of tools for conceptualising diverse situations and articulating a range of responses to them. Although cast as universal truths, these are in fact flexible templates that are meant to be adapted to the particular context of their utterance. This is a pragmatic form of knowledge, a flexible set of gnomic principles for thought and action, born out of experience and designed to facilitate movement through the world.

With their pithy form and pragmatic content, these verses build on an older tradition of Middle Persian wisdom, also called *andarz*, which consists of aphorisms on topics ranging from Zoroastrian ritual and belief to politics and practical morality.[25] New Persian wisdom verse inherited many of the sensibilities of the latter, although it exhibits a vague monotheism more acceptable to its primarily Muslim audience in place of the latter's explicitly Zoroastrian outlook.[26] Furthermore, while New Persian wisdom poetry is versified in rhyme and metre, the Middle Persian *andarz* were almost all written in prose, although they do exhibit parallelisms, lists and puns that, like rhyme and metre, would have aided in memorisation and facilitated oral circulation.[27] When compiled into textual collections, *andarz* were frequently framed as the collected utterances of sages or kings; in the case of the latter, they might be cast as the king's testament to his son or subjects on the occasion of his enthronement or from his deathbed.[28] They are thus presented as the verbal utterances of authoritative figures that have been passed down through the generations.

The figure of the sage – and to some extent the king – persists in the New Persian material as the archetypal articulator of wisdom. Sometimes the attribution is explicit, as in the final aphorism translated above ('With resignation, the sage [*kheradmand*] said . . .'). Other times it is more implicit, part and parcel of the genre. Even when a verse (or, more accurately, its content) is not traced back to such authority, it is frequently indexed as the product of oral transmission, as in 'I have heard (*shanidam*) a thing is secure when it has many protectors . . .' Unlike the Middle Persian *andarz*, however, these pieces of New Persian wisdom are also very much authorial productions, and the poets themselves frequently elide with the sages that they invoke. By placing the community's proverbial knowledge in rhyme and metre, poets communicate wisdom in an eloquent and memorable form and thus promote its continued circulation. Indeed, many poets throughout the medieval period are remembered with the honorific 'sage/philosopher' (*hakim*) before their pen names, including Ferdowsi and Sana'i, and a number of early poets, such as Shahid-e Balkhi, were known by their contemporaries as philosophers.[29] Abu Shakur's verses often appeal to an authoritative *sakhon-dan*, or 'knower of speech', who could be understood as both poet and sage, and he casts wisdom as inseparable from its fluent expression: 'a philosopher (*faylasufi*) must be eloquent (*shiva*) to the utmost,' he writes, 'so that he can be strong in speaking (*sakhon goftan*).'[30] In this way, the knowledge transmitted by early New Persian wisdom verse is cast as oral, trans-generational and fundamentally linked to speech and expression.

The themes encapsulated in these verses run through the didactic mode more broadly, including later didactic *masnavi*s. Shorn of their explicitly Islamic terminology, many of 'Attar's ethical lessons and those of other, later *masnavi* writers would not be out of place in the early *andarz* literature. But beyond these thematic similarities, there is also a broader congruence of sensibility and approach. In his homiletic discourses, as will be seen below, 'Attar does not provide his readers with a comprehensive ethical or theological system but strings of generalising sententiae and pithy aphoristic sayings in an ad hoc fashion. The modularity of his address recalls the self-contained character of the *andarz*, and it likewise facilitates the oral transmission of single lines or short passages as proverbial tools for thought while providing readers with the freedom to focus on particular sections of the poem.[31] In most didactic *masnavi*s, spiritual instruction is also imagined as an oral process: whether the poem is read or recited, the poet plays the role of a preacher or a spiritual guide, and his teachings are reflexively cast as verbal utterances. In the *masnavi*s of ʿAttar, these imagined performance contexts take on a more concrete form through the frame-tale structure, which describes the imagined social settings in which the poem's teaching-activity takes place: the homiletic assemblies of the hoopoe in the case of the *Conference of the Birds*, or the *pir*'s discussions with his disciple over the course of the ritual retreat in the *Mosibat-nama*. In the *Elahi-nama*, the old Middle Persian figure of the king as a dispenser of wisdom merges with the figure of the spiritual guide: a wise monarch dialogues with his six sons, directing them towards the spiritual analogues of their worldly desires through homiletic discourse and illustrative stories.

In their modularity and imagined orality, didactic *masnavi*s such as those of ʿAttar and Sanaʾi elaborate key characteristics of the didactic mode that are already visible in the scattered early New Persian wisdom verse. But in their explicitly Islamic orientation, complex authorial personae and carefully calibrated addressees, they have more in common with another kind of didactic verse which has been better preserved: ascetic poetry (*zohdiyat*), a genre in which the poet speaks as a preacher on the pulpit, haranguing an imagined audience gathered at his feet.

Is Anybody Listening? Speaker and Addressee in Homiletic Verse

Ascetic poetry (*zohdiyat*), which treats religious and renunciatory themes including the shortness of life, the inevitability of death and the duplicity of the world, was one of several new monothematic genres that developed in Arabic during the eighth century.[32] Musings on mortality were already found in pre-Islamic poetry, usually in sections of proverbial reflections within polythematic *qasida*s; these were later classified as a minor poetic mode under the label of 'wisdom' (*hekmat*). In the late Umayyad and ʿAbbasid period, however, such themes were married with a more explicitly monotheistic eschatological perspective and began to dominant complete poems. The borders of the *zohdiyat*, like most genres, are rather porous, but it is recognised as a distinct type within premodern Arabic and Persian literary criticism. Although not the first to compose ascetic poetry, the genre became inextricably fused with the memory of its greatest practitioner, Abu'l-ʿAtahiya (d. c. 825), an ʿAbbasid court poet who is said to have given up luxury and love poetry in favour of ascetic verse and a life of detachment.[33]

Ascetic poetry has often been described as a form of sermon in verse, and its most prominent themes – the transience of the world, the inevitability of death and the gravity of the coming judgement – certainly recall those of homiletic assemblies as portrayed in the anecdotal material.[34] Its language also recalls that of a sermon, being simple yet forceful, with frequent use of repetition and rhetorical questions, including variations on the *ubi sunt?* motif, which C. H. Becker traces back to Syriac Christian homiletic practices.[35] The poet speaks from a position of religious authority as someone who has grasped the stakes of the mortal situation, and he seeks to wake others from the slumber of ignorance and guide them towards this bitter truth. Of course, the poet's homiletic persona ought not to be confused with the historical poet himself. Abu Nuwas (d. c. 815), the well-known poet of wine and love, was no preacher, but he nonetheless composed a couple dozen ascetic poems; Abu'l-ʿAtahiya is said to have asked him to stop, feeling that he was muscling into his domain.[36] Nonetheless, whatever an individual poet's relationship to preaching may have been, the conventions of the genre evoke the themes, rhetorical stance, didactic goals and overall communicative situation of preaching. Medieval rhetoricians and anthologists even used 'homily' (*vaʿz*, *mowʿeza*) as a generic term nearly synonymous with 'ascetic poetry' (*zohd*).[37] And if Abu Nuwas is not remembered as sermoniser, other practitioners of the genre are, including Salih b. ʿAbd al-Quddus, one of its early forerunners.[38]

In ascetic verse, and didactic poetry more broadly, the poet's persona does not exist independent of his addressee or addressees, to whom he is dialectically bound. Whereas the lyric persona is allegedly overheard by a spectral listener, the didactic poet faces his audience directly, haranguing them according to particular pedagogical conventions. This is frequently cited as one of the defining characteristics of classical didactic poetry in Greek and Latin. The genre 'implies a certain relationship between author and reader, a relationship of teacher and pupil, and the logic of that situation is important in moulding the form . . . [I]t is always directed towards an audience.'[39] In the context of the *zohdiyat*, this audience is more specifically that of a homiletic assembly, a group of listeners who have gathered around the pulpit to receive religious exhortation. As de Bruijn concisely explains, 'the homiletic mode of discourse always presupposes someone, or a group of people, to whom the preaching poet addresses himself, if only virtually. This allows us to postulate the presence of a persona opposite the speaker who can be identified as "the person or persons be admonished" . . . the audience of the homily.'[40] And within the Perso-Arabic literary imaginary, a homiletic audience – even if only a 'virtual' one – already implies a complex, asymmetrical relationship. The preacher addresses an audience who recognises his authority by virtue of their continued presence and attention at his assembly, and he admonishes them for spiritual failings that they have been, and continue to be, unable or reluctant to reform. Audience members are by no means passive subjects, and their assent and submission is not guaranteed. In ascetic verse, readers and listeners are invited to play a literary adaptation of this dialectical game, acknowledging the speaker's authority and exposing themselves to his exhortations and admonishments, which presuppose both their need for reform and the possibility of their resistance.

The genre of ascetic poetry, more than other kinds of Perso-Arabic verse, is thus marked by a palpable intentionality and persuasive purpose. Even when composed by a non-preacher, such as Abu Nuwas, the ascetic poem makes serious judgements and assertions about the world, from which it derives ethical conclusions that it seeks to impress upon its readers.[41] In the past fifty years, poetry has often been analysed as a kind of speech-act; most frequently, it has been considered a species of what J. L. Austin termed an *illocutionary* act, a conventional statement that 'does something' in its very utterance (classic examples include swearing a vow or christening a ship). Within Austin's scheme, however, ascetic poetry can be more usefully understood as a *perlocutionary* act, a statement that is intentionally calibrated to produce effects in the world that are separable from its utterance, and which may or may not actually result from it.[42] Through forceful imagery and other poetic structures, ascetic poetry seeks to guide the reader's gaze, if even only for a moment, towards the terror and inevitability of death, and to thereby cultivate an ethos of pious detachment that goes beyond the spatial borders of the page and the temporal bounds of recitation. Whether any given poem succeeds in this endeavour, of course, is an entirely different question.

This rhetorical dynamic can be observed in action in a short passage from Naser-e Khosrow (d. 1077), translated below.[43] Some of the earliest extant ascetic poetry in New Persian was composed by Naser-e Khosrow, an Isma'ili missionary, poet and philosopher, whose *divan* includes allegorical poems on Isma'ili cosmogony, imaginative descriptions of spring and the night sky and bitter complaints against his exile. Much of his verse is also panegyric and dedicated to his protector in Badakhshan, the Fatimid caliph, or other Fatimid elites.[44] This thematic and generic diversity is evident not only between poems but also within individual compositions, which, unlike the monothematic Arabic *zohdiyat*, frequently move through multiple generic modes. The homiletic mode dominates his poems, however, and when describing his own work, he names only the instructive genres, including ascetic poetry (*she'r-e zohd*), advice poetry (*she'r-e pand*) and wisdom poetry (*she'r-e kherad*). The fifteenth-century anthologist Dowlat-Shah follows suit, describing Naser's *divan* as 'predominantly wisdom and sermonising' (*hekmat va mow'eza*).[45]

The following passage is taken from a thirty-three-line *qasida* whose thematic focus, the treachery of the world, had already been well developed in the tradition of ascetic verse. It begins with an address to 'You who have travelled the world and seen its snares', an addressee whom the poet proceeds to lecture on the false promises of temporal good fortune. The world raises kings up only to bring them down, so, according to Naser, those who 'know its ways and work' turn to the firmer ground of religion. Naser continues to exhort his audience and describe the world's treacheries, and for a few verses he even addresses the world itself, imploring it to save its duplicity for those who actively seek out its temporal charms. Near the end of the poem, Naser turns to call on his human addressee again (a rhetorical device known as *eltefat*, or 'turning'), whom he addresses as 'son' (*pesar*, which could also be translated as 'boy'), a vocative that runs throughout Naser's *divan*:

Listen to my fatherly (*pedarana*) advice, O son,
    The same advice that Noah gave to Shem.
Avoid anyone who does not recognise
    the instability of the world and its blessings,

and who, from his heart, cannot drive out the darkness,
with the light of religion and knowledge of God.
Wash your hands of him, and except with silence
give no answer to his questions, O son.[46]

This modular bit of advice – bookended between the two vocatives – is framed as an utterance within a paternal relationship: the addressee is a boy or young man in need of the speaker's fatherly (*pedarana*) guidance. Here, like in so much of Naser's poetry, the persona of the preacher central to the *zohdiyat* merges with the figure of the father in an echo of the early *andarz*. In this case, however, the practice of paternal counsel is not projected back to pre-Islamic kings, but to Abrahamic prophets: Naser claims Noah bestowed the same bit of advice on his son Shem, who thereby provides an authoritative model for his own pedagogical paternalism. The passage's imperative verbs are, as is conventionally expected, conjugated in the second-person singular instead of the more formal plural, which suggests both a power imbalance and a measure of intimacy in keeping with the father–son dynamic. The imperative 'listen!' and the repeated vocatives also evoke an oral frame of reference for the transmission of this advice. Assuming Naser-e Khosrow imagined a primarily male and mature readership, the rhetorical stance constructed here implies a measure of condescension, calling their masculinity and worldly experience into question.[47] At the same time, it entails a sense of paternal responsibility for the recipient and assumes his potential for growth.

It is possible that Naser-e Khosrow had a specific historical addressee in mind as he composed these lines, and the 'son' exhorted here was an actual student, disciple or a minor at court.[48] Sussing out such references, if indeed they exist, would require a serious study of his biography and the chronology of his oeuvre. Like most *qasida*s and *ghazal*s, this poem would have been recited orally, so the addressee could also take on all sorts of context-specific meanings determined by the performer and audience independent of the poet's intentions.[49] While declaiming the passage, the reciter might point out a younger listener or someone known to associate with 'a bad crowd' and thereby make them the target of the above admonishment, in jest or in seriousness. Then, when Naser's addressee shifts or takes on a new valence, as it sometimes does, a new member of the audience might be indicated.[50] At one point in this particular poem, for example, the poet calls on his addressee as 'brother' and urges him to carry the poet's message to others: 'Inform them, O brother, of the world's treachery / Whether they are near or close, from the elite or the masses.'[51] Here the relationship between speaker and addressee is less asymmetrical and more collaborative: the latter already knows of the dangers of the world, and the speaker calls on him to join him in his homiletic mission. During an actual performance, one might imagine these lines being spoken to an older man, or one with some authority over others in the room.

The dynamism of the addressee and its ability to take on new, context-dependent referents does not, however, negate the more general pull that it exerts on readers and listeners as a group. In some performances these lines might be directed towards specific individuals, but in others the addressee will remain an anonymous stand-in for the audience as a whole. The frequent use of indexical, second-person pronouns leads readers and listeners to imagine themselves as the poem's didactic targets, and the repeated calls to 'son' or 'boy' imply an ideal recipient that they are invited to inhabit. As David Konstan puts it, the wider audience of didactic poetry 'peers over the shoulder' of the formal addressee to whom the didactic poet directly speaks.[52] Regardless of the identity of this particular 'son' – if he even existed at all – the addressee offers an opening onto the text from a particular social perspective, that of a young male receiving oral instruction from a wise father figure. The audience thereby approaches the above-quoted passage not as an object for detached aesthetic contemplation, nor as a piece of evidence for reconstructing the poet's ethical system, but as a wise paternal utterance, a perlocutionary call to cultivate an ethos of detachment and associate with like-minded folk. Despite the ontological gap between textual addressees and flesh-and-blood recipients, the former function as critical hermeneutic signposts for readers and listeners, through which they structure their rhetorical and affective relationships with the poet and his speech. At the very least, the speaker–addressee dialectic sets up certain parameters for experiencing the text's message, parameters to which readers and listeners must either accede or actively resist.

Stories, Sermons and Authorial Interpretation

The speaking persona of the ascetic poet and the corresponding addressee are taken up by the genre of the didactic *masnavi*, where they are coupled with a discursive mode largely absent from monorhyme didactic verse: storytelling. In addition to direct exhortation and admonishment, didactic *masnavi*s are studded with dozens, sometimes hundreds of narratives that illustrate the homilies' theological, ethical and psychological teachings. The homilies, in turn, point the narratives with specific moral and religious lessons, and they thereby take on an interpretative function in addition to their exhortative work. The inclusion of exempla in the didactic *masnavi* is facilitated by the formal properties of the *masnavi* form. *Masnavi*s are composed of rhyming hemistiches, and the rhyme changes with every line. This allows for greater freedom in word choice than possible with the monorhyme forms and makes the versification of narratives, which frequently require a specific vocabulary, much easier.

The earliest extant didactic *masnavi* is the *Hadiqat al-haqiqa* of Sana'i. Earlier examples certainly existed, but they have not been preserved. As previously mentioned, Abu Shakur composed a *masnavi* entitled the *Afarin-nama*, from which only scattered verses remain, and some of which were quoted above. A few of the preserved fragments appear to be narrative in nature, but it is difficult to draw firm conclusions about the poem as a whole on the basis of this incomplete evidence. In any case, the extant verses lack the explicitly Islamic orientation of Sana'i's *Hadiqat* and most later didactic *masnavi*s. A couple of short didactic poems in the *masnavi* form are also attributed to Naser-e Khosrow, but their mood is more descriptive than exhortative and they are missing the alteration of narrative and homily so characteristic of the later genre.[53] The *Hadiqat*, however, displays the long length, religious orientation and use of narrative exempla that would become hallmarks of the didactic *masnavi*, and it is frequently invoked by later poets and commentators as a paradigm for their own work.

For example, the *Hadiqat* is considered to have been a model for Rumi's *Masnavi* by the hagiographers of the Mevlevi tradition, and it is usually thought to have inspired ʿAttar as well.[54] It is explicitly identified by Nezami as the model for his own *Makhzan al-asrar*, although he composed the latter in a different metre (*sariʿ*).[55] The *Makhzan*, in turn, set a paradigm for many later *masnavi*s that adopted its metre, structure and even the *-ar* ending of its title, including the *Matlaʿ al-anvar* of Amir Khosrow (d. 1325), the *Rozat al-anvar* of Khwaju (d. c. 1349), the *Mo'nes al-abrar* of ʿEmad al-Din Faqih Kermani

(d. 1371–2) and the *Tohfat al-ahrar* of Jami (d. 1492).[56] Metrically speaking, the *Bustan* of Saʿdi (d. 1291–2) is something of an outlier, being composed in the *motaqareb* metre, which is more frequently associated with epic poetry. (This metre is, however, used in Nezami's Alexandrian 'didactic epics', the *Eqbal-nama* and *Sharaf-nama*.) Other didactic *masnavi*s continued to use the *khafif* metre of the *Hadiqat*, such as the *Rahiq al-tahqiq* of Mobarak-Shah (d. 1206), or adopted the *ramal* and *hazaj* metres of Rumi and ʿAttar, such as the *Golshan-e raz* by Shabestari, in which ʿAttar is singled out for special praise. These formal resemblances, authorial references and networks of influence show how tightly bound the didactic *masnavi* was as a generic tradition, even though it was never explicitly named as such. Premodern commentators frequently discussed didactic poetry with terms like *pand*, *nasihat*, *mowʿeza*, and so on, but this was a loose, modal terminology that could be applied to verses in a variety of genres and forms; there was no specific generic term reserved for the didactic *masnavi*. There can be little doubt, however, that poets who composed didactic *masnavi*s saw themselves as producing a particular kind of verse, distinct from other forms of didactic poetry (i.e. ascetic poetry, wisdom verse) and other kinds of *masnavi*s (i.e. romances, epics).

This is not to say that the tradition of the didactic *masnavi* was uniform or unchanging. On the contrary, ʿAttar develops the genre in several key ways. He includes many more anecdotes than either Sana'i or Nezami, so a far greater portion of each of his *masnavi*s is devoted to narrative, as will be discussed in detail in Chapter 5. Three out of ʿAttar's four *masnavi*s are actually majority narrative, with over 50 per cent of their content devoted to exempla, as opposed to just 16 per cent of the *Makhzan* and 8 per cent of the earliest versions of the *Hadiqat*. ʿAttar not only adds more anecdotes to the genre, but he also brings to them a daramtist's eye. Most of his narratives are relatively short with only a couple of plot points, but they are tightly structured and generally end in a surprise reversal or twist. A few, however, are exceedingly long, pushing hundreds of verses, and resemble Perso-hellenic romances. These include the well-known tales of Marhuma, Shaykh Sanʿan and the romance of Rabeʿa and Bektash, which are are unlike anything found in Sana'i's *Hadiqat* or Nezami's *Makhzan* in terms of both their length and erotic content.

ʿAttar's shorter narratives feature a wide variety of protagonists: unnamed stock figures such as princes, beggars and old pious women; specific historical pre-Islamic kings such as Anushirvan, Ardashir and Alexander; Islamic rulers and bureaucrats including Sultan Mahmud, Harun al-Rashid and Nezam al-Molk; the Prophet Muhammad and his companions; pre-Islamic prophets; legendary lovers such as Layli and Majnun; heroes of the sufi tradition including Rabeʿa, Hallaj and Abu Saʿid; and even talking animals and mythical beasts. Many of these narratives had been previously used as religious exempla by Qushayri (d. 1072), Ghazali (d. 1111) or other writers in the sufi tradition, but some seem to have been adapted from courtly or literary sources, such as the *Shah-nama*, the *Siasat-nama* or the *Qabus-nama*. Whatever their source, the accompanying homilies always take the narratives seriously as sources of religious wisdom. In this context, the homilies not only exhort but also interpret, pulling lines of meaning out of the narrated anecdotes that are not always obvious in their absence. Poets are thus able to incorporate narratives from all kinds of sources and generic contexts into the didactic *masnavi* and reinterpret them in accordance with their own instructive aims.

ʿAttar's appropriation of narratives for didactic purposes will be analysed in detail below, using the mythical story of the Qoqnos as a case study. First, however, it must be recognised that the use of short narratives to illustrate and amplify moral points was not an exclusively literary-textual phenomenon; it reflected contemporary practices of oral sermonising. Storytelling had been closely linked to preaching since the first generations after the Prophet, when storytellers (*qossas*) incorporated Jewish and Christian legend into Islamic homiletic culture.[57] By the twelfth century, preachers were a major religious force across the Islamic world, and renowned sermonisers such as Ahmad Ghazali (d. 1124) and Ibn al-Jawzi (d. 1200) could draw thousands of attendees to their events.[58] These were not instances of the liturgically mandated Friday sermon, which was a necessary part of communal prayer, but 'homiletic assemblies' (*majles-e vaʿz*) that are sometimes referred to as 'popular' in the scholarship. This terminology has been criticised as erroneously implying that this mode of sermonising was restricted to the lower classes, which was not the case; these sessions could be quite exclusive and were frequented by highly trained religious scholars.[59] Nevertheless, certain preachers could also pose a challenge to the authority of more 'credentialed' religious scholars, and the former's influence among the masses was frequently a source of anxiety for the latter.[60]

This was a variegated tradition, both in terms of social participation and the setting of the event: besides large public sermons, there were also smaller, more private gatherings, especially in sufi circles where a shaykh might head an informal homiletic assembly for his disciples. Both large public sermons and smaller homiletic assemblies were semi-improvised affairs that were rarely recorded, but a rough idea of their content and performance procedures can be gleaned from normative manuals of preaching, travel narratives and homiletic source books. Literary texts like Rumi's *Fihi ma fih* and the sessions of Nezam al-Din Owleya (d. 1325) were based on intimate assemblies, or were at least constructed as if they were, so they also provide clues to how such sessions were imagined to unfold, if not how they were actually practised. Taken together, these sources suggest that a sermon – whether delivered to a large audience or a more intimate company – frequently involved a mixture of Quranic exegesis and direct homiletic exhortation peppered with narratives of the Prophet, his companions and sufi saintly figures.[61] Some preachers also narrated love stories from the pulpit, but this was a controversial practice that was frequently criticised by more austere sermonisers, most famously Ibn al-Jawzi.[62]

The genre of the didactic *masnavi* builds on the 'sermon in verse' of ascetic poetry by incorporating these narrative exempla into its literary-didactic project. This is not to say that didactic *masnavi*s are direct versifications of sermons, but rather poetic adaptations that imaginatively draw on the thematic and rhetorical conventions of sermonising to perform their work. One of the most obvious differences between a didactic *masnavi* and the sermon texts that have been preserved – besides versification itself – is the number and length of their narratives. Sermons attributed to Rumi, for instance, may include only a couple of anecdotes each, no more than a few sentences long; his *Masnavi*, on the other hand, contains dozens and dozens of stories, many of which are hundreds of verses long. Furthermore, the stories in didactic *masnavi*s tend to be generically more diverse than those recited in homiletic assemblies, at least in so far as our sources allow us to judge. Despite these differences, the *masanvi*s' narratives evoke the exempla of contemporary sermonising in terms of their illustrative function, narrating personae and the reception stances they invite audiences to adopt; they thus represent one aspect of the genre's adaptive 'translation' of oral homiletic discourse into the literary-textual arena.

Once we understand how the genre of the didactic *masnavi* is informed by the structures of contemporary sermonising and evokes an imagined homiletic setting, it becomes clear that the homilies are not expendable glosses, but in fact logically and literarily prior to the narratives that they surround and contextualise. It is through the homiletic sections of the didactic *masnavi* that the poet establishes his persona as a preacher or teacher, invites the reader to adopt the stance of a potentially resistant listener who will (hopefully) be convinced by his speech and brings forth the implied performance context of a homiletic assembly or teaching circle. It is these imagined settings, and the storytelling practices associated with them, that justify the inclusion of narratives and condition their reception.

As a short example, let us take a closer look at the tale of the Qoqnos and its accompanying homily, one of the more popular anecdotes in ʿAttar's oeuvre.[63] It describes the strange life and death of the phoenix-like Qoqnos, a 'wondrous bird' (*torfa morghi*) that lives somewhere in India.[64] According to ʿAttar, there can be only one Qoqnos in existence at a time, and it lives for nearly a thousand years. Among its many fabulous characteristics is its perforated beak, by means of which it produces melancholy music in the manner of a reed flute. The human science of music even owes its origins to the Qoqnos: the bird was observed by an unnamed philosopher who thereby learned the secrets of melody. The affective power of its song is so great that all the other animals lose their composure whenever they hear it:

In every hole, another note
    Beneath every song, another mystery.
Through those holes, when it mournfully wails,
    the birds and fish all lose their composure.[65]

Stranger still is the Qoqnos's process of dying. When it has reached the end of its allotted lifespan, it gathers brushwood around itself while emitting a mournful dirge from every hole in its beak. All the animals gather around, attracted by its swan song, and many of them die from the intensity of Qoqnos's self-threnody. It then trembles and flaps its wings, producing sparks and igniting the fuel piled at its feet. When its self-immolation is complete, and the fire has been reduced to embers and then to ashes, a fledgling Qoqnos emerges from the pyre.

Prior to 'Attar, a few references to the Qoqnos and similar beasts can be found in the scientific and wonders of creation literature (*'aja'eb al-makhluqat*). The philosopher Abu'l-Barakat Baghdadi, for example, names the Qoqnos as the sole example of asexual animal reproduction, and he describes its music and death ritual much as 'Attar does.[66] A peculiar animal is also mentioned in an early wonders work, the *Tohfat al-ghara'eb*, which displays many of the characteristics of 'Attar's Qoqnos but remains unnamed. According to the *Tohfat*, this creature resembles a deer with a perforated horn. When the wind blows, the horn produces music that attracts the other animals and throws them into ecstasy, and the philosopher Plato removed this horn and used it as a musical instrument.[67] Broadly speaking, 'Attar's Qoqnos seems to combine elements of the phoenix, in its status as a species-of-one and rebirth in fire, with the swan's mythical self-dirge.[68] Whatever 'Attar's sources may have been (and they could have just as easily been oral legends as texts), the story recalls the scientific wonders literature. The continued invocation of terms like 'wonder' (*'ajab*), 'wonders' (*'aja'eb*) and 'wondrous' (*torfa*) may constitute a wink towards these generic origins.

Although short, the narrative is exceedingly rich, and it incorporates several interlocking thematic strands. As an origins story for the human practice and science of music, it explains the affective power of song, especially the lament. The Qoqnos's power to attract other beasts and throw them into fatal ecstasy recalls the sufi *sama'* ceremony as well as the stories of the prophet David. Perhaps most obviously, one can read the Qoqnos as a symbol of rebirth and resurrection. There is even the slightest hint of metempsychosis here: at one point, the narrator rhetorically questions, 'Has this ever come to pass, for anyone else? / That after death he emerges, un-born?' suggesting that the fledgling Qoqnos may be not only a new member of the same species, but even a new reincarnation of the same individual.[69] This nod towards reincarnation recalls Hindu and Buddhist beliefs, and the Qoqnus's self-immolation could also be seen as a reference to the practice of sati. A mood of Indic exoticism thus runs through the anecdote, consistent with India's frequent portrayal in Persian texts as a land of unimaginable riches, wondrous animals and strange human practices.

Within the wonders genre, such descriptions might serve to dazzle readers and install a sense of awe for God's creation. In the *Conference of the Birds*, however, the story is assigned a very different purpose by ʿAttar in his accompanying homiletic commentary (whose voice, as discussed in Chapter 5, elides with that of the hoopoe on the level of the frame-tale). In the explanatory address that follows the narrative, ʿAttar does not elaborate on any of the above-mentioned thematic threads but interprets the Qoqnos as an exemplum of death's inevitability. Every creature, even the singular Qoqnos, must ultimately die:

In the end, death got its due
    It came and scattered its [the Qoqnos's] ashes on the wind
so that you might know that from death's claws
    none escapes alive. How long with these stratagems!?
In all the world, there is no one without death,
    but behold this wonder, that none can bear it!
Death is a harsh tyrant,
    and rebels must be brought to heel.
Although much has befallen us,
    nothing is more difficult than this business of death.[70]

In other words, the tale of the Qoqnos functions as an illustrative limit case that demonstrates the universality of death and underscores the seriousness of this condition. If the Qoqnos, a bird who lives a thousand years, is mournfully preoccupied with its own death, then how much more so ought we – whose lifetimes last only 'two breaths' in comparison – attend to our own mortality? Through ʿAttar's interpretive homily, the story becomes part of a larger rhetorical manoeuvre designed to force audiences to face the gravity of the mortal condition and give up their futile 'stratagems' for maintaining a happy ignorance. The true wonder, according to ʿAttar, is not the fabulous Qoqnos, with its thousand-year lifespan and perforated beak, but the terror of death, which is so great no one has the strength to confront it.

As an interpretive and rhetorical act, ʿAttar's speech guides readers to a specific understanding of the Qoqnos as an emblem of death's inevitability, but he does not comment on any of the other thematic strands that run through the anecdote. Metempsychosis, music, ecstasy, self-immolation and Indian exoticism – all of them are absent from the homily, despite their palpable presence in the narrative itself. This kind of relationship between homily and narrative has been described as 'tangential' by Peter Toohey, not in the sense of 'unrelated', but in the technical, mathematical sense of a single point of contact: the didactic address follows a single thread of the narrative's potential meanings, amplifying it and using it as springboard to run in new directions.[71] This is ʿAttar's standard modus operendi: he lifts out one or two particular strands of thought, leaving other interpretative possibilities latent in the anecdote for readers to suss out on their own, if at all. Such a procedure does not necessarily foreclose alternative interpretations, but it does elevate one particular understanding of the anecdote while de-emphasising other levels of meaning.

Attempts at authorial interpretation sometimes offend modern literary sensibilities, but it is far from clear if the premodern, sufi-inclined audience ʿAttar imagined for his works would feel the same unease. When ʿAttar interprets his narratives and points them with morals, he glosses them not only as an author, but also – among other personae – as a sufi preacher guiding his flock. Submission to a spiritual guide's authority, hermeneutic or otherwise, was understood as the *sine qua non* for progress along the sufi path, and mystically minded readers would naturally bring this cultural habit with them to ʿAttar's work. To read 'with the grain' means to enter into this pedagogical relationship, to accept ʿAttar's authority and to allow oneself to be guided by his interpretations. This pedagogical relationship may be asymmetrical, but power is not unidirectional and readers are by no means passive subjects. They can simultaneously accept ʿAttar's authority and resist his interpretations. Indeed, ʿAttar imagines an addressee who is, at the very least, always potentially resistant to his didactic teachings, and sometimes actively so. This is not the 'resistant reader' of modern criticism who rejects authorial intentions and is suspicious of a text's surface meanings, but the resistance of a novice disciple or a sufi-inclined listener who has yet to make the definitive turn (*towba*) to God, and who is continually led astray by the carnal soul despite their professed desire for reform. ʿAttar's exhortations, as perlocutionary utterances, presuppose and even call forth this mode of resistance, which they then aim to overcome.

He thus speaks with the exasperation and performative anger of a preacher on the pulpit, haranguing an imagined audience who have yet to reform themselves and heed his teachings. In the homily that follows the story of the

Qoqnos, he rebukes his recipients for ignoring their own inevitable deaths ('how long with these stratagems!?'), and many of his homilies are even more forceful. They frequently open with belittling epithets as 'Attar calls out his addressee as an 'ignoramus' (*ghafel*), a 'fault-finder' (*'ayb-juya*) and a spiritual 'non-man' (*mokhannas*). He excoriates his interlocutors for their major spiritual failings and calls on them to make a drastic change in their mode of life:

> As long as you are mired in pride and conceit,
>   you will remain far, far from the truth.
> Destroy that pride and burn that conceit!
>   You are present to your carnal soul – burn that presence!
> O you who turn a different colour every minute
>   and have a Pharaoh at the base of every hair,
> as long as one speck of you remains,
>   there will be a hundred signs of your hypocrisy.[72]

The idealised relationship between 'Attar's homiletic persona and his addressee, while motivated by care and concern, is also marked by conflict and struggle. The charges he levies against his audience are serious: they remain mired in pride and pomp in the presence of the carnal soul. They are fickle and inconstant – a different colour every moment – instead of steadfastly focused on the divine. Egotistical self-assertion is woven into their very being, with a Pharaoh at the root of every hair. It is easy to domesticate mystical poets as gentle, ethereal souls, but as the above lines show, there is more than a touch of violence to pedagogical endeavour. Dowlat-Shah, writing in the fifteenth century, even calls 'Attar's speech 'the whip of the people of the path'. The metaphor is an arresting one, and it is worth taking seriously because it points to the antagonism that accompanies collaboration in this particular kind of pedagogical relationship. The guide and disciple work together, but the former also uses their dominance to steer the latter in directions that they would not go on their own, and which may be uncomfortable or even painful. As Dowlat-Shah would have it, to consume 'Attar's poetry is to willingly expose oneself to sting of his verbal lash in the hopes of breaking the resistance of the carnal soul and sparking spiritual progress.

This rhetoric, although harsh and confrontational, is ultimately deployed for the good of the listener, and necessarily presumes the possibility of reform that it aims to enact. Although mired in sin, the addressee can still 'burn the carnal soul' and destroy their pride; otherwise 'Attar's perlocutionary poetic performance would serve no purpose. They might even reach an illuminated state, as 'Attar explains in the continuation of the above-quoted homily:

> If you would be safe from I-ness
>   you must be an enemy to the two worlds.
> If, one day, you enter effacement,
>   even if shrouded by night upon night, you will be illuminated.[73]

The harsh accusations that opened the passage thus give way to the hope – if not the certainty – of spiritual progress and salvation, the effacement of the separate self riven from God and a return to a supra-personal existence in and through the divine. And in a few passages in his *masnavi*s, 'Attar is downright reassuring. For example, following a story about a sinner who, much to his ascetic neighbour's surprise, ends up in Paradise after death, 'Attar expounds on the theme of humanity's intrinsic metaphysical worth. He explains to his addressee that, as a human being, he is the telos of all creation:

> These eight spinning compasses, O son, day and night
>   do their work for you, O son.
> The obedience of spiritual beings is for you
>   Paradise and Hell are a reflection of your mercy and wrath.
> The angels all bowed to you
>   The particular and universal are they glory of your being.
> Don't look at yourself with condescension
>   since no one can be higher than you.
> Your body is the particular, and your soul the universal of universals
>   Don't enfeeble yourself in the essence of vulgarity!
> . . .
> One hundred thousand clouds of mercy over you are
>   raining so that your passion may increase.[74]

This is almost an apotheosis: while Heaven and Hell are generally explained as manifestations of God's mercy and wrath, here they are a reflection of human attributes.[75] The angels bowed down to you, 'Attar reminds his addressee, alluding to the Quranic myth of Adam's creation, and your soul is linked to the 'universal of universals', the Universal Soul that transcends time, space and multiplicity itself. This exuberant ecstasy, however, is still pedagogical. 'Attar's proclamations of humanity's cosmic worth are intertwined with homiletic imperatives ('Don't enfeeble yourself in the essence of vulgarity!' 'Don't look at yourself with condescension'), which situate these utterances within an asymmetrical teaching relationship. And as was the case with Naser-e Khosrow, the addressee of these lines is a boy, not a man, and he has much to learn about the world (and himself) at 'Attar's feet.

Paratactic Structures and Associative Transitions

Illustrative narratives, paired with interpretative homilies that either precede or follow them, constitute the basic structural unit of 'Attar's didactic *masnavi*s. As was the case with Sana'i before him, these narrative-homily pairs are joined together to form thematic clusters, which are usually set off as independently titled units in the manuscripts. This is almost always the case in manuscripts of the *Asrar-nama*, *Elahi-nama* and *Mostibat-nama*, which are divided into a series of numbered chapters (*maqala*). The earliest manuscripts of the *Conference of the Birds*, on the other hand, do not include chapter headings at the beginning of every cluster, but they are nonetheless marked as distinct discourses within the action of the frame-tale. For example, the story of the Qoqnos, analysed above, is part of the hoopoe's discourse on death, which contains four additional anecdotes treating the same themes: the narrative of the Son Rebuked at His Father's Funeral, the Flute-Player on His Deathbed, Jesus and the Jug and finally Socrates on His Deathbed.

By virtue of their progressive frame-tales, the thematic chapters in the *Mosibat-nama*, *Elahi-nama* and *Conference of the Birds* are, in terms of their relationships to one another, fitted into a clearly structured sequence. It is much more difficult, however, to perceive a similar kind of systematic progression among anecdotes and homilies within a single chapter. As Ritter puts it, '['Attar] is happy to digress by concluding a story with an aspect of the subject different from the one he introduced it with, and he then proceeds by way of free association. Thus the main idea frequently determines the first or the first few subordinate stories [of the chapter], whereas the others are connected through free association and often with rather forced transitions.'[76] The four anecdotes that follow the narrative of the Qoqnos are all focused on death and dying, but Ritter is correct that the associations between them seem, for the most part, to be based on lexical associations more than adherence to any conceptual hierarchy or sequence. This is not to say that there are no structuring principles at work. As the longest and most complex story of the chapter, the narrative of the Qoqnos comes first, which is often the case in ʿAttar's poems. There is also a glimmer of hope in the final anecdote, which gestures towards salvation through Neoplatonic self-knowledge, even though time to acquire such knowledge is short. This might explain why it concludes the chapter: the terror and inevitability of death are illustrated in the first four narratives as a kind of motivational strategy, and only then, after impressing on his audience the stakes of death, does ʿAttar explains what might be done about it. It is far from clear if this was an intentional choice, however, and one could swap the second and third anecdotes, or the third and fourth, without disrupting any obvious conceptual development. On the whole, as demonstrated below, the logic that governs their arrangement is paratactic and associative, with each anecdote connected to the preceding homily on the basis of a shared word or phrase, rather than syntactic, with each anecdote corresponding to a particular step in an argument or a hierarchical sequence of elements.

Such associative transitions are immediately visible in the homily that follows the story of the Qoqnos, which ends with a succinct observation on how hard the business of death and dying really is: 'although much has befallen us (*kar oftad*) / nothing is more difficult (*sakht-tar*) than this business of death.'[77] The pain of death is then illustrated in the next story, which features a mourning son crying before the coffin of his recently deceased father. The son laments that he has never before known such an agonising day. A passing sufi rebukes him, reminding him that such a day has not befallen the father before, either; indeed, that which has befallen (*kar oftad*) the now-deceased father is much more difficult (*moshkel*) than that which has befallen the still-living son![78] While the anecdote exemplifies the theme of death's difficulty, the specific reason for its narration seems to lie in its use of the idiomatic phrase *kar oftad* (befell), as well as terms like 'hard' and 'difficult'. These lexical items, which are central to the 'punch line' of the anecdote, previously appeared in the final line of the preceding homily. In this way, the connective tissue between the homily and anecdote is as much linguistic and terminological as it is thematic, with specific key words and phrases justifying the transition.

Following the anecdote of the Son Rebuked at His Father's Funeral, the narrator utters the proverbial line 'even if you're the chancellor of the kingdom / you will leave with nothing but wind in your hands', which then prompts the story of the Flute-Player on His Deathbed.[79] When a questioner asks the dying flute-player to say a few words about his state during this liminal time of passing, he laments that his life has been wasted in 'harnessing the wind' and now, at its end, he is about to 'go with the dust'.[80] Besides indicating a futile task, the idiomatic expression 'harnessing the wind' evokes the flute-player's breath, while it also ties the anecdote back to the preceding proverb and its mention of 'wind'.

'Dust' is an expected poetic pair with 'wind', and here 'to go with the dust' functions as a conventional, metaphorical reference to the flute-player's impending demise. The subsequent homily continues to use the language of dirt, dust and clay as it reflects on how everyone, even kings and princes, will disintegrate in the 'dirt of the grave' and become 'clay under the earth'. And it is this subterranean imagery of soil and clay that seems to bring the story of Jesus and the Jug to the poet's mind.[81] According to this anecdote, Jesus – the prophet most associated with life, animation and resurrection – once filled up a jug with water from a sweet spring and took a drink, only to find it bitter. Puzzled, he wondered aloud how the sweet water of the spring could become bitter as soon as it was placed in the jar. The jug then miraculously responded that it was composed from the clay of a deceased man's body, and although it had been shaped and reshaped into thousands of vessels over the millennia, it was still infused with the bitterness of that man's death. The speaking jug is a familiar trope, well known from Khayyam, and here it seems to emerge out of the preceding homily's focus on earth and clay as human beings' final resting place and the stuff that we will all become. The anecdote's repeated references to bitterness and sweetness also tie back to the final, transitionary line of that homily: 'If only you knew the bitterness of death / your sweet soul would be thrown asunder.'[82]

Keyword transitions continue to structure the remainder of the chapter. After the story of Jesus and the Jug, 'Attar turns to his readers with a characteristic rebuke: 'O you ignoramus, drink the secret (*raz*) from a jug – don't make yourself a jug-head from ignorance!'[83] The 'secret' spoken by the jug would seem to be the universality of death's terror, which is everywhere at hand but little considered. In the homily's subsequent lines, however, the poet elaborates on a different kind of secret – the human being's 'secret' ontological connection to the divine which must be activated before death: 'Since you have lost yourself, O secret-seeker (*raz-ju*) / find the secret (*raz*) before your soul leaves! / If you don't find yourself while you are alive / how will you know the secret (*raz*) when you die?'[84] This imperative is then illustrated in the final narrative of the chapter, a humorous anecdote that features Socrates on his deathbed and plays on his reputation for self-knowledge and self-examination. When his disciples ask where they should bury his body, Socrates responds that he doubts they will be able to find 'him' after death – because he did not find 'himself' in life, how could anyone else find him when he is gone?

It is often difficult for modern readers to appreciate these kinds of transitions, which can seem rambling or digressive. Many scholars have felt the need to apologise for the allegedly disorganised nature of didactic *masnavis*, or to defend them from charges of the same.[85] There is little indication, however, that premodern readers felt at all uncomfortable with didactic *masnavi*s' flexible, paratactic structure, or that they were deemed unorganised or incoherent. Associative transitions are common even in the most systematic premodern Perso-Arabic texts, such as those of the philosophical and theological traditions. It should be no surprise, then, that such elements are even more evident in the genre of the didactic *masnavi*, which quite intentionally evokes a semi-improvised, oral homiletic event.[86] One often gets the feeling that didactic *masnavis* are themselves semi-improvised, and that the poet may have started a particular thematic chapter without knowing exactly where it would end up. He riffs on a central theme, allowing anecdotes to develop dynamically on the basis of localised transitions rather than in accordance with any pre-planned sequence.

Because they unfold according to an associative logic, a single thematic chapter can accommodate a range of illustrative anecdotes that, while bound together by shared keywords and themes, imply very different understandings of the topic at hand. Diverging exempla sit quite comfortably next to each other within 'Attar's *masnavi*s, without the poet (or the reader) being forced to reconcile them in the name of 'consistency' or 'systematic thinking'. For example, in a chapter on God's inherent connection to human beings and immanence in the world, 'Attar narrates a parable of a beautiful king whose subjects are all hopelessly in love with him. Unfortunately, he is so overwhelmingly gorgeous that whoever sees his face immediately gives up the ghost. The king must therefore keep himself perpetually veiled, and his people burn from unfilled desire. To solve this conundrum, he builds a mirror on the roof of his palace and sits opposite it so that his subjects might safely gaze on his reflection therein. In the accompanying homily, ʿAttar explains that the mirror is an allegory for the human heart, through which human beings can behold the overwhelming beauty of God in a safely tempered form.[87] A second anecdote in the same chapter offers another allegory for the heart and its mediatory role, but with very different emotional tenor and metaphysical import. It tells of Sultan Mahmud, who was so enamoured of his slave Ayaz that whenever the latter fell ill, Mahmud felt so discombobulated himself that he had to immediately visit his beloved. He had a secret passageway leading to Ayaz's bedchamber, and, according to the narrative, he was therefore able to steal away there much faster than a messenger ordered to go by more conventional routes. 'The king', ʿAttar explains, 'has secret paths to every heart. / Even if the king is a stranger outside the chamber, / don't despair, for he is a companion within.'[88] In both stories, the heart serves a key role connecting human beings to God, but in the first narrative, God is a distant and overpowering beloved, and the best humans can hope for is a mediated view of him. In the second, the heart is the site of a much more personal, intimate encounter with the divine. Here it is God who plays the role of lover, not the believer, and God himself takes the initiative to steal into the human heart.

The chapter's paratactic, non-hierarchical structure suggests that each of these stories is a valid but necessarily limited perspective on God's ontological connection to human beings. The desire to systematise the poem – in the sense of forcing the anecdotes into a completely consistent theological, ethical or mystical framework – flattens out the magic of the genre of the didactic *masnavi*, which is its ability to accommodate diverging and even competing viewpoints. Each anecdote represents a single, partial 'take' on the topic at hand, and no single narrative or homily can claim to represent ʿAttar's total thought on the matter. When strung together within thematic chapters, they produce a succession of mutually illuminating essays that are by no means unitary or free from contradiction or tension, but collectively present a dynamic, multifaceted view of the chapter's main theme. These chapters often feel as if they could continue without end; there is no explicit conclusion or summation that indicates closure, nor is there a sense that the topic at hand has been exhausted. At the same time, each individual anecdote remains valid on its own terms as an independent, self-contained element; indeed, the poem's paratactic structure seems to invite the extraction of stories, which can then take on a life of their own in new contexts. The fact that many of ʿAttar's narratives were later retold by the writers of other *masnavi*s, including Rumi and Jami, testifies to this modularity. Because no anecdote necessarily abrogates or displaces any other, readers are granted a great deal of hermeneutic freedom in the relative weights they assign to each of them and how they divide their attention. They are invited to dwell on those stories that speak to them, either individually or as components of longer, unfolding thematic chains.

A paratactic arrangement through associative transitions is common to didactic *masnavi*s, from Sanaʾi to Jami. ʿAttar's poems, however, are also distinguished by his use of allegorical frame-tales, which adds another layer of poetic structure on top of this parataxis. While the anecdotes within each chapter are bound by associative transitions and do not appear to follow any obvious, preplanned sequence, the chapters themselves are syntactically arranged through the frame-tale into clear hierarchies that correspond to the progressive nature of the sufi path. As we shall see in later chapters, the relationship between the frame and its contents is a complicated one, and it results in a good deal of the poems' literary and religious interest. Before tackling these issues, however, we must examine ʿAttar's relationship to sufism more generally, as well as that of his varied audiences, historical and imagined. It is to these questions that we now turn.

Notes

1. J. T. P. de Bruijn, *Of Piety and Poetry: The Interaction of Religion and Literature in the Life and Works of Ḥakīm Sanāʾī of Ghazna* (Leiden: Brill, 1983), 164–75; De Bruijn, 'Preaching Poet'.
2. Ritter, *Ocean of the Soul*, 32.
3. Kermani, *Terror of God*; Claudia Yaghoobi, *Subjectivity in ʿAṭṭār, Persian Sufism, and European Mysticism* (West Lafayette, IN: Purdue University Press, 2017); Davis, 'Journey as Paradigm'.

4. Edward Browne, *A Literary History of Persia* (New York: C. Scribner's Sons, 1902–24), 2:319.
5. Browne, *Literary History*, 3:517, 527–8.
6. Browne, *Literary History*, 2:520.
7. Alexander Dalzell, *The Criticism of Didactic Poetry: Essays on Lucretius, Virgil, and Ovid* (Toronto: University of Toronto Press, 1996), 8–34; David Duff, *Romanticism and the Uses of Genre* (Oxford: Oxford University Press, 2009), 95–118. A suspicion that didactic verse might not really qualify as poetry can actually be found as far back as classical antiquity, although the objection is based on a different set of concerns. Aristotle, for example, refuses to grant Empedocles, the great didactic versifier whom he frequently quotes, the title of 'poet'. According to Dalzell, this is a consequence of Aristotle's insistence that all poetry must be essentially mimetic.
8. Percy Shelley, *Shelley's Poetry and Prose*, ed. Donald H. Reiman and Neil Fraistat, 2nd ed. (New York: Norton, 2002), 209; Edgar Allen Poe, *Critical Theory: The Major Documents* (Urbana: University of Illinois Press, 2009), 182.
9. Quoted in Duff, *Romanticism and the Uses of Genre*, 117–18.
10. W. K. Wimsatt Jr and M. C. Beardsley, 'The Intentional Fallacy', *The Sewanee Review* 54, no. 3 (1946): 468–88; Roland Barthes, 'Death of the Author', in *Image, Music, Text*, ed. Stephen Heath (New York: Hill and Wang, 1977), 143.
11. Dick Davis, 'Sufism and Poetry: A Marriage of Convenience?', *Edebiyât: The Journal of Middle Eastern Literatures* 10, no. 2 (1999), 285–7.
12. Christine van Ruymbeke, *Kāshefi's "Anvār-e sohayli": Rewriting "Kalila and Dimna" in Timurid Herat* (Leiden: Brill, 2016), 75–6, 123–7.
13. The notion of a poetic 'mode' as a recognisable literary stance that crosses the boundaries of formal genres was first popularised by Alastair Fowler. In Middle Eastern literary studies, it has been productively used to theorise the traditional Perso-Arabic genre system by Geert Jan van Gelder, 'Some Brave Attempts at Generic Classification', in *Aspects of Genre and Type in Pre-modern Literary Cultures*, ed. Bert Roest and Herman Vanstiphout (Groningen: Styx, 1999). See also Meisami, *Structure and Meaning*, 26–30.
14. On Abu Shakur, see Gilbert Lazard, *Les premiers poètes persans (IXe–Xe): Fragments rassemblés, édités et traduits* (Paris: Librairie d'Amérique et d'Orient, 1964), 1:27–30; Gilbert Lazard, 'Abū Šakūr Balḵī', in *Encyclopaedia Iranica*, posted 2020, https://doi.org/10.1163/2330-4804_EIRO_COM_4686; J. Matini, '*Āfarīn-nāma*', in *Encyclopaedia Iranica*, posted 2020, https://doi.org/10.1163/2330-4804_EIRO_COM_4799.

15. Lazard, *Les premiers poètes*, 2:91.
16. Lazard, *Les premiers poètes*, 2:98.
17. Lazard, *Les premiers poètes*, 2:114.
18. Lazard, *Les premiers poètes*, 2:107.
19. Lazard, *Les premiers poètes*, 2:119.
20. Lazard, *Les premiers poètes*, 2:108.
21. Lazard, *Les premiers poètes*, 2:121.
22. Lazard, *Les premiers poètes*, 2:107.
23. Lazard, *Les premiers poètes*, 2:124.
24. See the insightful comments on proverbs as tools in Kenneth Burke, 'Literature as Equipment for Living', in *The Philosophy of Literary Form: Studies in Symbolic Action*, 2nd ed. (Baton Rouge: Louisiana State University Press, 1967).
25. Shaul Shaked, '*Andarz* i. *Andarz* and *Andarz* Literature in Pre-Islamic Iran', in *Encyclopaedia Iranica*, posted 2020, https://doi.org/10.1163/2330-4804_EIRO_COM_5432; Mary Boyce, 'Middle Persian Literature', in *Iranistik: Literatur* (Leiden: Brill, 1968), 51–5; Maria Macuch, 'Pahlavi Literature', in *A History of Persian Literature*, ed. Ehsan Yarshater, companion vol. 1, *The Literature of Pre-Islamic Iran*, ed. Ronald E. Emmerick and Maria Macuch (London: I. B. Tauris, 2009), 160–72; Jean de Menasce, 'Zoroastrian Pahlavī Writings', in *The Cambridge History of Iran*, vol. 3, pt. 2, *The Seleucid, Parthian and Sasanid Periods*, ed. Ehsan Yarshater (Cambridge: Cambridge University Press, 1983), 1180–6.
26. On the continuation of *andarz* in Persian prose, see especially Ch.-H. de Fouchécour, *Moralia: Les notions morales dans la littérature persane du 3e/9e au 7e/13e siècle* (Paris: Recherche sur les civilisations, 1986), 19–131.
27. Shaked, '*Andarz*'. Shaked and Ahmad Tafazzoli have identified what appear to be versified passages embedded in *andarz* texts. The principles of Middle Persian versification are poorly understood but seem to be based on syllable stress. See Shaul Shaked, 'Specimens of Middle Persian Verse', in *W. B. Henning Memorial Volume*, ed. Mary Boyce and Ilya Gershevitch (London: Lund Humphries, 1970); Ahmad Tafazzoli, 'Andarz i Wehzād Farrox Pērōz, Containing a Pahlavi Poem in Praise of Wisdom', *Studia Iranica* 1, no. 2 (1972): 207–17.
28. Boyce, 'Middle Persian Literature', 51–2.
29. Gilbert Lazard, 'The Rise of the New Persian Language', in *The Cambridge History of Iran*, vol. 4, *The Period from the Arab Invasion to the Seljuqs*, ed. R. N. Frye (Cambridge: Cambridge University Press, 1975), 627; De Bruijn, *Persian Sufi Poetry*, 86; Lazard, *Les premiers poètes*, 1:20–1.

30. Lazard, *Les premiers poètes*, 2:88. On the significance of *sakhon* in later periods, see Kamran Talattof, 'Nizāmī Ganjavi, the Wordsmith: The Concept of *Sakhun* in Classical Persian Poetry', in *A Key to the Treasure of the Hakīm: Artistic and Humanistic Aspects of Nizāmī Ganjavī's 'Khamsa'*, ed. Johann-Christoph Bürgel and Christine van Ruymbeke (Leiden: Leiden University Press, 2011).
31. In a fascinating boast, 'Attar claims his verses are frequently mistaken for anonymous proverbs. 'Attar, *Mosibat-nama*, 447.
32. A. Hamori, 'Ascetic Poetry (*Zuhdiyyāt*)', in *Abbasid Belles Lettres*, ed. Julia Ashtiany et al. (Cambridge: Cambridge University Press, 1990); Paul Kennedy, '*Zuhdiyya*', in *Encyclopaedia of Islam, Second Edition*, posted 2012, https://doi.org/10.1163/1573-3912_islam_COM_1392.
33. Gregor Schoeler, 'Bashshār b. Burd, Abū'l-'Atāhiyah and Abū Nuwās', in *Abbasid Belles Lettres*, ed. Julia Ashtiany et al. (Cambridge: Cambridge University Press, 1990), 286–90; James D. Martin, 'The Religious Beliefs of Abu'l-'Atāhiya according to *Zuhdīyāt*', in *Transactions, Volume XXIII, 1969–1970*, ed. William McKane (Glasgow: Glasgow University Oriental Society, 1972).
34. Kennedy, '*Zuhdiyya*'.
35. C. H. Becker, 'Ubi sunt qui ante nos in mundo fuere', in *Aufsätze zur Kultur- und Sprachgeschichte* (Breslau: M. & H. Marcus, 1916).
36. Hamori, 'Ascetic Poetry (*Zuhdiyyāt*)', 268.
37. See the examples collected in Gregor Schoeler, 'The Genres of Classical Arabic Poetry: Classifications of Poetic Themes and Poems by Pre-modern Critics and Redactors of *Dīwāns*', *Quaderni di Studi Arabi* 5/6 (2010–11), 16, 18; Matthew Thomas Miller, 'Poetics of the Sufi Carnival: The "Rogue Lyrics" (*Qalandariyât*) of Sanâ'i, 'Attâr, and 'Erâqi' (PhD diss., Washington University in Saint Louis, 2016), 78–9.
38. Kennedy, '*Zuhdiyya*'; Mohsen Zakeri, 'Ṣāliḥ b. 'Abd al-Ḳuddūs', in *Encyclopaedia of Islam, Second Edition*, posted 2012, https://doi.org/10.1163/1573-3912_islam_SIM_6537.
39. Dalzell, *Criticism of Didactic Poetry*, 7. See also David Konstan, 'Foreword: To the Reader', in *Mega nepios: Il destinatario nell'epos didascalico*, ed. Alessandro Schiesaro et al. (Pisa: Giardini, 1993).
40. De Bruijn, 'Preaching Poet', 87. This quotation is taken from de Bruijn's discussion of what he calls the 'homiletic mode', which includes the *zohdiyat* but is not limited to it. On addressees in Persian poetry, see also Meisami, 'The Ghazal as Fiction'.

41 Philip Kennedy, *Abu Nuwas: A Genius of Poetry* (London: Oneworld, 2005), 121–9.
42. J. L. Austin, *How to Do Things with Words*, 2nd ed. (Cambridge, MA: Harvard University Press, 1975), 121–2; Jonathan Culler, *Theory of the Lyric* (Cambridge, MA: Harvard University Press, 2015), 125–31.
43. Naser-e Khosrow's life, philosophy and poetry are treated in Alice C. Hunsberger, *Nasir Khusraw: The Ruby of Badakhshan* (London: I. B. Tauris, 2000); Alice C. Hunsberger, ed., *Pearls of Persia: The Philosophical Poetry of Nāṣir-i Khusraw* (London: I. B. Tauris, 2012); Annemarie Schimmel, *Make a Shield from Wisdom: Selected Verses from Nāṣir-i Khusraw's 'Dīvān'* (London: The Institute of Ismaili Studies, 1993); Henry Corbin, 'Nasir-i Khusrau and Iranian Isma'ilism', in *The Cambridge History of Iran*, vol. 4, *The Period from the Arab Invasion to the Saljuqs*, ed. R. N. Frye (Cambridge: Cambridge University Press, 1975); W. Ivanow, *Problems in Nasir-i Khusraw's Biography* (Bombay: The Ismaili Society, 1956). See also the translations in Naser-e Khosrow, *Forty Poems from the 'Divan'*, trans. Peter Lamborn Wilson and Gholam Reza Aavani (Tehran: Imperial Iranian Academy of Philosophy, 1977).
44. Julie Scott Meisami, 'Nāṣir-i Khusraw: A Poet Lost in Thought?', in *Pearls of Persia: The Philosophical Poetry of Nāṣir-i Khusraw*, ed. Alice C. Hunsberger (London: I. B. Tauris, 2012), 225.
45. Meisami, 'Nāṣir-i Khusraw', 224; Dowlat-Shah Samarqandi, *Tazkerat al-sho'ara*, ed. Fatema 'Alaqa (Tehran: Pazhuheshgah-e 'Olum-e Ensani va Motala'at-e Farhangi, 1385 [2006–7]), 112.
46. Naser-e Khosrow, *Divan-e ash'ar-e Hakim Naser-e Khosrow*, ed. Mahdi Mohaqqeq and Mojtaba Minovi (Tehran: McGill University, Center for Islamic Studies; Daneshgah-e Tehran, 1357 [1978–9]), 493.
47. On the rhetorical potential of 'unmanning' one's audience in didactic poetry, see Lewis, 'Sexual Occidentation', 694–5.
48. Meisami, 'Nāṣir-i Khusraw', 224.
49. Franklin Lewis, 'Reading, Writing, and Recitation: Sanā'i and the Origins of the Persian Ghazal' (PhD diss., University of Chicago, 1995), 99, 108–9.
50. Meisami, 'Nāṣir-i Khusraw', 224–5; Alice C. Hunsberger, '"On the Steed of Speech": A Philosophical Poem by Nāṣir-i Khusraw', in *Pearls of Persia : The Philosophical Poetry of Nāṣir-i Khusraw*, ed. Alice C. Hunsberger (London: I. B. Tauris, 2012), 177.
51. Naser-e Khosrow, *Divan-e ash'ar-e Hakim Naser-e Khosrow*, 493.
52. Konstan, 'Foreword', 12.

53. Here I refer to the *Rowshana'i-nama* and *Sa'adat-nama*, the authenticity of which are contested. See Nasrollah Pourjavady, 'Hearing by Way of Seeing: *Zabān-e ḥāl* in Nāṣir-i Khusraw's Poetry and the Question of Authorship of the *Rawshanā'ī-nāma*', in *Pearls of Persia: The Philosophical Poetry of Nāṣir-i Khusraw*, ed. Alice C. Hunsberger (London: I. B. Tauris, 2012); Mohsen Zakeri, 'The *Rawshanā'ī-nāma* and the Older Iranian Cosmogony', in *Pearls of Persia: The Philosophical Poetry of Nāṣir Khusraw*, ed. Alice C. Hunsberger (London: I. B. Tauris, 2012).
54. Shams al-Din Ahmad Aflaki, *Manaqeb al-'arefin*, ed. Tahsin Yazıcı (Ankara: Türk Tarih Kurumu Basımevi, 1959–61; repr., Tehran: Donya-ye Ketab, 1382 [2003–4]), 2:739–40; 'Abd al-Rahman Jami, *Nafahat al-ons men hazarat al-qods*, ed. Mahmud 'Abedi (Tehran: Sokhan, 1394 [2015–16]), 470; De Bruijn, 'Comparative Notes'.
55. Nezami-ye Ganjavi, *Makhzan al-asrar: Matn-e 'elmi-enteqadi az ru-ye 14 nuskha-ye khatti*, ed. Behruz Sarvatian (Tehran: Amir Kabir, 1387 [2008–9]), 66.
56. Annemarie Schimmel, *A Two-Colored Brocade: The Imagery of Persian Poetry* (Chapel Hill: University of North Carolina Press, 1992), 32.
57. Ch. Pellat, '*Ḳāṣṣ*', in *Encyclopaedia of Islam, Second Edition*, posted 2012, https://doi.org/10.1163/1573-3912_islam_SIM_4002.
58. On preachers and preaching, see Linda Jones, *The Power of Oratory in the Medieval Muslim World* (Cambridge: Cambridge University Press, 2012); Johannes Pedersen, 'The Islamic Preacher: *Wā'iẓ, Mudhakkir, Qāṣṣ*', in *Ignace Goldziher Memorial Volume*, ed. Samuel Löwinger and Joseph Somogyi (Budapest: 1948); Johannes Pedersen, 'The Criticism of the Islamic Preacher', *Die Welt des Islam*, n.s., 2, no. 4 (1953): 215–31; Merlin Swartz, 'The Rules of Popular Preaching in Twelfth-Century Baghdad, according to Ibn al-Jawzî', in *Prédication et propagande au Moyen Age: Islam, Byzance, Occident*, ed. George Makdisi et al. (Paris: Presses universitaires de France, 1983); Daniella Talmon-Heller, *Islamic Piety in Medieval Syria: Mosques, Cemeteries and Sermons under the Zangids and Ayyūbids (1146–1260)* (Leiden: Brill, 2007), 115–48; Jonathan Berkey, *Popular Preaching and Religious Authority in the Medieval Islamic Near East* (Seattle: University of Washington Press, 2001).
59. See especially Jones's problematisation of the term 'popular' in *Power of Oratory*, 158–63.
60. Berkey, *Popular Preaching*, 19–20; Pedersen, 'The Criticism of the Islamic Preacher'.

61. On the normative structure and performative practices of preaching, see Chapter 4, especially p. 128–33.
62. Ibn al-Jawzi, *Kitab al-qussas wa'l-mudhakkirin,* ed. and trans. Merlin Swartz (Beirut: Dar el-Machreq, 1971), 115–17/trans. 199–202.
63. ʻAttar, *Manteq al-tayr*, 336–8.
64. ʻAttar, *Manteq al-tayr*, 336.
65. ʻAttar, *Manteq al-tayr*, 336.
66. See Shafiʻi-Kadkani's commentary, pp. 649–51, note 2334; Fatema Sanʻatinia, *Ma'akhez-e qesas va tamsil-e masnaviha-ye ʻAttar-e Nayshaburi* (Tehran: Zavvar, 1369 [1990–1]), 148–9; ʻAbdolhosayn Zarrinkub, *Ba karavan-e andisha: Maqalat va esharat dar zamina-ye andisha va akhlaq* (Tehran: Amir Kabir, 1363 [1984]), 234–5; Abu'l-Barakat Baghdadi, *al-Muʻtabar fi'l-hikma*, ed. Muhammad ʻUthman (Cairo: Maktaba al-Thaqafa al-Diniyya, 2015), 2:61.
67. Mohammad b. Ayyub Tabari, *Tohfat al-ghara'eb*, ed. Jalal Matini (Tehran: Ketabkhana, Muza, va Markez-e Asnad-e Majles-e Shura-ye Eslami, 1391 [2012–13]), 123–4.
68. Shafiʻi-Kadkani's commentary, pp. 649–51, note 2334; on the phoenix as a species-of-one more broadly in Islamicate literature and philosophy, see Jane Mikkelson, 'Flights of Imagination: Avicenna's Phoenix (*ʻAnqā*) and Bedil's Figuration for the Lyric Self', *Journal of South Asian Intellectual History* 2 (2019): 28–72.
69. ʻAttar, *Manteq al-tayr*, 337.
70. ʻAttar, *Manteq al-tayr*, 337–8.
71. Peter Toohey, *Epic Lessons: An Introduction to Didactic Poetry* (London: Routledge, 1996), 25–7.
72. ʻAttar, *Manteq al-tayr*, 365.
73. ʻAttar, *Manteq al-tayr*, 365.
74. ʻAttar, *Manteq al-tayr*, 316.
75. The notion that the external reality of the cosmos, including Heaven and Hell, are reflections of the inner attributes of the human soul can be found in the writings of Najm al-Din Kobra, and the presence of those themes here suggests ʻAttar was familiar with Kobravi discourse. See pp. 65, 68, 218n36.
76. Ritter, *Ocean of the Soul*, 4.
77. ʻAttar, *Manteq al-tayr*, 338.
78. ʻAttar, *Manteq al-tayr*, 338.
79. ʻAttar, *Manteq al-tayr*, 338.
80. ʻAttar, *Manteq al-tayr*, 338.
81. ʻAttar, *Manteq al-tayr*, 339.

82. ʿAttar, *Manteq al-tayr*, 339.
83. ʿAttar, *Manteq al-tayr*, 339.
84. ʿAttar, *Manteq al-tayr*, 339.
85. For observations on the apparently disorganised structure of didactic *masnavi*s, see Ritter, *Ocean of the Soul*, 4; De Bruijn, *Piety and Poetry*, 119, 226–7; Reynold Nicholson, introduction to *The Mathnawí of Jalálu'ddín Rúmí*, by Jalal al-Din Rumi (Cambridge: Gibb Memorial Trust, 2015), xvi. Others have emphasised *masnavi*s' thematic unity or argued that their apparent digressions conceal an carefully pre-planned design: Parisa Zahiremami, 'Sanāʾī's *Hadiqat al-Haqiqeh*: Between Narrative and Non-narrative', *Iranian Studies* 54, no. 3–4 (2021): 485–519; Seyed Ghahreman Safavi and Simon Weightman, *Rūmī's Mystical Design: Reading the "Mathnawī," Book One* (Albany, NY: SUNY Press, 2009); Simon Weightman, 'Spiritual Progression in Books One and Two of the *Mathnawī*', in *The Philosophy of Ecstasy: Rumi and the Sufi Tradition*, ed. Leonard Lewisohn (Bloomington, IN: World Wisdom, 2014). Cf. J. A. Mojaddedi, 'The Ebb and Flow of "The Ocean inside a Jug": The Structure of Book One of Rūmī's *Mathnawī* Reconsidered', *Journal of Sufi Studies* 3 (2014): 105–31.
86. On orality and paratactic structure, see Walter J. Ong, *Orality and Literacy: The Technologizing of the Word* (London: Routledge, 1991), 37–8; Toohey, *Epic Lessons*, 20–32. The genre's connection with orality, parataxis and improvisation has already been noted by De Bruijn, 'Preaching Poet', 87; Nasrollah Pourjavady, 'Genres of Religious Literature', in *A History of Persian Literature*, ed. Ehsan Yarshater, vol. 1, *General Introduction to Persian Literature*, ed. J. T. P. de Bruijn (London: I. B. Tauris, 2009), 292.
87. ʿAttar, *Manteq al-tayr*, 281.
88. ʿAttar, *Manteq al-tayr*, 283.

2

ʿAttar and Persian Literary Sufism

In the works generally accepted as authentic, ʿAttar reveals almost nothing directly about himself or his circumstances: he mentions no travels, legal affiliation or spiritual guide; he names only one contemporary and no disciples, patrons or historical addressees. Likewise, the earliest external accounts of the poet – from ʿOwfi (d. 1232) and Nasir al-Din Tusi (d. 1274) – are exceedingly terse and do not fill many of these gaps.[1] Later biographical sources such as those of Jami (d. 1492) and Dowlat-Shah (d. c. 1507) are much more extensive, but they were written more than 200 years after ʿAttar's death and motivated by a hagiographical agenda. They narrate his life according to the expected contours of saintly vitae, complete with sudden conversion, extravagant martyrdom and continuing spiritual presence in the world after death.[2]

More than any other aspect of his biography, the lack of information on ʿAttar's spiritual training – and thus his status as a 'true' sufi – has generated much scholarly handwringing. According to the idealised portrayals of the sufi manuals, an aspiring sufi ought to enter into formal discipleship with a shaykh who, after a period of training and service, will invest the novice with a sufi cloak (*kherqa*) signifying their admission into the sufi community. ʿAttar, however, makes no mention of a formal spiritual guide in his undisputed works, and neither do the early accounts of his life. Eager to solve the mystery, scholars from the Timurid period onwards have suggested a number of potential guides, ranging from the chronologically plausible (Majd al-Din Baghdadi [d. c. 1209]) to the paradoxically fantastic (Shaykh Sanʿan!).[3] On closer inspection, however, even the more plausible suggestions have proven unfounded.[4] Given the ambiguity over his organisational affiliation, several scholars have concluded that ʿAttar cannot properly be called a sufi at all. Ritter, for example, writes that "Aṭṭār was a pharmacist and doctor, and whilst not actually a Ṣūfī, he admired the holy men and was edified by the tales told about them, from his youth onward'. Rypka, echoing Ritter, writes that 'Attar was not a 'true sufi', while Kermani describes him as 'more of an empathetic observer of Sufism than an active exponent', who 'consciously kept his distance from the Sufi scene'.[5] Others have pushed back on such characterisations. Seyyed Hossein Nasr, for example, considers him 'a great Sufi, who happened to be a poet, not a poet who happened to be a Sufi', and Benedickt Reinert identifies him as a 'Persian poet, sufi, and theoretician of mysticism'.[6]

As Omid Safi points out, the claim that 'Attar was not 'actually a Ṣūfī' because no guide can be identified presumes a rather restrictive definition of term.[7] Part of the problem is that 'sufi' is frequently taken as a self-evident designation and reified into a discrete, totalising identity. In actuality, however, the pious trend we now label sufism overlapped with other commitments and identities – legal, scholarly, religious and political – and admitted different modalities of engagement and levels of commitment. This is especially true during the twelfth and thirteenth centuries, when sufism was undergoing profound changes. On the one hand, it was becoming more institutionalised: *tariqa*s such as the Kobraviya and Sohravardiya were emerging, and the importance of 'training masters' who oversaw the spiritual progress of a cadre of disciples was increasing.[8] In this sense, the impulse to identify 'Attar's spiritual guide is perfectly understandable. On the other hand, even as sufism was becoming more institutionalised, sufi discourses and practices were beginning to penetrate all levels of society and find purchase even among those who were not formally initiated. Sufi preachers such as Ahmad Ghazali (d. 1124) and 'Abd al-Qadir Jilani (d. 1166) attracted large crowds to public sermons in which they propagated sufi ideas to broad audiences in an open environment. Interested individuals might attach themselves to a sufi teacher (or teachers) on a temporary or contingent basis without relinquishing more conventional lifestyles or formally joining an order. Shrine visitation was increasing during this period, and the veneration of deceased sufi saints was becoming a major focus of piety.[9] Most important for our purposes, this period also witnessed the rise of a Persian-language 'literary sufism', in which sufi sensibilities and ideas were increasingly made accessible through Persian-language literary texts, often of a rather ecumenical bent, that stand in contrast to the more scholastic

Arabic-language manuals and biographical works that had dominated the sufi textual production of earlier centuries.

The present chapter explores how ʿAttar was a product of, and a participant in, these intertwined processes of sufism's vernacularisation, popularisation and literary textualisation. His poems imagine a variegated audience sympathetic to sufism, who may or may not be formally initiated, and they provide this imagined audience with multiple routes of access to sufi beliefs and practices. This is not to say that ʿAttar's works lack complexity or sophistication, or that they were necessarily targeting less educated or lower-class members of society. Rather, it is to recognise that they engage with complex ideas in an accessible (and entertaining!) manner in a literary Persian idiom without presuming allegiance to any particular organised sufi tradition or advanced spiritual training. These developments were not unique to ʿAttar – following Sanaʾi, authorial literary texts were generally becoming important vectors for the popularisation of sufi discourse in the Persian-speaking world – but ʿAttar sensed the power of literary text to reach a broad audience beyond scholastic circles in a way that few previously had, and he appreciated how the textual encounter itself could function as a spiritual exercise, opening up new avenues for sufi practice and the purification of the soul.

I begin by situating ʿAttar within the rise of Persian-language literary sufism and exploring how he envisions a broad, variegated readership for his works. His popularising aims are explicit in his meta-poetic reflections and implicit in the form and content of many of his compositions, including his *masnavi*s and prose hagiography, the *Tazkerat al-owleya*. This also accords with the few clues we have regarding his biography: although he cannot be tied to any specific guide, and he does not seem to have trained any formal disciples himself, contemporary accounts of his life suggest that he was involved in spiritual training of a more informal sort, both orally and through his literary texts. According to the prose preface to the *Mokhtar-nama*, in which he comments on the circumstances of his texts' production, a community of mystically minded readers had formed around him and specifically requested that he compose a treasury of quatrains for contemplation (*taʾammol*), a sufi practice in which sustained hermeneutic engagement with verbal or material signs was used to intentionally cultivate particular virtues and spiritual states. Traditionally, verses from the Quran, the hadith or the physical wonders of God's creation would serve objects of contemplation, but the *Mokhtar-nama* offers quatrains for this purpose, and its thematic arrangement allows verses on particular topics to be located and memorised with ease. By examining the *Mokhtar-nama* alongside 'Attar's biography and popularising aims, the present chapter shows how Persian-language literary works did more than express sufi ideas for new audiences in an accessible form: they also opened up new modalities for 'doing sufism' through poetic texts and the technology of the written word.

Persian Literature and the Vernacularisation of Sufism

Sufism traces its roots back to a number of semi-legendary ascetic figures, but it was in ninth-century Baghdad that a loose group of religious scholars first started identifying themselves with the term. The emerging network of vocabulary, concerns and practices that constituted sufism then spread eastwards and found especially fertile soil in Khorasan and Transoxania where it was systematised and institutionally organised. The city of Nishapur, 'Attar's hometown, played an important role in these developments. In Nishapur and its environs, religious scholars began to teach sufism in their madrasas, elevating it to the level of a distinct religious science, and spiritual masters established *khanaqah*s as centres for the spiritual training of their disciples.[10] Alongside the rise of organised sufi institutions in Khorasan, sufi thought was systematised in textual works. Particularly important were the early manuals of sufism, in which sufi concepts were explained in theological and legal terms. By expounding sufi terminology, doctrine and practice in a theological framework, these manuals made it understandable for the scholarly elites of Khorasan and Transoxania. Prominent examples include the works of Sarraj (d. 988) and Kalabadhi (d. c. 990), and, slightly later, Qushayri (d. 1072) and Hojviri (d. c. 1072).[11] Alongside these systematising manuals of sufi thought and practice, extensive biographical works were produced that traced successive generations (*tabaqat*) of sufis back from contemporary times to the pious heroes of early Islam. Examples include the biographical works of Sulami (d. 1021), Ansari (d. 1089) and Abu Nu'aym (d. 1038; writing in Isfahan), as well as the biographical portions of the manuals of Qushayri and Hojviri (the latter writing in Lahore but hailing from greater Khorasan).

These works share a scholarly orientation, visible not only in their content and methods, but also in the context of their production and initial circulation. Chains of transmission (*esnads*) frequently introduce the sayings and deeds of the sufis that they recount, and Prophetic hadith with full *esnad*s are adduced to support particular conclusions, along with appeals to sufi and scholarly authorities. The biographical genre of *tabaqat* itself functions something like a giant *esnad* for sufism, in that it connects contemporary sufi masters back to the pious ancestors (*salaf*).[12] This process of legitimation through genealogical appeal to the early generations of Islam was, as Vincent Cornell has argued, based on Shafiʿi jurisprudential habits of thought.[13] Many of these works also seem to have been composed and/or transmitted within the context of scholarly study. The *tabaqat* of Sulami, for example, appears to have been arranged from material that was transmitted orally in study circles.[14] The treatises and *tabaqat* works attributed to Ansari and Abu Nuʿaym were not only assembled from such materials, but also bear the marks of further oral transmission before they acquired their current shape; they seem to have circulated among the compiler's students as notes and school texts for at least a couple of generations before they took on a fixed textual form.[15] Finally, all of these works were written in Arabic, with the exception of those of Hojviri and Ansari, which were composed in dialectical Persian. One suspects that the texts attributed to Ansari, in particular, were preserved in their distinctive Herati dialect because they functioned as aids to oral instruction within a school context.[16]

Over the course of the twelfth and thirteenth centuries, the nature of sufi textual production on the Iranian plateau shifted. It became increasingly Persian, a process of vernacularisation that was made possible by the rise of Persian as a literary language and sufism's increasing popularity, which accessible Persian-language texts further facilitated. While most of the aforementioned authors had composed in Arabic, and Hojviri and Ansari had composed works in dialectical Persian, by the twelfth century many writers were composing sufi texts in what had by then become standard literary Persian. The switch to Persian, in many cases, was explicitly linked to a desire to attract a wider range of readers. One clear example is Abu Hamid Ghazali's *Kimia-ye saʿadat*, a Persian adaptation of his monumental Arabic work *Ihyaʾ ʿulum al-din*. According to its preface, Ghazali composed the *Kimia* in Persian in order to reach an audience who were unable to access or understand the more academic *Ihyaʾ*:

> In this book, we explain [the religious sciences] for Persian speakers. We have refrained from lofty, abstruse words and subtle, complex meanings so that the common people (*ʿavamm*) might understand it. If someone desires verification and discernment beyond what is present here, they should look to the Arabic books that I have penned, including the *Ihya' ʿulum al-din* and the *Jawahir al-Qur'an*. The target of this book is the common people (*ʿavamm-e khalq*), who have beseeched me that these issues be treated in Persian in speech that does not exceed their limits of apprehension.[17]

The *Kimia*, then, is not just a translation of the *Ihya'*, but an adaptation for a new kind of reader. It is allegedly shorn of 'lofty, abstruse words' and 'subtle, complex meanings', and a reading of the text largely bears this out. It is quite a bit shorter than the *Ihya'*, although it covers the same general content. It adduces fewer proof-texts to support its points, and it does not provide the same methodical, rigorously comprehensive treatment of its subjects as the *Ihya'* does. Although Ghazali writes that he composed the *Kimia* for the 'common people' (*avamm*), it is not exactly clear who specifically is included in this category. Presumably Ghazali does not mean illiterate peasants or the urban masses, although a work like the *Kimia* could perhaps be read out loud to those who could not read themselves. More likely Ghazali imagines a literate audience who received some madrasa education, but who had not advanced to a level in which they would be comfortable with a dense academic work like the *Ihya'*, and who would not be considered part of the scholarly elite (*khavass*). This would be a diverse group, including merchants, shopkeepers, craftsmen and landowners, as well as younger students and less scholarly inclined sufis.[18] Whatever the exact social make-up of this group, Ghazali clearly saw the Persian *Kimia* as reaching a broader audience than his *Ihya'*. A number of authors claim to have composed in Persian for similar reasons, including ʿAttar in his *Tazkera* (discussed below) and Najm al-Din Razi Daya in his *Mersad al-ʿebad*.[19]

Not all Persian-language works from this period are necessarily accessible – Ahmad Ghazali's *Savaneh*, for instance, is notoriously difficult. Bits of allusive verse, many of them Ahmad's own compositions, are embedded in more technical prose on the metaphysical nature of love that they then illustrate and amplify. While it seems unlikely that the *Savaneh* was designed for a broad audience, it does exhibit a strong authorial voice coupled with a literary concern for the surface texture of language, qualities that it shares with other Persian-language sufi texts of the period. The literary character of Sana'i, ʿAttar, ʿEraqi (d. 1289) and Rumi's works is obvious, most of which were composed in recognised poetic forms. Many of the purely prose works of the period are also marked by an authorial confidence and a literary sensibility. For example, when Ebn Monavvar (fl. last quarter of the twelfth century) composed the *Asrar al-towhid*, a hagiography devoted to his ancestor and sufi saint Abu Saʿid (d. 1049), he took much of his material from an earlier hagiography but substantially altered it in keeping with his own rhetorical concerns: he embellished and elaborated it, added connective tissue and explanatory commentary, and updated and standardised the language. The shrine community centred on Abu Saʿid's tomb had recently been destroyed in the Ghuzz revolts, and Ebn Monavvar was motivated to preserve Abu Saʿid's legacy by adapting it into fluid literary Persian.[20] While the earlier compilations of Abu Nuʿaym and Ansari cannot even be considered authorial productions, works like the *Asrar al-towhid* were quite clearly composed by individual authors who intended to disseminate their work in textual form, and they confidently intervened in the material to render it aesthetically pleasing, relevant and accessible for a broad audience beyond any specific scholarly or sufi community.[21]

These intertwined trends of vernacularisation, popularisation and literarisation are especially visible in ʿAttar, where they are also the subject of metapoetic reflection. One example, found in the conclusion of the *Conference of the Birds*, has already been quoted in the introduction of this monograph:

> My utterances suffice as your leader
> for this speech is a spiritual guide (*pir*) on the path for everyone.
> Although I am no one compared to the birds of the way,
> I have mentioned them – isn't that enough for me?[22]

Such a statement, hyperbolic as it may be, speaks to both ʿAttar's variegated audience and the pedagogic intention of his work: it functions as a spiritual guide – a training master – for all who read it. At the same time, even as ʿAttar boasts of his work's universal efficacy, he humbly confesses his lack of standing compared with those 'birds of the way' who have followed the spiritual path to its end. He does not count himself among the spiritual elite, but he has immortalised those spiritual exemplars in a poetic text that is sufficient to guide others like him. The universal reach of his work is the subject of a second set of lines in the same section, again as part of a poetic boast:

> The people of form are drowned in my speech
> The people of meaning are men of my secrets.
> This book is an ornament for the ages
> It gives a share to the elite (*khass*) and the masses (*ʿamm*).
> If one frozen like ice were to see this book,
> he would come out from behind the veil like fire.[23]

Here ʿAttar celebrates the book's multifaceted meanings for multiple audiences. As he puts it, 'the people of form' remain entranced with his eloquent speech, while 'the people of meaning' dive deeper into the work's inner significance; both the 'elite' and the 'masses' have a share in it. The same language is found in the introduction to the *Mosibat-nama*, which ʿAttar describes as 'a beautiful book for the elite and the masses'.[24] As was the case with Abu Hamid Ghazali, it is not exactly clear whom these two terms refer to, and whether they map onto identifiable social groups. They might refer to cultural elites vs unlettered devotees, scholarly vs non-scholarly literate readers or invested sufis vs uninitiated dabblers. But however we understand the specific scope of these terms, it is clear that ʿAttar imagines his text speaking to a broader audience than the scholarly readers of Qushayri and Sulami. He even claims that his book can transform its readers, sparking mystical desire in the 'frozen' hearts of those who were not particularly attracted to sufi piety before reading it. In short, although scholars and formally initiated sufis are by no means excluded from ʿAttar's intended audience, the poet envisions his readership extending outside of those specialised circles.

It has been suggested that the relatively simple language of ʿAttar's poems and the social range of characters they feature also speak to his popularising aims.[25] These narrative and linguistic characteristics, however, are not unique to ʿAttar but are common to the genre of the didactic *masnavi* more broadly. Still, the adaptation of the didactic *masnavi* as a vehicle for sufi discourse does speak to the latter's increasing popularity and represents a new vector for its textual circulation and dissemination. Scholarly works like Qushayri's were transmitted as part of academic study, usually in a madrasa context, and while one imagines that most readers of the *Conference of the Birds*, as literate manuscript owners, would have had some madrasa training, it, like other literary texts, was read, recited and transmitted without any need for a scholarly licence (*ejaza*). Likewise, the *Conference of the Birds* (and most other *masnavis*) can be appreciated without advanced training in theology, jurisprudence or the technicalities of sufi doctrine. The poem's diverse stories and homilies provide a number of different routes into the material, and because of the work's paratactic structure, readers and listeners can focus in on those stories and sections that they find most meaningful. Those who are familiar with technical theological debates may be attracted to ʿAttar's more complex allegorical stories, while others may find his romantic tales of adventure or humorous stories of wise-fools more engaging.

The accessible register of ʿAttar's didactic *masnavis* is part and parcel of the genre, but his *Tazkera*, which represents an original adaptation of the scholarly *tabaqat* and biographical compendia, demonstrates his individual concern for the popularisation of sufi discourse in literary Persian forms.[26] The *tabaqat*, as previously mentioned, trace sufism back from contemporary times to the earliest generations after the Prophet in order to establish its Islamic roots. The *Tazkera*, by contrast, does not seek to legitimise or justify sufism; rather, according to ʿAttar's testimony in the introduction, its primary purpose is to provide access to the religious blessings of saintly speech for a non-Arabophobe audience. Specialised knowledge of Arabic grammar and vocabulary are required to appreciate the Quran and hadith, or so ʿAttar claims, and therefore most people cannot take full advantage of them. Thankfully, the words of the saints are a 'commentary' on the Quran and *sunna* in which 'both the elites (*khass*) and the masses (*ʿamm*) have a share'. And while most saintly dicta are in the Arabic language, they can be felicitously translated, a project that ʿAttar undertakes 'so that all might be included' in their benefits.[27] He writes that he composed the *Tazkera* for a group of friends, but he also addresses an anonymous audience beyond this group, figuring his reader as anyone who, like himself, respects and admires the saints: 'I saw in a group of friends a great desire for the sayings of this clan, and I also have a great desire for studying their states and speech . . . So I made a collection for my friends and myself, and if you are one of this group, for you, too.'[28]

In keeping with this more popular orientation, ʿAttar also removes the chains of transmission (*esnad*s) found in the earlier hagiographical compilations that served as his sources.[29] This is not to suggest that historical accuracy was unimportant to ʿAttar, or that he rejects *esnad*s on methodological grounds. The transformative power of these dicta depends on the authenticity of their saintly origin, and ʿAttar thus claims to have included only authentic sayings and narratives and to have erred on the side of caution.[30] Reproducing the traditional scholarly apparatus documenting that process, however, was unnecessary given the expanded readership and devotional purpose that he imagined for the work, as well as sufism's increasing popularity and dominance. Instead of defending contemporary sufism to a scholarly elite by documenting its roots among the Prophet's successors through rigorous chains of transmission, ʿAttar aimed to provide Persophone readers and listeners with a direct and seemingly unmediated encounter with the saints' inspired words.[31]

I say 'seemingly unmediated' because ʿAttar intervenes extensively in his material even as he actively downplays those interventions. As Paul Losensky has ably shown, ʿAttar creatively adapts and reworks both his Persian and his Arabic sources. He updates archaic language, smooths transitions and clunky syntax and adds contextual information to produce a fluent text for a thirteenth-century Persian audience.[32] While ʿAttar does not directly comment on the specific kinds of elaborations, elisions and shifts in emphasis that Losensky has documented, he does claim a general reluctance to intervene in the material. He describes himself as a transmitter who has exercised 'utmost caution' in selecting narratives, and he claims to have refrained from adding his own commentary or annotations because, as he puts it, 'I did not think it would be proper (*adab nadidam*) to place my speech alongside theirs . . . except in a few places to ward off the misunderstanding of the uninitiated.'[33] Such annotations are usually unnecessary, as the saints' words speak for themselves: 'If anyone needs a commentary, he ought first to look at their words and interpret them again.'[34] Saintly speech is thus presented as a self-sufficient font of meaning and blessings, and ʿAttar is reluctant to increase the distance between his audience and these saintly dicta through editorial clarification or scholarly interpretation.[35] At the same time, his mediation of the material is undeniable: it has been translated from Arabic or updated from archaic Persian precisely in order to make it readily understandable for his audience. Such interventions paradoxically cloak their own presence; 'Attar's role as translator and editor disappears from view through his editorial 'smoothing' of his material, just as his work as transmitter disappears with the lifting of *esnad*s.

Besides the removal of *esnad*s, the *Tazkera* also deviates from its sources in terms of its scope. 'Attar's major sources for the *Tazkera* – including Sulami, Qushayri, Hojviri and Abu Nu'aym – present a chronological history of sufism all the way up to the compiler's teachers. Indeed, the inclusion of the latter is central to the whole purpose of these collections: they justify contemporary sufism by tracing it back to the authoritative example of the pious forefathers (*salaf*) while simultaneously constructing normative boundaries for the sufi community by determining who is 'in' and who is 'out'. Thus the final generation of Sulami's *tabaqat* includes Ibn Nujayd Sulami, his maternal grandfather from whom he takes his name and at whose hand he may have been introduced to sufism.[36] Likewise, Qushayri's biographical section (which mostly follows that of Sulami with some key additions and omissions) ends with a list of 'contemporary shaykhs' at the head of which stands his own teacher, Abu 'Ali Daqqaq.[37] 'Attar's *Tazkera*, by contrast, does not continue to contemporary times but ends with Hallaj, the tenth-century exemplar of ecstatic, 'drunken' sufism who was famously executed on the gallows.

Hallaj was a controversial figure. Sulami and Hojviri include him in their biographical works while acknowledging the controversy around him, while Qushayri chooses to omit him consistent with his more restrictive understanding of legitimate sufism. By 'Attar's time, however, almost 200 years after his execution, Hallaj was generally remembered favourably by the sufi-inclined – if he deserved some blame, it was for his exuberance and failure to conceal the mystic secret, not for heresy. That the *Tazkera* makes the martyrdom of Hallaj its climax, instead of continuing up to the generation of 'Attar's predecessors, points not only to the changing status of Hallaj but also to sufism's dominance as a mode of piety. It was no longer necessary to defensively tie contemporary sufism back to the Prophet by tracing its genealogy step by step – its Islamic legitimacy was now taken for granted. It also gives the work a much more ecumenical feel than the earlier *tabaqat* and biographical compendia because 'Attar is not forced to decide who among more recent shaykhs to include and who to exclude, and he can thus avoid explicitly tying his work to a particular school or tradition. By focusing on the 'golden age' of sufism without reference to contemporary shaykhs, the *Tazkera* acquires a special mobility and applicability across sufi lineages, which partly explains the text's success.

Poet, Preacher, Sufi, Saint

Until the mid-twentieth century, scholarly retellings of 'Attar's biography were based on works that are now rejected as spurious, and his authentic works offer few autobiographical details.[38] As for external sources, the most detailed by far are those of the Timurid-era biographical anthologist Dowlat-Shah and hagiographer Jami, but they are full of legendary material of questionable validity. While admittedly vague and brief in comparison, the earlier accounts of 'Owfi, Tusi and Hajj Bola (the first two of whom were 'Attar's contemporaries) are not motivated by the same hagiographical agenda and provide a firmer basis for reconstructing the context of his works, at least in its general outlines. They give no indication that 'Attar managed a *khanaqah* or formally invested disciples with a sufi cloak, but they do present 'Attar calling people to sufi piety in other ways consistent with the popularising ethos of his texts and the spread of sufism during the eleventh and twelfth centuries: namely, by transmitting saintly dicta to non-initiates, preaching in semi-public settings and by composing and circulating literary texts for devotional purposes.

The paucity of biographical traditions about 'Attar's life is due partly to his particular historical circumstances. Nishapur was a bustling economic and intellectual centre throughout the tenth and eleventh centuries, but by the twelfth century it had entered a period of decline. In the mid-twelfth century, the area was occupied by the Khwarazm-Shah and then pillaged by the Ghuzz Turks.[39] In the wake of these depredations, and under the pressure of the famine that followed, open conflict broke out between rival Hanafi and Shafi'i factions, and those sections of the city that had been spared by the Ghuzz were destroyed. The survivors rebuilt on a smaller scale in Shadyakh, previously a suburb of the old city. 'Attar was thus born into a Nishapur that looked much different than it had a century prior; its rich networks of scholars had contracted, and its intellectual and economic life had substantially diminished. An even worse catastrophe, however, was still in store: the Mongol invasions, during which Nishapur was subjected to another round of violence, over the course of which, according to traditional accounts of his life, 'Attar himself was killed. The scale of the destruction and the decimation of the populace doubtlessly contributed to the lack of reliable information about him, as many of his friends, family and any possible disciples or associates with knowledge of the poet must have perished as well.

The vast majority of accounts regarding ʿAttar's life are later legends constructed according to the conventional expectations of a saintly vita. Jami and Dowlat-Shah, writing over 250 years after his death, narrate elaborate accounts of his sudden conversion, after which he boarded up his apothecary and embarked on a life of mystical asceticism; his heroic martyrdom at the hands of the Mongols, in which he calmly welcomed death; and his alleged meeting with a young Rumi, symbolising the latter's initiation into the pantheon of Persian sufi poets. They were also particularly eager to identify ʿAttar's spiritual guide. Carefully documented *selsela*s (chains of initiation) were de rigueur by the Timurid period, but ʿAttar's texts do not provide a satisfactory answer to the question of his *pir*. The romance *Khosrow-nama*, attributed to ʿAttar, praises one Saʿd al-Din b. Rabib in terms consistent with a training master, but some scholars have raised doubts about its authenticity, and this individual is not known from other sources.[40] Among the works commonly accepted as authentic, ʿAttar names only a single contemporary, in the introduction to his *Tazkera*, where he reports visiting one Majd al-Din Khwarazmi and finding him weeping as he reflects on the saints and his passion for them.[41] There is nothing in ʿAttar's account, however, to suggest that this Majd al-Din Khwarazmi was his *pir*. Nevertheless, the Timurid scholar Jami understood this figure to be ʿAttar's guide, and he further identifies him (perhaps on the basis of manuscript corruptions) as the famous Kobravi sufi Majd al-Din Baghdadi. It seems likely that ʿAttar must have at least known of Baghdadi, who managed a *khanaqah* in Nishapur until after 1200, but there is no evidence that the latter ever used the *nesba* 'Khwarazmi'.[42] Jami also reports that ʿAttar was considered an Ovaysi by some, or a sufi initiated by the spirit (*ruhaniyat*) of a deceased master. Jami identifies Hallaj as ʿAttar's possible spectral guide, while some modern scholars have proposed that ʿAttar enjoyed a special relationship with the legacy of Abu Saʿid.[43] But this notion of Ovaysi initiation, at least as Jami intends it, is anachronistic. ʿAttar himself understands an Ovaysi to be someone 'who has no need of a guide, being nurtured by the spirit of prophecy'; he does not appear to be familiar with the notion that someone could be formally initiated into sufism by the spirit of a deceased master.[44] Dowlat-Shah, for his part, reports that 'Attar repented at the hand of Rokn al-Din Akkaf, a view derived from an overly biographical reading of his *masnavis*. Akkaf features as a protagonist in a number of 'Attar's anecdotes, but he was an ascetic who died before 'Attar was born or while he was very young.[45] Modern scholars have inherited this Timurid-era fascination with 'Attar's guide, but they, too, have been unable to provide any clear-cut answers to the question.[46]

'Attar is also mentioned by two of his contemporaries, 'Owfi and Nasir al-Din Tusi, and while their accounts are not nearly as detailed as the later Timurid hagiographies, they are much more reliable as historical sources. They both describe 'Attar as a practitioner of sufi piety, but they shed no light on the question of whether he was formally initiated or who his guide might have been; the problem that so bedeviled Timurid and modern scholars seems to have been, for these earlier observers, a non-issue. Both of these accounts were also set down outside of Khorasan, which explains how they survived the early Mongol conquests. 'Owfi visited Nishapur in 1206–7, but he compiled his biographical anthology of poets two decades later while residing in Ucch.[47] He includes 'Attar in his chapter on poets 'after the reign of Sanjar'. He describes 'Attar as 'a traveller (*salek*) of the path of truth (*haqiqat*) and a resident of the prayer rug of the way (*tariqat*)', terminology that is strongly associated with sufi piety.[48] He also signals the mystical content of 'Attar's work by speaking of its great appeal for the 'people of taste' and 'lords of passion and taste', epithets that suggest mystically inclined readers. This should not be taken to mean, however, that 'Attar's audience was limited to formally initiated sufis *khanaqah* residents. 'Owfi, for his part, does not seem to have had any formal relationship to sufism, although he is said to have attended the sermons of Majd al-Din Baghdadi.[49] Nevertheless, he was quite taken with 'Attar's work, and he praises him in hyperbolic terms that suggest his verse had achieved a wide circulation: "Attar, the grace of whose perfume has wafted over the tracks of the heavens, and whose sweet smelling compounds have infused the four corners of the inhabited world . . .'

The second account is from Nasir al-Din Tusi, the famous Shi'i philosopher; he was not just a contemporary, but actually met 'Attar. Like 'Owfi, Tusi was never a member of an order or *khanaqah* community, but he nevertheless displays a certain sympathy to mystical modes of thought.[50] Tusi's account is preserved by Ibn al-Fuwati, the former's student and librarian at the observatory at Maragha, in his unfinished biographical dictionary.[51] His entry on ʿAttar describes him as 'an eloquent shaykh, of great discernment and knowledge regarding the speech of the wayfaring shaykhs, gnostics and imams'.[52] The heading that introduces the biography includes the epithet 'knower of god' (*ʿaref*) appended to ʿAttar's name, which also suggests a mystical orientation. Most of the passage is a quotation directly from Tusi:

> Mawlana Nas[i]r al-Din Abu Jaʿfar Muhammad b. Muhammad b. al-Hasan al-Tusi saw him [ʿAttar] at Nishapur. He said: 'He was an eloquent shaykh, of great discernment and knowledge regarding the speech of the wayfaring shaykhs, gnostics and imams. He has a large *divan* and the *Conference of the Birds* is among his *masnavis*. He was martyred by the Tatars at Nishapur. He said "I heard that Dhu'l-Nun Misri would say: 'sufis prefer God over all things, and God prefers them over all things.'"'

This is the first mention of the *Conference of the Birds* in an external source, and also the first report that ʿAttar died at the hands of the Mongols. The Arabic saying of Dhu'l-Nun Misri quoted here, which Tusi allegedly heard directly from ʿAttar in Nishapur, is also found in Persian translation in the *Tazkera*, suggesting that ʿAttar may have orally transmitted some of the same material found in his texts.[53]

Perhaps the most interesting thing about this account is not its specific content, but the very idea that Nasir al-Din Tusi, the future Shiʿi philosopher, met with ʿAttar, the Sunni sufi poet, and was sufficiently impressed to transmit laudatory details about him to his own students. Tusi was born in 1201, so he must have been quite young when he met ʿAttar: no more than twenty years old if we accept 1221 as the latter's death date (Shafiʿi-Kadkani argues for an alternate death date of 1230, in which case the meeting may have occurred later).[54] The historicity of such accounts is always open to debate, but this particular tradition must be counted among the most reliable related to ʿAttar that has been preserved. It is certainly on much firmer footing than the better known legend that ʿAttar met the young Rumi and presented him with a copy of the *Asrar-nama*, a legend that first appeared in the Timurid hagiographies.[55] Whereas Rumi and his immediate disciples are silent on that alleged encounter, which does not appear in the historical record until a century and a half later, Tusi's own student, Ibn al-Fuwati, reports his teacher's meeting with ʿAttar within fifty years of his passing and transmits a direct quotation from him on the matter. Furthermore, the Timurid hagiographers were especially concerned with tracing chains of initiation (formal or otherwise) as part of their project of canonisation, so there are ideological reasons motivating their account of Rumi's meeting with ʿAttar. Tusi's friends and disciples, by contrast, would not seem to have had any specific ideological motivation to attach the Shiʿi philosopher to the sufi poet from Nishapur.

Among the two contemporaries who comment on ʿAttar, neither would be considered a sufi in a formal, restrictive sense of the word: one was a polymath with literary proclivities, and the other was philosopher and scientist. Although sufi life in Nishapur had likely contracted following the Ghuzz rebellions and the city's factional strife, the Kobravis were active throughout Transoxania and Khorasan and ʿAttar must have had contacts with them. Nevertheless, the earliest (and likely most reliable) accounts of ʿAttar originate from outside of this organised sufi milieu. It is difficult to reconstruct the early reception history of ʿAttar's works, especially with the disruptions caused by the Mongol invasions, but the identities of his two earliest observers would suggest that his works appealed to those who were inclined to sufi piety but not necessarily formally initiated or specialists in the area. At the same time, this broader orientation does not exclude those attached to organised sufism, as ʿAttar's later reception by Shabestari and the Mevlevis shows.

A much more elaborate account of Tusi's meeting with ʿAttar is narrated in the *Safina-ye Tabriz*.[56] This miscellany, compiled in the fourteenth century in Tabriz by the scholar Abu'l-Majd Mohammad, contains a variety of works on diverse topics. The anecdote in question is found in a collection of narratives and scholarly discussions that Abu'l-Majd assembled from the lectures of his teacher, Amin al-Din Hajj Bola (d. 1320), and it likely originated among Nasir al-Din Tusi's students or disciples.[57] According to the anecdote, ʿAttar regularly delivered sermons (i.e. 'proclaimed the oneness of God') to a group in the main mosque of Nishapur. It was in one of these preaching sessions that Tusi first became acquainted with him:

> When Khwaja ʿAttar had become enamoured with the divine and would recount miraculous stories, he would go to the Maniʿi mosque, which was the congregational mosque of old Nishapur – according to some every day,

and according to others three times every week – and proclaim the oneness of God. One day he was occupied with discoursing on the oneness of God. Khwaja Nasir al-Din Tusi – may he rest in peace! – who was then in the period of his youth, was behind a pillar.

As Tusi watched from his concealed position, ʿAttar explained the fundamental non-existence of all contingent being, which exists only through the necessary being of God. When a questioner pointedly asked about the status of individual human existence, ʿAttar replied, 'It is the second image of a strabismic eye':

When Khwaja Nasir al-Din [Tusi] heard this, his heart warmed. He stood up and kissed the hand of Khwaja ʿAttar. He said to the crowd (*jamaʿat*): 'Kiss his hand, since he has arrived!' He then went out from that gathering (*mahfel*) and sang this quatrain:

The true existent is the primary One
    Everything else is just illusion and fantasy.
Whatever enters your gaze besides him,
    is only the second image of a strabismic eye.

Tusi continued to associate with ʿAttar after that, attending his sermons and even copying a selection of his quatrains for personal use:

[Tusi] said: 'I had never heard this expression "the second image of a strabismic eye".'[58] Nasir al-Din was always a believer (*moʿtaqed*) in ʿAttar's poetry. They say that during the period when Nasir al-Din attended ʿAttar's circle (*majmaʿ*), he had studied the *Esharat* (*The Pointers* [of Avicenna]) and solved Euclid, and at the end of that period, he had written down 400 of ʿAttar's quatrains in his own hand.[59]

This elaborate account of Tusi's meeting with ʿAttar cannot be taken at face value. It is structured around a conventional narrative topos, that of the sceptical outsider who is unexpectedly converted after surreptitiously listening to a religious authority's sermon or discourse.[60] The Maniʿi mosque, in which this anecdote's action is set, was a well-known landmark in old Nishapur, but it was destroyed in the Ghuzz rebellion while ʿAttar was very young, so it could not have actually taken place there.[61] The extent of Tusi's devotion is also likely exaggerated: his own account of his alleged meeting with ʿAttar (transmitted via Ibn al-Fuwati), while still laudatory, is much more subdued.

At the same time, this is a relatively early tradition, and a homiletic assembly is a plausible context for Tusi's reported meeting with ʿAttar and his audition of saintly dicta. Although certain details are clearly unreliable embellishments, it may very well preserve a kernel of truth about ʿAttar's activities and the nature of his community. But even if the anecdote is completely invented, it still shows how people two generations after ʿAttar – without any clear ideological motivation to burnish his reputation – chose to imagine him: as a sufi-inclined preacher calling people to piety in verse-studded homiletic sessions. Preaching, during this period, was a major vector for the dissemination of sufi thought to new layers of society, as demonstrated in the lives of sufi homilists such as Abu Saʿid, Ahmad Ghazali and ʿAbd al-Qadir Jilani, and the genre of the didactic *masnavi*, as we have seen, transmutes this homiletic speech situation into a literary text intended for broad dissemination. The portrayal is thus a natural one: in this anecdote, the homiletic inclinations of ʿAttar's *masnavi*s are imaginatively applied to his own biography. Tusi had already studied philosophy with other teachers by the time he met ʿAttar, and although young, he certainly would have been counted among the intellectual 'elite' and not the 'masses'. Nevertheless, he was not an initiated sufi, much less one of ʿAttar's exclusive disciples (if ʿAttar even had any), and his attendance at ʿAttar's sessions must have overlapped with other social and intellectual commitments. He is said to have become a 'believer' (*moʿtaqed*) in ʿAttar's poetry – terminology that was often applied to the followers of popular preachers – and he allegedly copied out 400 quatrains for his own use.[62] Even if fabricated by Tusi's later followers, the story recorded in the *Safina* thus still speaks to the homiletic, popularising ethos that informs ʿAttar's work, as well as sufism's burgeoning appeal more broadly.

A Request from Friends

In addition to the external sources, some information about the intended readership of ʿAttar's works can be gleaned from the works themselves. As mentioned previously, ʿAttar claims to have composed the *Tazkera* for '[his] friends and for [him]self' while simultaneously gesturing towards a larger, anonymous readership.[63] When introducing the concluding allegorical story of the *Conference of the Birds*, he writes that it was narrated at the prompting of 'our companions' (*ashabona*), an Arabic borrowing often applied to groups of disciples in sufi contexts.[64] His most extensive gestures towards his initial audience, however, are made in the prose introduction to the *Mokhtar-nama*.[65] There ʿAttar explains that he compiled the quatrain collection for a group of companions at their request, and he describes them in language that suggests an interest in sufi piety, if not necessarily formal discipleship. Attar portrays his leadership of this community as deriving not from homiletic activities, but from their interest in his poetic texts as sites of devotional practice. Sufi preachers had previously used poetry in *sama*ʿ sessions and sermons, and their disciples made informal collections for their own use, much as Nasir al-Din Tusi is alleged to have done. With the *Mokhtar-nama*, however, ʿAttar produced an organised, authorial rendition of his own quatrains, from which he envisions his textual community memorising and contemplating verses on specific themes.

The *Mokhtar-nama* is unusual for a couple of reasons. First, prior to the thirteenth century, Persian poets generally did not compile their own lyric poetry into textual collections, and especially not their quatrains, which were more occasional in nature and not considered polished pieces on the level of the *ghazal* or the *qasida*. Although poets were expected to improvise witty quatrains with ease, facility with the form alone was not enough to qualify one as a 'poet' in the courtly sense, and quatrains occupied a smaller proportion of most poets' *divan*s than *ghazal*s or *qasida*s.[66] This was a popular form of poetry, likely with folk origins, and people from all walks of life would compose them. Before the Mongol period, lyric verses – whether quatrains, *ghazal*s or *qasida*s – were not usually collected by the poets themselves for textual dissemination. That task was left to the poet's friends, disciples or professional colleagues, often after the former's death.[67] During their own lifetimes, poets might gift friends or patrons smaller, non-standardised collections of poems (*daftar*s) tailored to their specific interests or for special occasions, and individuals might compile private copies of a poet's work for their own use. In an unusual move, however, ʿAttar prepared an authorial recension of his own *divan* and the *Mokhtar-nama*, a separate collection of around 2,000 of his quatrains. This is the first substantial, extant authorial collection of quatrains in Persian literary history, and ʿAttar considers it unprecedented: 'no poet has made a collection like this,' he writes, 'if someone had, it would have certainly been apparent.'[68]

Second, the *Mokhtar-nama* is arranged into clearly defined thematic chapters. Many early *divans* were arranged into loose, frequently unmarked thematic clusters, but not with the specificity of the *Mokhtar-nama*, which includes fifty chapters of approximately equal length that bear descriptive titles. Around half of the *Mokhtar-nama*'s early chapters are devoted to ethical and theological themes, such as the virtue of silence, the ineffable origin of the soul and the effacement of the self in God; the remaining chapters consist of études on conventional poetic topoi, especially amatory ones, such as the beloved's mouth, eyes and waist. Further testament to 'Attar's continual obsession with poetic disposition, the first three chapters of the *Mokhtar-nama* mirror the sequence of topics in the doxological exordiums that open most *masnavi*s, and which, in a less structured form, are also apparent in some thematically arranged *divans*.[69] The first chapter describes God's oneness, the second praises the Prophet and the third eulogises the Prophet's companions, including one quatrain each for Abu Bakr, 'Umar, 'Uthman, 'Ali, Hasan and Husayn. The fiftieth and final chapter is even a sort of 'account of the poet's state' (*hasb-e hal*) parallel to those found in the concluding sections of 'Attar's four *masnavi*s: its quatrains consist primarily of self-praise, exhortations to careful reading, as well as complaints of loneliness and misunderstanding. Ritter has identified only one extant quatrain collection that precedes the *Mokhtar-nama* organised in explicit thematic chapters, and it is an anthology of multiple poets' work, not an authorial production.[70]

Most intriguing, however, is the *Mokhtar-nama*'s prose introduction, in which 'Attar explains the circumstances of its production and the purpose behind its thematic arrangement. He claims that he had previously compiled an authorial recension of his *divan* (already an unusual move for a poet of this period) that included a full set of 3,000 quatrains. Then, at the behest of a group of friends, he removed the quatrains from the *Divan* and compiled the *Mokhtar-nama* as a separate work. He praises these friends in glowing terms:

> A group of intimate companions, like-minded lovers, far-sighted confidants and allied associates, who have hearts illuminated like the sun, breathe sincerity like the true dawn and – like candles – smile as they burn.[71]

Although not explicitly labelled as sufis or disciples, such terms have something of the fragrance of sufi piety. Sincerity was a common preoccupation of sufi thinkers, as was the illumination of the heart. The metaphor of the candle that 'smiles as it burns' is frequently given a mystical cast in ʿAttar: one ought to not only bear the slings and arrows of outrageous fortune, but to welcome them as blows from God, the divine beloved.

According to ʿAttar, these companions approached him with a request. First, they overviewed his oeuvre:

> The dominion of the *Khosrow-nama* (lit. *Book of the King*)[72] has been established in the world, and the secrets of the *Asrar-nama* (*Book of Secrets*) have been divulged (*montasher*), and the language of the birds of the *Toyur-nama* (lit. *Book of the Birds*, i.e. the *Conference of the Birds*) has transported rational souls to the site of unveiling, and the burn of the *Mosibat-nama* (*Book of Affliction*) has passed bounds and limits, and the register of the *Divan* has been made complete. And the verses of the *Javaher-nama* (*Book of Essences*) and *Sharh al-qalb* (*Husking the Heart*) were left unfinished out of passion, surrendered to the flame and washed away.[73]

This community is portrayed as familiar with ʿAttar's works, which (except for the last two) were apparently 'divulged' or 'published' (*montasher*) such that they were circulating among them in a finished textual form. These friends go on to explain, however, that the quatrains in the *Divan* are too numerous and unorganised, and they therefore ask ʿAttar to produce an independent, thematically organised selection of his quatrains. He is only too happy to oblige, although it involves a substantial reworking of his textual output:

> The quatrains that had been composed amounted to about 6,000 verses. One thousand of them were not fit for this world, so they were washed from the page and sent to the next world. As they say, '*Guard your secret, even from your button* [on your clothes],'[74] and one cannot enter the next world without having been washed and purified. From the 5,000 that remained, I selected and ordered a number of them in this collection, and I left the rest in the *Divan*. *Whoever seeks and strives, finds*. And I titled this the *Mokhtar-nama* (*Choice Book*).[75]

Even though the *Divan*'s text was circulating amongst this community in some fashion, 'Attar was able to transfer 2,000 quatrains to a new collection and destroy the textual traces of 500 others: he 'washed' them from the page and 'sent them to that world', punning on the ritually mandated washing of the dead. Nor was this the first time 'Attar destroyed some of his work: as explained in the overview of his oeuvre, he had previously suppressed two other poems entitled the *Javaher-nama* and *Sharh al-qalb*. The fact that 'Attar was able to exert this degree of control over the textual transmission of his work, ensuring the destruction of 500 poems that had been previously recorded and were circulating in some capacity, is likely an indication of the limited scope of his texts' circulation; it may also reflect the authority that he was accorded as a spiritual leader.[76]

A 'request by friends' is a conventional trope in premodern Islamicate literatures, through which authors explain how their works came to be. Given the ubiquity of the convention, we may naturally doubt the historicity of 'Attar's claim to have compiled the *Mokhtar-nama* in accordance with a request from a specific group of friends. Nevertheless, the persistence of this convention, and its continuing intelligibility to generations of premodern readers, testifies to the extent that textual production and dissemination was a fundamentally social activity during the manuscript age. An author's or compiler's text could only circulate if audiences were willing to accept the expense of copying and further dissemination, so a successful author would be wise to ensure his or her work appealed to a known audience. A committed local readership would have been especially critical for a poet like 'Attar, since he did not write for a patron, and, as far as we know, never left Khorasan. He therefore likely had a specific community in mind when compiling the *Mokhtar-nama*, and he arranged the work with an eye towards their particular needs and expectations.

And as 'Attar tells the story, the abridged, thematically arranged *Mokhtar-nama* met a very specific need for this community of sufi-inclined companions. They had previously found his quatrains to be spiritually useful and aesthetically pleasing, but the massive *Divan* difficult to navigate:

> [They said:] 'The quatrains in the *Divan* are great in number and memorising them (*zabt-e an*) is difficult. They lack the ornament of arrangement, and they are ignorant of the epitome of brevity. Although compiled, they

> are not arranged, and many of the seekers (*juyandagan*) remain bereft of their lot and aspirants (*taleban*) return without having reached their destination (*maqsud*). If an abridgement were made and a selection were chosen on the basis of order and arrangement, their structure and adornment would increase, and from the beauty of brevity, their brilliance would grow.'[77]

Such an arrangement would not only endow the quatrains with a certain 'brilliance', but it would serve a practical purpose by making specific quatrains or types of quatrains easier to locate. As the friends explain in religiously charged terminology, 'aspirants' (*taleban*) and 'seekers' (*juyandagan*) are more likely to attain to their 'destination' (*maqsud*) when the poems are arranged according to an overarching structure. That 'destination' immediately evokes images of the sufi path and its conclusion in proximity with God, but in a more mundane sense it also indicates those sought-after quatrains that readers are unable to locate due to the disorder of the *Divan*. The *Mokhtar-nama* thus seems to have been envisioned as a sort of treasury, organised by theme so that its readers could easily retrieve verses on desired topics for memorisation. It has even been suggested that its title – which translates as the *Choice Book* – refers neither to the quality of the poems nor to ʿAttar's authorial act of selection, but to the reader's ability to quickly choose verses relevant to their particular interests.[78] The text was not intended to be read completely through, like a *masnavi*; rather, the reader would use the text to find quatrains to memorise for later recitation or contemplation.

Contemplative Reading

ʿAttar underscores the quatrains' spiritual benefits throughout the *Mokhtar-nama*'s preface, but he also hints at the necessity of a particular interpretive approach rooted in sufi contemplative practice:

> This is a treasure of divine meanings of '*I was a hidden treasure, and I wanted to be known*', and a treasury of points from the unseen of '*And he holds the keys to the unseen, and no one known them but him*' (Quran 6:59). If the reader (*khwananda*) comes to the secret of this treasure through deliberation and contemplation (*tadabbor va ta'ammol*) then in no case will his goal (*maqsud*) not be achieved.[79]

The terms deliberation (*taddabor*) and contemplation (*ta'ammol*) might indicate close reading or attentive reflection in a general sense, but they also refer to a specific set of sufi practices, in which signs are interpreted as part of an intentional practice of self-regulation.[80] Through contemplation, the interpreting subject derives and internalises knowledge in order to alter their spiritual state and guide subsequent actions. These more technical, ritualistic meanings would not be lost on mystically minded readers, especially because the terms appear together in a discussion of the quatrains' spiritual benefits accompanied by language and allusions redolent of sufi piety.

The exact procedures of contemplation, like those of other sufi practices, were likely transmitted orally and varied from tradition to tradition. Nevertheless, a few authors do discuss contemplation in writing, most notably Abu Hamid Ghazali, who overviews the practice in detail in both his *Kimia-ye sa'adat* and the *Ihya'*, texts with which 'Attar was almost certainly familiar.[81] Ghazali generally uses the term *tafakkor* for contemplation, but he notes that *ta'ammol* and *tadabbor* – the terms used by 'Attar in the passage quoted above – are exact synonyms, 'with no difference in meaning among them'.[82] Of course, even the closest synonyms do usually carry some difference in connotation, but Ghazali's larger point seems to be that all these terms can refer to formal mediative practice. More specifically, they refer to a mode of sustained, repeated hermeneutic engagement with 'signs' (*ayat*), especially the Quran and hadith, as well as phenomena in the natural world and within the human self, consistent with the oft-cited Quranic proof-text, 'we will show them our signs [*ayat*] in the horizons and in themselves' (41:53). For Ghazali, the practice of contemplation involves the derivation of these signs' spiritual significance through a form of syllogistic thinking: 'contemplation is bringing forth two propositions in the heart, so that one might profit from a third proposition derived thereby.'[83] The goal, however, is not an abstract, intellectual conclusion, but a form of internalised and embodied knowledge. The promise of 'profit' is telling: ultimately, despite its syllogistic basis, contemplation is pragmatic and practical. 'The fruits of contemplation,' writes Ghazali, are 'knowledge, states and actions. Its primary fruit is knowledge . . . and when knowledge is present to the heart, the state of the heart is altered, and when the state of the heart changes, the actions of the members are altered.'[84] Through the derivation of knowledge, contemplation serves to cultivate religiously desirable actions and states of being.[85]

Contemplation is thus not only a hermeneutic or deductive procedure, but a spiritual exercise for shaping the self.[86] Ghazali urges his readers to reflect on their ethical states and then embark on a targeted regimen of contemplation in order to desist from sins and cultivate positive attributes. More specifically, he advises that one interrogate the individual members of the body every morning, scanning them for anything that might be displeasing to God. When a past transgression is identified, or the possibility of a future sin is discerned, one ought to construct a syllogism-like structure out of relevant passages from the Quran, the hadith or already-accepted religious premises in order to steer the ship of one's self away from those dangerous shoals. For example, if one identifies excessive love of food, one ought to call to mind that gluttony is an attribute of beasts, and that if there were any perfection in it, it would be an attribute of God and the angels.[87] If one desires to induce a state repentance, one ought to bring to mind one's sins in conjunction with God's threat and the punishments prescribed in the religious law.[88] If one is too attached to the world, one should remind oneself that the eternal is better than the temporal, and that the hereafter is eternal while the world is temporal. By repeating these deductive procedures in the mind, one will, ideally, come to internalise the resulting conclusions and modify one's behaviour as a result.

Ghazali also recommends the contemplation of God's creation in order to better appreciate his attributes and intentionally cultivate corresponding affective stances: 'If one desires a state of love and passion, then let him contemplate God's beauty and majesty, greatness and omnipotence by gazing on the wonders of his wisdom and his marvels of creation.'[89] In the *Kimia*, in particular, Ghazali gushes effusively about the wisdom hidden behind the gestation of the fetus, the workings of human anatomy, plant and animal biology, and the size and motion of celestial bodies.[90] These phenomena are not to be marvelled at in and of themselves, but as testimony to the wisdom, power and glory of their creator. Unlike the physician, who contemplates the organs in order to treat them more effectively, Ghazali gazes on the human body as a sign of God's wisdom to induce a state of wonder and awe.[91] The human body and the wider world are all signs that point beyond themselves towards the divine, and through which the contemplator ascends to new spiritual heights.

When ʿAttar urges readers to approach the *Mokhtar-nama* with 'deliberation and contemplation', he promotes a style of literary consumption informed by the procedures and aims of this sufi practice of meditative self-fashioning. The quatrain form is brief and easy to memorise, and it is often endowed with an almost syllogistic structure that naturally lends itself to contemplative exercises as described by Ghazali.[92] For example, the following quatrain presents the universality of death in a few striking images, on the basis of which ʿAttar exhorts the addressee to abstain from chasing material wealth:

> Since the lion of the appointed hour lies in ambush for you,
> your disintegration to dust is certain.
> With the passing of time, don't amass land (*amlak*), but reflect –
> your lot from fate will be two metres of earth.[93]

The first two hemstitches explain that death is a certainty, and that your time on earth will necessarily come to an end. The third hemistich then derives the moral significance of this fact: in light of the temporality of human existence, you ought to refrain from amassing material wealth – *amlak* especially calls to mind land and property – the utility of which is voided by the shortness of life. And the final distich presents a powerfully concrete *memento mori*, exhorting the addressee to reflect (*bedan!*) on the mere two metres of earth that will constitute their final resting place, no matter how large their estates in life. The quatrain encourages the contemplation of death while itself serving as a vehicle for such contemplation, offering a stark emblem of the subterranean fate that awaits us all. And this terrible truth carries with it serious ethical consequences: when properly appreciated, death should motivate ascetic resolve and dampen avarice and greed.

About half of the chapters in the *Mokhtar-nama* are devoted to ethical and theological themes, while most of the remainder treat the various features and characteristics of lovers and beloveds. The latter are explained as allegorical signs that point to higher divine realities in much the same that way that, according to Ghazali, the wonders of creation can be contemplated as visible signs of God's attributes. In his introduction, ʿAttar alludes to the ontological and hermeneutic assumptions animating this approach:

> Some verses . . . are exoterically clothed in tresses, beauty spots, lips and mouths and can be recited according to the outward linguistic forms and

> terminology customary among the formalists (*ahl-e rasm*) . . . The people of taste and attributes, however, are unhindered by speech's form and go towards its inner meaning. They witness the Holy Spirit clothed in diverse forms, so they will not leave this table without benefit (*bi-fayeda*).[94]

The quatrains' amatory imagery is all 'clothing' donned by the Holy Spirit, and mystically minded readers (i.e. the people of taste and attributes) ought to be able to peel back those veils to witness the higher meanings concealed within. Sufi symbolist hermeneutics is sometimes derided as mechanistic in modern scholarship, especially with regards to 'sufi lexicons' like the *Estelahat* (attributed to 'Eraqi) and the *Golshan-e raz* of Shabestari, which allegedly reduce erotic topoi into conventional signs with fixed mystical signifieds.[95] 'Attar, however, never provides a pre-determined 'code' for deciphering his poems, and the extent to which the former actually promote a reductive style of reading is also open to debate. By 'Attar's own account, his poems contain 'inner meanings' beneath their outer verbal forms, but he does not provide an explanation of those inner meanings – or a route to them – separate from the poems themselves.[96] As he puts it, one cannot see the face without the mole, or the mole without the face. Clearly, the above-quoted passage functions as a rhetorical defense, but it still ought to be taken seriously: for a good number of premodern poets and readers, this was apparently a perfectly satisfactory way of articulating the spiritual significance of erotic verse.

'Attar's quatrains must have continued to circulate orally – after all, the form lends itself to an oral mode of transmission – but he was particularly interested in the spiritual possibilities of text, and his innovative act of authorial thematic arrangement is by definition a textual project. It has been suggested that the *Mokhtar-nama* and other later quatrain collections were used as treasuries of material for *samaʿ* or preaching, and this certainly may have been the case.[97] 'Attar's own vision of his text's spiritual benefits, however, as laid out in the preface, does not include *samaʿ* but the more subdued practice of contemplation (*tadabbor va ta'ammol*). As described by Ghazali, this was an intentional, self-guided exercise, in which the practitioner first identifies a particular virtue to cultivate, an ethical state to induce, or a sinful tendency to eliminate; we can thus imagine readers identifying aspects of themselves for reform and then thumbing to a relevant thematic section of the

Mokhtar-nama where specific quatrains could be selected for memorisation and contemplation. As Brian Stock notes in his analysis of *lectio et meditatio*, the actual physical encounter with the text is only a prelude to the act of contemplation itself, which would involve continued mental engagement after the text has been closed.[98] We know that orally transmitted quatrains were used in similar ways: Abu Saʿid, for instance, learned a quatrain by heart from one of his earliest spiritual masters, who instructed him to repeat it to himself continuously.[99] With a textual collection, however, readers can quickly access thousands of quatrains for contemplation on a variety of topics in a matter of seconds, including the bewildering unity of God, the terror of the coming judgement and the treachery of the world, as well as the many erotic topoi for which ʿAttar urges an allegorical mode of interpretation. By virtue of the thematically organised text, they possess a menu of topics through which they can direct their own spiritual development.

Other works in ʿAttar's oeuvre seek to 'literarise' and 'textualise' other sufi rituals and practices. As will be demonstrated in the coming chapters, a reader's narrative progress through the *masnavi*s' frame-tales is cast as symbolic movement along the sufi path; the *Mosibat-nama* is offered to readers as a virtual ritual retreat (*chella*); and the saintly sayings contained in the *Tazkerat al-owliya* are presented as daily readings and litanies to maintain spiritual health. Underlying all of this is a widespread cultural belief in the power of literary speech and text to instigate fundamental changes in the heart, spirit and even body of listeners and readers, a belief that suffuses ʿAttar's poetry and leads to the frequent comparison of speech with medicine. It is to this metaphor, and its implications for the poetics of didacticism, that we now turn.

Notes

1. Kamal al-Din b. al-Fuwati, *Talkhis majmaʿ al-adab fi moʿjam al-alqab*, ed. Mustafa Jawad (Damascus: Wizarat al-Thaqafa wa'l-Irshad al-Qawmi, 1963–5), 4.3:461–2; Mohammad ʿOwfi, *Lobab al-albab*, ed. Edward Browne (Leiden: Brill, 1903–6), 2:337–9.
2. Jami, *Nafahat*, 596–8; Samarqandi, *Tazkerat al-shoʿara*, 323–3.
3. Shaykh Sanʿan is the protagonist of the longest story in the *Conference of the Birds*, which may have historical roots, but is largely fictionalised. According to Gazorgahi, some claimed that this character was ʿAttar's spiritual guide. The

tradition continued in several later sources, especially in South Asia. Mir Kamal al-Din Hosayn Gazorgahi, *Majales al-ʿoshshaq*, ed. Gholam Reza Tabataba'i-Majd (Tehran: Zarrin, 1375 [1996–7]), 140; Christopher Shackle, 'Representations of ʿAṭṭār in the West and in the East: Translations of *Manṭiq al-ṭayr* and the Tale of Shaykh Ṣanʿān', in *ʿAṭṭār and the Persian Sufi Tradition: The Art of Spiritual Flight*, ed. Leonard Lewisohn and Christopher Shackle (London: I. B. Tauris, 2006), 182.

4. Austin O'Malley, 'Poetry and Pedagogy: The Homiletic Verse of Farid al-Din ʿAṭṭâr' (PhD diss., University of Chicago, 2017), 36–42; Hermann Landolt, "Aṭṭār, Sufism, and Ismailism', in *ʿAṭṭār and the Persian Sufi Tradition: The Art of Spiritual Flight*, ed. Leonard Lewisohn and Christopher Shackle (London: I. B. Tauris, 2006), 9–10; Badiʿ al-Zaman Foruzanfar, *Sharh-e ahval va naqd va tahlil-e asar-e Shaykh Farid al-Din Mohammad ʿAttar-e Nayshaburi* (Tehran: Chapkhana-ye Daneshgah, 1339 [1960–1]; repr., Tehran: Asim, 1389 [2010–11]), 24–5.
5. Hellmut Ritter, "Aṭṭār', in *Encyclopaedia of Islam, Second Edition*, posted 2012, https://doi.org/10.1163/1573-3912_islam_COM_0074; Jan Rypka, *History of Iranian Literature* (Dordrecht: D. Reidel, 1968), 237; Kermani, *Terror of God*, 26–7; De Bruijn, 'Preaching Poet', 88.
6. B. Reinert, "Aṭṭār, Farīd-al-Dīn', in *Encyclopaedia Iranica*, posted 2020, https://doi.org/10.1163/2330-4804_EIRO_COM_6077; Seyyed Hossein Nasr, 'Some Observations on the Place of ʿAṭṭār within the Sufi Tradition', in *Colloquio italo-iraniano sul poeta mistico Fariduddin ʿAṭṭār (Roma, 24–25 Marzo 1977)* (Rome: Accademia Nazionale dei Lincei, 1978), 9.
7. Omid Safi, "Aṭṭār, Farīd al-Dīn', in *Encyclopaedia of Islam, Three*, posted 2016, https://doi.org/10.1163/1573-3912_ei3_COM_23976.
8. Erik Ohlander, *Sufism in an Age of Transition: ʿUmar al-Suhrawardī and the Rise of the Islamic Mystical Brotherhoods* (Leiden: Brill, 2008); Meier, 'Khurāsān and the End of Classical Sufism'.
9. For overviews of these developments, see Ahmet T. Karamustafa, *Sufism: The Formative Period* (Berkeley: University of California Press, 2007), 141–71; Nile Green, *Sufism: A Global History* (Chichester: Wiley-Blackwell, 2012), 71–115.
10. Useful overviews of sufi history can be found in Green, *Sufism*; Karamustafa, *Sufism*. On the rise of institutionalised sufism in Khorasan more specifically, see Christopher Melchert, 'Sufis and Competing Movements in Nishapur', *Iran* 39 (2001): 237–47; Margaret Malamud, 'Sufi Organizations and Structures of Authority in Medieval Nishapur', *International Journal of Middle East Studies*

26, no. 3 (1994): 427–42; Jacqueline Chabbi, 'Remarques sur le développement historique des mouvements ascétiques et mystiques au Khurāsān', *Studia Islamica* 46 (1977): 5–72; Meier, 'Khurāsān and the End of Classical Sufism'.

11. On this process, see Karamustafa, *Sufism*, 96–107.
12. J. A. Mojaddedi, *The Biographical Tradition in Sufism: The* Ṭabaqāt *Genre from al-Sulamī to Jāmī* (Richmond: Curzon, 2001), 107.
13. Vincent J. Cornell, *Realm of the Saint: Power and Authority in Moroccan Sufism* (Austin: University of Texas Press, 1998), 14–19.
14. Mojaddedi, *Biographical Tradition*, 29–32.
15. Mojaddedi, *Biographical Tradition*, 42, 93–4.
16. On Ansari's works as mnemonic aids and notes for oral exposition, see A. G. Ravān Farhādī, 'The *Hundred Grounds* of 'Abdullāh Anṣārī of Herāt (d. 448/1056): The Earliest Mnemonic Sufi Manual in Persian', in *Classical Persian Sufism: From Its Origins to Rumi*, ed. Leonard Lewisohn (London: Khaniqahi Nimatullahi Publications, 1993).
17. Abu Hamid Ghazali, *Kimia-ye sa'adat*, ed. Ahmad Aram (Tehran: Ganjina, 1997), 5.
18. On the slipperiness of the terms *khavass* and *'avamm* and understanding *'avamm* as a kind of 'sub-elite', see Shawkat Toorawa, *Ibn Abī Ṭāhir Ṭayfūr and Arabic Writerly Culture: A Ninth-Century Bookman in Baghdad* (London: RoutledgeCurzon, 2005), 54.
19. Farid al-Din 'Attar, *Tazkerat al-owleya*, ed. Mohammad Este'lami, rev. ed. (Tehran: Zavvar, 1383 [2004–5]), 7. According to Najm al-Din Razi Daya, most books on sufism were written in Arabic and were therefore not very useful for Persian speakers (apparently he envisioned a non-Arabophone audience). He thus resolved to write a sufi manual in Persian that would be 'short in length but rich in meaning', profitable for both 'deficient novices and perfected experts'. Najm al-Din Razi Daya, *Mersad al-'ebad*, ed. Mohammad Amin Riahi (Tehran: Bongah-e Tarjoma va Nashr-e Ketab, 1391 [2012–13]), 15–16. In other genres, too, the decision to compose in Persian is frequently explained as a way to reach non-Arabic speakers. See Lazard, 'The Rise of the New Persian Language', 630–1. Cf. Elton Daniel, 'The Rise and Development of Persian Historiography', in *A History of Persian Literature*, ed. Ehsan Yarshater, vol. 10, *Persian Historiography*, ed. Charles Melville (London: I. B. Tauris, 2012), 104–6.
20. Austin O'Malley, 'From Blessed Lips: The Textualization of Abu Sa'id's Dicta and Deeds', *Journal of Persianate Studies* 12, no. 1 (2019): 5–31.
21. For evaluations of the literary merit of the *Asrar al-towhid*, see Zabihollah

Safa, *Tarikh-i adabiyat dar Iran* (Tehran: Ferdowsi, 1371 [1992–3]), 2:982; Mohammad Reza Shafiʿi-Kadkani, introduction to *Asrar al-towhid fi maqamat al-Shaykh Abi Saʿid*, by Mohammad b. Monavvar (Tehran: Agah, 1389 [2010]), 171–4.

22. ʿAttar, *Manteq al-tayr*, 439.
23. ʿAttar, *Manteq al-tayr*, 436.
24. ʿAttar, *Mosibat-nama*, 159.
25. Ghazzal Dabiri, 'Reading ʿAttār's *Elāhināma* as Sufi Practical Ethics: Between Genre, Reception, and Muslim and Christian Audiences', *Journal of Persianate Studies* 11 (2018), 34–5; Safa, *Tarikh-i adabiyat dar Iran*, 2:865.
26. See the observations of Paul Losensky, 'The Creative Compiler: The Art of Rewriting in 'Aṭṭār's *Tazkirat al-awlīyā*'', in *The Necklace of the Pleiades: Studies in Persian Literature Presented to Heshmat Moayyad on His 80th Birthday*, ed. Franklin Lewis and Sunil Sharma (Leiden: Leiden University Press, 2010), 118–19; Jürgen Paul, 'Hagiographic Literature', in *Encyclopaedia Iranica*, posted 2020, https://doi.org/10.1163/2330-4804_EIRO_COM_2645; John Renard, *Friends of God: Islamic Images of Piety, Commitment, and Servanthood* (Berkeley: University of California Press, 2008), 242–3, 250–2.
27. ʿAttar, *Tazkerat al-owleya*, 7. Although ʿAttar speaks of only translating the saint's words from Arabic, he also relied on previous Persian translations. In the case of Qushayri's *Risala*, Esteʿlami argues that he likely leaned more heavily on the prior translation by Abu ʿAli ʿOsmani than the Arabic. Mohammad Esteʿlami, introduction to *Tazkerat al-owleya*, by Farid al-Din ʿAttar, rev. ed. (Tehran: Zavvar, 1383 [2004–5]), xxx–xxxii.
28. ʿAttar, *Tazkerat al-owleya*, 4.
29. ʿAttar, *Tazkerat al-owleya*, 5.
30. ʿAttar, *Tazkerat al-owleya*, 5.
31. Ebn Monavvar also excludes *esnad*s from his hagiography 'in order to ward off boredom and tedium', *Asrar al-towhid fi maqamat al-Shaykh Abi Saʿid*, ed. Mohammad Reza Shafiʿi-Kadkani (Tehran: Agah, 1376 [1997]), 1:8.
32. Losensky, 'Creative Compiler'.
33. ʿAttar, *Tazkerat al-owleya*, 5.
34. ʿAttar, *Tazkerat al-owleya*, 5.
35. Leili Anvar-Chenderoff, 'Le genre hagiographique à travers la *Tadhkirat al-awliā*' de Farīd al-Dīn ʿAttār', in *Saints orientaux*, ed. Denise Aigle (Paris: De Boccard, 1995), 42.
36. Mojaddedi, *Biographical Tradition*, 9–10.

37. Mojaddedi, *Biographical Tradition*, 107; Abu'l-Qasim Qushayri, *al-Risala al-qushayriyya*, ed. 'Abd al-Halim Mahmud and Mahmud b. al-Sharif (Cairo: Dar al-Sha'b, 1989), 128.
38. For an overview of the spurious works attributed to 'Attar, see O'Malley, 'Poetry and Pedagogy', 12–30.
39. On the social and political history of Nishapur in this period, see Richard W. Bulliet, *The Patricians of Nishapur: A Study in Medieval Islamic Social History* (Cambridge, MA: Harvard University Press, 1972), 76–81; E. Honigmann and Clifford Edmund Bosworth, 'Nishapur', in *Historic Cities of the Islamic World*, ed. Clifford Edmund Bosworth (Leiden: Brill, 2007); Clifford Edmund Bosworth, 'The Political and Dynastic History of the Iranian World (A.D. 1000–1217)', in *The Cambridge History of Iran*, vol. 5, *The Saljuq and Mongol Periods*, ed. J. A. Boyle (Cambridge: Cambridge University Press, 1968), 135–57.
40. Farid al-Din 'Attar [attrib.], *Khosrow-nama*, ed. Ahmad Sohayli-Khwansari (Tehran: Anjoman-e Asar-e Melli, 1339 [1961–2]), 27–8; Austin O'Malley, 'An Unexpected Romance: Reevaluating the Authorship of the *Khosrow-nāma*', *Al-'Uṣūr al-Wusṭā: The Journal of Middle East Medievalists* 27 (2019): 201–32.
41. 'Attar, *Tazkerat al-owleya*, 8–9.
42. Jami, *Nafahat*, 596–7; Mohammad Reza Shafi'i-Kadkani, introduction to *Manteq al-tayr*, by Farid al-Din 'Attar, 2nd ed. (Tehran: Sokhan, 1387 [2008–9]), 63–4; Landolt, "Aṭṭār, Sufism, and Ismailism', 9–10; Eyad Abuali, 'al-Baghdādī, Majd al-Dīn', in *Encyclopaedia of Islam, Three*, posted 2019, https://doi.org/10.1163/1573-3912_ei3_COM_25114.
43. Jami, *Nafahat*, 597; Foruzanfar, *Sharh-e ahval-e 'Attar*, 25.
44. 'Attar, *Tazkerat al-owleya*, 25. Jami actually quotes 'Attar's definition of an Ovaysi when he explains the term in his *Nafahat*, but he adds the following amendment: 'Some seekers are trained by the spirits of deceased masters (*ruhaniyat*), such that they have no need of external guidance, and they too must be counted among the Ovaysis' (16). That Jami felt it necessary to add this clarification testifies to how the notion of Ovaysi initiation had evolved since 'Attar's time.
45. Samarqandi, *Tazkerat al-sho'ara*, 326; Foruzanfar, *Sharh-e ahval-e 'Attar*, 24–5.
46. Besides the traditional candidates posited from the Timurid-era onwards, Shafi'i-Kadkani has recently drawn attention to a *selsela* for 'Attar included in the fifteenth-century *Mojmal-e Fasihi*, which connects him to Abu Sa'id and Ebn Monavvar through a string of largely unknown figures. This is a late source,

however, and it seems motivated by a desire to formally tie ʿAttar back to Abu Saʿid. See Shafiʿi-Kadkani, intro. to *Manteq al-tayr*, 63–74; Landolt, "ʿAṭṭār, Sufism, and Ismailism', 10.

47. For the fullest treatment of ʿOwfi's biography, see Muhammad Qazvini, introduction to *Lobab al-albab*, by Mohammad ʿOwfi (Leiden: Brill, 1906).
48. ʿOwfi, *Lobab al-albab*, 2:337–9. Shafiʿi-Kadkani interprets the phrase *saken-e sajjada-ye tariqat* to mean that ʿAttar was in seclusion when ʿOwfi visited Nishapur (he speculates that ʿAttar would have withdrawn to the village of Kadkan). Although possible, it seems more likely that this phrase signifies not a specific devotional practice (seclusion or otherwise), but rather a general adherence to a sufi way of life. Shafiʿi-Kadkani, intro. to *Manteq al-tayr*, 44–7, 70.
49. Qazvini, intro. to *Lobab al-albab*, xiii.
50. Wilferd Madelung, 'Ethics in Islam', in *Naṣīr al-Dīn Ṭūsī's Ethics: Between Philosophy, Shiʿism, and Sufism*, ed. Richard Hovannisian (Malibu, CA: Undena Publications, 1995), 99–101.
51. Charles Melville, 'Ebn al-Fowaṭī, Kamāl-al-Dīn ʿAbd-al-Razzāq', in *Encyclopaedia Iranica*, posted 2020, https://doi.org/10.1163/2330-4804_EIRO_COM_8686; Mohammad Taqi Modarres-Razavi, *Ahval va asar-e Mohammad b. Mohammad b. al-Hasan al-Tusi molaqqab be Khwaja Nasir al-Din* (Tehran: Bonyad-e Farhang-e Iran, 1354 [1974–5]), 252–7.
52. Ibn al-Fuwati, *Talkhis*, 4.3:461–2.
53. ʿAttar, *Tazkerat al-owleya*, 136.
54. Foruzanfar, *Sharh-e ahval-e ʿAttar*, 12–13; Modarres-Razavi, *Ahval-e Nasir al-Din Tusi*, 5–9; Shafiʿi-Kadkani, intro. to *Manteq al-tayr*, 62.
55. Landolt, "ʿAṭṭār, Sufism, and Ismailism', 12; Franklin Lewis, *Rumi: Past and Present, East and West* (Oxford: Oneworld, 2008), 262–3.
56. Abu'l-Majd Mohammad b. Masʿud Tabrizi, *Safina-ye Tabriz: Chap-e ʿaksi az ru-ye noskha-ye khatti-ye Ketabkhana-ye Majles-e Shura-ye Eslami* (Tehran: Markez-e Nashr-e Daneshgahi, 1381 [2001–2]), 521.
57. Little is known about this Amin al-Din Hajj Bola (d. 720/1320), but he certainly seems to have greatly influenced his student Abu'l-Majd. Thirteen works/compilations are ascribed to him in the *Safina*, including treatises on jurisprudence, history, philosophy and prosody. See Ali Asghar Seyed-Gohrab, 'Casing the Treasury: The *Safīna-yi Tabrīz* and Its Compiler', in *The Treasury of Tabriz: The Great Il-Khanid Compendium*, ed. Ali Asghar Seyed-Gohrab and S. McGlinn (West Lafayette, IN: Purdue University Press, 2007), 20; Sayyed Ali Al-e Davud, 'A Review of the Treatises and Historical Documents in *Safīna-yi Tabrīz*', in

The Treasury of Tabriz: The Great Ilkhanid Compendium, ed. Ali Asghar Seyed-Gohrab and S. McGlinn (West Lafayette, IN: Purdue University Press, 2007); ʿAbdolhosayn Haʾeri, introduction to *Safina-ye Tabriz: Chap-e ʿaksi az ru-ye noskha-ye khatti-ye Ketabkhana-ye Majles-e Shura-ye Eslami*, by Abuʾl-Majd Mohammad b. Masʿud Tabrizi (Tehran: Markez-e Nashr-e Daneshgahi, 1381 [2001–2]), viii.

58. ʿAttar uses this image several times in his poetic works to discuss the illusory nature of worldly multiplicity: Farid al-Din ʿAttar, *Asrar-nama*, ed. Mohammad Reza Shafiʿi-Kadkani, 2nd ed. (Tehran: Sokhan, 1388 [2009–10]), 99; ʿAttar, *Manteq al-tayr*, 403.
59. Tabrizi, *Safina-ye Tabriz*, 521.
60. For an example of a previous instance of this topos in action, see Mohammad b. Monavvar, *Asrar al-towhid*, 1:131–2.
61. ʿAbbas Eqbal-Ashtiani, ʿJameʿ-e Maniʿi-ye Nayshaburʾ, *Mehr* 3, no. 11 (Farvardin 1315 [March–April 1936]): 1089–94.
62. Berkey, *Popular Preaching*, 26.
63. ʿAttar, *Tazkerat al-owleya*, 4.
64. ʿAttar, *Manteq al-tayr*, 427.
65. The authenticity of this preface (and the authorial nature of *Mokhtar-nama* itself) has been questioned by Zarrinkub, whose arguments have been countered by Shafiʿi-Kadkani. The scholarly consensus has followed the latter and continued to accept the preface as authentic. See Sayyed ʿAli Mirafzali, ʿAya Mokhtar-nama az ʿAttar ast? ʾ, *Nashr-e danesh* 17, no. 1 (1379 [2000]): 32–43; Daniela Meneghini, ʿ*Moḵtār-nāma*ʾ, in *Encyclopaedia Iranica*, posted 2020, https://doi.org/10.1163/2330-4804_EIRO_COM_398.
66. On the quatrain form, see L. P. Elwell-Sutton, ʿThe "Rubāʿī" in Early Persian Literatureʾ, in *The Cambridge History of Iran,* vol. 4, *The Period from the Arab Invasion to the Saljuqs*, ed. R. N. Frye (Cambridge: Cambridge University Press, 1975); Ali Asghar Seyed-Gohrab, ʿThe Flourishing of Persian Quatrainsʾ, in *A History of Persian Literature*, ed. Ehsan Yarshater, vol. 2, *Persian Lyric Poetry in the Classical Era: Ghazals, Panegyrics, Quatrains*, ed. Ehsan Yarshater (London: I. B. Tauris, 2019); Sirus Shamisa, *Sayr-e robaʿi dar sheʿr-e farsi* (Tehran: Ashtiani, 1363 [1984]).
67. On the compilation of *divan*s and poets' involvement (or lack thereof) in the process, see Franklin Lewis, ʿAuthorship, *Auctoritas*, and the Management of Literary Estates in Pre-modern Persian literatureʾ, *Jerusalem Studies in Arabic and Islam* 45 (2018): 73–125; Lewis, ʿReading, Writing, and Recitationʾ, 229–32;

Lewis, *Rumi*, 295–7; Julie Scott Meisami, 'Hafez v. Manuscripts of Hafez', in *Encyclopaedia Iranica*, posted 2020, https://doi.org/10.1163/2330-4804_EIRO_COM_2596. The authorial compilation of *divans* began a couple of centuries earlier in Arabic; see Gregor Schoeler, *The Genesis of Literature in Islam: From the Aural to the Read*, trans. Shawkat M. Toorawa (Edinburgh: Edinburgh University Press, 2009), 115.

68. Farid al-Din ʿAttar, *Mokhtar-nama*, ed. Mohammad Reza Shafiʿi-Kadkani, 2nd ed. (Tehran: Sokhan, 1389 [2010–11]), 71. ʿOwfi mentions an earlier quatrain collection by Bakharzi (d. 1075) that was arranged alphabetically, but it is no longer extant. See Seyed-Gohrab, 'The Flourishing of Persian Quatrains', 493; ʿOwfi, *Lobab al-albab*, 70.
69. De Bruijn, *Piety and Poetry*, 187–9; Matthew Thomas Miller, 'Genre in Classical Persian Poetry', in *Routledge Handbook of Persian Literature*, ed. Kamran Talattof (Abingdon: Routledge, forthcoming).
70. Hellmut Ritter, 'Philologika XVI: Farīduddīn ʿAṭṭār IV', *Oriens* 13/14 (1960–1), 195; Hellmut Ritter, 'Philologika XI: Maulānā Ǧalāladdīn Rūmī und sein Kreis', *Der Islam* 26 (1942), 245–6.
71. ʿAttar, *Mokhtar-nama*, 70.
72. The *Khosrow-nama*, a romance in the style of *Vis o Ramin* and *Varaqa o Golshah*, has been long attributed to ʿAttar. Shafiʿi-Kadkani has claimed that this is a spurious attribution, and that when ʿAttar invokes the *Khosrow-nama* in the above quotation, he is actually referring to the *Elahi-nama*. His argument, however, is not entirely convincing. See O'Malley, 'An Unexpected Romance'.
73. ʿAttar, *Mokhtar-nama*, 70.
74. Italics indicate Arabic.
75. ʿAttar, *Mokhtar-nama*, 71.
76. It was not unusual for medieval authors to produce several different recensions of a single work, sometimes with drastic differences; the search for a single, authorial archetype is often a fool's errand. See Lewis, 'Reading, Writing, and Recitation', 270–5, 295–309; Franklin Lewis, 'The Modes of Literary Production: Remarks on the Composition, Revision and "Publication" of Persian Texts in the Medieval Period', *Persica* 17 (2001): 69–83; Barbara Flemming, 'From Archetype to Oral Tradition: Editing Persian and Turkish Literary Texts', *Manuscripts of the Middle East* 3 (1998), 8; De Bruijn, *Piety and Poetry*, 119–20; Adam Gacek, *Arabic Manuscripts: A Vademecum for Readers* (Leiden: Brill, 2009), s.vv. 'Textual Criticism and Editing', 'Textual Variants'.
77. ʿAttar, *Mokhtar-nama*, 70–1.

78. Meneghini, *'Moḵtār-nāma'*.
79. 'Attar, *Mokhtar-nama*, 71.
80. See Muhammad Isa Waley, 'Contemplative Disciplines in Early Persian Sufism', in *Classical Persian Sufism: From Its Origins to Rumi*, ed. Leonard Lewisohn (London: Khaniqahi Nimatullahi Publications, 1999), 541–7; the practice of *ta'ammol* also appears in Bidel's poems, in which Jane Mikkelson argues it should be understood as a form of lyrical, imaginative training, 'Flights of Imagination', 48–50.
81. Abu Hamid Ghazali, *Ihya' 'ulum al-din* (Cairo: Lajnat Nashr al-Thaqafa al-Islamiyya, 1356–7 [1937–8]), 4:2801–44; Ghazali, *Kimia-ye sa'adat*, 2:779–97.
82. Ghazali, *Ihya' 'ulum al-din*, 4:2797.
83. Ghazali, *Ihya' 'ulum al-din*, 4:2806.
84. Ghazali, *Ihya' 'ulum al-din*, 4:2808.
85. Ghazali, *Ihya' 'ulum al-din*, 4:2806–7.
86. Compare with the practices of *lectio divina* and *meditatio* in the Western Christian tradition: Brian Stock, *After Augustine: The Meditative Reader and the Text* (Philadelphia: University of Philadelphia Press, 2001), 13–17, 101–14; Jean Leclercq, *The Love of Learning and the Desire for God: A Study of Monastic Culture*, trans. Catherine Misrahi (New York: Fordham University Press, 1974), 18–22, 89–90.
87. Ghazali, *Ihya' 'ulum al-din*, 4:2804.
88. Ghazali, *Ihya' 'ulum al-din*, 4:2804.
89. Ghazali, *Ihya' 'ulum al-din*, 4:2814.
90. Ghazali, *Kimia-ye sa'adat*, 2:785–97.
91. Ghazali, *Ihya' 'ulum al-din*, 4:2815.
92. Seyed-Gohrab ('The Flourishing of Persian Quatrains', 492–3), De Bruijn (*Persian Sufi Poetry*, 8) and Elwell-Sutton ('The "Rubāʿī" in Early Persian Literature', 640) have all commented on the progression of thought within the quatrain, which frequently recalls logical deduction.
93. 'Attar, *Mokhtar-nama*, 194.
94. 'Attar, *Mokhtar-nama*, 71.
95. De Bruijn, *Persian Sufi Poetry*, 71; Davis, 'Sufism and Poetry', 283–4; Meisami, *Structure and Meaning*, 392–3.
96. See especially the discussion of Fatemeh Keshavarz, *Reading Mystical Lyric: The Case of Jalal al-Din Rumi* (Columbia, SC: University of South Carolina Press, 1998), 18–21.

97. Meneghini, *'Mok̲tār-nāma'*; Seyed-Gohrab, 'The Flourishing of Persian Quatrains', 521.
98. Stock, *After Augustine*, 15–16.
99. Ebn Monavvar, *Asrar al-towhid*, 1:19.

3

Talk Therapy: Poetry as Spiritual Medicine

The introduction to the *Mokhtar-nama*, like many works of Persian poetry, contains a litany of conventional poetic boasts. 'Attar praises his verses' beauty, the unprecedented nature of the collection and the depth of their spiritual secrets. Near the end of the introduction, he invokes a metaphorical trope that might strike some modern readers as odd, but which was critical to premodern understandings of the transformative power of elegant speech – poetry in particular, but also prose. After expressing confidence that a mystically minded audience will be able to decode the hidden spiritual meaning of his quatrains, 'Attar nonchalantly likens his verse to a kind of drug, almost as an aside. 'Truly,' he writes, "Attar's poetic speech (*sokhan*) is an antidote (*taryak*).'[1] More precisely, *taryak* (theriac) was a compound medicine – usually containing opium – that was used as an antidote to toxins and venoms, but also more broadly as a general panacea for all sorts of aches and pains.[2] The offhand nature of his remark testifies to the ubiquity and familiarity of the association for his readers, who would have found the comparison to be a natural one needing no further explanation. A number of intellectual discourses within the Islamicate world, especially philosophy and homiletics, routinely invoked the practice of medicine as analogues to their own therapeutic aims, and poetry was frequently likened to a drug, especially in meta-poetic verses and prefaces. 'Attar, however, pushes this conceptual metaphor further than his predecessors, adducing it throughout his oeuvre and making it a central pillar of his public poetic identity through his pen name, 'Attar, which means not only 'the perfumer', but also 'the pharmacist'.

This medicinal metaphor is more than mere boiler plate or the parroting of convention. It is a wide-ranging heuristic for thinking through the rhetorical power of speech, explicitly invoked by ʿAttar in regards to his own verse (especially the *masnavi*s and the *Mokhtar-nama*) and the saintly dicta in the *Tazkera*. The first half of this chapter examines what this characterisation implies about the function of ʿAttar's texts, the effects they are imagined to have on their readers and listeners and their intended manner of consumption. When speech is cast as medicinal, its pragmatic value is highlighted; such a characterisation speaks not only to poetry's form or meaning, but also to its ability to impact and transform its audiences. In the *Conference of the Birds*, for example, ʿAttar claims to have composed verse that counteracts irreligious influences and thereby brings its audiences back to a state of spiritually normative 'health'.[3] Its operations are not confined to the sonic and semantic planes, but extend to the body, the psyche and even the ontological state of its readers and listeners. In the introduction to the *Tazkera*, ʿAttar describes the words of the saints as 'cardiac stimulants' (*mofarreh*) that energise the heart, the organ of spiritual vision in sufi psycho-physiology.[4] Saintly dicta thus not only convey lessons and teachings, but actually strengthen their recipients' bodily connection to the divine realm. And like any drug, these utterances must be consumed according to particular regimes to be effective; a single dose is generally not sufficient. ʿAttar's readers are therefore encouraged to embark on durational pharmacological treatments that involve disciplined and ritualised regimens of reading.

Besides articulating a particular vision of the function of ʿAttar's texts vis-à-vis his audiences, the medicinal metaphor also implies specific notions of poetic authority, which are explored in the second half of this chapter. Insincere, hypocritical physicians are stock figures in the premodern imagination, who, because they fail to 'take their own medicine', lack the authority to prescribe effective cures. The trope of the insincere physician was frequently transferred to the field of homiletics, where, among other uses, it was employed to critique those hypocritical preachers who did not hold themselves to the same standards to which they called others. ʿAttar composed homiletic verse that is both likened to medicine and informed by the conventions and rhetoric of preaching, so he too had to prove his sincerity before his verbal 'cures' could bear fruit. Unlike a doctor or a preacher delivering an oral sermon, however, *masnavi* writers had to do this within their texts through their poetic personae. As we shall see, this is one of the functions of the extensive meta-poetic sections in ʿAttar's *masnavi*s, in which he paradoxically demonstrates his sincerity by confessing his hypocrisy and lack of medical-homiletic qualifications.

By carefully attending to the medicinal metaphor, we can reconstruct an implicit, recipient-centred poetics of didacticism that was never directly theorised in Persian-language works of rhetoric or literary criticism, but which informed readers' understandings and mediated their experiences of ʿAttar's texts. Although systematic poetic manuals in Persian do occasionally discuss poetry's effects, they generally focus on formal characteristics, especially typologies of rhetorical embellishments, and they privilege erotic and panegyric verse in the classical Arabic-derived forms. Didactic and mystical poetry – especially in the Persian *masnavi* form – did not receive much attention.[5] And while the philosophical tradition treats the truth-value of poetic imagery and its impact on the imagination, it too is not directly concerned with how poetry might inculcate ethical teachings or instigate religious reform.[6]

Nevertheless, more organic, imaginative and pragmatic understandings of poetics emerge from the poems themselves, especially in the rich array of metaphors routinely applied to poetic activity and speech. Drugs and medicines are not the only metaphorical vehicles for speech in the Persian tradition, nor are they the most common: verses are also described as precious commodities of exchange, the products of careful craftsmanship, a form of licit magic or an allusive scent. Each one of the above metaphors presents a conceptual lens for exploring the work of poetry (and elegant speech more generally) in medieval Persianate society, and several scholars have already teased out some of their implications.[7] The medicinal metaphor has not yet been investigated to the same degree, but it offers a critical vantage point for exploring how didactic speech in particular was thought to impact its recipients, especially in the case of the poet-pharmacist ʿAttar.[8] The present chapter, through an examination of how ʿAttar casts his speech as a therapeutic drug, seeks to recover some of the poetic and rhetorical assumptions that conditioned readers' encounters with didactic literary texts, as well as ʿAttar's own manipulations of those assumptions. We can thereby begin to reconstruct a performative, participatory and recipient-centred poetics of didacticism that was never systematically delineated within the poetic manuals or philosophical treatises, but which informed the production and consumption of this central literary mode.

Of Drugs and Discourse

Speech has long been understood in medicinal terms in Islamic culture. In the Quran, disbelief is described as a sickness of the heart, and the divine word itself is presented as 'a cure (*shifa'*) and a mercy for the believers' (17:82).[9] Later commentators routinely characterised prophets as physicians for their respective communities, prescribing laws to cure their people's specific spiritual maladies.[10] Sufi shaykhs were described as heirs to the prophets in a post-prophetic age and also likened to doctors: they designed spiritually therapeutic regimens for their disciples on the basis of their individual needs and temperaments.[11] Such notions are informed by older trends in Hellenistic thought, in which the practice of philosophy was seen as a kind of therapy for the soul aimed at the cultivation of virtues and the tamping down of vices.[12] This understanding of philosophy (along with the Greek medical knowledge with which it is intertwined) was adapted into Arabic during the translation movement of the ninth century, giving rise to works like the *al-Tibb al-ruhani* (*The Spiritual Medicine*) of Abu Bakr al-Razi (d. c. 935), which explains how to combat the excesses of the lower soul by changing one's patterns of thought. This philosophical cultivation of virtue was medically adjacent, as Razi's title suggests, and the presence of vices within the soul was frequently tied to humoral imbalance.[13]

Perhaps most relevant for our purposes, the metaphor was commonly used in the discourse of (and about) popular preachers.[14] Similar to prophets and sufi shaykhs, preachers were likened to physicians and their sermons were compared to medicine: although their speech (especially the fire-and-brimstone variety) might be bitter, it was ultimately aimed at healing their listeners of the disease of impiety.[15] Ibn al-Jawzi, the preacher and intellectual of twelfth-century Baghdad, repeatedly invokes the metaphor in his writing on the practice of preaching, and he even compiled a treasury of homiletic material entitled *Ru'us al-qawarir* (*The Best of the Vials*) from which aspiring preachers could fashion their own sermons. The text contains stories, exegesis and rhyming invocations, all of which were important components of a homiletic assembly, and which could be memorised and combined into a full-length performance. This process, in which a sermon is assembled from pre-existing, modular components, is likened by Ibn al-Jawzi to the process of compounding more complex drugs from the simpler *materia medica*, and he thus introduces his sourcebook as a kind for pharmacopeia, a collection of 'vials of syrups, from which physicians can combine samples to produce a compound medicine exceeding its singular components'.[16] The notion of speech as medicine was thus widespread, eagerly embraced by practitioners of a wide array of competing discourses. However different philosophy, sufism and homiletics might otherwise be, their shared use of the medicinal metaphor suggests an overarching pragmatic orientation that privileges discourse's effects in a human context.

Utterances were thought to be particularly impactful when they were 'eloquent', meaning constructed with a concern for the surface level of language and embellished with metaphor and other rhetorical devices. For Ibn al-Jawzi, the judicious employment of literary ornament (partly) explains a powerful sermon's impact. When a preacher's message is eloquently expressed, it is more likely to stir the hearts of listeners:

> Now if a preacher (*wāʿiẓ*) were to say in his *khuṭba* [the sermon's rhyming invocation]: 'Praise be to God!' and then add: 'Fear God!' and would restrict himself to a repetition of words like this, he would have no effect whatsoever in countering those who are capable of composing eloquent utterances and expressions that elicit admiration because of their beauty. Those who have studied the Quran and its allusions, metaphors, and figurative speech know what an impact eloquent speech can have on the hearts of people.[17]

Ibn al-Jawzi takes the Quran as the pinnacle of eloquence, as is to be expected. Poetry, however, displays a density of signification rarely matched in prose, and it is not only ornamented but also rhymed and metred, and so it too is capable of impacting listeners in dramatic ways. For example, ʿAbd al-Qahir Jurjani, the Arabic literary theorist, marvels at how poetry can make a frigid man a flirt, distract people from their sorrow and dispel loneliness.[18] Shams-e Qays, who composed a Persian rhetorical manual, also alludes to this affective power when he hyperbolically describes the power of amatory quatrains to provoke female desire: 'How many girls, out of passion from a melody (*tarana*), have breached the doors and walls of their abode of chastity, and how many women, out of love from a quatrain (*do bayti*), have loosened the weave and weft of their shirts of modesty.'[19] And not infrequently poetry's impact is expressed in medicinal terms. The reed flute that 'sings' Rumi's *Masnavi* is thus both 'a poison (*zahr*) and an antidote (*taryaq*)', and Khaqani's speech is 'a cure (*shefa'*) for those who grieve'. Hafez closes a *ghazal* run through with medical imagery with a self-addressed boast: 'Hafez, your poetry has given me a drink (*sharbat*) from the water of life / Put the doctor aside, come and read out my prescription (*noskha-ye sharbat*)!'[20] Many more examples could be adduced.

'Attar, as a poet in general and a homiletic poet in particular, was thus well positioned to make use of the medicinal metaphor to conceptualise his own elegant speech. The metaphor is not only elaborated in his poetry and prose, but it is also inextricably bound to his authorial persona through his pen name. In both lyrics and *masnavi*s, poets punned on their pen names as a kind of poetic signature. It was through those pen names that they would be remembered by prosperity, so the choice of a moniker was not to be taken lightly. They were often derived from the name of a patron, a birthplace or profession, or another term that carried some special significance for the poet. In 'Attar's case, his name refers to a compounder of perfumes and medicines who might also perform basic medical procedures. (In Iranian markets today, an *'attari* is, first and foremost, a shop of traditional herbal medicines.) 'Attar's pen name, then, might be variously translated as 'perfumer', 'apothecary' or 'pharmacist', involving shades of meaning from all three. It is often assumed that he actually made his living with the craft, although this has been challenged by Shafi'i-Kadkani, who claims it was 'Attar's father who worked as an apothecary.[21] His poems themselves do not necessarily indicate any specialised knowledge of medicine, and poets such as Khaqani include far more technical language from the field.[22] Nevertheless, whatever 'Attar's relationship to the actual practice of medicine may have been, his pen name would hardly have been adopted without consideration of its metaphoric and poetic implications.

While technical medical terms are largely absent, 'Attar's lyrics do draw from the semantic field of pain, cures and remedies in a more general sense. This is not unusual in the *ghazal* tradition, but the density of such terms in 'Attar's poems and their frequent coupling with his pen name in the lyrics' final lines suggests that they are at least partly motivated by his nom de plume. For example:

> 'Attar (i.e. the pharmacist) now seeks out pain
> because in pain he has found the cure (*darman*).[23]

Throughout his works, ʿAttar repeatedly plays with the paradoxical notions of ʿcurative pain' and the ʿremedy of no-remedy', and by invoking his presumed profession he adds an ironic twist. A pharmacist is supposed to cure others, but ʿAttar suffers from his own ignorance, which he cannot cure:

Out of ignorance, my pain has passed all bounds;
how can I cure (*daru konam*) an ignorant pharmacist (*ʿattar*)?[24]

Other lines allude to medicinal products:

When ʿAttar's heart mixes your threshold's dirt with
blood, it resembles an electuary (*maʿjun*).[25]

What is ʿAttar's religion here? Loss of self!
For here neither wounds (*jarahat*) nor salves (*marham*) are found.[26]

In these verses, ʿAttar's pen name resonates with the accompanying medicinal terms and thereby activates their more concrete meanings in a pharmacological context. For example, the ʿwounds' and ʿsalves' in the final line quoted above could be conventionally understood as the power of the beloved to both inflict pain on the lover and relieve that pain by granting union. And once the self disappears in mystical annihilation, the lover no longer has any independent existence to be harmed or healed. On a more concrete level, however, the line also suggests that ʿAttar has transcended the phenomenal world and the pharmacist's daily work of treating minor injuries and applying treatments. ʿWounds' and ʿsalves' are not only potential results of the beloved's actions, but also markers of ʿAttar's presumed profession, left behind as he moves beyond self. A similar ambiguity is present in a final example, a *ghazal* full of transgressive, *qalandar* topoi. In its concluding line, the drunken narrator is brought before ʿAttar:

Then, when I was totally blasted from that wine
they hauled me before ʿAttar.[27]

One can see here both a boast – ʿAttar is the *qalandar* master to whom they bring those who are mystically intoxicated – as well as more tongue-in-cheek reference to the mundane work of preparing a hangover cure.

In the *masnavis*, the *Tazkera* and much of the *Mokhtar-nama* – which are more didactic in tone than the *Divan* – medicinal imagery is used more specifically in regards to the curative power of speech. We have already seen how ʿAttar likens his speech to an antidote in the introduction to the *Mokhtar-nama*, and the same metaphor is deployed, in a somewhat more elaborate fashion, in the meta-poetic conclusion to the *Conference of the Birds*:

> Whoever suffers from the poison of religious deviation (*zahr-e bedʿat*),
> these lofty words are antidote (*taryak*) enough for him!
> Although I am an *ʿattar* and a dispenser of antidotes (*taryak-deh*),
> I have just burnt liver, like those who sell adulterated musk.[28]

The first verse casts ʿAttar's speech as an antidote to 'the poison of religious deviation', but the poet immediately undercuts this boast in the next verse by confessing his hypocrisy and comparing himself to those apothecaries who fraudulently sell musk adulterated with burnt liver, a well-known scam in the bazaar.[29] There is something of a double entendre here, since to speak of one's liver as 'burnt' also suggests a high rank among the suffering lovers of God. We will return to issues of persona and the performance of sincerity later in the chapter; at the moment it suffices to note that ʿAttar explicitly connects his pen name to his ability to cure spiritual ailments through speech.

After his death, the broader literary tradition continued to understand ʿAttar's poetry through the lens of his nom de plume and presumed profession. According to Gazorgahi, the Timurid-era hagiographer and anthologist, ʿAttar studied medicine (*tebb*) as a youth, and his store was 'full of syrups, drugs and related goods'.[30] Nurollah Shushtari, the sixteenth-century Shiʿi hagiographer, introduces ʿAttar as a druggist for mystical lovers:

> ʿAttar, the bearer of packets of the drug of effacement (*daru-ye fana*),
> whose verse is a cure (*shefa-bakhsh*) for afflicted lovers . . .[31]

In the mind of Shushtari, and presumably many of his other readers, the significance of ʿAttar's pen name lay not just in his (assumed) historical profession, but in the transformative potential of his carefully crafted speech, which was capable of countering irreligion, instigating ethical reform and even giving some 'taste' of the effacement of self on the path towards reunion with the divine.

An *'attar* produced perfumes as well as medicines, and both aspects of the craft are simultaneously operative in the construction of 'Attar's poetic identity. He ends many of his *ghazal*s with puns on his pen name and references to sweet scents and perfumes. For instance, he praises his own verse as musk filling the world with its scent, and he thereby provides a fantastic explanation of the morning dawn's fragrance:

> The sweet smell of morning's wind wafts musk
> You'd think it had sucked musk from the Chinese deer's breath.
> But no – the morning scatters musk because it has caught a scent
> of 'Attar's [i.e. the perfumer's] musk bag (*nafa*) in the air.[32]

In the *Mosibat-nama*, he figures himself as the perfumer who prepares the raw 'musk bag of secrets', transforming it into processed musk for consumption:

> The musk bag (*nafa*) of secrets cannot rain musk
> until 'Attar lays his hands on it.[33]

At several points in the *Divan* he claims, according to the poetic logic of fantastic etiology, that the enchanting scent of the beloved's perfume made him a perfumer: the product gave rise to the producer. And he compares his love-struck self to incense that gives off a sweet scent as it burns:

> I might be a perfumer (*'attar*), but only in a derivative sense:
> without the perfume (*'etr*) of his locks, I would never be 'Attar.[34]

> On the censer (*mejmar*) of passion for you, just like sandalwood and sugar
> 'Attar is burning and melting – what's to be done?[35]

> I've burnt so much in this heat
> that I am not the perfumer (*'attar*) but the sandalwood.[36]

Later anthologists and imitators continued to praise 'Attar through the semantic field of perfume and olfactory sensation: Shabestari, for instance, humbly presents his own work as a mere 'whiff from the shop of 'Attar', and 'Owfi also invokes the semantic field of perfumery in his discussion of the poet.[37] This is not to imply any necessary contradiction between his verses' medicinal functionality and their status as aesthetic objects, however. Just as an *'attar* compounds both perfumes and drugs – and the two often overlap – 'Attar's poetic compositions are intended to be not only beautiful but functional. Indeed, their sweetness may be key to their effectiveness. As Rumi (according to Aflaki) explains, people are not inclined to spiritual truths, but they are inclined to music and verse. The former should be expressed through the latter, just as a doctor's syrup should be poured into a beer jug to encourage its consumption so that the patient might be cured.[38]

Psycho-somatics

Besides emphasising poetry's curative function, the medicinal metaphor also gestures towards the bodily mechanisms through which it works. Eloquent speech was thought to impact individuals in much the same way as medicine, bloodletting and special diets: by manipulating the listener's 'disposition' (*teba*ʿ), the balance of humors that, according to Galenic medicine, gives rise to specific emotional and behavioural tendencies, and, when out of balance, physical disease. Perso-Arabic anecdotal literature is full of accounts of eloquent speech impacting listeners in dramatic ways, and its mechanisms are often explained in humoral and psycho-somatic terms. According to Nezami-ye ʿAruzi, poetry 'excites the faculties of irascibility and concupiscence through the imagination, so that the natural disposition (*teba*ʿ) is constricted or dilated, which leads to the performance of great deeds in the order of the world'. As one of his examples, he recounts the narrative of how Rudaki constructed his famous ode in order to entice the Samanid amir to return to Bokhara.[39] The efficacy of homiletic speech was explained in similar ways, through its retentive action on the disposition. According to Ibn al-Jawzi, 'the natural disposition (*teba*ʿ) is inclined to love of base desires and detrimental frivolities . . . just as water naturally flows towards the lowest point. If it is held back by a dam, it will seek a way around it.' Homiletic speech, he continues, is the dam that holds back the 'waters' of the natural disposition, but just as a dam must be continuously repaired to maintain its integrity, periodic exhortations are also necessary to hold back the natural tendency towards lust and desire.[40] Speech, in this paradigm, not only communicates, but physiologically alters its recipients on the level of the 'disposition', leading to psychological and behavioural changes.

ʿAttar and other didactic poets seek to harness the psycho-somatic power of poetry – and, in homiletic verse, combine it with that of the sermon – to produce speech that, by acting on the disposition, induces a desire for proximity to God and inculcates the principles of a religiously valuable way of life. Once the psycho-somatic nature of the poetic endeavour is acknowledged, certain metaphors in ʿAttar's work take on new levels of meaning tied to bodily sensation and change. For example, we have already quoted the following line, from the conclusion to the *Conference of the Birds*:

> If one frozen like ice were to see this book,
> he would come out from behind the veil like fire.[41]

This poetry-induced transformation, as it is described here, recalls the bodily effects of certain medicinal compounds. Like an opiate theriac, ʿAttar's poetry is a warming, quickening force that overtakes its listeners, leading to changes in the disposition that, once begun, cannot be easily stopped. It makes cold bodies hot and provokes a dynamism where there was only frigid stoicism before. The description of a 'frozen' reader coming out like 'fire' can thus be read as more than a vague allusion to salvation or passion for the divine beloved; it gestures towards the bodily effects of ʿAttar's medicinal speech.

ʿAttar also speaks of his own bodily state in terms of heat and uncontrollable internal motion:

> I am drowned in fire – don't blame me!
> I burn if I don't speak.
> The sea of my soul boils in a hundred ways,
> how can I be silent for even a moment?[42]

ʿAttar's speech is almost involuntary: the only way to alleviate his painful passion is to give voice to it in poetry. He is both drowning and burning, a paradoxical situation that suggests not only pain, but also a constriction, an inability to breathe and a frantic, instinctual search for air. His soul is in a constant state of bubbling, an internal restlessness that can be sensed but not stopped. His poetry is both an emblem of this suffering and a testament to his broken body:

> I have burnt myself like a lamp
> to light up the world like a candle.
> My brain is like a lamp niche from smoke –
> but what is some lamp smoke when the candle of eternity is mine?!

I don't eat in the day or sleep at night
    and from the fire of my heart, my liver is desiccated.[43]

Like a candle, he lights up the world in verse, but only at the price of his own immolation. He neither eats nor sleeps. His liver is desiccated and brain full of smoke, metaphors that point to exhaustion and pain and call attention to the bodily toll of old age and exertion. This psychic and physical suffering, however, is also an expression of his longing for God. He is hopeful for the candle of eternity, and the mystical path requires pain. His verses, moreover, provide his audience with a small taste of this salvational suffering:

Look at my cahier with an eye for pain
    so that you might believe one hundredth of my passions.
He who looks with pain on these words
    strikes the polo ball of fortune to eternity.
Move beyond asceticism and naiveté;
    you need pain, and the experience of pain![44]

Poetry is born of painful mystical longing, encapsulates it and passes something of that experience on to readers who approach it correctly.

The impact of speech upon the heart was of particular interest to ʿAttar and other sufi poets because of the mediating role that that organ plays between the body and the divine realm in sufi psychology. ʿAttar devotes ample attention to the heart throughout his oeuvre, and in the introduction to the *Tazkera* he invokes the medicinal metaphor to tout the work's cardiac benefits.[45] For example, in one passage ʿAttar quotes a saying attributed to Junayd (d. 910), according to which saintly speech 'is one of the armies of the Lord, which strengthens the devotee's heart if they are heart-broken'.[46] In another passage, he explains that he has loved the saints since childhood and likens their speech to a specific class of medicinal compounds, *mofarreh*, that strengthen the heart:

> For no apparent reason, from childhood onwards, love for this clan has swelled in my soul, and their words were always a *mofarreh* for my heart.[47]

Mofarreh was a sweet-tasting, sweet-smelling drug composed of valuable ingredients – according to some recipes, including powdered gold and ruby – that was thought to excite the heart and liver and thereby strengthen them while bestowing a sense of joy or happiness.[48] Here again we see the close interrelationship of form and function in the *'attar*'s role as druggist and perfumist: the compound is not only medicinally effective, but luxurious, expensive and olfactorily pleasing.

Today the heart is metaphorically understood as a vague centre of emotion, but in sufi psychology it is much more than this: the heart is the seat of a faculty by means of which human beings can approach God and an organ through which they maintain a very real connection to Him, on an ontological and even bodily level. As Ghazali explains, the heart is both 'the cone-shaped organ situated on the left side of breast', as well as a 'subtle, divine, spiritual substance' that 'is perceiving, knowing and experiencing'. These spiritual and bodily hearts are linked, although the connection between them is difficult to articulate: it is like 'that of accidents with bodies, a user of tools with the tool and that which resides in a place with that place'.[49] Najm al-Din Razi Daya is more explicit: the heart is 'a piece of flesh that has a spiritual soul' and thus serves as the ontological link between the microcosm and the divine realms.[50] He puns on the etymology of *qalb*, the Arabic term for 'heart' – its triliteral root encompasses notions of turning, facing and rotation – in order to highlight this ontological liminality:

> The human heart has one face turned towards the world of divinity and the other face towards the world of the bodily frame, and it is for this reason that it is called *qalb*. It contains the two worlds, corporal and spiritual, and it is the place of division for every sustaining emanation that it receives from the spirit.[51]

The heart faces the divine world and receives emanations from it, which are then distributed throughout the body through anatomical channels in the manner of a material substance:

> There are narrow veins running from the heart to every member of the body, which carry the emanations of the spirit. The heart divides the emanations that it receives, sending an appropriate amount to each member. If for one moment the sustenance of those emanations would be cut off from the heart, the bodily form would wither and life would cease. And if that sustenance were cut off from a single member because of a blockage in the veins that carry it, that member would cease to move and become paralysed.[52]

Among all the members of the body, the heart alone receives 'emanations' from the non-material spirit, but it simultaneously remains firmly rooted in the bodily materiality, sustaining life through its anatomical work. Through ascetic practice, the heart can be directed more and more towards the higher realm from which it receives these emanations; then, according to Razi, when 'it reaches perfection through nurturing, purification and intention towards God, it becomes the manifestation of the total attributes of divinity'.[53]

In this context, saintly speech's impact on the heart signifies more than its power to impassion. As Bausani points out, when ʿAttar refers to 'heart-broken' devotees, he speaks not only of a state of depression or sadness, but of ontological estrangement from the divine that involves both the spirit and the body.[54] Saintly speech, by 'strengthening the heart', re-establishes an internal, mediating connection with God. By likening these dicta to 'cardiac stimulants' (*mofarreh*), ʿAttar not only intends their power to bring joy or excite, but also to reinforce the internal isthmus of the heart. Intertwined with their edifying and aesthetic qualities, these 'verbal compounds' help the body receive sustenance from the unseen, and they thereby open a route through which readers and listeners can cultivate a return to a pre-eternal proximity to the divine.

This transformative potential is explicitly claimed by ʿAttar near the end of the *Tazkera*'s introduction, where he writes that after the Quran and hadith, 'there is no better book in creation'.[55] Its alchemical power is expressed in a gendered hierarchy, through which the book allegedly elevates its audience:

> This is a book that changes effeminates (*mokhannesan*) into men, and men into lion-men, and lion-men into incomparables and incomparables into the essence of pain (*dard*). How could it not? Whoever recites this book and reflects upon it as is prescribed will learn what pain lay in the saints' souls to bring forth such deeds and words from their hearts.[56]

The *Tazkera* not only provides its audience with ethical instruction, but also changes the very nature of their being. For ʿAttar, as in much sufi writing, spiritual success is gendered as a particular form of masculinity; spiritual heroes are the real 'men', and 'manliness' is a prerequisite of spiritual progress. The *Tazkera* thus transforms effeminates into men and men into lion-men and so forth, elevating its readers through the ranks of 'manliness' until they realise the painful, passionate drive for God that dominates the souls of the saints and which gives rise to their words and deeds. Born from the saints' onto-psychological passion for God, these utterances can induce a similar state in readers, although presumably in a more tempered fashion. To activate this transformative power, however, the reader must engage with the work in a specifically 'prescribed' way: he or she is to recite the saints' words aloud (*bar khwandan*), attending to them visually, aurally and bodily through vocal production.[57]

Taking Medicine, Making Meaning

The medicinal metaphor, like all metaphors, does not imply a perfect mapping between two domains; select properties of the source are transferred to the target while others are left behind. One obvious way in which poems are not like drugs is that poems are meaningful forms of communication. Drugs, on the other hand, carry no semantic content, and their efficacy does not depend on patients' comprehension of their mechanisms or anything else. In the case of ʿAttar's verbal medicines, however, both form and content contribute to their therapeutic effects. He stresses the need for a slow, durational mode of reading, urging readers to repeatedly return to his texts again and again to discover new meanings. These are not one-time interventions, but long-term therapies, and they depend on readers' continuous engagement with their semantic content.

The issue is, yet again, most directly addressed in the *Tazkera*. The hagiography was composed, according to ʿAttar, so that non-Arabophone readers could access and benefit from the saintly traditions; the question of understanding, then, is at the heart of its production.[58] ʿAttar explains, through a quotation from Akkafi, that the Quran produces an effect in readers regardless of whether it is understood, but that this effect is magnified through proper comprehension:

> Akkafi was asked: 'If someone reads the Quran and does not understand what he is reading, will it have any effect (*asar*)?' He replied: 'If someone takes a medicine (*daru*) and does not know what he is taking, it still has an effect. So why wouldn't the Quran have an effect? On the contrary, it will have a great effect. But how much greater it will be if they do understand!'[59]

Although Akkafi discusses the Quran, not saintly speech, ʿAttar repeatedly draws analogies between the two throughout the *Tazkera*'s preface, so the import of the above quotation is clear. Saintly speech, like the Quran, is therapeutically beneficial for readers and listeners even if they do not understand it. But, he adds, those medicinal effects will be much greater if they do understand – thus the translation of Arabic dicta into Persian. ʿAttar's use of the medicinal metaphor, then, does not imply a repudiation of speech's communicative power so much as a shift of emphasis towards its broader effects, which are still (at least partly) produced through comprehension.

The importance of understanding is emphasised to an even greater degree in ʿAttar's poetic works, where he advocates a slow, reflective mode of literary engagement. We have already seen, for example, that he urges his readers to approach his quatrains with 'deliberation and contemplation', alluding to a spiritual practice that stresses deep hermeneutic engagement with various signs in the world, both textual and non-textual, as part of a practice of self-fashioning. And a number of ʿAttar's meta-poetic verses enjoin their addressees to penetrate the formal surface of his poetry to arrive at a deeper layer of signification, as in the following quatrain from the final chapter of the *Mokhtar-nama*:

> We threaded one hundred pearls as allusions (*esharat*), then left
> We picked one hundred roses as signs (*ʿebarat*), then left
> If you are wise, don't look to the verbal form (*lafz*), but consider (*bendish*),
> the secret that we said in symbols (*ramz*), then left.[60]

His verses are imbued with a secret meaning, accessible through carefully formulated allusions and symbols, and the reader is invited to reflect on these deeper significations instead of merely basking in their verbal beauty. Another quatrain from the same chapter makes a similar point, urging readers to ruminate on the poems slowly and carefully:

> I have strung many pearls of certainty for you
> You should know that I am not sleeping like you.
> Don't pass so quickly from this back to frivolity,
> but think a bit about what I have told you.[61]

The *masnavis* also end with entreaties to read repeatedly and carefully in order to unlock their transformative potential. In the conclusion to the *Mosibat-nama*, for example, 'Attar claims that if one of the 'people of secrets' – a common epithet for a practitioner of mystical piety – spends 'a long life in this book', then at every moment 'it will bestow new light upon him'.[62] And at the end of the *Conference of the Birds*, he likens the book to a coquettish bride who removes her veil only slowly, and he urges his audience to read the poem multiple times so that with each reading new secrets might be revealed to them.[63]

Speech's spiritual efficacy – articulated in medicinal terms – must therefore be understood in conjunction with 'Attar's stress on the reflective action required to uncover its inner meanings, which reveal themselves only after extended contemplation and multiple literary encounters. The medicinal metaphor thus implies not so much a black-box instrumentality as a perlocutionary efficacy, in which poetry's significance begins in the semantic realm but extends beyond it to include the bodily, emotive and ontological changes that it induces in its reader-listeners. The hermeneutic encounter is key to producing those curative effects, and 'Attar even provides instructions on the best interpretive approach, stressing the durational aspects of meaning-making. In all of the above examples, readers are urged to carefully consider the meaning of 'Attar's works over extended periods of time. They are to hold shorter poems in their minds, contemplating their significance, and to return to the longer *masnavis* multiple times over the course of their lives. Medicinal speech is not a single-dose drug, but a prolonged pharmacological therapy.

In the preface to the *Tazkera*, 'Attar provides even more specific procedures for how saintly speech in particular is to be consumed: he advocates not only a durational encounter, but a practice of daily reading to maximise the medicine's effect. Consistent with the venerative ethos of the *Tazkera*, he does not provide these instructions directly, but rather relies on a quotation attributed to Yusof-e Hamadani (d. 1140), a spiritual master from a previous generation:

> Yusof-e Hamadani (God have mercy on him!) was asked: 'When this age passes, and this clan [i.e. saintly masters] withdraws behind the veil of concealment, what will we do to remain in health (*be-salamat bemanim*)?' He said: 'You will read eight pages of their sayings every day.' I therefore considered it an incumbent religious obligation to compose some daily readings (*verd*) for the ignorant.[64]

Implicit in the question posed to Hamadani is the belief that the saints maintain the well-being of the world and those within it, and that they will vanish in accordance with sufism's ongoing decline, a common trope in sufi manuals. In response, Hamadani explains that future generations will still have access to the saints' blessings through textual accounts of their feats and sayings. He thus recommends a daily reading of eight pages of their utterances in order to maintain spiritual health. The *Tazkera* was composed to serve just such a purpose, being a set of daily readings (*verd*) for those who would otherwise remain mired in the ignorance of the age. The term ʿAttar employs here, *verd*, usually refers to litanies of Quranic verses and pious phrases that would be recited at specific hours, often late at night or early in the morning as a form of supererogatory devotion.[65] ʿAttar's application of the term to the *Tazkera* may therefore suggest that he imagined it being read every day at prescribed times. The term also has theurgic overtones – it can refer to a verbal charm, especially one derived from the Quran – which also gestures towards saintly speech's spiritual efficacy above and beyond its semantic content.[66]

The Compounding Compiler

A medieval *ʿattar* was expected to be familiar with a wide range of simple substances and their medical properties (*materia medica/mofradat*), and to be able to combine those simple substances into more complex compound medicines (*morakkabat*). As a poet-pharmacist, ʿAttar's literary activity can also be conceptualised as a kind of compounding: the combination, arrangement and transformation of discrete literary components into therapeutically effective wholes. One one level, the didactic *masnavi* is a fundamentally combinatory genre. Stories and sayings are extracted from a range of genres and sources – epics, romances, folk tales, stories of the prophets and even the scientific and wonders literature – and then refashioned in line with the poet's homiletic aims. ʿAttar incorporates an especially wide range of generic material, including a plethora of amatory narratives and long extended romances.[67] On another, more individual level, he is also drawn to overarching macrostructures that unify component parts into ordered wholes. A concern for the armature of the text is present not just in his *masnavis*, but across the oeuvre, and his structural innovations in this regard set him apart from his predecessors.

Book-length organising structures can be found, to some degree, in most of ʿAttar's undisputed works. The *Mokhtar-nama*, as discussed in the previous chapter, represents the first authorially curated, thematically organised quatrain collection in Persian. It contains fifty distinct thematic chapters, the first three of which follow the pattern of *masnavis*' opening doxologies and many thematically organised *divans*, beginning with praise of God, then of the Prophet and then of the four 'rightly guided' caliphs. The chapters then run through a series of theological and ethical topics, followed by a set of études on (primarily erotic) topoi. The final chapter is devoted to self-reflective and meta-poetic quatrains, much like the 'accounts of the poet's state' conventionally found at the conclusions of ʿAttar's *masnavis*. In the collection's introduction, besides boasting of its unprecedented nature, ʿAttar emphasises his act of selection (*ekhtiar*) and ordering: the previously unorganised quatrains of the *Divan* are, in the *Mokhtar-nama*, endowed with a 'sequence' (*tartib*), 'order' (*nezam*) and 'arrangement' (*nazm*) that increases both their aesthetic value and spiritual benefit.[68]

As for the *masnavis*, they feature innovative frame-tale devices that justify the inclusion of a diverse set of anecdotes, incorporate them into an overarching framework and endow them with a sense of unity. The *Mosibat-nama*, for instance, contains forty chapters, each one of which corresponds to a single visionary encounter on the sufi wayfarer's journey through the cosmos. The number forty conventionally implies totality and completeness, and the wayfarer's forty interlocutors together represent the totality of creation, from the highest metaphysical heights to the interior of the psyche.[69] The poem thus presents an ordered microcosm, an idealised reflection of the universe, and ʿAttar boasts that he has collected 'the essence of things' (*lobb-e ashya*) and placed them before his readers.[70] Frame-tales like this were not frequently used to structure didactic *masnavis* before ʿAttar. The only earlier extant example is Mobarak-Shah Marvrudi's *Rahiq al-tahqiq*, and its framing device is relatively thin compared to those in ʿAttar's poems. ʿAttar was clearly taken with the device, deploying frame-tales in three of his four *mansavis*, where they not only allowed him to unify the poems' disparate components, but also to combine distinct literary models in surprising ways. For example, the *Mosibat-nama* seems to be modelled on both Sana'i's *Hadiqat* – a paradigmatic mystical didactic *masnavi* – as well as Sana'i's *Sayr al-ʿebad*, a versified, visionary allegory. In the *Mosibat-nama*, ʿAttar has combined the alternating homilies and anecdotes of the former with the overarching, book-length allegorical narrative of the latter, creating a new 'compound' poem that recalls two very different generic models.

Finally, the *Tazkera* is also composed of discrete constituent parts that together form a comprehensive composite whole, although less obviously than the previous two examples. Each biography in the book, ʿAttar explains, represents a different spiritual type: 'Some are people of gnosis, some are people of action, some are people of love, some are people of unity and some are everything.'[71] There are a total of seventy-two biographies in the *Tazkera*, arranged in a roughly chronological order, from Ovays-e Qarani to Hallaj, whose climactic execution closes the work. The number seventy-two, like forty, suggests fullness and completeness: the *Tazkera* thus presents idealised types of mystical piety, all drawn from an imagined 'golden age' of sufism, that together represent 'the full range of Islamic spirituality'.[72]

Beyond individual works, the oeuvre as whole is also conceptualised as a structured compound. In the preface to the *Mokhtar-nama*, ʿAttar divides his works up into two trilogies (*mosallas*): the first consists of the *Khosrow-nama*, the *Asrar-nama* and the *Conference of the Birds*; the second consists of the *Divan*, the *Mosibat-nama* and the *Mokhtar-nama*.[73] The term used for trilogy, *mosallas*, has a range of meanings related to triplicity, but it was also a kind of incense made up of three equal parts of musk, ambergris and sandalwood, and it was thereby directly connected to the craft of perfumery and ʿAttar's pen name.[74] In this way, the oeuvre was likened to a balanced mixture in which sweet-smelling individual texts come together to produce new entities greater than the sum of their parts. The same term also appears in the introduction to the *Tazkera*, where ʿAttar writes that he would like to compose a separate book on the sayings and feats of the prophets, the companions of Muhammad and Muhammad's family and descendants.[75] This tripartite work – which does not appear to have ever been composed – is also described as a *mosallas*, a composite spiritual perfume, and ʿAttar expresses hope that if he were to write it, it would serve as his memorial in the world.

Practise What You Preach

In the medieval period, as is the case today, not just anyone could compound medicines: a physician or druggist had to prove their authority before their cures would be taken seriously. ʿAttar, as a druggist of souls, also had to prove his authority in order assure readers of his verbal cures' efficacy. This is especially the case in his *masnavis*, where – unlike the *Tazkera* – he does not seek to hide his own interventions and disappear into the background as a 'mere' compiler and transmitter. Rather, his literary persona takes centre stage as the root-level narrator of the text. Not only are the myriad stories of saints and others rendered into metrical verse, a constant formal reminder of the poet's hand, but after each story he addresses his audience directly in a homiletic mode, explaining and amplifying its significance while urging them to take its message to heart. (This is complicated somewhat by the elision between ʿAttar's speaking persona and characters in the frame-tale, as we shall see in Chapter 5.) But if these homiletic endeavours are to bear fruit, ʿAttar must convince his readers to accept him as a spiritual authority and submit to his exhortations.

A premodern doctor's authority depended in large part on their sincerity, as did the authority of preachers, whose speech was conceptualised as a kind of therapeutic cure for the soul in accordance with the medicinal metaphor. This is not the sincerity of the Romantics, which celebrated the honest rendering of the individual's subjective encounter with higher truths, but an older notion of sincerity, rooted in the alignment of one's words and deeds.[76] Doctors demonstrated their expertise through their own good health, which they maintained by following the dietary and lifestyle regimens that they recommended to others. The many proverbs in Near Eastern and European languages that assert the untrustworthiness of sick doctors or condemn their hypocrisy (Physician, heal thyself!) testify to the historical pervasiveness of this model of medical authority. Similarly, in order to be effective, a preacher had to embody the state of piety to which they verbally called their flock. Ibn al-Jawzi makes the analogy with physicians explicit in his twelfth-century manual for preachers:

> It is necessary for the preacher to eschew the excesses of life and wear modest clothes so that others might imitate him . . . When the physician himself

> abstains, his prescriptions are effective, but when he partakes, his admonishments to others do no good . . . Preaching is to be performed by a scrupulous ascetic through a woolen robe, an emaciated body, and by eating little . . . How can the hearts of the people respond to a preacher who goes around in an obese condition and dressed in luxurious clothes so that he might associate with sultans?[77]

Piety here serves a rhetorical purpose. Exhortations carry more force with an audience when they see that the preacher himself lives in accordance with his principles; inversely, sermons by impious preachers are not endowed with the same persuasive power. Those preachers who associate with sultans are singled out in particular by Ibn al-Jawzi as hypocrites whose speech cannot be effective, given the aura of irreligiousity that hovered around courts in the eyes of the pious. The royal wine symposium, which was a crucial platform for the performance of royal authority, was clearly at odds with Islamic legal injunctions, and many princes relied on, or were imagined to have relied on, un-Islamic and unjust taxes to fill their treasuries. The reality, of course, was far more complicated, and there were myriad interconnections between political elites and religious scholars. Still, Ibn al-Jawzi's condemnation reflects a common sentiment. A preacher who associated with sultans – or even worse, accepted money from them – could be charged with insincerity as one who called others to a set of standards that he himself did not live up to, and his speech would thus fail to have its desired effect. A successful preacher must align his actions with his words, which meant, along other ethical practices, keeping one's distance from political authorities, and these pious displays must not be born out of dissimulation, as Ibn al-Jawzi goes on to explain, 'but an expression of genuinely upright motives'.[78] Only then will the preacher become a model for emulation, steering their audience towards piety not only with their speech, but through their personal example.

The hypocritical preacher is frequently condemned in Persian poetry. These condemnations, however, also raise questions about the nature of the poet's authority and sincerity, especially as regards homiletic verse. As we have seen, the didactic *masnavi* is a kind of imagined homiletic performance that takes its cues from the idealised discourse and practices of preachers. The model of homiletic authority outlined above, however, assumes an oral performance environment in which the audience could see the preacher and evaluate non-verbal signs of their piety. In smaller communities, audiences would also have been likely to know something of the preacher's personal life and social habits, either directly or through reputation, just as they would be able to judge a physician by their appearance and reputation for health. But poets like 'Attar were also writing for imagined readers and listeners outside of their immediate milieu whom they would never meet face to face. They therefore had to find a way perform their sincerity within the text itself.

'Attar rises to this task most directly in a number of meta-poetic passages focused on the ethical aspects of his literary practice, including an extended discourse on poetry in the introduction to the *Mosibat-nama*. After their conventional opening doxologies, many *masnavi*s contain sections devoted to reflections on the poetic art. In these sections, poets generally praise the power and value of speech and, in a courtly context, thereby remind their patrons of their suitability for reward. In the *Mosibat-nama*, however, 'Attar uses this section to directly criticise the patronage economy and those poets who would associate with sultans.[79] Several religious poets had previously expressed some ambivalence about the patronage relationship, most notably Sana'i, who, in a meta-poetic section of the *Hadiqat*, exhorts himself to abandon the business of being a poet (*sha'eri*) now that he has been admitted to the court of the law (*shar'*).[80] Sultan Valad, a century and a half later, will express similar sentiments.[81] Still, despite their reservations, these two dedicated ample poetry to political leaders and received material support in return. 'Attar, on the other hand, does not seem to have ever received meaningful patronage from any political or religious figure, unusual for a poet with an oeuvre of his size.[82]

'Attar gives a number of reasons for eschewing patronage, from the danger of a king's fickleness to the legality of their monies, but his strongest objection is that the patronage relationship entails submission to worldly authorities of questionable legitimacy, which places aesthetic and ethical constraints on poets who must then flatter their 'unworthy' patrons in the highest terms. At its worst, according to 'Attar, such hypocrisy may even constitute a form of idolatry, as he explains in a meta-poetic section at the conclusion to the *Conference of the Birds*:

Thank God that I am no courtier,
　　that I am unbound to any reprobate.
Why should I bind my heart to anyone
　　and call some degenerate 'lord'?
I have not eaten the victuals of a tyrant,
　　nor have I closed my book with a patron's name.
My high aspiration suffices for my patron
　　Sustenance of body and power of spirit are enough for me.[83]

Underlying this condemnation is the notion that the praise of worldly rulers impinges on the rights of God, the ultimate object of eulogy. ʿAttar thus gives thanks that he has not taken any 'degenerate' as his 'lord' (*khodavand*), the implication being that only God is truly worthy of the title: it is borderline idolatrous to accept a human king as 'lord' through the institutions of patronage. God furnishes ample sustenance for the body, so there is no need to resort to 'the victuals of a tyrant'. To slightly adapt the above quotation from Ibn al-Jawzi, ʿAttar shows that he is not one of those *poets* 'who goes around in an obese condition and dressed in luxurious clothes so that he might associate with sultans'. Thus, like a physician 'who himself abstains from things injurious to health', ʿAttar's prescriptions – that is to say, his didactic verse – will be effective.

Besides direct condemnations of patronage, ʿAttar also performs sincerity by making himself the target of edifying anecdotes. In the opening discourse of the *Mosibat-nama*, he narrates several anecdotes which he uses to think through his own rejection of court patronage in terms of ethical paradigms set by ancient spiritual heroes. Generally speaking, the illustrative stories in didactic *masnavi*s are narrated for the benefit of readers, who are also the targets of the accompanying homiletic exhortations; here, however, ʿAttar shows that he uses these stories to make sense of his own life, too. One of the most striking narratives from this section features Hippocrates, or, as he was known in the Islamicate world, Boqrat, who is often portrayed as a pious pre-Islamic ascetic and sage.[84] According to this anecdote, Boqrat inhabited a cave in the wilderness and subsisted solely on grass – 'like an animal' – so that he could avoid an ethically problematic life at court. One day, a courtier finds him and calls him to come serve the king, only to meet with Boqrat's harsh rebuke:

A king went into the mountains for the hunt.
Boqrat was at that moment in the corner of a cave.
Just like an animal he was eating grass,
looking this way and that way absentmindedly.
One from among the royal retinue saw him from the road.
He said: 'The king has been calling you for a whole lifetime
so that you might be his companion day and night,
but you flee and don't come when summoned.'
– A soul content to be a beggar is,
in truth, a king! –
Boqrat said to him: 'O you who are deluded by the king,
if only you were content (*qane'*) with vegetation;
If, like me, you were satisfied with grass,
would you ever have made your free (*azad*) self a slave?'[85]

Boqrat, like the wise-fool characters of whom 'Attar was so fond, engages in socially transgressive behaviour for spiritual ends. In the medieval Islamic world, vegetarianism was not a mainstream spiritual practice. It is often presented as laudable but strange and a bit extreme, while sometimes it is attacked as denying humankind the favours that God has appointed for them.[86] In the beginning of the anecdote, Hippocrates' vegetarianism seems to be associated with a sub-human, animalistic existence. Like a dumb beast, he inhabits a cave and glances this way and that as he contentedly munches grass. Once confronted by the courtier, however, Hippocrates inverts this animal–human binary: because he is content with an 'animalistic' lifestyle, eating grass and sleeping in a cave, he has remained free (*azad*) as is proper for a human. The courtier, on the other hand, is 'deluded by the king' and lacks the spiritual fortitude to practise contentment, so he has foolishly accepted the burden of slavery as is fitting of an animal. 'Even if the king has an Alexandrian rank,' writes 'Attar, 'only an ass would make itself a slave.'[87]

Following this anecdote is a self-reflective homily in which 'Attar uses the narrative to justify his rejection of court patronage on ethical grounds. Just as Boqrat could avoid kings' summons by subsisting on grass, so too 'Attar resists the patronage economy by practising contentment and satisfaction:

When a soul is content with this small satisfaction,
what could a king do for him?
What would I do with a group of dissolutes?
How much trouble for one so restless?
I have my provisions for this moment until my death,
Whatever I could want, I have more than that before me.
What would I do with gold, since I am not Qarun?
How long should I spin about, since I am not the sphere?[88]

Besides justifying his lack of patronage and developing his pious persona, ʿAttar here interprets the previous narrative in a self-reflexive way, showing how the poem's anecdotes can be used to triangulate and assess one's spiritual standing. The story of Hippocrates, in terms of its structure and themes, does not differ substantially from the hundreds of anecdotes that populate the bulk of the text, but the homilies which follow the latter are almost always directed towards the audience and not applied by ʿAttar to himself. Here in the introduction, however, ʿAttar uses the anecdotes to conceptualise and evaluate his own ethical state: he thus models how to interpret and apply these exempla. For ʿAttar, pious heroes like Hippocrates are not to be imitated exactly, but rather approached as hyperbolic, illustrative embodiments of pious principles and attitudes. Unlike Hippocrates, ʿAttar does not eat grass, and it has been argued that he had some amount of material wealth.[89] Nevertheless, he still conceptualises the moral dynamics of his life in terms of a paradigm set by the grass-eating Hippocrates. He thus models a hermeneutic mode in which these exemplary figures become signposts for triangulating pious principles and attitudes, if not necessarily templates for direct imitation. By using the material to evaluate and assess his own ethical and religious state, he demonstrates that he holds himself to the same standard as his imagined readers. He practises what he preaches, striving to understand and shape himself through the text's illustrative anecdotes just as he expects his reader-listeners to do.

Confessions of Insincerity

Ironically, ʿAttar's most effective demonstrations of homiletic sincerity are found in his proclamations of *insincerity* that conclude each of the four *masnavi*s. At a discrete point in each *masnavi*'s conclusion, ʿAttar shifts from literary self-praise to religious self-criticism in which he renounces his poetic-homiletic project as an inherently self-absorbed and sinful endeavour.[90] He berates himself for remaining content with speech instead of action and for failing to embody a corresponding spiritual state. He suggests that his work has been motivated by pride in his own poetic talents rather than a sincere homiletic impulse, renounces poetry as egotistical delusion and confesses spiritual bankruptcy. The following quotation, taken from the conclusion of the *Elahi-nama*, is typical of this sort of self-admonishment. Analogous passages can be found in his other didactic *masnavi*s.

> How long will you speak these subtle words
> when you must eventually sleep in the dark?
> You are like Abraham in your speech
> but like Nimrod in your actions!
> If you can't die like a man for the task,
> it would be a shame to die a piece of carrion!
> How long will you stumble around speech?
> Stride forth in ecstasy, if you're lion-man!
> If your heart is eased by speech,
> how can it take a name from the states of men?
> In the end, this speech is nothing more than a husk;
> strive, like the men, for a state (*hal*)!
> You have spent your sweet life
> all in speaking. When will you act?
> Even if poetry is at the degree of perfection,
> if you look carefully, it is still just the menstruation of men.
> If you had even a hair of awareness,
> you wouldn't have anything to do with storytelling!
> Poetry has always been your idol
> You have no occupation other than idol-worshipping.[91]

At issue is the gap between speech, state (*hal*) and action: speech, however lofty and pious it may be, is ultimately useless if not enacted and embodied. ʿAttar thus berates his own heart for being content with speech, the husk of religiosity. There is even the suggestion that speech and action are mutually exclusive, and that true spiritual progress can only begin once speech has ceased. In condemnation of his excessive blabbering, ʿAttar goes so far as to proclaim his poetic practice a form of idolatry, an activity that distracts him from God even as it purports to be religiously motivated. Particularly eye-catching is the image of poetry as the 'menstruation of men'. The phrase, rooted in a discourse in which spiritual weakness is gendered feminine, was applied to the miracles of the saints – or 'the men', as they were often styled – by those who considered their supernatural acts to be prideful displays of ostentation. In using the term here, ʿAttar suggests that his seemingly pious verse is rooted not in sincere love of God, but a 'feminine' self-satisfaction in his own talent and desire for recognition.[92]

These passages of self-criticism come on the heels of fulsome self-praise in which ʿAttar lauds his poetry as unprecedented, divinely inspired and capable of spiritually transforming his reader-listeners. Some scholars have tried to reconcile these differences into a stable 'attitude' or 'philosophy' of poetry; others have pointed to the tension between classical, courtly poetic norms – especially the boast (*fakhr*) – and the ego-effacing demands of sufi mysticism.[93] The seemingly abrupt and contradictory turn from self-praise to self-blame, however, can also be read as a specific kind of rhetorical performance. Self-criticism is a common feature of Islamic popular preaching and reminiscent of Malamati spirituality, the Khorasani mystical movement that stressed the importance of sincerity and the dangers of hypocritical conceit, and which encouraged its adherents to avoid cultivating a pious reputation. By the tenth century, the Malamatiya had been subsumed into mainstream sufism – which retained the former's emphasis on humility and self-accusation – and from there it filtered into Islamic popular piety more generally.[94] In the *Tazkera*, ʿAttar speaks approvingly of various figures associated with the Malamatiya and narrates stories and sayings that stress their sincerity and humble self-estimation.[95] Popular preachers associated with Malamati-style religiosity are said to have confessed their impiety from the pulpit, wept before their audiences and even to have refused to preach on the basis of a self-alleged sinfulness. Such displays did not drive audiences away, however; on the contrary, these performances proved the preachers' sincerity and truthfulness and could therefore inspire even greater devotion among their followers.

An instructive example is found in Ibn al-Jawzi's preaching manual. It explains how the Nayshaburi preacher and Malamati Abu ʿUthman al-Hiri

(d. 910) one day refused to preach to those assembled before him, justifying his silence through the medicinal metaphor:[96]

> [Abu 'Uthman al-Hiri] left his house and came and sat in the place where he usually did when he gave public exhortations. But this time he was silent, and his silence drew out for some time. So a man called to him: 'You appear to be saying something in your silence.' Then he recited the following verse:
>
> The people are commanded to be pious
> by those who are impious;
> And they are treated by physicians who
> are infected by disease.
>
> Thereupon the people began to cry out and weep.[97]

Abu 'Uthman invokes the metaphorical identification of preacher with physician, along with the proverbial notion that a diseased doctor cannot successfully treat patients. His silence, he implies, results from a recognition of his own impiety and thus inadequacy as a preacher. Since he himself is 'diseased', any homily he would deliver would necessarily be insincere and ineffective. But the audience's reaction suggests something more complicated is going on here: they weep and cry out, as audiences are wont to do at the most climatic portions of the sermon. Abu 'Uthman's silence and self-criticism is, in fact, itself a successful homiletic act. By confessing his own spiritual laxity, he proves his humility and fear of God, and he calls on the audience to evaluate their own lives in comparison.

'Attar's professions of insincerity at the end of his *masnavis* are motivated by the same rhetorical logic. By confessing his failure to live in accordance with his words, he does not invalidate his earlier exhortations, but rather confirms them. He demonstrates that he holds himself to the same high standards as he holds his readers, and that he is willing excoriate his heart with the same ferocity. A specific kind of sincerity is thus established and performed: even if his actions do not always live up to the lofty goals of his speech, he truthfully – and performatively – condemns his failures and makes himself the first target of didactic judgement. In short, he knows the taste of his own medicine, and he is willing to take it publicly at full strength. By confessing his failures and recusing himself from the position of poet-preacher, he demonstrates that he is precisely the man for the job.

The medicinal metaphor is thus far more than a rhetorical ornament: it is the outward sign of a multifaceted conceptual network that undergirds the rhetorical work of didactic poetry, and which was especially important for ʿAttar. As a drug, poetry not only communicates, but affects its readers and listeners on a bodily level, bringing about spiritual reform through action on the humors and disposition. A kind of therapeutic regime, ʿAttar's texts were meant to be consumed in a particular way – ideally repeatedly and over time – to deliver maximum benefits. And these benefits are dependent on the ethical state of the author, who, like a doctor, must prove their sincerity for their speech to be effective. By carefully attending to this metaphor and other meta-poetic figures like it, we can reconstruct a poetics of didacticism that was never systematically theorised in rhetorical manuals or philosophical treatises, but which mediated how didactic verse was conceptualised, produced and consumed within the premodern Persianate imaginary.

Notes

1. ʿAttar, *Mokhtar-nama*, 71.
2. See *Loghat-nama-ye Dehkhoda*, s.v. 'taryak'; S. Shahnavaz, '*Afyūn*', in *Encyclopaedia Iranica*, posted 2020, https://doi.org/10.1163/2330-4804_EIRO_COM_4866.
3. ʿAttar, *Manteq al-tayr*, 440.
4. ʿAttar, *Tazkerat al-owleya*, 7–8.
5. J. T. P. de Bruijn, '*Mathnawī* 2. In Persian', in *Encyclopaedia of Islam, Second Edition*, posted 2012, https://doi.org/10.1163/1573-3912_islam_COM_0709; Van Gelder, 'Traditional Literary Theory', 124, 138; N. Chalisova, 'Persian Rhetoric: *Elm-e badiʿ* and *elm-e bayân*', in *A History of Persian Literature*, ed. Ehsan Yarshater, vol. 1, *General Introduction to Persian Literature*, ed. J. T. P. de Bruijn (London: I. B. Tauris, 2009).
6. See Landau, 'Naṣīr al-Dīn Ṭūsī and the Poetic Imagination'; Vincente Cantarino, *Arabic Poetics in the Golden Age* (Leiden: Brill, 1975), 70–99; Harb, *Arabic Poetics*.
7. Clinton, 'Esthetics by Implication'; Bürgel, *Feather*, 53–88; Meisami, *Structure and Meaning*, 9–19; Julia Rubanovich, 'Metaphors of Authorship in Persian Prose', *Middle Eastern Literatures* 12, no. 2 (2009): 127–35; Michael Pifer,

'The Rose of Muḥammad, the Fragrance of Christ: Liminal Poetics in Medieval Anatolia', *Medieval Encounters* 26 (2020): 258–320.

8. Alan Williams has collected a number of verses that deal with these themes from Rumi's *Masnavi* in 'Open Heart Surgery: The Operation of Love in Rūmī's *Mathnawī*', in *The Philosophy of Ecstasy: Rumi and the Sufi Tradition*, ed. Leonard Lewisohn (Bloomington, IN: World Wisdom, 2014). The metaphor's use in various intellectual traditions (but not poetry) has been examined in Tahera Qutbuddin, 'Healing the Soul: Perspectives of Medieval Muslim Writers', *Harvard Middle Eastern and Islamic Review* 2 (1995): 62–87. Medical imagery in Khaqani's poetry has been examined by Anna Livia Beelaert, *A Cure for the Grieving: Studies on the Poetry of the 12th-Century Persian Court Poet Khāqānī Širwānī* (Leiden: Nederlands Instituut Voor Het Nabije Oosten, 2000), 87–93.
9. See also Quran 74:31 and the discussion in Qutbuddin, 'Healing the Soul', 64.
10. Qutbuddin, 'Healing the Soul', 67–8.
11. 'Ali b. 'Osman Hojviri, *Kashf al-mahjub*, ed. Mahmud 'Abedi (Tehran: Sorush, 1392 [2013–14]), 75; Daya, *Mersad al-'ebad*, 230.
12. See especially Martha Nussbaum, *The Therapy of Desire: Theory and Practice in Hellenistic Ethics* (Princeton: Princeton University Press, 1994).
13. On virtue and the humors, see Cyrus Ali Zargar, *The Polished Mirror: Storytelling and the Pursuit of Virtue in Islamic Philosophy and Sufism* (London: Oneworld, 2017), 33–52.
14. On the application of the medical metaphor to preachers, see Merlin Swartz, 'Arabic Rhetoric and the Art of the Homily in Medieval Islam', in *Religion and Culture in Medieval Islam*, ed. Richard G. Hovannisian and Georges Sabagh (Cambridge: Cambridge University Press, 1999), 56n26; Lois Anita Giffen, *Theory of Profane Love among the Arabs: The Development of the Genre* (New York: New York University Press, 1971), 28–9.
15. For example, Ibn al-Jawzi recounts an anecdote in which a dying man pleads for exhortations despite their bitter taste: 'I have a festering sore whose cure has resisted all the efforts of the preachers and the remedy of which even the physicians have found impossible. I heard of the effectiveness of your ointment for the treatment of wounds and pain. Therefore, I beg you not to neglect the application of the medicine [*taryaq*] even though its taste may be bitter, for I am one of those who patiently endures the pain of the remedy out of hope for the cure' (*Qussas*, 60/trans. 142).
16. Ibn al-Jawzi, *Ru'us al-qawarir*, ed. Muhammad Nabil Sunbul (Tanta, Egypt: Dar al-Sahaba li'l-Turath, 1410 [1990]), 14.

17. Ibn al-Jawzi, *Qussas*, 138/trans. 221–2.
18. ʿAbd al-Qahir Jurjani, *Asrar al-balagha*, ed. Hellmut Ritter (Istanbul: Istanbul Government Press, 1954), 262; Bürgel, *Feather*, 57.
19. Shams-e Qays, *al-Moʿjam fi maʿayer ashʿar al-ʿajam*, ed. Mohammad Qazvini et al. (Tehran: ʿElm, 1388 [2009–10]), 142.
20. Jalal al-Din Rumi, *Masnavi*, ed. Mohammad Esteʿlami (Tehran: Sokhan, 1393 [2014]), 1:95; Shams al-Din Mohammad Hafez, *Divan*, ed. Parviz Khanlari (Tehran: Entesharat-e Bonyad-e Farhang-e Iran, 1359 [1980–1]), 750.
21. Mohammad Reza Shafiʿi-Kadkani, introduction to *Mokhtar-nama*, by Farid al-Din ʿAttar, 2nd ed. (Tehran: Sokhan, 1389 [2010–11]), 28–9. In an anecdote in the *Asrar-nama*, ʿAttar reports being asked to create a syrup (*sharbat*) for a dying miser, which might indicate he actually worked as a druggist (cf. the anecdote from Ibn al-Jawzi in note 15). In the *Khosrow-nama*, he claims to have composed poems in an apothecary (*daru-khana*), which would seem to be a clear indication of his profession, but the romance is considered spurious by many. See ʿAttar, *Asrar-nama*, 214–15; ʿAttar [attrib.], *Khosrow-nama*, 667–8; O'Malley, 'An Unexpected Romance'.
22. Beelaert, *A Cure for the Greiving*, 59–65, 87–93, 161–79.
23. Farid al-Din ʿAttar, *Divan-e ʿAttar*, ed. Taqi Tafazzoli (Tehran: Entesharat-e ʿElmi va Farhangi, 1386 [2007]), 101.
24. ʿAttar, *Divan-e ʿAttar*, 468.
25. ʿAttar, *Divan-e ʿAttar*, 298.
26. ʿAttar, *Divan-e ʿAttar*, 24.
27. ʿAttar, *Divan-e ʿAttar*, 215.
28. ʿAttar, *Manteq al-tayr*, 440.
29. Anya King, *Scent from the Garden of Paradise: Musk and the Medieval Islamic World* (Leiden: Brill, 2017), 271.
30. Gazorgahi, *Majales al-ʿoshshaq*, 140.
31. Sayyed Nurollah Shushtari, *Majales al-mo'menin* (Tehran: Ketab-forushi-ye Eslamiya, 1365 [1986–7]), 2:99.
32. ʿAttar, *Divan-e ʿAttar*, 115.
33. ʿAttar, *Mosibat-nama*, 448.
34. ʿAttar, *Divan-e ʿAttar*, 203.
35. ʿAttar, *Divan-e ʿAttar*, 333.
36. ʿAttar, *Divan-e ʿAttar*, 315.
37. Mahmud Shabestari, *Majmuʿa-ye asar-e Shaykh Mahmud Shabestari*, ed. Samad Movahhed (Tehran: Tahuri, 1365 [1986–7]), 69; ʿOwfi, *Lobab al-albab*, 2:337.

38. Aflaki, *Manaqeb al-ʿarefin*, 1:207–8. See the discussion in Michael Pifer, *Kindred Voices: A Literary History of Medieval Anatolia* (New Haven: Yale University Press, 2021), 55.
39. Nezami-ye ʿAruzi, *Chahar maqala*, ed. Mohammad Qazvini (Tehran: Eshraqi, 1368 [1989]), 26. See also Landau, 'Naṣīr al-Dīn Ṭūsī and the Poetic Imagination'.
40. Ibn al-Jawzi, *Qussas*, 20–1.
41. ʿAttar, *Manteq al-tayr*, 436.
42. ʿAttar, *Manteq al-tayr*, 437.
43. ʿAttar, *Manteq al-tayr*, 437.
44. ʿAttar, *Manteq al-tayr*, 436.
45. On the heart in ʿAttar more generally, see Eve Feuillebois-Pierunek, 'Mystical Quest and Oneness in the *Mukhtār-nāma* Attributed to Farīd al-Dīn ʿAṭṭār', in *ʿAṭṭār and the Persian Sufi Tradition: The Art of Spiritual Flight*, ed. Leonard Lewisohn and Christopher Shackle (London: I. B. Tauris, 2006). See also Ingenito, *Beholding Beauty*, 352–89.
46. ʿAttar, *Tazkerat al-owleya*, 6.
47. ʿAttar, *Tazkerat al-owleya*, 7–8.
48. *Loghat-nama-ye Dehkhoda*, s.v. '*mofarreh*'.
49. Ghazali, *Ihya' ʿulum al-din*, 2:1349–50.
50. Daya, *Mersad al-ʿebad*, 192.
51. Daya, *Mersad al-ʿebad*, 189. Translated by Hamid Algar as *The Path of God's Bondsmen from Origin to Return* (Delmar, NY: Caravan Books, 1982).
52. Daya, *Mersad al-ʿebad*, 189.
53. Daya, *Mersad al-ʿebad*, 191.
54. Alessandro Bausani, 'Considerazioni sulla *Tadhkiratu 'l-Auliyā'* di ʿAṭṭār', in *Colloquio italo-iraniano sul poeta mistico Fariduddin ʿAṭṭār (Roma, 24–25 Marzo 1977)* (Rome: Accademia Nazionale dei Lincei, 1978), 78; Alan Williams, 'Open Heart Surgery', 212–16.
55. ʿAttar, *Tazkerat al-owleya*, 8. See also the discussion in Anvar-Chenderoff, 'Le genre hagiographique', 49–50.
56. ʿAttar, *Tazkerat al-owleya*, 8.
57. Bausani, 'Considerazioni', 83–4.
58. ʿAttar, *Tazkerat al-owleya*, 7. See the discussion on p. 61.
59. ʿAttar, *Tazkerat al-owleya*, 7.
60. ʿAttar, *Mokhtar-nama*, 341.
61. ʿAttar, *Mokhtar-nama*, 344.
62. ʿAttar, *Mosibat-nama*, 447.

63. 'Attar, *Manteq al-tayr*, 436.
64. 'Attar, *Tazkerat al-owleya*, 7.
65. F. M. Denny, '*Wird*', in *Encyclopaedia of Islam, Second Edition*, posted 2012, https://doi.org/10.1163/1573-3912_islam_SIM_7914.
66. Mahmoud Omidsalar, 'Charms', in *Encyclopaedia Iranica*, posted 2020, https://doi.org/10.1163/2330-4804_EIRO_COM_7668.
67. Austin O'Malley, 'Erotic Narratives and 'Attār's Refashioning of the Didactic *Masnavi*', in *Routledge Handbook of Persian Literature*, ed. Kamran Talattof (Abingdon: Routledge, forthcoming).
68. 'Attar, *Mokhtar-nama*, 71.
69. As Najm al-Din Razi Daya puts it, 'the number forty has a quality of completeness that other numbers do not' (*Mersad*, 282). See also Annemarie Schimmel and Franz Carl Endres, *The Mystery of Numbers* (New York: Oxford University Press, 1993), 245–53.
70. 'Attar, *Mosibat-nama*, 448.
71. 'Attar, *Tazkerat al-owleya*, 5.
72. Schimmel and Endres, *The Mystery of Numbers*, 264–8. Paul Losensky ties the number of biographies to the hadith of 'seventy-two sects' in 'Words and Deeds: Message and Structure in 'Aṭṭār's *Tadhkirat al-awliyā*', in *'Aṭṭār and the Persian Sufi Tradition: The Art of Spiritual Flight*, ed. Leonard Lewisohn and Christopher Shackle (London: I. B. Tauris, 2006), 78–9.
73. 'Attar, *Mokhtar-nama*, 71–2.
74. King, *Scent from the Garden*, 278.
75. 'Attar, *Tazkerat al-owleya*, 5.
76. See Lionel Trilling's classic distinction between sincerity and authenticity in *Sincerity and Authenticity* (Cambridge, MA: Harvard University Press, 1972).
77. Ibn al-Jawzi, *Qussas*, 26–7/trans. 112–13 (translation modified).
78. Ibn al-Jawzi, *Qussas*, 27/trans. 113.
79. 'Attar, *Mosibat-nama*, 149–57.
80. Majdud b. Adam Sana'i, *Hadiqat al-haqiqa va shari'at al-tariqa (Fakhri-nama)*, ed. Maryam Hosayni (Tehran: Nashr-e Daneshgahi, 1382 [2003–4]), 131. See the discussion in De Bruijn, 'Comparative Notes', 375–7.
81. Franklin Lewis, 'Solṭân Valad and the Political Order: Framing the Ethos and Praxis of Poetry in the Mevlevi Tradition after Rumi', in *Persian Language, Literature and Culture: New Leaves, Fresh Looks*, ed. Kamran Talattof (Abingdon: Routledge, 2015), 24; Franklin Lewis, 'The Unbearable Lightness of Rhyming Meter: Jāmī's Confessions of a Versification Junkie' (paper presented

at A Worldwide Literature: Jami in the Dār al-Islām and Beyond, University of Chicago Paris Center, 14–15 March 2013); J. T. P. de Bruijn, 'Chains of Gold: Jami's Defence of Poetry', *Journal of Turkish Studies* 26, no. 1 (2002): 81–92; De Bruijn, 'Comparative Notes', 375–7.

82. On 'Attar's panegyric poetry, see O'Malley, 'An Unexpected Romance', 220–2; Mohammad Reza Shafiʿi-Kadkani, ed., *Zabur-e parsi: Negahi be zendagi va ghazalha-ye 'Attar* (Tehran: Agah, 1378 [1999–2000]), 95–9; Shafiʿi-Kadkani, intro. to *Mokhtar-nama*, 40–1.
83. 'Attar, *Manteq al-tayr*, 440–1.
84. Most versions of this story feature Socrates as the protagonist. Boqrat, however, is said to have refused to join Ardashir-Bahman's court, which recalls the action here: perhaps this led 'Attar to conflate the two. See Shafiʿi-Kadkani's commentary (531n823) and Lutz Richter-Bernburg, 'Hippocrates', in *Encyclopaedia Iranica*, posted 2020, https://doi.org/10.1163/2330-4804_EIRO_COM_3097.
85. 'Attar, *Mosibat-nama*, 155.
86. The richest source for medieval Islamic thought on vegetarianism is Abu'l-ʿAla' al-Maʿarri's exchange of letters with the chief Ismaʿili missionary (*daʿi*) of Cairo, al-Mo'ayyad fi'l-Din al-Shirazi, introduced, reproduced and translated in D. S. Margoliouth, 'Abu'l-ʿAlā al-Maʿarri's Correspondence on Vegetarianism', *Journal of the Royal Asiatic Society* (1902): 289–332. Hayy ibn Yaqzan, in Ibn Tufayl's allegory, eats only fruits and vegetables when at all possible so as to not cut animals off from achieving their own happiness in accordance with God's intentions (144–5). Majnun adopts a vegetarian diet in Nezami's *Layli and Majnun* as part of his transgressive withdrawal from society and reversion to animalistic existence due to love madness; see Ali Asghar Seyed-Gohrab, *Laylī and Majnūn: Love, Madness and Mystic Longing in Niẓāmī's Epic Romance* (Leiden: Brill, 2003), 92–101. 'Attar, in the *Tazkera*, includes an anecdote that suggests Rabeʿa practised vegetarianism (66). See also Paulina B. Lewicka, *Food and Foodways of Medieval Cairenes* (Leiden: Brill, 2011), 253–64; Richard Foltz, 'Islam, Animals, and Vegetarianism', in *The Encyclopedia of Religion and Nature*, ed. Bron R. Taylor and Jeffrey Kaplan (London: Thoemmes Continuum, 2005); Ahmet T. Karamustafa, 'Antinomian Sufis', in *The Cambridge Companion to Sufism*, ed. Lloyd Ridgeon (Cambridge: Cambridge University Press, 2014), 101.
87. 'Attar, *Mosibat-nama*, 154.
88. 'Attar, *Mosibat-nama*, 155.
89. According to Foruzanfar, 'Attar may have even been a landowner in Kadkan. He argues this on the basis of a reference in the *Conference of the Birds* to 'our village'

(*deh-e ma*). It is not entirely clear to me, however, why this must signify possession and not simply origin. See Foruzanfar, *Sharh-e ahval-e 'Attar*, 52; 'Attar, *Manteq al-tayr*, 398.

90. 'Attar, *Mosibat-nama*, 451; Farid al-Din 'Attar, *Elahi-nama*, ed. Mohammad Reza Shafi'i-Kadkani, 2nd ed. (Tehran: Sokhan, 1388 [2009–10]), 400; 'Attar, *Asrar-nama*, 228; 'Attar, *Manteq al-tayr*, 437.
91. 'Attar, *Elahi-nama*, 400.
92. Even though the term is clearly intended negatively as a form of self-criticism, in this context it simultaneously contains a measure of self-praise since it gestures towards his poetry's 'miraculous' nature.
93. Pourjavady, 'Naqd-e falsafi'; Pourjavady, 'She'r-e hekmat'; Rafal Stepien, 'A Study in Sufi Poetics: The Case of 'Aṭṭār Nayshābūrī', *Oriens* 41 (2013): 77–120. See also Dick Davis's introduction to his and Afkham Darbandi's translation of the *Conference of the Birds* (London: Penguin, 1984), 25.
94. On the history of Malamati spirituality and its characteristics, see Sara Sviri, 'Ḥakīm Tirmidhī and the Malāmatī Movement in Early Sufism', in *Classical Persian Sufism: From Its Origins to Rumi*, ed. Leonard Lewisohn (London: Khaniqahi Nimatullahi Publications, 1993); Melchert, 'Sufis and Competing Movements in Nishapur'; Alexander D. Knysh, *Islamic Mysticism: A Short History* (Leiden: Brill, 2000), 94–9. The connection between Malamati-style piety and 'Attar's poetic self-criticism has been noted by Waley, 'Didactic Style'.
95. See, for example, the biographies of Hamdun-e Qassar, Abu Hafs Haddad and Abu 'Uthman al-Hiri in 'Attar's *Tazkera*, 340–9, 350–3, 414–21.
96. The chapter devoted to Abu 'Uthman al-Hiri in 'Attar's *Tazkera* (414) specifically mentions his homilies (*va'z*) and 'measured and effective speech' (*sokhan-e mowzun va mo'asser*). For other examples of the rhetorical use of silence in preaching, see Berkey, *Popular Preaching*, 53.
97. Ibn al-Jawzi, *Qussas*, 80/trans. 158.

4

The Hoopoe on the Pulpit

Without a doubt, 'Attar's most famous work today is the *Conference of the Birds*. Since 1863 it has been translated multiple times into European languages, and it has recently inspired two original illustrated books as well as multiple stage performances.[1] It is also easily 'Attar's most studied work. Its academic and non-academic popularity is largely due to its allegorical frame-tale, which is commonly summarised as follows: a hoopoe leads a group of birds on a dangerous journey towards their king, the Simorgh, who resides on Mount Qaf at the edge of the world. To arrive there, they must journey through seven valleys. Many of the birds perish along the way, and when they finally encounter the Simorgh, only thirty of them are left alive. When those thirty remaining birds gaze on the Simorgh, they are astonished to see themselves reflected in the Simorgh, and the Simorgh reflected in themselves. They are ontologically linked to the Simorgh, who nevertheless remains utterly transcendent. In this way, they experience effacement (*fana'*) in the divine, which is encapsulated in the poem's central pun on 'thirty birds' (*si-morgh*) and 'Simorgh'. The poem is thus an allegory of the sufi path, in which the birds symbolise sufi seekers, the hoopoe their *pir* and the Simorgh, God.

The above summary, however, corresponds only to a portion of the frame-tale. Before they actually set out on the quest, the birds voice objections and concerns about the proposed journey, which the hoopoe proceeds to demolish; they then ask a series of questions about spiritual virtues and vices, to which the hoopoe responds in the fashion of a preacher delivering a homiletic assembly. These are more than brief preliminaries introducing the quest. In fact, the hoopoe's homiletic performances are, in many ways, the heart of the *masnavi*. They represent the vast majority of the poem (approximately 88 per cent of its total length), and it is through these performances, the contents of which are recapitulated by ʿAttar for the benefit of his readers, that the birds are rendered fit for their journey. Only at the very end of the poem do they actually set out on the path towards the Simorgh, and the events of the journey are only briefly alluded to before their final admission to the divine presence. This is not to deny the importance of the birds' allegorical journey or the significance of their final climactic encounter with the Simorgh. Rather, it is to place that climactic scene in context, and to recognise that most of the poem's content is devoted to the homiletic speech that *motivates* the journey and which makes that final encounter possible. The poem is not just the story of an allegorical journey towards God through seven valleys: it is the story of a series of homiletic performances that prepare, instigate and serve as a vehicle for that allegorical journey.

Through the frame-tale, the implicit homiletic speech situation that suffuses the genre of the didactic *masnavi* is made visible in a concrete narrative form. As we have seen, by the twelfth century preaching had become a significant avenue for spiritual instruction and the dissemination of sufi ideas to broad audiences. The genre of the didactic *masnavi* idealises and adapts the discourse of preachers to a literary context through its use of short illustrative narratives, its style of direct exhortation and its evocation of orality; in the *Conference of the Birds*, this imagined homiletic context is further embodied in the characters, setting and actions of the frame-tale. This allows a for more concrete depiction of the genre's imagined homiletic context, including the rhetorical effects of the speaker's discourse, the participation of the audience and various bodily and para-lingual channels of communication. As we shall see, the hoopoe delivers his discourses in accordance with the established practices and conventions of preaching, not only in terms of the content of his speech, but also in his position on the pulpit, the opening Quranic recitations and his relationship to his audience. Most strikingly, the frame-tale allows ʿAttar to capture something of the dynamic, interactive quality of an oral sermon. The hoopoe engages his (fictive) listeners according to their specific needs, responding to questions and meeting their objections with a calibrated mixture of admonishment and encouragement. By virtue of the frame-tale, ʿAttar can show the effects that the hoopoe's homiletic performance induces in the birds, including ecstasy and wailing, as he convinces them to undertake the dangerous journey towards the Simorgh.

The *Conference of the Birds* can thus be read as a narrative demonstration of the perlocutionary power of homiletic speech, in particular its ability to motivate spiritual reform and push listeners forward on the mystical path. The poem is composed of a series of homiletic assemblies that, in the end, lead to the birds' effacement in the Simorgh, and it thereby shows how homiletic performance instigates the ethical reform that leads to mystical experience and proximity with the divine. This valorisation of homiletic speech is not disinterested, however: the text is composed of the very same mode of discourse whose efficacy it strives demonstrate. To read the *Conference of the Birds* is to place oneself on the receiving end of the hoopoe's exhortations and admonishments, so the poem's framing of the latter's rhetorical power is critical to the transformative work that it aspires to perform.

The present chapter thus investigates how homiletic speech and its perlocutionary effects are portrayed in the *Conference of the Birds*. It begins by reconstructing, in so far as possible, the practices and procedures of preaching in ʿAttar's time, which provide the context for the hoopoe's performance. It then turns to the frame-tale structure, which allows ʿAttar to construct an imagined performance setting with an embodied speaker and reactive audience for the sermons and anecdotes typical of the genre. He can thus narrate the effects of the hoopoe's speech – which is ultimately his own speech – on the fictive audience of birds, showing how it counters their doubts, enflames their passion for God and ultimately convinces them to set out on the spiritual path. Finally, the chapter examines the changing nature of speech once the birds reach the court of the Simorgh, where identities and hierarchies dissolve, referents prove elusive and speech – if it is to be any use at all – must be allusive and oblique. Ultimately, the *Conference of the Birds* is a tale of speech, its power and its limits. The hoopoe's performances provoke a journey towards an ineffable God who cannot be grasped in language: homiletic utterances push readers and listeners towards a realm that speech itself can never fully capture.

The Practice of Preaching

As we saw in Chapter 1, didactic *masnavi*s recall homiletic discourse in both their content and overall mood: they are composed of direct exhortations in a hortatory mode, illustrated by short anecdotes and generally assume a paternalistic, advisory relationship between speaker and audience. Again, this is not to claim that didactic *masnavi*s are the genetic descendants of oral sermons or their exact formal equivalents. Rather, it is to acknowledge that the genre's tone, rhetorical stance and subject matter would, for most medieval audiences, evoke the sessions of hortatory preachers, which would cue specific expectations that would inform their experience of the text. For the medieval reader-listener, the implied setting of a didactic *masnavi* like the *Hadiqat al-haqiqa* or the *Makhzan al-asrar* was a hortatory preaching session; the poet's primary persona was that of a mystically minded preacher, sermonising from atop a pulpit or at the head of a teaching circle, and his reader-listeners were invited to imagine themselves as members of the audience assembled around him. And many of these poets would themselves preach, or at least were remembered as doing so. ʿAttar, as we have seen, is said to have preached weekly in the congregational mosque at Nishapur; Rumi delivered formal sermons as well as more intimate homiletic sessions for his disciples, both of which were preserved by his community; Sanaʾi associated with preachers like Mohammad-e Mansur; and Saʿdi also has a collection of sermons to his name.[2]

ʿAttar, however, was not content with the generic implication of a homiletic setting for his didactic *masnavi*s. Instead, he creates more concrete homiletic settings for his poems by means of the frame-tale device. Unlike the *Hadiqat* or *Makhzan*, the anecdotes and exhortations in the *Conference of the Birds* are cast as the intra-diegetic utterances of the hoopoe, the frame-tale's fictional protagonist. In the style of a preacher delivering a large public sermon, the hoopoe exhorts an assembly of birds to undertake the arduous journey towards the Simorgh. The bulk of the poem is devoted to these homiletic performances, by means of which the hoopoe ultimately succeeds in prodding his listeners onto the spiritual path. The poem's various embedded (or 'hypodiegetic') anecdotes thus unfold in an imagined communicative situation, complete with an embodied speaker, detailed setting and responsive audience. Unlike earlier *masnavi*s, which evoke a homiletic context by virtue of content and mood alone, the *Conference of the Birds* narrates it on the level of the frame-tale.

The conventions of popular preaching varied across time, space and social setting, and because the tradition was predominantly an oral one, it is difficult to reconstruct. Nevertheless, by triangulating references in different classes of sources, we can deduce some of the common features of homiletic practice as it was performed (and imagined) in the eastern Islamic world during the Seljuk and Mongol periods. First, some textual works purport to preserve the actual content of specific homiletic performances: we have already mentioned the sermons and assemblies attributed to Rumi, Saʿdi, Semnani and Nezam al-Din Owleya. These are probably not accurate transcriptions, however, but edited accounts set down at a later date, or even literary idealisations of how such events were imagined to have unfolded. Still, they give some indication of a homiletic assembly's expected countours. Also useful for reconstructing homiletic practice are hagiographies and travel accounts, which more directly capture the context and non-verbal aspects of the sermon. Finally, normative accounts of preaching – especially Ibn al-Jawzi's manual on the subject and Ghazali's discussions of preaching in the *Ihya'* – are invaluable for reconstructing the horizon of expectations against which ʿAttar's idealised accounts of preaching made meaning.

As portrayed in these sources, homiletic assemblies could take place in a variety of settings: in mosques, madrasas and *khanaqah*s, or their attached courtyards; in shrines and cemeteries; or when the session was sponsored by a private donor, in the courtyard of a palace or residence.[3] Preachers like Ibn al-Jawzi and Ahmad Ghazali could attract huge crowds, and the hoopoe's assembly is hyperbolically described as consisting of 100,000 attendees.[4] The preacher would usually ascend a pulpit or other platform, especially in these larger gatherings, increasing his visibility and marking him as a spiritual authority. He would generally sit, a standing posture being reserved for the formal, liturgically mandated Friday sermon.[5] According to Ibn al-Jawzi, the preacher should open the session with praise of God and Quranic recitation, performed either by himself or a professional reciter (*moqri*). The traveller Ibn Jubayr (d. 1217), who attended three of Ibn al-Jawzi's sermons in Baghdad, describes twenty reciters seated before the famous preacher, chanting in rounds.[6] The recitation is then followed by a eulogy for the Prophet, a prayer for the reigning caliph and his subjects and what Ibn al-Jawzi calls a *khotba*, a benediction of rhymed prose in praise of God, usually climaxing in a Quranic verse or phrase.[7] The Quranic recitation and rhyming *khotba* endow the performance with a ritual quality and cultivate a sense of pious awe and wonder, encouraging audience attention and receptivity to the sermon proper (*vaʿz*), which tends to be more discursive and didactic than the opening material; it should, according to Ibn al-Jawzi, consist of Quranic exegesis along with related exhortations to pious behaviour and 'stories of pious men' (*hekayat al-salehin*).[8]

As for specific vocal and bodily techniques, the preacher might emphasise certain points by striking the pulpit with a sword or staff, his traditional accoutrements; such an action 'arouse[s] the hearts of the people and prepares them to snatch up the exhortations avidly'.[9] Tone and modulation were important as well; Ibn al-Jawzi recommends 'raising the voice and displaying zeal in warning and exhortation', and he cites a hadith that the Prophet would visibly display his excitement while preaching and his eyes would become bloodshot. According to Ibn Jubayr's travel account, Ibn al-Jawzi reacted visibly and emotionally to his own material in a way that increased its rhetorical effect:

> Emotion visibly overtook him and tears prevented him from speaking so that we feared lest he would choke. Then suddenly he got up from his seat and descended from the minbar [pulpit], and having instilled fear into the hearts of those present, he left them as though on burning coals. They followed him with tears of agitation, some weeping profusely, and some rolling in the dust.[10]

Some preachers would even allegedly apply a salve of mustard seed and vinegar under their eyes to produce tears on demand. Such behaviour is harshly criticised on the grounds of its insincerity, but it nevertheless demonstrates how preachers sought to trigger affective responses in the audience through their own non-verbal emotional displays.[11]

By its very nature, oral homily presupposes a 'circumambient actuality' in which the audience and preacher are present in the same space over the course of the performance and are thus capable of reacting to and influencing each other.[12] The audience's participation was not only possible, but encouraged; indeed, it was a central component of the performance. Listeners would intervene by posing questions and voicing objections, and they would register the effect of the preacher's words through bodily displays. For example, during particularly intense moments of admonishment, some listeners would raise their hands upwards to signal their engagement and approval of the material.[13] Displays of extreme affect, including weeping, fainting and ecstatic movements were common – if contested – modes of audience response. Weeping is portrayed as a frequent occurrence in the assemblies, especially when preachers admonished listeners to consider their own sins and reminded them of the terrible fate in store for those who violate God's law.[14] Ecstatic behaviour (*wajd*) is also reported, similar to that which occurred in sufi *samaʿ* ceremonies. Attendees would allegedly flail about, striking each other and themselves, and sometimes even ripping off their clothing.[15] Some were said to fall down in swoons and even die.[16]

These intense displays of affect were a focus of much scholarly debate. In general, Ibn al-Jawzi did not approve of them, not because he thought the audience should remain unmoved by the preacher, but because he worried that these particular practices were often feigned and insincere, and that ecstatic movements could lead to a potentially lascivious mingling of the sexes. He does not condemn them absolutely, but suggests that, in most cases, they are to be discouraged.[17] On the question of crying, Ghazali is more permissive, allowing it on the part of both the preacher and the audience.[18] Sibt b. al-Jawzi (d. 1256; the grandson of Ibn al-Jawzi) considered the audience's weeping to be a sign of a sermon's efficacy, and he boasts of his own ability to reduce great men to tears.[19] In any case, despite scholarly debates over their legitimacy, these practices appear to have been widespread. According to Ibn Jubayr, the assemblies of Ibn al-Jawzi were full of weeping and ecstatic displays, even though the latter opposed such behaviour in his prescriptive writings.

Through these displays – as well as more subtle cues – the audience could not only demonstrate their attention and receptivity to the material (or lack thereof), but also influence how the sermon unfolded. Most sermons were semi-improvised events, so a skilled preacher could pick up on the audience's expectations and reactions and adjust his performance accordingly. This dynamic has been well documented by ethnographers in modern oral performance settings, and while our own premodern sources are much more reticent on such matters, they do hint at the extent to which audience reaction shaped the course of a homiletic assembly. For example, the sufi preacher Abu Saʿid is said to have been able to intuitively sense when a listener was struggling with a particular concept and immediately clarify his position with an apt verse or anecdote:

> The shaykh would speak at an assembly every day, and whenever a concern would pass through someone's heart, he would turn to them in the middle of his discourse and respond to whatever was in their heart with an allusion (*ramz*), a verse (*bayt*) or a narrative (*hekayat*) in such a way that they would understand.[20]

The above quotation is taken from Ebn Monavvar's hagiographical work, which often ascribes the shaykh's perceptiveness in such matters to a miraculous, preternatural intuition (*ferasat*). But these abilities can also be interpreted in a more sober fashion as the knack of an expert orator and teacher for identifying resistant or confused listeners on the basis of bodily cues and adjusting the performance accordingly.

Audiences could influence the course of the homily in a more direct fashion by asking questions, and numerous anecdotes attest to its interactive, dialectical character. The ideal structure of a large, public sermon, as imagined by Ibn al-Jawzi, includes a section devoted exclusively to audience questions. According to Ibn Jubayr, the majority of Ibn al-Jawzi's sessions were spent answering questions posed verbally or passed to him in the form of notes (*reqaʿ*).[21] Works such as Rumi's *Fihi ma fih* and the *Fava'ed al-fo'ad*, which purport to record more intimate homiletic sessions, also include frequent questions and interjections from the audience. These texts may be literary constructions designed to evoke oral homiletics more than records of actual events, but they still show the general form that such assemblies were imagined to take.[22]

The conventions of preaching – including the mounting of the pulpit, the opening Quranic recitation, the queries from the audience and the latter's wailing and ecstasy – are incorporated into the hoopoe's performance in the *Conference of the Birds*, which is thereby cast as an idealised homiletic assembly. This performance setting runs throughout almost the entire poem, but it is most obviously encapsulated in a passage immediately after the birds agree to journey towards the Simorgh. Although amenable to the journey in principle, they confess that they remain mired in confusion which must first be resolved because 'this path cannot be trod in ignorance'. After casting lots to choose a leader, they invite the hoopoe to ascend the pulpit as their 'imam of tightening and loosening' so that they might be prepared for the way.[23]

The hoopoe complies with their request and ascends the pulpit to conduct an assembly:

> Then the hoopoe made the preliminaries for his speech
> He ascended the pulpit (*korsi*) and began.
> When the crowned hoopoe mounted his throne (*takht*),
> whoever saw his face found high fortune.
> The troop of birds formed ranks, shoulder to shoulder,
> more than a hundred thousand before the hoopoe.
> The nightingale and turtle dove came forward together
> so that they might together serve as Quran-reciters (*moqri*).
> They chanted such melodies (*alhan*) then,
> that the world was thrown by them into a tumult.
> As for those whose ears were struck by their melody –
> agitated (*bi-qarar*) they came, stupefied (*madhush*) they left.
> An ecstatic state (*halat*) came over everyone
> None were with themselves, nor without.
> Then the hoopoe began his homily
> He withdrew the veil from the face of meaning.[24]

The hoopoe first ascends the pulpit and performs the 'preliminaries': presumably the invocation, praise of the Prophet and perhaps the *khotba* as discussed by Ibn al-Jawzi. By virtue of the crown of feathers lining his head, he is cast as a king on his throne (*takht*), bestowing fortune on those who approach him – it is useful here to recall Becker's argument that at the dawn of Islam, the pulpit functioned not only as a platform for oratory, but as a 'throne' for the Prophet.[25] If we understand the hoopoe to be sitting on this 'throne', which seems reasonable, that would also indicate that this is a hortatory assembly and not the liturgically mandated Friday sermon, during which the preacher would traditionally stand. Before the hoopoe begins the homily proper, the nightingale and the turtle dove, both renowned for their beautiful voices, play the role of Quran-reciter (*moqri*). More specifically, they chant 'melodies' (*alhan*) with the Quran, a particular style of recitation that was sometimes criticised for being too close to secular singing. (Ibn al-Jawzi, for instance, fiercely attacks it, writing that melodious recitation 'pleases and stirs human nature' and thereby 'diverts the people from contemplating the Quran itself'.)[26] As we have seen,

Quranic recitation could also sometimes trigger ecstatic states in its listeners, which was a source of religious anxiety for more sober critics, who worried that these behaviours were insincere affectations. The birds behave in precisely this way; the melodious recitations of the nightingale and the turtle dove throw them into an ecstatic 'tumult'.

Compared to a live homiletic performance, literary texts are something of a one-way street, at least as far as the author's relationship to their later readers is concerned. While a preacher might respond in real time to their audience, and a reciter might deviate from their script in response to listeners' reactions, ʿAttar composes his poetry, at least in part, for an anonymous textual readership that he will never meet. Literary communication with these anonymous readers necessarily lacks the circumambient actuality of oral homiletics and thus their dialogical character. Through the frame-tale, however, ʿAttar manages to mimic, within the text itself, something of the interactive, circumambient performance and reception environment that literary, authorial communication is otherwise denied.[27] The birds not only react to the hoopoe's sermons with extreme displays of affect, but, as we shall see, actually steer the direction of the performance through their questions and objections, consistent with non-literary homiletic practice.

Question and Answer

The frame-tale can be heuristically divided into four major sections. In the first section, the birds are introduced and the hoopoe urges them to seek the Simorgh; one by one they present their excuses, which the hoopoe counters with exhortations and illustrative anecdotes. In the second section, the hoopoe mounts the pulpit and continues his assembly, answering specific questions about the way. In the third, the hoopoe discourses on the seven valleys, describing each of them before launching into a thematically related set of anecdotes and homilies. In the last section, the birds finally set out and ʿAttar provides a brief narration of their journey followed by their encounter with the Simorgh.

Even before reading a single verse of these exchanges, the poem's title hints at the importance it attaches to language in general and homiletic utterance in particular. Titles were notoriously fluid in the medieval period, and the poem circulated under several names in the manuscript tradition, including the *Manteq al-tayr* (*Conference of the Birds*), *Maqamat-e toyur* (*Spiritual Stages of the Birds*) and the *Toyur-nama* (*Book of the Birds*). All of three of these titles, however, can be traced back to how ʿAttar himself describes the work, and they are all somehow related to speech. The first two, found in a single verse in the poem's conclusion, might not have been intended as titles but as references to the events of the frame-tale more generally:

> The 'conference of birds' and the 'spiritual stages of the birds'
> have found their completion in you [O ʿAttar], like light in the sun.[28]

Regarding the former, the Arabic root *n-t-q* encompasses a semantic field related to language and meaning: *manteq* is usually translated as 'speech', 'language' or 'logic', but also 'oration', whence the poem's common English title, *Conference of the Birds*.[29] The phrase also alludes to Solomon, who, according to the Quran, was taught 'the language of the birds' (*manteq al-tayr*). Not only could he perceive the significance in what others mistakenly believe to be meaningless chirping, but he was able to use this knowledge to command an avian host and dispatch the hoopoe to the Queen of Sheba as a messenger. Consistent with Solomon's image as a sorcerer-prophet-king, the phrase is endowed with theurgic overtones.[30] The second expression from the above-quoted verse, *maqamat-e toyur*, is usually translated as the *Spiritual Stages of the Birds*, and ʿAttar also uses this expression as one of the poem's proper titles in his introduction to the *Mokhtar-nama*.[31] In technical sufi terminology, a 'stage' (*maqam*) refers to one of the psycho-ethical waypoints along the sufi path towards the divine, and the seven valleys traversed by the birds can easily be read allegorically as such a sequence of mystical stages. Yet there is notable polysemy here: *maqamat* is also the plural of *maqama*, which signifies the place in which one stands to deliver a discourse, especially a homiletic one, and by way of metonymy, the homily itself.[32] It is used in this sense in the picaresque *maqamat* genre, in which eloquent, rogue heroes repeatedly dazzle audiences with their oratory in a variety of locales. The *Maqamat-e toyur*, then, could also be translated as the *Homilies of the Birds*, a rather apt title given the bulk of the poem's content. Finally, yet another title is suggested in the prologue to the *Mokhtar-nama*, where ʿAttar enumerates his previous works. The particular title he gives here is rather generic – the *Toyur-nama* (*Book of the Birds*) – but it is praised in terms drawn from the conceptual field of language and coupled with a Persian calque of the Arabic *manteq al-tayr*:

'the language of the birds (*zaban-e morghan*) of the *Toyur-nama* has transported rational (*nateqa*) souls to the site of unveiling (*kashf*).'[33] The work is thus cast a transformative utterance that gives rational – literally 'speaking' (*nateqa*) – souls access to knowledge inspired directly from God.

In contrast to the *Mosibat-nama*, which features a pedagogical discussion between a sufi shaykh and a single disciple, the *Conference of the Birds* depicts a much larger homiletic performance for a multitude of seekers. The journey towards the Simorgh and the discourses that motivate it are a group affair. After the customary doxologies, 'Attar's narratorial voice welcomes various birds one by one onto the field of action, including a parrot, peacock, eagle, pheasant and falcon, among others.[34] The various fowl then assemble themselves into a group (*jam'*, *majma'*) and observe that every city and clime, except for their own, is ruled by a king. Without a king, they complain, there can be no 'order or arrangement' in the army, nor can they progress further along 'the way'. In this manner, 'they all arrive at one conclusion': they must seek out a king for themselves, too.[35] The birds' quest is thus, from the very beginning, an explicitly social undertaking. The birds commit to seek out their ruler not as individuals, but as a group. A ruler is necessary precisely because they are bound together by social ties: they constitute a 'city' (*shahr*) and therefore need a 'monarch' (*shahryar*).

Although the birds jointly decide to set out, their endeavour is profoundly hierarchical. Immediately after they settle on the search for their king, the hoopoe emerges as their de facto leader on the quest. He recounts his bonafides as Solomon's companion, and he tells the birds he already knows the identity of their lord – the fabled Simorgh – and he claims to be uniquely positioned to guide them towards its royal court. Already we can discern the asymmetrical, pedagogical axis that will structure most of the remainder of the poem. The hoopoe must continuously prod his resistant and fickle flock to move forward. Only at the end of the tale, when they enter the court of the Simorgh, does that hierarchy dissolve. At the same time, even though the hoopoe stands above his fellow birds, he does not stand apart from them; he is an integral member of the group. As he confesses in his opening speech, he has travelled much and knows the identity of their king, but he cannot make the journey alone.[36] The quest for the Simorgh is a social, dialectical project, undertaken collaboratively by both teachers and students.

The Simorgh has its origins in pre-Islamic Iranian mythology, but it remained a resonant cultural symbol even after the Islamisation of Iran. In early New Persian literature, it is famously found in the *Shah-nama* where it is endowed with a variety of magical powers, especially healing, and nurtures and protects the hero Zal after he is abandoned as a newborn.[37] In the following centuries, the Simorgh and similar mythical birds were incorporated into Islamic mystical and philosophical writings, where they were often associated with Gabriel, the Holy Spirit and the Active Intellect.[38] It appears, for example, in the *Safir-e simorgh* (*Simorgh's Cry*) of Sohravardi (d. 1191), where it calls a hoopoe upwards towards unification with itself.[39] The allegorical *Treatise of the Birds* by Ibn Sina (d. 1037) explores similar themes: it is the story of a bird (told in the first person) who is freed from the nets of terrestrial hunters by his avian brothers who have already escaped. Although no longer captives, bits of cord remain bound to their feet that hobble them slightly. Together they journey across eight mountains to the summit of a ninth, the residence of the supreme king. Although not explicitly identified as the Simorgh, the king's mountainous perch certainly recalls that of the mythological fowl.[40] Ahmad Ghazali later composed his own rendition of the treatise, in which a group of birds journey to the island of their avian king. His version exists in both Arabic and Persian; the birds' monarch is a phoenix (*'anqa*) in the former and a Simorgh in the latter. Many of the birds perish along the way, and when they finally arrive, they are denied entry because their king, in his complete self-sufficiency, has no need of their devotion or love. They are admitted through his grace only when they realise the futility of their own action and his ultimate independence from them.[41]

'Attar's frame-tale seems to be based primarily on Ahmad Ghazali's version, but it also includes elements from Ibn Sina's treatise as well as his own innovations.[42] As in Ghazali's telling, many birds in the *Conference of the Birds* perish along the way, and they are initially rebuffed by the Simorgh's chamberlain of glory before being admitted by the chamberlain of grace. But like Ibn Sina's birds, their journey is also a sequential quest to the mountainous home of their king through a symbolically significant number of stages (here seven valleys instead of nine mountains). The play on 'thirty birds' (*si-morgh*) and 'Simorgh' seems to be 'Attar's own invention, by means of which he explores the disintegration of identities at the moment of effacement (*fana'*). Ibn Sina's treatise can be read as an allegorical, Neoplatonic ascent from concrete, sensory particulars towards the Active Intellect (or beyond), while Ghazali's version of the narrative emphasises the necessity of grace to reach the divine beloved. ʿAttar's *Conference of the Birds* incorporates elements from both of these, but it is also run through with specifically sufi concerns, especially the interior connection between self and God.

In addition to its particular theological vision, the *Conference of the Birds* also represents a striking formal deviation from these earlier works: the standalone, allegorical narrative of the birds has here been reworked into a frame-tale structure. The figure of the guide is completely absent from Ghazali's treatise, and while the avian protagonist in Ibn Sina's version is shown the way by others, they are not granted extensive speaking time. In the *Conference of the Birds*, by contrast, the majority of the story is given over to the hoopoe's hypo-diegetic performances. In the first section of the poem, the hoopoe meets the excuses of specific birds, starting with the nightingale, who, in accordance with its conventional characteristics in Persian poetry, proclaims the rose his sole object of desire.[43] Why search for the Simorgh, he asks, when the rose suffices? Why endure ascetic deprivations (*bi-bargi*), when he could dally with his beloved, adorned with a hundred petals (*barg*)? The hoopoe responds critically, accusing the nightingale of falling prey to the superficial charms of an inappropriate beloved:

The hoopoe said to him, 'O you who are mired in form,
    don't boast of your love for a flirt!
Love for a rose-face has brought nothing but thorns;
    she has really done a number on you!
Although the rose is lovely,
    in only a week her beauty begins to fade.
Love of something that decays
    vexes those who are wise.
Although the rose's smile gets you going,
    she throws you into plaintive singing, day and night.
Pass by the rose, for every new spring the rose
    laughs at you, not for you! Have some shame!'[44]

Although the rose is beautiful, her beauty is temporarily bounded.[45] Born of contingency, she is destined to wither within a week, and it is the height of folly to love something so ephemeral. According to the hoopoe, her smile – a conventional metaphor for the opening rosebud – is in fact a mocking grin as she laughs at the nightingale's foolishness. For all these reasons, the hoopoe castigates the nightingale, asking whether he has any shame and exhorting him to 'pass by the rose' and towards the Simorgh who is the only object truly worthy of love. He then transitions into an illustrative narrative that concretises this point. It tells of a dervish who falls in love with a princess, and he is encouraged in his devotion by her smile. When he persists in public professions of his love, he faces execution for his breach of decorum. Before he is killed, however, he learns that the princess's smile, like that of the rose, was one of mockery, and that all his love-pains have been for naught.

The hoopoe's excoriating tone in the above passage reflects the rough-and-tumble nature of homiletic rhetoric as well as the power imbalance between the preacher and his audience. His address opens with the disparaging epithet, 'O you who are mired in form', and he admonishes the nightingale to 'have some shame'. Although harsh and seemingly contemptuous, such a tone is pedagogically motivated. The nightingale, like many of his avian fellows, resists a transformation that would ultimately be to his own benefit; therefore, he must be made to see the precariousness of his current spiritual situation, and a belittling, cajoling address is, according to contemporary homiletic norms, one way to do this. Ibn al-Jawzi, for example, would address his listeners with vocatives such as 'O you who forget', and 'O you who are banished from the company of the pious'.[46] Likewise, homiletic poets such as ʿAttar and Rumi routinely chastise their reader-listeners for their weakness or ignorance. As we have seen, these homiletic reproaches are often gendered on the basis of an assumed association between masculinity and spiritual strength and effeminacy and spiritual weakness; thus, the wayward individual is derided in ʿAttar's poems as a 'woman' (*zan*) or a 'non-man' (*mokhannas*), while the spiritual hero is praised as a 'man' (*mard*).[47]

In this way, the hoopoe adopts the preacher's conventional language of rebuke in an effort to disabuse the nightingale of his foolish attachment to terrestrial beauty. Over the course of the section, he counters the objections of the nightingale and nine other birds: for each of them, he begins a cajoling admonishment with a dismissive epithet and then narrates an illustrative anecdote. Each of these dissenters embodies a particular spiritual fault on the

Table 4.1 *The birds' objections*

Bird	*Objection*	*Hoopoe's response*
Nightingale	Loves only the rose	The rose passes away
Parrot	Desires only eternal life	Life must be sacrificed for the beloved
Peacock	Desires only to return to Paradise	Seek the whole, not the part
Duck	Pridefully content with his own asceticism and purity	Purity is for the unclean
Partridge	Desires only gems	Don't be dazzled by colour
Homa[a]	Sees no reason to seek out the Simorgh because he is himself a king-maker	Don't take so much pride in yourself
Falcon	Already serves kings	The Simorgh is the ultimate king; human kings are fickle and dangerous
Heron	Content to sit mournfully beside the sea	Unlike the Simorgh, the sea is inconstant and unstable
Owl	Desires only treasure	Love of treasure is idolatry
Sparrow	Considers himself, like Jacob, too weak to travel to the Simorgh	This is hypocrisy; set out on the path!

[a] According to folk beliefs, whoever was touched by the shadow of the *homa* (a kind of vulture) was destined to be king. See H. Massé and Cl. Haurt, '*Humā*', in *Encyclopaedia of Islam, Second Edition*, posted 2012, https://doi.org/10.1163/1573-3912_islam_SIM_2947.

basis of its species' conventionally understood appearance and behaviour.[48] The duck is thus portrayed as a fastidious ascetic, constantly performing ablutions; he is too concerned with purity to seek the Simorgh. The owl, known to haunt ruins associated with buried treasure, is a miser so myopically obsessed with gold that he sees no profit in the long journey. The falcon proudly serves temporal kings, and because the latter have restricted his sight with blinders and hood, he cannot see their deficiencies in comparison with the Simorgh. The hoopoe lambasts each of them for their spiritual weaknesses and exhorts them to move past such short-sighted objections (Table 4.1).

This general pattern of question and answer continues through the second section of the poem, which comprises approximately 1,500 lines, or 40 per cent of the narrative (Table 4.2). Unlike the hoopoe's initial discourses, which he delivered in response to the excuses of specific birds, the questioners here are left anonymous. The hoopoe responds to around twenty enquiries, most of which are introduced by the formula 'another said to him' or 'another asked

Table 4.2 *The birds' questions*

Interlocutor's question/topic	*Hoopoe's response*
What is our relation to the Simorgh?	We are connected to the Simorgh through the heart
How can we, being so weak, travel this way?	Tale of Shaykh Sanʿan
Why is the way empty?	Because of the glory of the king
How did you [i.e. the hoopoe] take precedence over us?	Divine grace
What if I die on the journey?	We all must die anyways; better to try and fail
What if I am sinful?	The door of repentance is open
Effeminacy/fickleness	Such is the human condition; work to constrain the lower soul
Power of the lower soul	The lower soul will never be worthy
Power of the Devil	Withdraw from the world
Love of gold	Look to inner meaning, not external form
Love of possessions/worldly entanglement	The world is a rubbish pit and death is coming
Love of a beautiful human beloved	The human form is grossly material and contingent; true beauty belongs to the unseen
Fear of death	Death is inevitable
Worldly sorrows	These will pass away with the world
Obedience to God's command	We are all his slaves
Going 'all in' (*pak-bazi*)	To travel this way, you must lose all you have
Spiritual ambition	High spiritual ambition propels us forwards
Justice	Justice is desirable; it is best preformed in secret to minimise the threat of hypocritical egoism
Can one speak frankly with God?	Only those intimates who have lost their reason to love
I love God, and it is time for union	You cannot attain to the Simorgh by vain boasts
What if I have already reached perfection through ascetic practice?	You are deluded by your self
What will bring me happiness on the way?	Happiness is through him
What reward should I ask of him at the end of the way?	Ask him for nothing but himself
What gift should I bring?	The burning of your soul and the pain of your heart

of him'. Approximately the first ten questions involve specific spiritual weaknesses. One bird admits that he is scared of death, another that he is enmeshed in earthly love and another that he suffers from excessive pride; the hoopoe castigates them for their failings and attempts to guide them to the straight path. Other birds enquire of the specific mystical virtues that they have already begun to develop, such as love of justice, submission to the divine will and high mystical aspiration (*hemmat*): these birds are met with the hoopoe's praise.[49] Still others ask the hoopoe what they ought to bring to the Simorgh as a gift, or boast of their exclusive focus on the divine. The hoopoe answers each of these interlocutors with some mixture of praise and admonishment, followed by a series of illustrative anecdotes coupled with explanatory exhortations. A typical response contains around four or five of these anecdote-exhortation pairs.

Generally speaking, as soon as the hoopoe's discourse on a particular topic comes to a close, another question is posed. At key points in the poem, however, the birds' reactions to a specific story or set of stories are narrated. For example, the first question posed by the birds in this section concerns their relationship to the Simorgh. How might they, as weak as they are, ever attain the Simorgh's lofty perch? How could there be any relation (*nesbat*) between them and the Simorgh? In response, the hoopoe narrates a series of parables, including the story of Mahmud's secret passage to Ayaz's bedchamber, which illustrate the internal connection between God and the human heart. After the hoopoe finishes these narrations and commentary, ʿAttar describes their impact on the assembled birds:

> When the birds heard this speech (*sokhan*),
>   they traced back the ancient secrets.
> They all found their relation (*nesbat*) to the Simorgh,
>   and that's how they found a desire (*raghbat*) for wayfaring.
> Due to this speech (*sokhan*) they all came to the path
>   in empathy and agreement with each other.[50]

The hoopoe's speech (*sokhan*), as the passage makes clear, is a powerful causal agent that works on the birds as they interpret it. By decoding its allegorical message, they learn how their innate connection to the Simorgh makes spiritual wayfaring possible, which sparks their desire (*raghbat*) and leads them to step up to the path, together. In this way, the hoopoe's stories carry perlocutionary effects over and above their spiritual meanings and moral points. Speech's effects are not confined to the linguistic realm: it changes its listeners' dispositions and provokes them to action, just as the hoopoe's anecdotes lead the birds to the path and convince them to set out.

Still, some birds continue to worry that they lack the strength necessary to finish the quest: how might the birds, weak as they are, ever hope to tread the entirety of this path? In response, the hoopoe explains that lovers always strive to reach their beloved no matter how low the chance of success: 'Whoever becomes a lover, thinks not of his life,' he proclaims. Indeed, life, the soul, even religion are only obstacles on the way of love, and the hoopoe narrates the story of Shaykh Sanʿan to illustrate this point. This is one of the most complicated stories in ʿAttar's oeuvre, and it has been well discussed in the scholarship, but I would like to draw attention to the profound effects that it produces in its fictive auditors:

> When the birds all heard this speech [*sokhan*, i.e. the tale of Shaykh Sanʿan],
> they gave up any care for life.
> The Simorgh had stolen repose from their hearts
> The love in their souls increased from one to a hundred thousand.
> They all turned to the road with firm intention
> They stood fast in the devotion to wayfaring.[51]

Through their act of audition, love in their hearts increases 100,000 fold, and the Simorgh, on the model of the Christian girl who beguiles Shaykh Sanʿan, steals all repose from their hearts. The story causes the birds to behave exactly as ʿAttar says true lovers should: after hearing it, they 'g[i]ve up any care for life' and turn with firm intention towards the path, eager to risk it all – although they do not set out just yet. As taken as readers and scholars have been with the tale, it seems to exert just as strong an influence on its fictive audience within the text. Their audition marks a key turning point in the poem, after which the hoopoe no longer needs to convince them to set out but rather must prepare them for the journey.[52] And this, too, is accomplished through speech: the hoopoe now mounts the pulpit and answers the above-listed questions about the nature of the road before them.

Discoursing on the Seven Valleys

The famous seven valleys appear in the third section of our heuristic, quadripartite division of the poem. But again, the birds do not actually traverse them at this point. Instead, the hoopoe delivers seven sermons, one for each 'valley', explaining its particular significance to his avian flock. One of the best-known aspects of the *Conference of the Birds*, these valleys represent a specific ordering of the various mystical 'stages' (*maqam*) that, according to the sufi manuals, populate the mystical path. At each stage, sufi wayfarers are expected to master a particular virtue, state of being or modality of experience, and only when that stage has been completely internalised under the eye of the spiritual guide can they move on to the next. The number and order of the stages varies widely between traditions, authors and texts, and the *Conference of the Birds* by no means provides a standard or universal ordering.

In response to a question about the route to the Simorgh, the hoopoe explains that they will have to pass through seven valleys: desirous seeking (*talab*), love (*'eshq*), gnosis (*ma'refat*), detachment (*esteghna*), unification (*towhid*), bewilderment (*hayrat*) and, finally, spiritual poverty and effacement (*faqr o fana'*). For each valley, the hoopoe delivers an introductory homily in which he explains the spiritual state associated with it, followed by anecdotes and further exhortations on related themes. This set of discourses comes to almost 800 verses.

There is no direct, narrative account of the birds traversing each of the seven valleys at this point, or at any other point in the poem: their names appear only in the context of the hoopoe's homiletic speech, in which he explains the various spiritual states that they symbolise.[53] In my experience, students and readers unaccustomed to the conventions of the didactic *masnavi* are frequently left somewhat disappointed by this aspect of the *Conference of the Birds*, expecting a denser allegorical plot akin to Spencer's *Faerie Queene*. Tellingly, modern adaptations of the poem almost always inflate the frame-narrative while diminishing or even eliminating the embedded homiletic performances. For example, Edward FitzGerald and Raficq Abdulla keep the focus more directly on the story of the birds in their renderings by reducing the number, frequency and length of the embedded narratives and sermons. In both versions, the hoopoe generally responds his flock's questions with a single anecdote or exhortation instead of branching off into a full thematic chapter bound by an associative logic. More recently, the *Conference of the Birds* has been reimagined as an illustrated children's book by Alexis York Lumbard and a gorgeous graphic novel by Peter Sís. The hoopoe plays a guiding and encouraging role in both of these, but he recounts no stories: the frame-narrative has become the only narrative, and the original's focus on the transformative power of embedded homiletic performances is necessarily lost.

These modern illustrated adaptations also include many images of the birds in flight as they journey towards the Simorgh. Premodern illustrated manuscripts, on the other hand, generally depict the events of the embedded anecdotes, and in the rare cases that they do depict a scene from the frame-tale, it is invariably that of the birds' homiletic assembly. In the famous illustrated manuscript at the Metropolitan Museum (Figure 4.1), dating from the Safavid period, the diminutive hoopoe occupies the compositional centre of the painting, perched on a rock like a preacher on a pulpit, while the other birds form a loose ring (*halqa*) before him. They gaze intently at the hoopoe, and his beak is partly open as if in speech. This same scene is illustrated in the Staatsbibliothek and Czartoryski Museum manuscripts. In the British Library composition (Figure 4.2), the hoopoe again stands on an elevated rock-pulpit, but he berates the peacock alone as his audience of one. The 1493 Bodelian manuscript (Figure 4.3) contains the same scene as the Met, Staatsbibliothek and Czartoryski manuscripts, but it includes a dazzling, multi-coloured Simorgh among the other birds. This is not, however, an illustration of their final encounter – rather, as the painting's position in the manuscript and the accompanying paratextual header makes clear, it is another illustration of the 'birds' assembly' (*majmaʿ-e toyur*). The Simorgh has been added into the scene as a creative act of interpretive illustration and painted in accordance with its appearance in the epic tradition. There is likely no single reason that can explain why this particular scene was favoured by the pictorial tradition: the availability of models, anxiety about the possible theological implications of depicting the birds at the moment of union and the illustrators' personal interests may have all played a role. Whatever the case may be, these premodern illustrations stand in sharp contrast to modern pictorial approaches to the work, and their presence serves to emphasise the centrality of the birds' preparatory, homiletic assemblies to their journey.

Figure 4.1 'The Assembly of the Birds', Metropolitan Museum of Art, Fletcher Fund, 63.210, 11r.

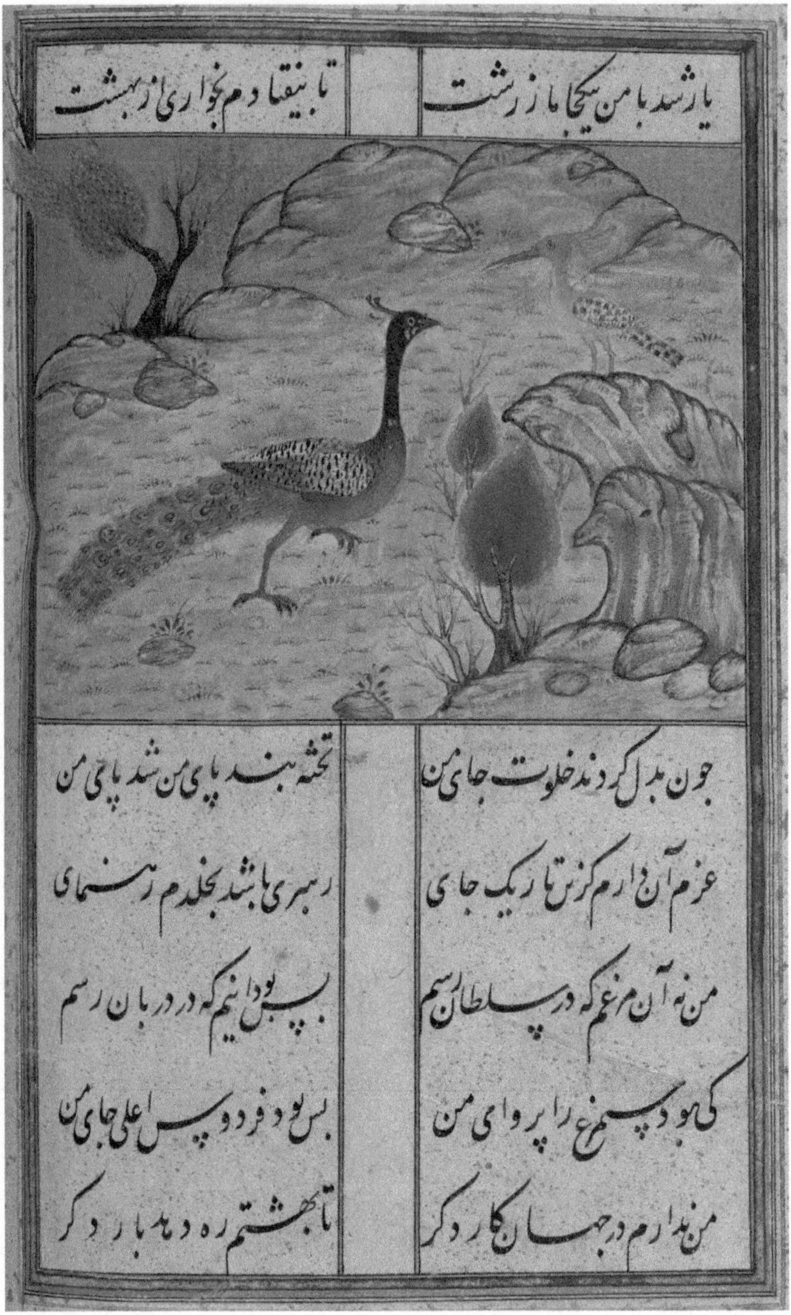

Figure 4.2 'The Hoopoe Lectures the Peacock', MS Add 7735, 30v. By Permission of the British Library.

Figure 4.3 'The Assembly of the Birds', MS Elliott 246, 25v.
By Permission of the Bodleian Library.

The hoopoe's sermons on the seven valleys further feed the birds' desire for the Simorgh and provide them with the final push they need to actually embark on the journey. His speech is so powerful that many die on the spot, a conventional trope of extreme audience reaction to powerful oration:

> Their souls became restless from these words,
> and many died right in that staging area.
> All of the birds left in that place
> headed out on the road in longing.
> For years, they travelled high and low,
> a long lifetime exhausted on their way.[54]

Their journey takes years, but as to its details, 'Attar largely demurs. He explains that many perished along this way, and he lists some the dangers they faced including panthers on the mountaintops and excessive hunger and thirst, which can be allegorically interpreted as the hazards that await novices along the spiritual path. This passage, however – which comes to less than a dozen lines – is the extent of his direct narration. The seven-fold spiritual geography of the valleys is drawn through the hoopoe's preparatory sermons, not through extra-diegetic narration of the journey itself, which is allegedly beyond explanation:

> How could any explanation answer
> for that which befell them on this way?
> If, one day, you come to this path,
> then you will see its passes one by one,
> and you will know what the birds experienced;
> it will be clear to you the blood they swallowed.[55]

For one to understand what it is like to actually make this arduous journey, one has to undertake it themselves. Thus, rather than recount this experience in detail (an impossible task in any case) 'Attar devotes the bulk of his narratorial energies within the first three sections of the poem to the didactic lessons that provoke the birds' quest and that constitute its ethical core.

Effacement in the Simorgh

The fourth and final section of the poem recounts how the birds arrive at the threshold of the Simorgh's court, where, after initially being turned away, they are finally admitted to its presence. The hoopoe, the central figure of the first three sections of the poem, is noticeably absent here. In fact, after he completes his sermons on the seven valleys and his flock sets out, he is not mentioned again. At this point in the narrative, when the birds speak, they speak together with one voice, freed from the pedagogical axis of teacher and student that previously conditioned their discourses. There are theological reasons for this flattening: the Simorgh's court is a place of unity, where divisions, hierarchies and even identities are transcended. A few narratives are embedded in this section, but they are no longer homiletic performances undertaken by the hoopoe. Rather, they are spoken by ʿAttar himself *in propria persona* or read or recited by the birds as a group. Several of these narratives – including the story of Joseph and the king who orders the execution of his beloved – are (like the frame-story itself) introduced as allegories that obliquely gesture towards matters that, according to ʿAttar, are not amenable to more direct explanation. The power of language thus remains a major concern of this section, but it is the limitations of speech – as well as its capacity to indicate, allude and parabolically signify – that come to the fore.

The frame-narrative is noticeably thicker in this section of the poem with more direct narration from ʿAttar. He begins by recounting how, out of the thousands of birds who set out, only thirty birds survive to arrive at the Simorgh's court, consistent with the sufi notion that proximity with God is a privilege only afforded to an elect few. And those that do arrive are in rough shape, with 'wings and feathers lost, sick and weak / broken hearted, souls departed, bodies unsound'.[56] The Simorgh's 'chamberlain of glory' appears before them and demands to know their business at the exalted threshold. They respond that have come in hope of an audience with their king, the Simorgh, and that they have suffered many tribulations on the path. The chamberlain denies them entry (much like Ghazali's version), berating them for thinking that the Simorgh, in its transcendent detachment, has any need for them or their suffering. The birds are on the brink of despair, but they resolve to be like Majnun who so loved Layli that he rejoiced even in her rebuke. When the chamberlain warns that they do not have the strength to bear the Simorgh's glory, they reply that, like the moth who welcomes immolation in the candle, they will not turn away from the Simorgh's blazing majesty even if it means their own death. Their devotion thus established, the 'chamberlain of grace' approaches, raises the curtains and sets them on the 'couch of proximity'. He hands them a manuscript that contains the story of Joesph's reunion with his brothers (a fascinating case of narrative embedding considered in detail in Chapter 5), and the 'light of proximity' shines on them. It is then that the birds gaze upon the visage of the Simorgh, where, much to their surprise, they see themselves.

This mystical merging of identities, often considered the highlight of the *Conference of the Birds*, is rooted in the sufi notion of 'effacement' (*fana'*): that state in which the mystic's consciousness is so overwhelmed by God's unity that everything else seems to melt away, even their own self.[57] In some interpretations, this loss of self takes on the flavour of an apotheosis. The sufi ceases to exist as an independent being and instead experiences their true reality as a manifestation of the divine. All conceptual categories fade away in the face of God's oneness, including, paradoxically, the boundary between God and not-God. But just as God's unity cannot, according to most sufis, be adequately expressed in words, neither can this state of effacement. Mystical writers and poets thus push syntax, morphology and vocabulary in new and unexpected ways in an attempt to gesture towards the experience of union without reifying it into a fixed, easily digestible form.[58]

In 'Attar's case, he playfully meditates on the birds' bewildering experience of mystical union by punning on Simorgh and 'thirty birds' (*si-morgh*). The pun is an example of 'compounded paronomasia' (*tajnis-e morakkab*), a rhetorical device in which a word is juxtaposed with a phrase of an identical or similar pronunciation.[59] Persian also lacks capitalisation, and in most manuscripts Simorgh and *si-morgh* are both written as one word (or the orthographic distinction between them is not consistently maintained), rendering them visually as well as aurally identical. In the passage below, the bewildered birds look back and forth between themselves and the Simorgh, and they are shocked to find that they cannot distinguish between themselves and their king. To preserve the dizzying quality of the original, in which one quickly loses track of which '*simorgh*' refers to the thirty birds and which to the Simorgh, the term is left untranslated here and its referent unspecified:

The light of proximity shone from ahead
All their souls were dazzled by that beam.
And reflected in the face of the *simorgh* of the world,
they then saw the visage of the *simorgh*.
When those *simorgh* looked closer,
without a doubt, this *simorgh* was that *simorgh*!
In confusion all were bewildered
These didn't know how they'd become that.
They saw themselves as the complete *simorgh*,
and the *simorgh* itself was the eternal *simorgh*.
When they looked towards the *simorgh*,
that *simorgh* was this over here.
And when they glanced at themselves,
this *simorgh*, they were that one there.
And when they glanced at both at once,
both were one *simorgh*, in all respects.
This one was that, and that one this,
no one in all the world has heard such a thing![60]

The term is repeated twelve times in only seven verses, the sheer weight of repetition serving to detach the verbal signifier from its distinct signifieds. At the same time, the contrasting indexicals 'this' and 'that' show that difference itself is never totally transcended; indeed, the very assertion of co-identity presumes some kind of distinction between the two elements to be equated. The frequent alteration of these demonstratives also makes it difficult to discern whether the antecedent in any given case ought to be understood as the divine Simorgh or the thirty birds, at least when reading the poem at a normal speed. Unlike English, demonstrative adjectives in Persian are not marked for number: 'this' and 'these', and 'that' and 'those', are identical, so we cannot rely on the presence of a plural to distinguish between the thirty birds and the Simorgh. The passage thus does not present a simple case of absolute identification, but a bewildering state of simultaneous identity and difference, linguistically expressed in the homonym of Simorgh and *si-morgh*, parallel grammatical structures and dizzying repetition.

Sufism's interest in dismantling conceptual boundaries at the point of union is concomitant with a concern for preserving God's ultimate transcendence: the divine should never by bounded by the reductive frameworks of human language, thought or even experience. The result, especially in more imaginative sufi writing, is a dynamic vacillation between attempts to describe the ineffable in parabolic, allusive or otherwise indirect speech, followed by disavowals of those same descriptions as insufficient or inappropriate. The pun on Simorgh and *si-morgh* is itself only a temporary heuristic that cannot fully capture the truth of the Simorgh or its relationship to the birds. Whatever its merits, it too must ultimately be discarded as insufficient.

The Simorgh thus reaffirms its ultimate transcendence and unknowability after the birds' experience of co-identity, disabusing them of any notion that they could understand, much less achieve union with it:

> This sunlike-presence is a mirror;
> whoever arrives here sees himself in it –
> body and soul sees body and soul in it.
> Since you came here as thirty birds (*si-morgh*),
> you appeared as thirty in this mirror.
> If you were to return as forty or fifty,
> you would still just remove the veil from yourselves.
> Far have you roamed, but
> you see and have seen only yourselves.
> How could anyone's vision reach us?
> how could an ant catch sight of the Pleiades?
> Have you seen an ant carry an anvil?
> or a fly grab an elephant in its teeth?
> Whatever you've known or seen – it wasn't that!
> Whatever you've said or heard – it wasn't that!
> . . .
> You remain thirty birds (*si-morgh*), perplexed,
> heart-broken, patience-tried, soul-stripped,
> but we in our 'simorgh-ness' are so much greater,
> since we are the true Simorgh in essence.[61]

The birds' experience of identity with the Simorgh is born out of their own limited perspective, which is incapable of grasping its true nature. The mystic pun that seemed to have captured, however obliquely, something of this state is unmasked as an accident of language and a one-sided imposition. If forty or fifty birds had made the journey to the Simorgh's court, they would have seen forty or fifty birds there. All attempts to articulate or even understand this experience originate with the human (or avian) observer.

One reaches a point at which further speech simply muddies the waters. Ultimately, the birds' climactic union with the Simorgh cannot be articulated, even by its own subjects: 'As long as they travelled, they spoke these words,' writes 'Attar, 'But then they arrived, and there was no beginning or ending / Here, no doubt, speech was cut short.'[62] The birds do not speak again in the poem, and 'Attar soon joins them in silence. At several points in this final section, he voices his reluctance to speak, especially near its conclusion. After the birds are effaced in the Simorgh, they are returned to themselves in 'subsistence' (*baqa'*), a mystical state that is frequently paired with effacement but even less clearly defined; it usually seems to involve some sort of recovery of individual existence, albeit in an altered form. 'Attar reports that the birds enter into 'subsistence after effacement', but he demurs direct discussion:

> No one, ancient or contemporary,
> has ever had words for this 'effacement' and 'subsistence'.
> Just as he is far, far from vision,
> this explanation is far from commentary or report.
> Nevertheless, some of our companions have, by way of allegory,
> requested a commentary on 'subsistence after effacement'.
> How could we discuss that here?
> It would require the compilation of a new book,
> since the secrets of 'subsistence after effacement'
> are known by them that are worthy.
> As long as you exist in the world of being and not-being
> how can you step foot into this realm?[63]

No speech can encompass the states of effacement and subsistence; they cannot be explained, nor do they fit in 'commentary' or 'report'. Its secrets can only be known by those worthy ones who have already transcended the world of being and not-being.

Nevertheless, at the urging of his companions, ʿAttar does narrate a story in an allegorical mode that, unlike other kinds of discourse, is apparently flexible and allusive enough to gesture towards these spiritual truths without circumscribing their ineffability. A king, after he finds his male beloved dallying with a female slave, orders him executed him in a bout of jealously. Unbeknownst to him, his vizier (who is also the boy's father) hides the boy and has a murderer executed in his place. The king soon regrets his decision and is wracked with guilt and sorrow. On the fortieth day, he sees his beloved in a dream and begs his forgiveness; the actual boy emerges from hiding with a sword and shroud, prepared to accept execution in recognition of his own transgression. Lover and beloved are thus reunited. As Davis has observed, it is not immediately obvious which of the pair represents God and which the believer, a structural ambiguity that echoes the thirty birds' mystical dissolution into the Simorgh.[64] This story of reunion, restoration and unexpected returns is presented by ʿAttar in his introductory comments as clarifying something of the nature of subsistence after effacement, but it remains indirect and parabolic enough not to violate the ineffability of that state.

Sometimes, however, even such indirect measures are too blunt an instrument. Once the king and his beloved are restored to each other, ʿAttar refuses to narrate what passes between them:

After this, anything I might say is unspeakable
    A pearl in the depths cannot be pierced.
When the king found deliverance from his separation,
    both went happily into the private pavilion.
After this, no one knows the mysteries
    for here is no place for strangers.
Whatever this one said and that one heard
    only a blind eye has seen it, a deaf ear heard.
Who am I to them to explain these secrets?
    If I did, I would sign my own death warrant.
Since I have not arrived, how would I explain it?
    I must remain silent, pinned on this chessboard.[65]

Such intimate secrets are known only through experience, and even if one could articulate them, it would be improper and dangerous to do so. In the end, silence is the only choice.

Although language is unable to fully communicate this mystery of effacement and subsistence, it is far from useless. From a Neoplatonic, sufi perspective, allegory and other kinds of parabolic speech can give readers and listeners a taste of certain higher realities in an allusive, indirect fashion that allows them to ontologically participate in those realities while preserving their ineffable mystery; this function of allegory will be discussed in detail in Chapter 6. On a more concrete level, speech can also motivate the ethical reforms necessary to bring one closer to God. The birds only experience mystical union, allusively described in the Simorgh/*si-morgh* pun, because they were convinced to set out and prepared for the journey by the hoopoe's homiletic performances. The first three sections of the poem are dominated by those performances, and the perlocutionary, rhetorical function of speech is repeatedly demonstrated on the level of the frame-tale. The *Conference of the Birds*, when taken as a whole, can thus be read as a narrative exploration of the power (and limits) of speech: it shows how homiletic exhortations and didactic anecdotes can propel seekers along the path towards God, where, if favoured by his grace, they might activate an internal connection to the divine to which allegorical speech can allude but never fully capture.

The poem's exploration of speech is curiously self-reflexive: by demonstrating the perlocutionary effects of the hoopoe's discourse, ʿAttar also asserts the transformative power of the *Conference of the Birds*, through which he presents that speech to his readers. Indeed, one of the most fascinating characteristics of the frame-tale device is its potential to blur narrative boundaries even as it establishes them. The birds' intra-diegetic, fictive audition of the hoopoe's oral sermons cannot be equated with actual readers' experiences of the poem, but the frame-tale structure elides that distinction: readers are invited to approach the text as if they were among the imaginary audience depicted within it. These complexities are the subject of the next chapter, in which we investigate the frame-tale's function as a tool of authorial control that conditions readers' encounters with the embedded homilies and anecdotes.

Notes

1. The poem was translated into French by Garcin de Tassy in 1863, followed by an adaptation into English by Edward FitzGerald (posthumously published in 1889) and an abriged translation by Rustom Masani (1924). The version of Stanley Nott (1952) is an indirect translation produced via de Tassy's French, and the version of Raficq Abdulla (2003) is a rhyming adaptation based primarily on Nott's prose. Afkham Darbandi and Dick Davis's fluent English verse translation (1984) is done in rhyming couplets directly from the Persian. Peter Avery's prose translation (1998) cleaves extraordinarily close to the Persian text: essentially a gloss, it is the most accurate and appropriate for scholarly uses. Most recently, Shole Wolpé has published a prosimetric version (2017). Illustrated retellings of the story have been done by Peter Sís (2011) and Alexis Lumbard (2012). The poem was adapted for the stage by Peter Brook and Jean-Claude Carrière (1977). On the various translations and adaptations, see Shackle, 'Representations of 'Aṭṭār'.
2. Jalal al-Din Rumi, *Majales-e sab'a: Haft khetaba*, ed. Towfiq Sobhani (Tehran: Kayhan, 1365 [1986]); Jalal al-Din Rumi, *Fihi ma fih va payvastha-ye no-yafta*, ed. Towfiq Sobhani (Tehran: Parsa, 1388 [2009–10]); Lewis, *Rumi*, 128–33, 292–4; Sa'di, *Kolliyat-e Sa'di*, ed. Mohammad 'Ali Foroughi (Tehran: Amir Kabir, 1367 [1988–9]), 895–916; De Bruijn, *Piety and Poetry*, 169.
3. Ibn Jubayr, *Rihlat Ibn Jubayr* (Beirut: Dar Sadir, 1964), 198; Swartz, 'Rules of Popular Preaching', 224–7.
4. 'Attar, *Manteq al-tayr*, 305.
5. Jones, *Power of Oratory*, 161–2.
6. Ibn Jubayr, *Rihla*, 196–200. A full translation can be found in Ibn Jubayr, *The Travels of Ibn Jubayr*, trans. R. J. C. Broadhurst (London: Jonathan Cape, 1952), 229–34.
7. This *khotba* must be distinguished from other uses of the term, including the formal, liturgically mandated Friday sermon.
8. Ibn al-Jawzi, *Qussas*, 140/trans. 224; Swartz, 'Rules of Popular Preaching', 229; Swartz, 'Arabic Rhetoric', 41.
9. Ibn al-Jawzi, *Qussas*, 137/trans. 220. On the preacher's staff and sword, see C. H. Becker, 'Die Kanzel im Kultus des alten Islam', in *Orientalische Studien: Theodor Nöldeke zum siebzigsten Geburtstag (2. März 1906)*, ed. Carl Bezold (Gieszen: A. Töpelmann, 1906), 336–7.
10. Ibn Jubayr, *Rihla*, 199. Translation from Swartz, 'Rules of Popular Preaching', 234.

11. Ibn al-Jawzi, *Qussas*, 94/trans. 171. See also Talmon-Heller, *Islamic Piety*, 121; Clifford Edmund Bosworth, *The Medieval Islamic Underworld: The Banū Sāsān in Arabic Society and Literature* (Leiden: Brill, 1976), 1:112.
12. Walter Ong, 'Writer's Audience', 10.
13. The motion of 'raising the hands' (*rafʿ al-yadayn*) can be traced back to pre-Islamic practices of prayer and supplication, but it also evokes the gestures of Islamic ritual prayer. Its use in hortatory assemblies, like weeping and ecstatic movements, was sometimes contested, but Ibn al-Jawzi seems to have approved. See Swartz's long note on the subject in his translation of Ibn al-Jawzi's *Qussas*, 120–1n5.
14. Jones, *Power of Oratory*, 243–4; Talmon-Heller, *Islamic Piety*, 141–4.
15. Ibn al-Jawzi, *Qussas*, 95/trans. 174–5. We should keep in mind that Ibn al-Jawzi opposed these practices as we read his descriptions.
16. Swartz, 'Rules of Popular Preaching', 234–5. Several of the anecdotes in the *Qussas* mention such deaths.
17. Ibn al-Jawzi, *Qussas*, 117, 140–2/trans. 203, 225–6.
18. Pedersen, 'The Islamic Preacher', 247.
19. Talmon-Heller, *Islamic Piety*, 141–2.
20. Ebn Monavvar, *Asrar al-towhid*, 1:62.
21. Ibn Jubayr, *Rihla*, 198; Ibn al-Jawzi, *Qussas*, 139/trans. 233.
22. Pourjavady, 'Genres of Religious Literature', 292.
23. 'Attar, *Manteq al-tayr*, 304. In classical Islamic political theory, the 'people of tightening and loosening' (*ahl al-hall wa'l-ʿaqd*) were the scholars and religious elites who were theoretically responsible for the selection of the caliph. Muhammad Qasim Zaman, '*Ahl al-ḥall wa-l-ʿaqd*', in *Encyclopaedia of Islam, Three*, posted 2007, https://doi.org/10.1163/1573-3912_ei3_COM_0027.
24. 'Attar, *Manteq al-tayr*, 305.
25. Becker, 'Die Kanzel', 335–44.
26. Ibn al-Jawzi, *Qussas*, 120–1/trans. 205. Regarding the debate over appropriate styles of Quranic recitation, see F. M. Denny, '*Tadjwīd*', in *Encyclopaedia of Islam, Second Edition*, posted 2012, https://doi.org/10.1163/1573-3912_islam_COM_1145.
27. See also the discussion in David A. Wacks, *Framing Iberia:* Maqāmāt *and Frametale Narratives in Medieval Spain* (Leiden: Brill, 2007), 53–65.
28. 'Attar, *Manteq al-tayr*, 435.
29. Lane, *Lexicon*, s.v. 'n-t-q'; *Loghat-nama-ye Dehkhoda*, s.v. '*manteq*'.
30. Quran 27:15–27.

31. 'Attar, *Mokhtar-nama*, 72. Peter Avery suggests that the two titles refer to two distinct sections of the poem; the *Conference of the Birds* (or as he renders it, *Speech of the Birds*) would refer to the hoopoe's homilies about the way, and the *Stages of the Birds* would refer to their traversal of the stages. See Farid al-Din 'Attar, *The Speech of the Birds: Concerning Migration to the Real*, trans. Peter Avery (Cambridge: The Islamic Texts Society, 1998), 397, 539n458.
32. In actuality, both *maqam* and *maqama* could refer to a homily. According to Devin Stewart, the singular *maqama* may be more properly applied to picaresque writings, and *maqam* to the non-ironic harangue. See Devin Stewart, 'The *Maqāma*', in *Arabic Literature in the Post-classical Period*, ed. Roger Allen and D. S. Richards (Cambridge: Cambridge University Press, 2006), 154–5; C. Brockelmann and Ch. Pellat, '*Maḳāma*', in *Encyclopaedia of Islam, Second Edition*, posted 2012, https://doi.org/10.1163/1573-3912_islam_COM_0634; Jones, *Power of Oratory*, 18–19, 164, 171.
33. 'Attar, *Mokhtar-nama*, 70. See also p. 33 above.
34. For a list of all the birds named by 'Attar and a discussion of their poetic characteristics, see Shafi'i-Kadkani, intro. to *Manteq al-tayr*, 169–80.
35. 'Attar, *Manteq al-tayr*, 262.
36. 'Attar, *Manteq al-tayr*, 263.
37. Purnamdarian, 'Simorgh va Jebra'il', 76–81; 'Ali Soltani Gerd-Faramarzi, *Simorgh dar qalamrov-e farhang-e Iran* (Tehran: Mobtakeran, 1372 [1993–4]), 39–126.
38. Throughout the history of Islamic philosophy there has been a tendency to interpret the angels as allegorical references to the various cosmic intellects. Among philosophers of the Illuminationist school, the Simorgh is often added into this mix as well. See Henry Corbin, *Avicenna and the Visionary Recital*, trans. Willard R. Trask (New York: Pantheon Books, 1960), 46–122; Purnamdarian, 'Simorgh va Jebra'il', 81–93; Gerd-Faramarzi, *Simorgh*, 193–229.
39. Shehab al-Din Yahya Sohravardi, *Majmu'a-ye mosannafat-e Shaykh-e Eshraq*, ed. Seyyed Hossein Nasr (Tehran: Anjoman-e Shahanshahi-ye Falsafa-ye Iran, 1976–7), 226–39, 314–32.
40. Avicenna's treatise was later translated into Persian by Sohravardi. See the commentary and translation in Corbin, *Visionary Recital*, 183–95. See also Purnamdarian, "Attar va resalaha-ye 'erfani-ye Ebn Sina'.
41. Ahmad Ghazali, *Majmu'a-ye asar-e farsi-ye Ahmad-e Ghazali*, ed. Ahmad Mojahed (Tehran: Daneshgah-e Tehran, 1979), 77–92. On the question of the treatise's authorship, see Mojahed's introduction to the work, 75–6. An English

translation of Ghazali's text is included as an appendix in Avery's translation of 'Attar, *The Speech of the Birds*, 551–60.

42. See the comparison of Ghazali, Avicenna and 'Attar in Corbin, *Visionary Recital*, 183–203.
43. 'Attar, *Manteq al-tayr*, 265–6.
44. 'Attar, *Manteq al-tayr*, 266.
45. I have gendered the rose female here because the hoopoe compares it, in the following anecdote, to a princess. There is no indication of gender in the nightingale's address itself, however.
46. See the examples collected in Swartz, 'Arabic Rhetoric', 44, 60n59.
47. Lewis, 'Sexual Occidentation', 694–5.
48. For an extensive summary and commentary on this section, including the embedded tales, see Lucian Stone, 'Blessed Perplexity: The Topos of *Ḥayrat* in Farīd al-Dīn 'Aṭṭār's *Manṭiq al-ṭayr*' (PhD diss., Southern Illinois University, 2005), 79–96.
49. Davis divides the questions into exactly two groups of ten, the first of which focuses on negative spiritual attributes, and the second on positive. This is part of his effort to show that a total of thirty birds pose questions (twenty anonymous questioners in this section along with the ten objectors from the beginning of the poem), who together represent the thirty birds who complete the journey. As Davis himself admits, however, this division requires a little 'juggling'. In actuality more than thirty questions are asked – I count a total of thirty-three, excluding two questions that the birds ask as a group. It seems to me that such methodologies can easily fall into the trap of numerological confirmation bias. See Davis, 'Journey as Paradigm', 174, 181–2n4; Julian Baldick, 'Persian *Ṣūfī* Poetry up to the Fifteenth Century', in *History of Persian Literature: From the Beginning of the Islamic Period to the Present Day*, ed. G. Morrison (Leiden: Brill, 1981), 120–2.
50. 'Attar, *Manteq al-tayr*, 284.
51. 'Attar, *Manteq al-tayr*, 302. Treatments of the Shaykh San'an tale can be found in Ardalan 'Attarpur, *Eqteda be kofr: Pazhuheshi dar dastan-e Shaykh San'an* (Tehran: An va Hama, 1382 [2003–4]); Claudia Yaghoobi, 'Subjectivity in 'Attār's Shaykh of San'ān Story in *The Conference of the Birds*', *CLCWeb: Comparative Literature and Culture* 16, no. 1 (2014): https://doi.org/10.7771/1481-4374.2425; De Bruijn, *Persian Sufi Poetry*, 103; Taqi Purnamdarian, 'Tafsiri digar az dasatan-e Shaykh San'an', in *Didar ba simorgh* (Tehran: Pazhuheshgah-e 'Olum-e Ensani va Motala'at-e Farhangi, 1374 [1995–6]); Lewis, 'Sexual Occidentation'.
52. The key structural position of the tale has been discussed by Davis, 'Journey

as Paradigm', 175–9; Seyyed Hossein Nasr, 'The Flight of the Birds to Union: Meditations upon "Aṭṭār's *Manṭiq al-ṭayr*"', in *Islamic Art and Spirituality* (Albany, NY: SUNY Press, 1987), 105–7; De Bruijn, *Persian Sufi Poetry*, 102–3.

53. There is also something of a false start earlier in the narrative, directly after the Shaykh San'an tale, when the birds 'catch a glimpse of a valley from the way' and are struck with terror: this prompts a narration from the hoopoe and then his ascent of the pulpit ('Attar, *Manteq al-tayr*, 303).
54. 'Attar, *Manteq al-tayr*, 422.
55. 'Attar, *Manteq al-tayr*, 422.
56. 'Attar, *Manteq al-tayr*, 422.
57. Gerhard Böwering, '*Baqā' wa Fanā*', in *Encyclopaedia Iranica*, posted 2020, https://doi.org/10.1163/2330-4804_EIRO_COM_6606; Fazlur Rahman, '*Baḳā' wa-Fanā*', in *Encyclopaedia of Islam, Second Edition*, posted 2012, https://doi.org/10.1163/1573-3912_islam_SIM_1083; Andrew Wilcox, 'The Dual Mystical Concepts of *Fanā'* and *Baqā'* in Early Sūfism', *British Journal of Middle Eastern Studies* 38, no. 1 (2011): 95–118. See also Zargar, *Polished Mirror*, 237–62.
58. On this point, see especially Michael Sells, *Mystical Languages of Unsaying* (Chicago: University of Chicago Press, 1994).
59. Browne, *Literary History*, 2:49–50.
60. 'Attar, *Manteq al-tayr*, 426.
61. 'Attar, *Manteq al-tayr*, 427.
62. 'Attar, *Manteq al-tayr*, 427.
63. 'Attar, *Manteq al-tayr*, 428.
64. Davis, 'Journey as Paradigm', 179–80.
65. 'Attar, *Manteq al-tayr*, 435.

5

Making Texts Speak

The hoopoe's speech is directed not only to the fictive birds, but also to 'Attar's flesh-and-blood readers. The poem's imagined reception, on the part of its avian audience, functions as both an invitation and a promise to its actual readers: like the birds, they should be moved by this speech to reform and thereby launched on the path towards proximity with God. Certainly, not all readers will accept 'Attar's reflexive portrayal of his own discourse's rhetorical power, and even among those who do and answer his call to turn towards piety, spiritual progress is by no means guaranteed. (Among the birds, after all, only thirty make it to the Simorgh.) Still, the frame-tale suggests that this speech has special transformative potential, and amenable readers are urged to receive it accordingly: to open themselves up to 'Attar's exhortations and allow themselves to be motivated, persuaded and transformed thereby.

This invitation depends in part on a series of reflexive elisions in which readers (and their textual encounter with the poem) are conflated with the birds (and their aural audition of the hoopoe). A literary text, of course, differs from an oral sermon in myriad ways, but the *Conference of the Birds* routinely blurs the boundaries between them. Readers are encouraged to identify with the birds, while 'Attar takes the hoopoe as his avatar: the bird–hoopoe relationship thus becomes the narrative embodiment of, and a prescriptive model for, readers' relationship with his teaching persona. In this way, the events of the frame-tale are projected onto the wider rhetorical work of the text.

The present chapter examines these elisions as tools of authorial control; it shows how 'Attar imagines and reflexively portrays his readers through the frame-tale and embedded anecdotes and in order to guide and condition their encounter with the poem. It begins with the *Conference of the Birds*' curious mixture of textuality and fictive orality. By virtue of the frame-tale, the poem

– a literary text in the *masnavi* form – is imagined as a vicarious oral homiletic assembly, justifying the inclusion of certain kinds of stories and providing a particular context for their interpretation. Even more importantly, the frame-tale draws on oral instruction's epistemic and spiritual privilege – especially in a sufi context – which it appropriates for a literary text. The chapter then turns to how the birds become avatars for 'Attar's readers, an identification that is facilitated through a certain slipperiness in the poem's narrative levels. It is not always clear if 'Attar is speaking to his readers, the hoopoe to the other birds or one of the embedded characters to their particular addressee – or even all three at once. These levels easily merge as analogous instances of the teacher/speaker–student/addressee relationship, the central rhetorical axis around which the poem spins. Finally, I consider a key embedded anecdote near the text's conclusion – the story of Joseph's reunion with his brothers – which is not narrated by the hoopoe but read by the birds from a scrap of paper, and which is presented as an allegory for the birds' spiritual state that foreshadows their coming reunion with the Simorgh. The notion of allegorical reading implied in this episode – that the events narrated within certain texts are re-enacted in the lives of their readers – exemplifies the transformative promise of the *Conference of the Birds*.

Through these elisions and entanglements, readers are invited into the poem and their experience of it is shaped and conditioned. As a poet who composed long *masnavis*, wrote down his own quatrains and compiled his own *divan*, 'Attar was clearly invested in the power of literary texts to offer spiritual guidance, but he also shared his contemporaries' concerns about text's shortcomings as a direct medium of authorial instruction. Unlike oral preachers and sufi guides, 'Attar's textual, literary persona would be unable to dynamically confront readers, gauge their reactions to his teachings or ensure proper understanding. He responds to these challenges – without exactly solving them – by creating fictive oral settings within his textual works, eliding oral utterances with the written word and seeking to paradoxically write his readers' responses into the poem itself.

Fictive Orality in a Textual Frame

The frame-tale device, which is often said to have originated in India, has a long history in Islamicate literatures.[1] In Persian and Arabic it is most often used to structure prose story collections, with prominent examples including the *One Thousand and One Nights*, *Kalila and Demna*, the *Sendbad-nama* and the *Tuti-nama*. This is a diverse set of texts: the *One Thousand and One Nights* is an anonymous prose work in Arabic marked by a colloquial style, while *Kalila and Demna*, in Ibn al-Muqaffa''s version, became a model of Arabic literary eloquence. The Persian versions of the *Senbad-nama* and *Tuti-nama* by Samarqandi and Nakhshabi, respectively, likewise bear a clear authorial stamp and a refined and embellished mode of expression. Each of these texts is marked by its own individual emphases and thematic concerns, but their embedded narratives generally belong to that amorphous class of entertaining tales frequently labelled as 'popular' in the scholarship. These stories recount the adventures of lovers, sailors and heroes on fantastic adventures; feature talking animals, jinn and other magical beings; and often descend into bawdy slapstick. Throughout the medieval period, such stories were associated with the practice of night-time storytelling. The tenth-century bookseller Ibn al-Nadim, for instance, considers 'night-stories' (*asmar*) and 'fables' (*khorafat*) to be a variegated genre including stories of ancient kings, parables in which animals speak, tales of passionate lovers – including humans who fall in love with jinn and vice versa – as well as stories of 'the wonders of the sea'.[2] These kinds of narratives were by no means shunned by elites or restricted to the lower classes, as the term 'popular' is sometimes taken to imply. Rather, there is ample evidence from Ibn al-Nadim and others that collections of such tales were produced and enjoyed at all levels of society, including government officials and the 'Abbasid caliphal household.[3]

Despite their popularity, the truth and utility of such stories was frequently suspect, and they were sometimes dismissed as pointless diversions that appealed especially to women and children.[4] The famed litterateur Abu Hayyan Tawhidi (d. 1023), for instance, writes that tales such as those found in the *One Thousand and One Nights* narrate impossible events that cannot be verified, appeal primarily to the senses and are beloved by those who are 'weak in intellect'.[5] The scholar Abu Bakr Suli (d. 947), who served as a tutor for the future caliph al-Radi, reports that his young charge once had his books taken away by his grandmother, who apparently wanted to keep an eye on his reading material. When they were finally returned, the boy angrily observed that his books were all serious works and not 'like the books you [i.e. his grandmother] read excessively, such as *The Wonders of the Sea*, the *Tale of Sindbād*, and *The Cat and the Mouse*'.[6] Even Ibn al-Nadim himself, who devotes a whole chapter to the *asmar* in his bibliographical work, displays some discomfort with the genre's fictionality and entertaining purposes: he writes that Alexander the Great listened to such stories, but only to preserve them and not for 'pleasure', and he criticises fellow booksellers and copyists for 'lying' in the composition of these tales.[7]

The association of such tales with women, pleasure and night-time storytelling is apparent in several of the above-mentioned collections, whose frame-tales imagine fictive situations in which such stories might be narrated.[8] In the *One Thousand and One Nights*, Shahrazad forestalls her own execution by entertaining her murderous royal husband with narratives all night long, night after night, in a series of high-stakes nocturnal storytelling events.[9] In the *Tuti-nama*, a parrot whose merchant master is away narrates entertaining tales to the latter's wife and thereby distracts her from visiting her lover. The *Haft Paykar* of Nezami, although composed in verse (and much too 'thick' to be considered a frame-tale on par with the others mentioned here), features embedded stories that are narrated in a similar performance context: the protagonist Bahram visits seven 'pleasure domes' and listens to a night-time story narrated by a beautiful princess in each of them. In the *Sendbad-nama*, the embedded stories are alternately narrated by one of the king's seven viziers and a wily concubine (*kanizak*), each of whom attempts to influence the king thereby.[10] The act of narration, in these examples, is usually undertaken by women (Shahrazad, the seven princesses, the *kanizak*) and motivated by female craftiness, for better or worse (*One Thousand and One Nights*, *Sendbad-nama*). It often takes place at night as a prelude or coda to sexual activity (*Haft Paykar*, *One Thousand and One Nights*). The *Tuti-nama* is an interesting inversion of this pattern: here it is a male narrator who tells stories to a female listener with the ulterior motive of frustrating her sexual adventures. The stories in *Kalila and Demna*, on the other hand, are narrated in a courtly, homosocial setting with didactic intent by the philosopher Bidaba to the king Dabshalim. Many of the stories narrated by Bidaba contain further instances of embedding, in which additional stories are told with an intent to either advise or deceive.

Walter Ong, in a short but thought-provoking article, observes that the frame-tale served as a mechanism of 'audience readjustment' in medieval

Europe. According to Ong, because there was little precedent for a written collection of bawdy and fantastic stories in English, Chaucer relied on the frame-tale of the pilgrims' storytelling contest to root the *Canterbury Tales* in more familiar practices of oral narration.[11] Arabic and Persian were established literary languages by this time, and popular narratives were written down in these languages in other forms before they found their way into the aforementioned works. Still, Ong's observations are apropos. In works like the *Senbad-nama* and *One Thousand and One Nights*, the frame-tale justifies the textualisation of narratives whose status as belles-lettres was open to question – e.g. stories of speaking animals, romances without clear historical referents, bawdy anecdotes and fictional tales of marvellous adventure – by imaging an oral context in which such stories might be told. That context might be a nocturnal storytelling session, a courtier's attempt to delicately advise a king or an agonistic storytelling contest. While the details of the frame differ from text to text, and they themselves might contain many fantastic elements, they nevertheless connect these stories to familiar practices of oral narration and thus ease their reception as components of a literary, textual work.

The didactic *masnavi* was an established tradition by the time ʿAttar was writing, and he enjoyed clear generic models for his *Conference of the Birds*. Still, the embedded narratives ʿAttar includes in his *masnavi*s diverge from those of earlier generic exemplars in both quantitative and qualitative terms. His works feature more anecdotes and longer stories, and the total proportion of narrative to homiletic content is much higher. The earliest manuscripts of Sanaʾi's *Hadiqat* contain only 56 anecdotes, and they tend to be short verbal exchanges that rarely run more than a few lines; collectively, they comprise only 8 per cent of the poem.[12] Similarly, Nezami's *Makhzan* contains only 20 anecdotes, one per chapter, for a total of 16 per cent narrative. The *Conference of the Birds*, by contrast, features 181 anecdotes, the longest of which comes to a whopping 411 lines, for a total of 52 per cent narrative.[13] This mass of narratives, far greater than those found in previous didactic *masnavi*s, also includes a number of erotic tales that are almost totally absent from earlier instances of the genre. Many of the longest and most famous narratives in ʿAttar's oeuvre – the tale of Shaykh Sanʿan, the adventures of Marhuma and Sarpatak, the romance of Rabeʿa and Bektash – are quite different than anything in Sanaʾi's *Hadiqat* or Nezami's *Makhzan*. When shorn of the accompanying didactic interpretations, they more readily recall the 'popular' romance and adventure stories that were sometimes derided as untruthful evening tales fit for women and children than the illustrative narratives of prior didactic *masnavi*s.

Among their other functions, 'Attar's frame-tales can thus be read as attempts to justify his textualisation of long, 'popular' romantic tales, not to mention the unprecedented number of shorter anecdotes that populate his *masnavi*s, by imagining fictive contexts that acknowledge the material's association with oral storytelling while also emphasising its didactic function. The storytelling contexts that they evoke are not those of evenings' entertainment (*Haft Paykar*, *One Thousand and One Nights*, *Tuti-nama*) or courtly advice or debate (*Kalila and Demna*, *Senbad-nama*), but religious guidance: a spiritual guide's conference with his disciple (*Mosibat-nama*), a king's discussions with his sons (*Elahi-nama*) and the hoopoe's sermons for his avian flock (*Conference of the Birds*). Historically, such stories – including fables and love stories reminiscent of the *asmar* – were likely narrated in all of these contexts, although their use in sermons was not without controversy. Abu Hamid Ghazali denounces preachers who would narrate fables (*khurafat*) from the pulpit and embellish or alter Quranic narratives and thereby mix truth (*sidq*) with lies (*kidhb*).[14] Ibn al-Jawzi expresses similar concerns, especially regarding preachers who would tell exaggerated stories of Joseph and Zolaykha or amorous narratives (*hadith*) featuring the likes of Suda and Lubna, two famous female beloveds of Arabic verse; he blames these suspect homiletic practices on Persian preachers and sufis in particular.[15] It is difficult to say how often such stories were actually used as homiletic exempla, but storytelling was clearly associated with preachers in the popular imagination – indeed, 'storyteller' (*qass*) is nearly synonymous with 'preacher' (*va'ez*/*mozakker*) in this period.[16]

'Attar himself displays a certain anxiety about his storytelling. In a revealing passage at the conclusion of the *Mosibat-nama*, he rebukes those who would dismiss him as a mere storyteller while asserting the value of narrative in a spiritual context (and making a series of poetic plays on the term 'story'):

> You have seen a lot of stories; look,
>   don't complain, this is the 'best of stories'.[17]
> If you start telling stories that I am a storyteller,

then you'll be disappointed, since I've stolen the polo ball in
storytelling.
Storytelling is not worthless, like wind in a cage;
don't you see that the Quran's spirit is in stories?
I'll cut the story short: if one from the people of secrets
spends a lifetime in this story,
then this story will bestow light at every breath.[18]

Authorial apologiae are a conventional component of longer *masnavis*, but the particular terms in which a poet chooses to defend their work often speak to their specific concerns and anxieties. For ʿAttar, it is the charge of being a storyteller – a recounter of useless, unverifiable narratives in a homiletic context – that seems to have hit a nerve.[19] He defends himself by claiming that his work is the 'best of stories', an epithet given in the Quran to the story of Joseph, its longest and most coherent narrative (and which was a favourite of the storytelling preachers criticised by Ibn al-Jawzi). At other points he appropriates the dismissive label of storyteller with pride: in the *Mosibat-nama*, he hopes that his speech will attract the attention of the angels and that he might thus earn the epithet 'God's storyteller' (*qessa-gu-ye haq[q]*).[20] Homiletic storytelling – and the suspicion it could attract – also appears in ʿAttar's biography. According to an anecdote preserved by Dowlat-Shah, a local judge dismissed ʿAttar as a 'doddering teller of fables' (*pirak-e afsana-gu*) after his death.[21] Like much of Dowlat-Shah's information, the authenticity of this anecdote is questionable, but at the very least it shows that later readers considered such dismissals plausible.

As a genre, the didactic *masnavi* already evokes an oral, pedagogical context through its homiletic content and the rhetorical stance of the narrator vis-à-vis the addressee. The frame-tale goes further, though: it casts the textual encounter as a kind of vicarious aural experience, and it thereby appropriates the cultural cachet of oral instruction for a literary text. The oral transmission of knowledge between teacher and student was highly regarded in most intellectual fields in ʿAttar's time, and it played an especially important role sufism, which privileged personal instruction from a spiritual guide. Books were widely read and produced, of course, in sufism as in other disciplines, but they were usually studied within the context of personal pedagogical relationships in which the teacher directed the reading, interpreted the text and prescribed other forms of spiritual or intellectual training.[22] To study a scholarly text without the benefit of oral guidance from an authoritative master posed a number of problems, chief among them the inability to ensure that the text had been properly understood. Such anxieties go back to Plato, but they have special resonance in Islamicate languages given the inherent ambiguities of the Perso-Arabic script, which usually does not indicate short vowels and sometimes lacks even consonantal diacritical marks. Books, therefore, ought to be studied under the oral guidance of a teacher who already knows them and who can thus ensure proper pronunciation and understanding, as the litterateur Ibn Qutayba and physician Ibn Butlan both point out.[23] Specialised knowledge, furthermore, was not for public consumption and should only be disclosed to those who were worthy and prepared to receive it (especially in sufism, which always had an esoteric and elitist streak, even during the period of its popularisation). The insistence on personal contact between teachers and students was one way to restrict learning to those who had developed the necessary qualifications.

ʿAttar's poems must have been orally recited in a variety of social settings and pedagogical relationships. They were likely read aloud in sufi *khanaqah*s as part of group spiritual training, declaimed in literary gatherings as examples of elegant verse and studied within other forms of spiritual and literary apprenticeship. They may also have been read individually; given the musicality of the verse, however, even a lone reader would likely have mouthed the words aloud as they read them in order to appreciate their rhyme and metre. Given the state of our sources, a comprehensive history of their reception and consumption eludes us. What makes the frame-tale device so intriguing, however, is that it encodes personal relationships of oral guidance into the text itself, and it thereby indexes an imagined orality that paradoxically underscores the *masnavi*'s status as an authorial text. ʿAttar, like most *masanvi* writers, confidently intervenes in his material and leaves a clear authorial stamp. He likely produced and disseminated his works in a textual form, and when he speaks of his own composition process, he refers to 'books' and 'placing pen on paper'.[24] The frame-tale allows him to organise a mass of variegated material into a coherent and unified work, and it thereby seems to address an inherently literary, textual problem. At the same time, however, it also presupposes the desirability and spiritual efficacy of oral instruction, which it seeks to duplicate within the text. A frame-tale does not accurately transcribe speech, nor does it exhaustively narrate an oral performance event. Rather, it surrounds a series of textual units and encourages audiences to imagine them *as if* they were utterances.[25] It thus establishes, as Bonnie Irwin puts it, 'a continuity of reception between the act of reading and that of listening' in which the text becomes an extension of the fictional audition depicted within it. In this way, ʿAttar's affinity for the frame-tale device does not contradict his broader interest in texts as agents of spiritual instruction, but is very much consistent with it. However his poems were actually read – individually or within teaching relationships, silently or aloud – the recursive magic of the frame-tale works to capture and transmute the activity of oral guidance and its spiritual benefits into a literary, textual form.

Fuzzy Narrative Boundaries

In addition to eliding the act of reading with that of audition, the frame-tale draws a series of more precise analogies between the poem's readers and the birds depicted within it. Both the readers and the birds are 'student figures' subject to homiletic exhortations, the former uttered by ʿAttar's persona and the latter by the hoopoe. ʿAttar further encourages readers' identification with the birds by allowing the poem's narrative levels to merge and collapse into each other. His own narrative voice routinely melds with that of the hoopoe; the hoopoe's speech, in turn, elides with the exhortations of speakers in the embedded anecdotes. The addressees who stand opposite these speakers – the poem's readers, the birds and the various targets of exhortation within the anecdotes – merge as well. A continuum is thus constructed between the nested, oral teaching relationships imagined within the poem and the didactic, textual relationship that ʿAttar seeks to cultivate with his audience. The readers' textual encounter with the *Conference of the Birds* becomes one more instance in a long chain of didactic acts, recursively depicted within the poem and projected back upon it.

These narrative elisions are only possible because the poem is constructed around a set of seemingly stable narrative levels in the first place; levels can only merge if a distinction between them has already been drawn. In narratological terminology, the *Conference of the Birds* is composed of three narrative levels: the extra-diegetic, intra-diegetic and hypo-diegetic.[26] This terminology – and the notion of narrative levels more broadly – provides a useful way to differentiate the many speakers and addressees in the work and to start thinking about the relationships between them. The extra-diegetic level is that on which ʿAttar speaks *in propria persona*, such as when he exhorts his addressees directly in the poem's introduction and conclusion, or when he describes the birds and narrates their quest. Another set of didactic utterances takes place on the intra-diegetic level, within the story of the birds. These are the anecdotes and exhortations of the hoopoe, who preaches to the birds in order to convince them to undertake the journey to the Simorgh. A final set of didactic utterances is found on the hypo-diegetic level, within the anecdotes narrated by the hoopoe. The vast majority of these anecdotes centre on a short encounter between two characters, in which one of them exhorts or admonishes the other, narrates an instructive anecdote for their benefit or otherwise provides them with a witty piece of modular advice. There is a great diversity of moods and rhetorical stances in these embedded didactic speech situations. The speaker's advice can be serious or sarcastic, sound or exaggerated; sometimes it even seems to be unintentional. The addressee might have actively sought out the speaker's advice, or it may have been foisted upon them against their will. Quite often the didactic relationship established between these characters cuts against expected religious, political or social hierarchies. These are just a few of the many possible variations on the same general pattern, in which an (often unexpected) spiritual authority delivers oral advice to another who would do well to listen.

As an example, consider the following anecdote, which is typical in many respects. It is found in the hoopoe's discourse on worldly entanglement and features an ostentatious, prideful king. He spends 100,000 dinars to construct an elaborate, paradisiacal palace full of carpets and ornaments. Onlookers from across the land come to gaze on the building, and the king has gold and jewels scattered before them. He then summons his boon companions and sages, seats them on thrones and asks them whether they have ever seen such a magnificent palace anywhere else on earth; predictably enough, they all reply in the negative. Suddenly, an ascetic leaps up and proclaims that the palace has one fundamental flaw: a crack in the wall. The king rebukes him and angrily demands to know why he is 'stirring up strife (*fetna*)'. The ascetic replies by upbraiding him for his pride in the face of death:

O you who are proud in kingship,
    that crack is the crack open for 'Azra'il.
If only you could have fastened that breach –
    otherwise, what's the use of a palace, a crown and a throne?
Although this palace is delightful like Paradise,
    death will render it ugly to your eye.
Nothing lasts; life is here and now
    It does not last – there's no stratagem to extend it.
Don't take so much comfort in your domain and palace!
    Don't spur on this mount of pride and rebellion![27]

The ascetic wittily harangues the king, calling on him to re-evaluate his attachment to material objects and temporal power. However paradisiacal his palace may seem, it cannot, unlike the eschatological gardens, protect its inhabitants from the constant march of time. Although the ascetic speaks with spiritual authority, such a rebuke was clearly a breach of courtly decorum with potentially deadly consequences, and none of the 'sages' whom the king had summoned to his palace had dared to point out this fatal flaw themselves. The king himself suggests the political implications of the ascetic's criticism when he accuses him of fomenting 'strife' (*fetna*), a term that conjures up images of political collapse. The ascetic de-legitimises the structures of kingship by publicly pointing out the 'flaw' in the king's palace and dismissing the symbols of temporal rule as foolish vanities in the face of death.

Variations on this pattern re-occur hundreds of times throughout the *Conference of the Birds* (as well as 'Attar's other *masnavi*s), and the poem derives a great measure of its coherence from the repeated portrayal of paraenetic speech events on all of its narrative levels. On the extra-diegetic level, 'Attar harangues his audience; on the intra-diegetic level, the hoopoe lectures the birds; and on the hypo-diegetic level, figures such as the ascetic admonish characters like the king. There are, of course, significant differences between these didactic speech situations. The hoopoe addresses a collective audience according to the accepted conventions of the hortatory assembly, whereas the ascetic rebukes a single recipient (the king) without the benefit of such formal legitimating structures.[28] The birds are ultimately convinced by the hoopoe and set out for the Simorgh, whereas we do not know if the king heeds the ascetic's advice or what becomes of him; like most of the hypo-diegetic anecdotes, it ends with its protagonist's verbal calls to reform. Despite these differences, the parallelism between these speech situations is clear: they both involve didactic utterances from self-assured (if not uncontested) positions of spiritual authority. They are also recursively nested: when the ascetic harangues the king, those exhortations are also spoken by the hoopoe for his own avian audience, whom he aims to thereby educate and transform, as well as by 'Attar's persona, the root-level narrator of the entire poem, as he urges his reader-listeners to piety. In short, the same basic didactic pattern is recursively repeated and intensified at each narrative level. The role of teacher-speaker is jointly played by 'Attar's extra-diegetic narratorial persona, the hoopoe, and the corresponding figures within the embedded material, while the position of didactic addressee is shared by 'Attar's imagined audience, the hoopoe's flock, and the various recipients of didactic harangues within the embedded anecdotes.

The exact boundaries between these narrative levels are often ambiguous, especially when the transition is 'upstream' to a higher narrative level (i.e. from an embedded speaker to the hoopoe, or from the hoopoe to 'Attar's persona). For example, in the story of the ostentatious king translated above, the last two lines could easily be read as the hoopoe's intra-diegetic amplification of the story for the benefit of the assembled birds, rather than a continuation of the ascetic's hypo-diegetic rebuke of the king. With some hermeneutic effort, one can often determine when a change of speaker likely took place: vocatives, a shift in pronouns or indexicals and a turn to universalising sententiae can all be good indicators of a possible change in speakers. But some ambiguity always remains, and – unlike modern editors – it seems unlikely that 'Attar's readers would have gone through the trouble of determining that precise moment of change. 'Attar himself is content to allow the narratological boundaries between them to remain fluid and imprecise.

This ambiguity is clearly evident in a hypo-diegetic anecdote featuring Hasan al-Basri, the eighth-century religious thinker, and Rabe'a, a legendary mystical figure celebrated by the later sufi tradition. The two are often paired together in the anecdotal literature as a contrasting odd couple: the male Hasan epitomises learning and religious scholarship, while the unschooled Rabe'a, a woman, takes a more intuitive approach of spirituality. In 'Attar's works,

Rabeʿa is almost always portrayed as Hasan's spiritual superior, outdoing him through her extreme asceticism, her pure love of God and sometimes even miraculous performances. In this particular anecdote, in keeping with those roles, Hasan asks her to recount a bit of spiritual learning that she has intuited on her own instead of acquiring through the traditional routes of knowledge transmission; he confesses that his heart is always gladdened by her insights. She replies by recounting that she once refused to hold two coins in a single hand out of fear that they might arouse her greed, an example of extreme scrupulousness and vigilance against vice:

> Rabeʿa said to him: O shaykh of the age,
> I had once woven a few strands of rope,
> I took them and sold them, and was glad of heart;
> two coins of silver were my profit.
> But I wouldn't take both in one hand at one time;
> I took this one in this hand, that one in that,
> because I was terrified that if they joined forces,
> they would waylay me on the path and I wouldn't be able to resist.
> The worldly man puts his heart and soul in blood
> and places a hundred thousand other snares
> so that he can obtain even a bit of unlawful gold;
> once he's obtained it and dies, that's it –
> for his heir, that gold will be lawful,
> but he will be mired in the consequences of sin.
> O you who have sold the Simorgh for gold,
> you've lit your heart like a candle in love of gold!
> Since there is no room in this way for a single hair,
> no one can have both a store of treasure and a sallow face.[29]

Rabeʿa is explicitly cued as the speaker at the beginning of this passage, but at some point the speaker shifts. Because it mentions the Simorgh, the penultimate line, 'O you who have sold the Simorgh for gold', seems unlikely to be an utterance of Rabeʿa; rather, it must be spoken directly by the hoopoe to the other birds. But where exactly does this shift occur? There are no paratextual or grammatical marks in the manuscript to indicate a change, and the text itself is ambiguous. This ambiguity is likely intentional: ʿAttar could have easily marked the point at which the hoopoe takes over with a phrase like 'the hoopoe said' or even '*ke*', the medieval Persian equivalent of the quotation-introducing colon, but none of these are present.

Premodern Persian lacks quotation marks, but Shafi'i-Kadkani, like many other editors, includes them in his editions, so he is forced to explicitly mark the end of Rabe'a's speech in a way that the manuscript sources do not. According to his reading, Rabe'a's utterance ends with her explanation of why she refused to carry both coins in one hand; he places the closing quotation mark after the line 'because I was terrified that if they joined forces / they would waylay me on the path and I wouldn't be able to resist'. Such a reading is certainly defensible. At this point, the passage shifts from the concrete example of Rabe'a's extreme vigilance, narrated in the first person, to more general observations on the spiritual dangers of wealth and material attachment, narrated in the third. Exhortations on the dangers on ill-gotten gains might also seem to be a more appropriate topic for the hoopoe's discourse than for Rabe'a's: the neophyte birds need this kind of basic instruction, whereas Hasan should be beyond such elementary lessons. At the same time, however, Hasan is routinely outdone by Rabe'a and in awe of her intuitive brand of piety, and 'Attar generally inverts expectations by making Rabe'a the 'master' in their relationship. One could thus understand these verses as didactic generalisations from Rabe'a's own experience delivered here for the benefit of the more 'book pious' Hasan. The point is not that Shafi'i-Kadkani's reading is wrong – on the contrary, it makes good sense – but that the inclusion of quotation marks forces this question to be answered in a definitive way that would not otherwise be necessary. 'Attar, composing without punctuation, was under no such obligation, and there is no indication that he or his readers were troubled by the resulting narratological ambiguity. On the contrary, this 'fuzziness' in the border zones between the poem's narrative levels seems to be deliberately cultivated. The voices of Rabe'a and the hoopoe, although distinguished by their own rhetorical situations and contexts, are both spiritual authorities who deliver edifying utterances – a pattern that is repeated hundreds of times throughout the poem in various guises – and their voices thus easily merge.

Just as hypo-diegetic utterances bleed into the hoopoe's intra-diegetic homilies, the latter also converge with 'Attar's own extra-diegetic discourse. This convergence, too, is operative in almost all of the anecdotes, even if it is not always immediately obvious. The ascetic's rebuke of the vain king, for instance, merges into a more generalised admonishment against pride and avarice that can be attributed to both the hoopoe and ʿAttar. The same is true of Rabeʿa's utterance translated above. Sometimes, however, this porousness is particularly clear. For example, in his sermon on the valley of oneness (*towhid*), the fifth valley on the path to the Simorgh, the hoopoe explains that aspirants must move beyond the dualities of good and bad and faith and infidelity in order to lose themselves in God's unity. His lecture soon turns to duality's origins in the lower soul, and he urges his addressees to be wary of the 'snakes and scorpions' of the carnal self. Then ʿAttar addresses himself, revealing that he, *in propria persona*, has been the direct speaker of at least some of the preceding passage:

> How much of this metaphorical language (*harf-e majaz*), O ʿAttar?
> Come back to the secrets of oneness (*towhid*).
> When the wayfaring man arrives at this place,
> the place where he stands is effaced from the road . . .[30]

ʿAttar calls on himself to leave aside these metaphorical musings on allegorical vermin and to get back to the topic of *towhid*. Such self-apostrophes are a common feature of homiletic discourse, but, in this case, the apostrophe also reveals the persistent convergence of homiletic speakers within the *Conference of the Birds*. If a reader had expected the poem's narrative levels to be strictly maintained and any transitions between them to be explicitly noted, then she might object that it was the hoopoe who had previously been treating the theme of *towhid*, so ʿAttar's above self-admonishment to get 'back on topic' makes little sense. The boundary between ʿAttar and the hoopoe, however, is not a firm one; their voices freely interpenetrate. Except for the work's introduction and conclusion, which are delivered outside the context of the frame-tale, most of the poem's didactic passages can be comfortably attributed to either ʿAttar's poetic persona or the hoopoe, or even both at once. ʿAttar's self-apostrophe, quoted above, is not a 'slip' out of character, but rather an indication of the broader conflation of his own persona with the hoopoe, rooted in their analogous structural positions as homiletic speakers.

This melding of narrative levels has not been throughly theorised in modern narratology, which tends to focus on modern and postmodern works.

The closest narratological figure discussed by modern scholars is 'metalepsis', which is characterised as the paradoxical penetration of events or voices on one narrative level into another, and which is frequently thought to produce a disquieting or humorous effect in the minds of readers. Debra Malina, for instance, characterises metalepsis as an 'intrusion' and 'violation' endowed with a certain 'shock value', and Gérard Genette writes that it 'produces an effect of strangeness that is either comical or fantastic'.[31] In the case of the *Conference of the Birds*, however, the hoopoe does not directly project his voice into the world of his narrator, nor does 'Attar descend into the world of the birds. Rather than a uni-directional transgression of a fixed narrative boundary, their voices converge such that the boundary between them is blurred and softened.[32] This conflation, furthermore, is not treated as a paradoxical or shocking occurrence. It is simply an explicit manifestation of the broader alignment between 'Attar and the hoopoe that runs throughout the entire poem. As teacher-speakers, they occupy the same position on the pedagogical axis, and their conflation therefore seems quite natural and not at all disquieting, transgressive or paradoxical.

By drawing analogies between the poem's narrative levels and allowing them to almost imperceptibly blur together, 'Attar invites readers deeper into the text. Readers' own positionality, as recipients of his extra-diegetic didactic utterances, is reflected and refracted in new variations throughout the poem, and these didactic relationships flow into one another as mutually reinforcing permutations of the same fundamental structure. The birds, like the poem's readers, are on the receiving end of didactic discourse, although for them that discourse is delivered through an oral homiletic assembly instead of a poetic text. The student-teacher relationship unfolds in even more diverse ways in the poem's embedded anecdotes, which encompass a wide range of social relationships, rhetorical stances and affective tonalities, whether it be Hasan al-Basri's eager reception of wisdom from an unschooled woman who routinely outdoes him, or a greedy king's surprise upbraiding from a sarcastic dervish. Still, all these encounters partake in the same underlying didactic pattern: a character, whose spiritual authority may or may not be recognised, provides some form of oral guidance to another. Because of these structural analogies criss-crossing the poem, readers are invited to see themselves and their own didactic situation variously manifested within it. Instead of consuming its stories at a distance, they participate in them, receiving exhortations and admonishments as they play the role of addressee and didactic subject in a variety of guises.

ʿAttar also gains new tools to control his readers' experience of the text. Because the hoopoe's relationship with the birds is presented as a mirror of ʿAttar's relationship with his audience, he can direct the latter through his portrayal of the former. Like a Greek chorus, the birds function as model 'reception figures' through which we, the readers, are cued in our responses to the poem. They show us which stories are meant to provoke a strong emotional response (e.g. Shaykh Sanʿan), which are meant to silence our misplaced objections (e.g. the dervish and the princess), and they model the submission to didactic authority that ʿAttar aims to produce. Most importantly, they allow ʿAttar to imagine the success of his didactic utterances by proxy through his narration of their perlocutionary effects within the poem: just as the hoopoe's discourses provoke the birds to move towards the Simurgh, so too can ʿAttar's poem produce an analogous (if not identical) movement towards God in the spiritual lives of its readers and listeners.

Nested Allegories

The self-reflexive potential of the frame-tale is most consciously exploited near the end of the poem in a stirking *mise en abyme* – a 'hall of mirrors' structure in which embedded anecdotes recursively mirror higher narrative levels – that emerges just before before the thirty surviving birds attain to the Simorgh. When the birds arrive at the Simorgh's threshold, they are first denied entry by the chamberlain of glory (*ʿezzat*) before he returns in the aspect of God's grace (*lotf*), raises the curtain to the Simorgh's court and seats the birds on 'cushions of proximity'. They do not gaze on the Simorgh just yet, however. First, the chamberlain hands them a scrap of paper (*roqʿa*) with writing on it and instructs them to 'read it through to the end'. It contains a scene from the story of Joseph's reunion with his brothers, in which the latter (like the birds) are given a piece of paper and urged to read it. This paper, the chamberlain continues, will clarify the meaning of the birds' 'confused state' (*shurida hal*) 'by way of allegory' (*az rah-e mesal*).[33] The anecdote is thus marked as unusual and significant before it even begins: it occupies a key structural position in the poem, and whereas the previous embedded anecdotes were generally framed as oral narrations of the hoopoe, this one is cast as a text that the birds read together as a group. It is, moreover, one of only a few anecdotes for which an allegorical mode of interpretation is explicitly suggested.

The tale of Joseph, and the story of his reunion with his brothers in particular, seems to have been especially meaningful for ʿAttar. Another version of the story appears earlier in the *Conference of the Birds*, and an account of his reunion with Benjamin is found in the *Elahi-nama*.[34] The outline of the Joseph tale is narrated in the Quran, but it was retold in more elaborate detail in the 'stories of the prophets' literature that ʿAttar likely relied on here.[35] According to the version of the story read by the birds, the brothers wrote out a bill of sale when they first sold Joseph into slavery, and this document played a critical role in their reunion many years later:

Joseph, for whom the stars burnt rue,
    was sold by his ten brothers,
and purchased by Malek-e Zoʿr,
    who wanted a receipt (*khatt*) since he had bought him cheap.
He requested a receipt from them right there
    and received from those ten brothers their testimony.
When the ʿAziz of Egypt bought Joseph,
    that perfidious note came into Joseph's hands.[36]

Joseph kept the receipt over the course of his rise to power until he became the king's advisor and managed Egypt's preparations for the coming famine; according to this version, he actually became the king (*padashah*) himself. While Egypt enjoyed plenty thanks to Joseph's foresight, Canaan was stricken with a shortage of food. Joseph's brothers came to Egypt in search of aid and threw themselves at their now-royal brother's feet as supplicants, all without realising his true identity. Joseph promised them bread if they would read a Hebrew manuscript for him, a request to which they readily agreed. The manuscript, of course, proves to be none other than the bill of sale that they themselves had written:

In the end, when Joseph became king,
    the ten brothers came there.
Not recognising Joseph's face,
    they threw themselves before him.

They begged deliverance for their souls
They made themselves piteous, pleading for bread.
Said truthful Joseph, 'O people,
I have a note (*khat[t]i*) in the Hebrew alphabet.
No one from my retinue can read it
If you would recite it for me, I will give you much bread.'
They were all fluent in Hebrew and more than willing
They gladly said, 'O king, bring the note!'
– Let him be blind-hearted, who, in this condition (*hal*) from presence (*hozur*),
does not hear his own story. How long with this pride?! –
Joseph handed them the note they had written,
and a trembling fell upon their limbs.
They couldn't bring themselves to read a single line of it
They didn't know how to explain.
They were all mired in regret and sadness
They remained afflicted by the matter of Joseph.
All of their tongues became drunk at once
They were mortified by this difficult affair.
Joseph said: 'It is as if you were unconscious.
When you read the note, why did you fall silent?'
They all said to him, 'We choose silence
because it is better than reading and losing our heads.'[37]

Through this embedded story, the poem constructs a series of recursively nested acts of reading. On the hypo-diegetic level, the brothers read the receipt that they had written out many years ago. On the intra-diegetic level, the birds read the story of Joseph's brothers reading the receipt. And these two textual encounters cannot fail to bring to mind readers' own encounter with the *Conference of the Birds* as they read the story of the birds reading the story of Joseph's brothers reading.

This is the last story before the birds encounter the Simorgh, and it is the only story that they read from a text; the act of reading thus plays a critical role in their spiritual transformation. The episode does not, however, necessarily oppose the ethos of imagined orality that imbues the rest of the *Conference of the Birds*. If anything, the passage again demonstrates the interpenetration of writing and (fictive) orality. Even as the birds read their manuscript, ʿAttar's narratorial persona intervenes, turning to his audience in a manner reminiscent of oral delivery. He calls on his reader-listeners to 'hear' in the story of Joseph's brothers an allegory for their own spiritual 'condition' (*hal*). Significantly, ʿAttar frames an earlier anecdote adapted from the Joseph story in exactly the same way:

> He's blind who hears this story (*qessa*)
> and doesn't take from it his own portion!
> Don't look so hard into the story;
> it's all your story, you ignoramus![38]

These repeated calls to understand the story as an allegory of one's own state also recall the Quranic (and extra-Quranic) treatment of the same material. Joseph, of course, is the hermeneut par excellence of Abrahamic myth, capable of interpreting all sorts of dreams. And the Joseph narrative is itself proffered by the Quran to its audience as an interpretable sign: 'In their stories', reads the last verse of the chapter, 'is a lesson (*ʿibra*) for those with discernment.'[39] The lesson that the Quran suggests, however, is primarily a message of God's power and involvement in human affairs. ʿAttar, on the other hand, urges a more mystical interpretation of the Joseph story as an allegory for the soul's internal relation to the divine.

The birds themselves model what such a reflexive, internalising interpretation of the tale might look like. In reading the story of Joseph's brothers, they see an allegorical icon of their self-imposed exile from the Simorgh:

> When those thirty, miserable birds looked
> into the writing (*khat[t]*) of that credible manuscript (*roqʿa-ye por eʿtebar*),
> whatever they had done, all of that,
> was inscribed therein, until the end.
> It was all them, and here was the difficulty:
> when those captives looked closely,
> they saw that they had gone and made their own way,
> thrown their own Joseph into the well,

burned their Joseph-souls in debasement,
and then, on top of that, sold him.[40]

The figure of Joseph, legendary for his beauty, is often used in sufi literature as a symbol for the soul. Not the concupiscent self (*nafs*), which spurs the individual to evil and which ʿAttar often likens to a noxious creature, but the soul (*ruh*) that enjoyed proximity to God during pre-eternity on the day of the covenant.[41] Through the soul, which is intimately connected to the divine world, the individual can even transcend death, and yet the birds have sold this most valuable part of themselves – their own 'Joseph-souls' – for a pittance, just as Joseph's brothers sold their own kin. In other words, by letting their lower, carnal selves dominate their lives, the birds are cut off from their true selves which subsist in and through the divine. This ethical failing is bound up with a larger ontological deficiency, in which individual earthly existence implies an inherent distance from God that must be overcome.

The narrative paradigm of the Joseph tale, transformed through the prism of allegory, is thus repeated in the world of its avian readers, giving rise to a complex *mise en abyme* in which each narrative level duplicates the central aspects of the level below it.[42] On the embedded level, Joseph's brothers travel to his court in Egypt as supplicants, where they are admitted to his presence but fail to recognise him. They are then given the receipt by Joseph and commanded to read it. Confronted with evidence of their crimes, they fall silent with pain and regret in fear of execution. ʿAttar's version ends there, but premodern Muslim readers would certainly be familiar with the rest of the story and know that the brothers are ultimately forgiven and reconciled with Joseph.[43] This pattern of supplication, reading, recognition and reconciliation is then transformed and re-enacted on a higher narrative level by the birds. After questing for the Simorgh, the thirty surviving birds are admitted to his court and seated on the 'cushions of proximity', but, like the brothers, they do not yet recognise their innate connection to their king. They too are given a scrap of paper and commanded to read it: it contains the story of Joesph's brothers which allegorically testifies to their own sinfulness. Like the brothers whose story they have just read, the birds are afflicted by 'shame' (*tashvir*) and 'regret' (*haya*) such that their bodies turn to 'tutty' (*tutia*).[44] But unlike the brothers, whose reconciliation with Joseph remains unnarrated, the birds' subsequent reunion with the

Simorgh is made explicit. They realise they have shamefully sold their Joseph-souls, but through that realisation the divine spark within them is revealed, and their souls become 'pure life' (*hayati mahz*) in God:

> Once again they became fresh servants of God;
> again they were bewildered, but in a different way.
> All that they had previously done or not done,
> was erased and purified from their breasts.
> The light of proximity (*qorbat*) shone from ahead
> All their souls were dazzled by that beam.[45]

Having recognised their break from the Simorgh, their sinful exile is forgiven; they are permitted to gaze on the Simorgh and see themselves therein, as discussed in Chapter 4. This is not a familial relationship, like that of the brothers to Joseph, but a pre-eternal, ontological affinity that gives rise to a disorienting experience of simultaneous identity and difference. The brothers fell silent because they feared execution for their crimes, but the birds, having reached the ineffable state of effacement and subsistence, can no longer put their experience in words. Even if they could, however, to disclose such mystical secrets would be unwise and dangerous, and might itself be cause for execution, as in the case of Hallaj.

In these ways, the story of Joesph's brothers is allegorically redoubled in the lives of the birds who read and interpret it. The *mise en abyme* does not stop with the frame-tale, however. It extends to the very 'top' narrative level, in which 'Attar calls on his readers and listeners to see this story as their story, too. He castigates his addressees in the same terms that he criticised the birds for having sold their 'Joseph-souls' and effecting their own separation from the God:

> Don't you know, you worthless beggar,
> that you sell a Joseph with every breath?
> When your Joseph becomes the king,
> he will stand at the head of the court.
> In the end, hungry and begging,
> naked will you go before him.
> Since your affair will be illuminated by him,
> why did you have to sell him lightly?[46]

Although ʿAttar reproaches his imagined reader-listeners, all hope is not lost: like the birds, they can look forward to a transformation and reunion with their true Joseph-selves at some future point. 'In the end, hungry and begging / naked will you go before him,' he informs them with the certainty of the future indicative, '[And] your affair will be illuminated by him.'

The recursive logic of the episode suggests that such a reunion can even be brought about through an allegorical reading of the poem itself. ʿAttar has constructed an analogical relationship between the brothers, the birds and his own imagined readers, whose stories not only parallel each other, but also causally intersect through recursive acts of reading. Joseph's brothers read a text that testifies to their sinfulness but also presages their reunion with their royal brother. The birds, reading that story, enact it on a higher narrative level; through the story of Joseph, they recognise their inherent sinfulness and ontological separation from the Simorgh and are purified for their final 'face-to-face' encounter. Carrying the analogy further, ʿAttar's audience is also promised a spiritual transformation through reading, one instigated by the *Conference of the Birds*. Just as the story of Jospeh's brothers was allegorically re-enacted by the birds who read it, so too might the story of the birds come to structure the spiritual lives of ʿAttar's readers through their encounter with the text. For a sufi audience, this particular instance of *mise en abyme* is not vertigo-inducing, but hopeful: the poem's allegory is not only explanatory, but performative, an opportunity to imaginatively enact their own reunion with divine.

The transformative power of allegory is not limited to the climactic Joseph episode. It is thematised by ʿAttar at other key points throughout his oeuvre and enacted by his *masnavis*' frame-tales, especially that of the *Mosibat-nama*, which is closely tied to dreams, visions and spiritual ascent. These topics form the focus of the next chapter, which examines the spiritual work performed by the *Mosibat-nama*'s allegorical frame-tale in more detail, as well as the philosophical structures and habits of thought that make that work possible.

Notes

1. See the overview of the device in Klaus Kanzog, 'Rahmenerzählung', in *Reallexikon der deutschen Literaturgeschichte*, ed. Paul Merker and Wolfgang Stammler, 2nd ed. (Berlin: W. de Gruyter, 1977).

2. Ibn al-Nadim, *The Fihrist of al-Nadīm: A Critical Edition,* ed. Ayman Fo'ād Sayyid (London: Al-Furqān Islamic Heritage Foundation, 2014), 2:321–32.
3. Nabia Abbott, 'A Ninth-Century Fragment of the "Thousand Nights": New Light on the History of the *Arabian Nights*', *Journal of Near Eastern Studies* 8, no. 3 (1949): 149–69; Rina Drory, *Models and Contacts: Arabic Literature and Its Impact on Medieval Jewish Culture* (Leiden: Brill, 2000), 46; Nasrin Askari, 'Élite Folktales: *Munes-nāma, Ketāb-e dāstān*, and Their Audiences', *Journal of Persianate Studies* 12 (2019): 32–61.
4. Seeger A. Bonebakker, 'Some Medieval Views on Fantastic Stories', *Quaderni di Studi Arabi* 10 (1992): 21–43; Cameron Cross, 'The Poetics of Romantic Love in Vis & Rāmin' (PhD diss., University of Chicago, 2015), 94–6; Bo Utas, 'Classical Persian Literature: Fiction, Didactics or Intuitive Truth?', in *True Lies Worldwide: Fictionality in Global Contexts,* ed. Anders Cullhed and Lena Rydholm (Berlin: De Gruyter, 2014); Konrad Hirschler, *The Written Word in Medieval Arabic Lands: A Social and Cultural History of Reading Practices* (Edinburgh: Edinburgh University Press, 2012), 164–96; Askari, 'Élite Folktales'.
5. Abu Hayyan Tawhidi, *al-Imta' wa'l-mu'anasa* (Beirut: Dar al-Kutub al-'Ilmiyya, 1317 [1997]), 25.
6. Quoted in Abbott, 'A Ninth-Century Fragment', 155.
7. Ibn al-Nadim, *Fihrist,* 2:322, 325, 331.
8. Wacks, *Framing Iberia*, 41–85; Bonnie D. Irwin, 'What's in a Frame? The Medieval Textualization of Traditional Storytelling', *Oral Tradition* 10, no. 1 (1995): 27–53.
9. On storytelling in the *One Thousand and One Nights*, see David Pinault, *Story-Telling Techniques in the Arabian Nights* (Leiden: Brill, 1992).
10. On the function of storytelling in the *Sendbad-nama*, see Alexandra Hoffmann, 'Angry Men: On Emotions and Masculinities in Samarqandī's *Sindbād-nāmeh*', *Narrative Culture* 7, no. 2 (2020): 145–64.
11. Ong, 'Writer's Audience', 16.
12. J. T. P. de Bruijn, 'The Stories in Sanâ'î's *Faxri-nâme*', in *Pand-o sokhan: Mélanges offerts à Charles-Henri de Fouchécour*, ed. Christophe Balaÿ et al. (Tehran: Institut français de recherche en Iran, 1995); De Bruijn, 'Comparative Notes', 372–5.
13. O'Malley, 'Erotic Narratives'.
14. Ghazali, *Ihya' 'ulum al-din*, 1:59.
15. Ibn al-Jawzi, *Qussas*, 103, 115–17/trans. 182–3, 199–202. There may be some truth to the idea of a certain Persian cultural or linguistic affinity for narrative. Ibn al-Nadim attributes the invention of fables (*khurafat*) to the ancient Persians, and

from their titles and content it is clear that many of them did move from Persian into Arabic. In some cases translation from Arabic into Persian also involved a strengthening of the material's narrative thread. Balʿami, who adapted Tabari's history into one of the first works of New Persian prose, constructs coherent narratives out of the often-contradictory traditions he finds side by side in his annalistic source. Daniel, 'The Rise and Development of Persian Historiography', 106–7; Ibn al-Nadim, *Fihrist*, 2:321.

16. In the introduction to his work, Ibn al-Jawzi distinguishes between the activities of the *qass*, *waʿiz* and *mudhakkir*, but this seems to be a prescriptive attempt to impose a distinction rather than a description of how the terms were actually used. Indeed, he himself admits that many use the terms interchangeably (Ibn al-Jawzi, *Qussas*, 9–11/trans. 96–8).
17. The Joseph story is described in the Quran as 'the most beautiful of stories (*ahsan al-qasas*)'. The phrase used here by ʿAttar is *ahsan al-qessa*, which is not quite grammatical, but fits the metre. The allusion remains clear.
18. ʿAttar, *Mosibat-nama*, 447.
19. Rumi responds to similar charges in his *Masnavi*, 3:194.
20. ʿAttar, *Mosibat-nama*, 454.
21. Samarqandi, *Tazkerat al-shoʿara*, 327.
22. On the the interplay of orality and textuality in sufism, see Nile Green, 'The Uses of Books in a Late Mughal *Takiyya*: Persianate Knowledge between Person and Paper', *Modern Asian Studies* 44 (2010): 241–65; Muhsin Mahdi, 'The Book and the Master as Poles of Cultural Change in Islam', in *Islam and Cultural Change in the Middle Ages*, ed. Speros Vryonis (Wiesbaden: Harrassowitz, 1975). For an overview of the oral practices through which books were transcribed and studied, see Johannes Pedersen, *The Arabic Book*, trans. Geoffrey French (Princeton: Princeton University Press, 1984), 20–36. Shawkat Toorawa and Gregor Schoeler have argued that books, broadly speaking, came to play a more significant role in the transmission of knowledge during the ʿAbbasid period, with some intellectual fields making this turn earlier than others. Toorawa, *Ibn Abī Ṭāhir Ṭayfūr*; Schoeler, *Genesis of Literature*. On the emergence of non-elite readers and popular reading practices in Damascus and Egypt, see Hirschler, *Written Word*. See also Julia Rubanovich, ed., *Orality and Textuality in the Iranian World: Patterns of Interaction across the Centuries* (Leiden: Brill, 2015); Samer Ali, *Arabic Literary Salons in the Islamic Middle Ages: Poetry, Public Performance, and the Presentation of the Past* (Notre Dame, IN: University of Notre Dame Press, 2010), 38–46.

23. Ali, *Arabic Literary Salons*, 40–3; Schoeler, *Genesis of Literature*, 117–20.
24. See, for example ʿAttar, *Manteq al-tayr*, 436.
25. Werner Wolf, 'Framing Borders in Frame Stories', in *Framing Borders in Literature and Other Media*, ed. Werner Wolf and Walter Bernhart (Amsterdam: Rodopi, 2006).
26. These terms are Mieke Bal's adaptations of those first proposed by Gérard Genette: Mieke Bal, *Narratologie (Essais sur la signification narrative dans quatre romans modernes)* (Paris: Klincksieck, 1977), 35; Gérard Genette, *Narrative Discourse: An Essay in Method,* trans. Jane E. Lewin (Ithaca, NY: Cornell University Press, 1980), 227–34.
27. ʿAttar, *Manteq al-tayr*, 329.
28. Ibn al-Jawzi advises aspiring preachers to tread carefully when sermonising to sultans; one should soften one's admonishments and speak generally so as to not offend the ruler or call his authority into question. *Qussas*, 143/trans. 228–9.
29. ʿAttar, *Manteq al-tayr*, 327.
30. ʿAttar, *Manteq al-tayr*, 404.
31. Debra Malina, *Breaking the Frame: Metalepsis and the Construction of the Subject* (Columbus: The Ohio State University Press, 2002), 4; Genette, *Narrative Discourse*, 235. See also John Pier, 'Metalepsis', in *Living Handbook of Narratology*, ed. Peter Hühn et al., updated 13 July 2016, www.lhn.uni-hamburg.de/article/metalepsis-revised-version-uploaded-13-july-2016; Brian McHale, *Postmodernist Fiction* (New York: Methuen, 1987), 112–32.
32. The metaleptic blending of narrators has also been explored in classical literature. See Irene de Jong, 'Metalepsis in Ancient Greek Literature', in *Narratology and Interpretation: The Content of Narrative Form in Ancient Literature*, ed. Jonas Grethlein and Antonios Rengakos (Berlin: De Gruyter, 2009).
33. ʿAttar, *Manteq al-tayr*, 425.
34. ʿAttar, *Manteq al-tayr*, 355–6; Ritter, *Ocean of the Soul*, 327; ʿAttar, *Elahi-nama*, 161.
35. Out of the standard collections of stories of the prophets, this particular version of the episode is found only in Maybodi. See Sanʿatinia, *Ma'akhez*, 169–71.
36. ʿAttar, *Manteq al-tayr*, 425.
37. ʿAttar, *Manteq al-tayr*, 425.
38. ʿAttar, *Manteq al-tayr*, 356.
39. Quran 12:111; see also 12:7.
40. ʿAttar, *Manteq al-tayr*, 426.
41. Corbin, *Visionary Recital*, 200; Ritter, *Ocean of the Soul*, 348, 374–5, 526.

42. Like metalepsis, the *mise en abyme* is often studied in the context of modern and postmodern literature, where it is frequently understood as an anti-illusionist device and an emblem of self-conscious fictionality. See Dorrit Cohn, 'Metalepsis and *Mise en Abyme*', trans. Lewis S. Gleich, *Narrative* 20, no. 1 (2012): 105–14; Lucien Dällenbach, *The Mirror in the Text* (Chicago: University of Chicago Press, 1989); Genette, *Narrative Discourse*, 233; McHale, *Postmodernist Fiction*, 124–8.
43. Joseph's forgiveness is, according to some exegetes, the reason why the story is described as 'the most beautiful'. Abu Ishaq Tha'labi, *'Arā'is al-majālis fī qiṣaṣ al-anbiyā'; or, Lives of the Prophets*, trans. William M. Brinner (Leiden: Brill, 2002), 181–2.
44. 'Attar, *Manteq al-tayr*, 426.
45. 'Attar, *Manteq al-tayr*, 426.
46. 'Attar, *Manteq al-tayr*, 426. 'Attar exhorts readers to understand the story of Joseph and Benjamin allegorically in similar terms in the *Elahi-nama*, 161.

6

Allegory and Ascent

By reading and allegorically interpreting the story of Joseph's reunion with his brothers, the birds bring about their own reunion with the Simorgh; and by reading the *Conference of the Birds*, ʿAttar's readers precipitate an analogous reconciliation with God, or so the recursive logic of the frame-tale implies. Allegorical reading, as reflexively portrayed in that climactic episode, is accorded a special power to transform, and ʿAttar seeks to harness that power in other narratives at key junctures throughout his *masnavi*s, as well as in the allegorical frame-tales that bind the poems together. The present chapter examines these allegories, in particular the frame-tale of the *Mosibat-nama*, not just to explicate their deeper meanings, but to clarify their performative work and the philosophical assumptions that make that work possible. ʿAttar, like many of his sufi contemporaries, was hostile to philosophy in a strict sense; nevertheless, his work is infused with Islamicised Neoplatonic concepts and habits of thought.[1] His poems invoke a metaphysical system in which allegorical interpretation leads not only to the recovery of hidden meanings, but also constitutes a symbolic ascent to higher realms of reality, granting ontological access to referents that could not otherwise be grasped. Allegorical reading thus becomes a spiritual exercise, a ritual performance in which the reader not only interprets, but enacts.

In addition to Neoplatonic metaphysics, this understanding of allegory draws on Islamicate philosophical theories of the imagination, especially as it relates to dreams, visions and prophecy. Dreams and visions, according to thinkers as diverse as Farabi and Ghazali, do not necessarily originate with the dreamer but descend from these higher realms. Non-material meanings and entities (which, depending on the theorist in question, might include psychological faculties, angelic beings, the divine attributes or pure intelligibles) are clothed in sensible forms through the faculty of the imagination, and they are thereby made visible to the dreamer. Through allegorical interpretation, one can trace the resulting sensible forms back to their more abstract, non-material origins.[2] Such theories of meaning are especially relevant for an analysis of the *Mosibat-nama*, 'Attar's longest work, whose frame-tale recounts a visionary experience witnessed by a sufi wayfarer (*salek*) over the course of a forty-day retreat (*chella*). This wayfarer travels throughout the cosmos on a journey reminiscent of the Prophet's ascent to Heaven (*me'raj*), over the course of which he encounters and discourses with a variety of interlocutors including angels, the Throne and Footstool, the four elements and various prophets. The narrative is not meant to be taken as an account of physical events in the waking world, as 'Attar makes clear, but as an allegorical vision that encodes a particular understanding of the cosmos in which humans might reascend to God through the soul. At the same time, an allegorical reading of the poem itself functions as a symbolic act of ascent, so the narrative of the wayfarer is re-enacted in the audience's consumption and interpretation of the text.

The following pages explore 'Attar's poems as sites for spiritual performance aimed at ontological transformation. They begin by examining how 'Attar obliquely conceptualises the work of allegory, often through allegory itself, and those authorial intimations are placed in conversation with more explicit discussions of symbolic scriptural exegesis and dream interpretation found in the philosophical writings of 'Attar's intellectual milieu. The chapter then reads the frame-tale of the *Mosibat-nama* as an allegorical ascent narrative on the model the Prophet's journey to Heaven, but recast in a mystical, Neoplatonic vein. It shows how readers are invited to undertake an analogous journey of their own by reading and interpreting the text, as 'Attar makes clear in the poem's introduction. Finally, it examines the practice of *chella*, the forty-day sufi retreat in which practitioners would witness visions and other imaginal phenomena, and which serves as the setting for the wayfarer's cosmic journey. In addition to narrating the wayfarer's *chella*, the poem reduplicates its structure within the text, such that an encounter with the poem becomes a vicarious performance of retreat endowed with ritual efficacy.

In his edited volume on allegorical reading, J. Stephen Russel writes that the processes whereby readers decode an allegory are usually 'far more interesting and mysterious than the decoded messages (if any)'.[3] This is certainly true in the case of the *Mosibat-nama*. The vision of the cosmos articulated in the *Mosibat-nama* does not differ substantially from those found in other sufi works of a Neoplatonic bent. The process of decoding that allegory, however, is a symbolically charged act through which the reader ascends to higher metaphysical realms. To borrow a formulation made famous by Pierre Hadot, the text, when understood this way, does not just 'inform' its readers, but 'forms' them.[4] Reading becomes a ritualised, transformative action, the performance of a vicarious forty-day retreat in textual form, and a symbolic ascent towards the supra-personal soul.

Ladders to Heaven

The term 'allegory' is derived from the Greek *allos* (other) and *agoreuein* (to speak in public), and it thus indicates a kind of 'other-speaking', a mode of indirect communication in which one's intended meaning diverges from the plain import of one's speech.[5] Northrop Frye, in an oft-cited working definition of allegory, highlights this bifurcation of signification while underscoring its narrative character: allegory, according to Frye, is a 'technique of literature' in which 'the events of a narrative obviously and continuously refer to another simultaneous structure of events or ideas, whether historical event, moral or philosophical ideas, or natural phenomena'.[6] In premodern Persian and Arabic, there was no single terminological equivalent for this mode of 'other-speaking', but rather a variety of terms with their own points of emphasis. The distinction between 'exoteric' (*zaher*) and 'esoteric' (*baten*) is frequently encountered, as are terms such as *ramz* (symbol/secret), *eshara* (pointer) and *mesal* (similitude), all of which, alongside their own specific connotations, point to a deeper, hidden level of meaning underneath a more accessible surface.[7] These two levels of meaning, however, are linked in a much stronger way in the premodern imagination than Frye's definition allows. For the Perso-Arabic philosophers who explored the work of allegory, and for the poets and authors who composed them, an allegory's narrative surface does not just 'refer' to hidden signifieds but, as we shall see, grants ontological access to them. It thus makes higher metaphysical truths present to readers in a fundamentally tangible way, even as its indirect mode of explanation preserves their ineffable alterity.

When 'Attar himself refers to allegory and allegorical interpretation, he tends to use the term *mesal*. The Arabic root *m-s-l* deals with notions of likeness, similarity and resemblance, and *mesal*, in 'Attar's poetry, takes on a wide range of meanings related to representation and signification including allegorical meaning-making, but by no means limited to it. For example, the term is frequently used to make the imaginal status of a metaphorical comparison explicit, similar to 'like' or 'as' in the schoolbook definition of a simile:

Your hair is the snare and beauty spot the bait
Whatever you hunt is halal!
The sun is forever trapped
in the night-like (*shab-mesal*) loops of your snare![8]

In these verses the beloved's bright, fair face is contrasted with their dark, looping hair, such that the two are likened to the bright sun and dark night, respectively. The compound 'night-like' (*shab-mesal*) in the final line makes the imaginative, metaphorical status of these comparisons explicit.

Another common use of *mesal* in 'Attar's poetry involves teaching stories and descriptive scenes, reminiscent of biblical example stories and the Midrashic *mashal*.[9] For instance, in one memorable example, 'Attar describes a dung beetle that spends its days rolling up dung. The beetle labours over its ball of refuse, rolling it this way and that, but when it arrives at its burrow its impure gleanings have grown much too large to fit inside. The beetle must then slink into its hole alone, abandoning its hard-won accumulations for naught. This, 'Attar claims, is an example (*mesal*) that clarifies the state of a man who seeks after worldly goods, constantly accumulating wealth even though he cannot bring it with him into the afterlife:

This is an example (*mesal*) of a man and his wealth
which will clarify his condition for you.
Whoever spends a lifetime accumulating silver and gold
must abandon it all in the tight grave.[10]

Here, the term *mesal* is not just a marker of metaphoric thinking but indicates a specific kind of teaching story rooted in structural similarities between a concrete scene from the natural world and the spiritual situation of worldly people. It illustrates the mortal condition and its spiritual stakes in a fresh and striking way, and it aims to convince listeners to take a hard look at their own attachments to material wealth thereby.

Other times 'Attar uses the term *mesal* for a more complex kind of story – generally about God, the soul or another transcendent entity – that cannot be so quickly reduced to an illustrative function. Two stories near the end of the *Conference of the Birds*, both of which are introduced as *mesal*, exemplify this mode of indirect meaning-making. The first is the Joseph tale, written on a scrap of paper that the birds receive from the chamberlain and which was discussed in detail in Chapter 5.[11] While the example of the dung beetle illustrates, in a memorable and striking way, an already well-known ethical principle (death renders material wealth vain and futile!), the Joseph story gestures, in a much more allusive fashion, to a subtle metaphysical point that is never made explicit outside of the narrative.[12] Part of the attraction of the dung beetle example is how neatly everything is tied up – the analogy between the rich man and his wealth and the beetle and its dung ball is direct, easy to grasp and explicitly drawn by 'Attar in his two-line epymithium. The significance of the Joseph story, on the other hand, is never fully explicated in the same way: rather than an illustration of some 'separable content', it is a window through which to approach a more elusive meaning. The poet insists that it be interpreted allegorically, and he explains that the birds (and his readers) have sold their 'Joseph souls', but what this actually means is left up to the audience to decipher. The allegorical significance of the scroll, of the brothers' act of reading and of their subsequent silence is not hand delivered by 'Attar, but must be deduced through hermeneutic work. At the same time, the story displays a notable polysemy: Joseph is cast as a symbol for the soul, but as a royal figure who receives supplicants and holds the power of life and death, he also exhibits clear parallels with the Simorgh/God. This ambiguity – which bears on the central point of the poem – is not resolved but left for readers to ponder on their own. The result is a much more 'open' narrative, in which the audience must work harder (but also enjoys greater freedom) in the generation of meaning.

This particular narrative's semiotic openness is likely due, at least in part, to the ineffable nature of its allegorical referent. Within the mystical framework in which 'Attar was working, God and other higher entities – including the supra-personal soul (*ruh*) – were held to transcend language, reason and human conceptualisation. This transcendence was not only an ontological fact but a performative imperative: human beings must find ways to talk about these entities and states (or ways to not talk about them) that preserve their incommensurability.[13] In many cases, allegory's 'other-speaking' was a manner of doing just that: a performative use of language that conceals even as it reveals. This function is especially apparent in the final story that concludes the birds' journey, and which is presented by 'Attar as an oblique comment on the state of 'subsistence after effacement'. As discussed in Chapter 4, 'Attar insists that he cannot reveal the mystery of these spiritual states. They are beyond explanation and definition; they are known only to those who are worthy; and even if he could disclose them, to do so would mean death.[14] Nevertheless, his companions have requested a commentary on effacement and subsistence 'by way of allegory' (*az rah-e mesal*), and 'Attar, however reluctantly, agrees.[15] He thus narrates the tale of the king who executes his young beloved in a fit of jealously but comes to regret the decision. After forty days of suffering, the king learns that his order was never carried out, and the two are joyfully reunited.[16] This narrative, like the allegory of Jospeh's brothers, is relatively ambiguous and semiotically open. As Davis has remarked, it is difficult to know who represents God and who represents the believer. On the one hand, a king is generally a symbol for God, in which case the king's beloved slave ought to correspond to the human soul; on the other, the role of beloved is usually more appropriate for God, and the role of lover for the soul or believer. The story, then, invokes two common, conventional mappings that are at odds with one another; one of them must necessarily be inverted. Such ambiguity is fitting, as Davis notes, given the mystical merging of identities that marks the poem's climax, and it also serves to protect the 'mystery' of effacement and subsistence through indirect speech.[17]

The philosophical underpinnings of allegorical representation that inform 'Attar's work are theorised in more detail by Abu Hamid Ghazali, who also articulates its high spiritual stakes. He is not concerned with literary allegory per se, but with symbolic scriptural exegesis. Nevertheless, his writings on the subject encapsulate the broader philosophical discourse on dreams, visions and prophecy that formed the intellectual background against which literary allegory's significance was understood. Indeed, many literary allegories, including the *Mosibat-nama*, were frequently framed as dreams or visions and elided with them. In his treatise *Mishkat al-anwar*, Ghazali interprets the Quran's famous light verse (24:35) as an allegory for the prophetic and imaginative faculties, and he begins with a metaphysical justification for the symbolic hermeneutics that he deploys:

> Know that the world is actually two worlds: spiritual and bodily. If you prefer, you can call them sensory and rational, or higher and lower, which are just different ways of expressing the same meaning . . . The world of dominion is an unseen world because it is concealed from most, while the sensory world is a visible world because everyone witnesses it. The sensory world is a ladder (*mirqat*) to the rational world, and if there were no contact or relation between them, the path of ascent (*taraqqi*) would be blocked; and if that were blocked, then the journey to Lordship's presence and proximity with God would be impossible.[18]

The upper realm, inaccessible in and of itself, parallels the lower world and is made accessible through it. Ghazali calls the points of contact between these worlds 'similitudes' (*mesal*), the same term that ʿAttar applies to the Joseph story. For Ghazali, similitudes include physical objects, dream visions and prophetic utterances – he is especially interested in the latter – that imprint 'the spirits of meanings' (*arwah al-maʿani*) within material or imaginal forms (*qawalib*).[19] They are sensible objects in the lower world that 'resemble' immaterial analogues in the higher one through a 'manner of likeness' and a 'kind of correspondence'; the vague language here points to the unusual nature of their signification, which straddles two seemingly distinct cosmic realms.[20] Due to the immaterial nature of these higher referents, this correspondence cannot be rooted in physical mimesis, but must rather proceed from analogical and structural associations. Celestial bodies, for example, function as similitudes of angels because they both distribute 'light' to the world, the former physically and the latter metaphorically in flows of divine grace. In the same way, the sun might represent a sultan in a dream and the moon a vizier, not because of any physical resemblance between them, but because the moon reflects the light of the sun just as the vizier derives his authority from the sultan.[21] Through this web of analogical relations, the higher and lower worlds are bound together and exchange is permitted in both directions. The unseen is rendered visible through similitudes, which then function as 'ladders' through which one can ascend upwards towards the spiritual realm.

The notion that allegory provides ontological access to higher realities is not directly theorised by ʿAttar, whose poems are naturally less systematic than Ghazali's treatises. He does, however, hint at this aspect of allegorical signification in several of his narratives, especially the parable of the King Whose Beauty Kills His Subjects, which was already discussed in another context in Chapter 1.[22] The parable is narrated early in the *Conference of the Birds* when the hoopoe's flock enquires about the nature of their relation (*nesbat*) to the Simorgh: how might they, as lowly as they are, have any way of reaching their lofty king? In response, the hoopoe explains that there was once a beautiful monarch whose subjects were all madly in love with him.[23] Due to his overwhelming beauty, no one could gaze upon him without immediately dying. Indeed, to even think of union with him would mean to lose one's sanity. His infatuated subjects were thus caught in a double bind: they could not bear to be deprived of his visage, but to see his beauty unveiled meant certain death. To solve this problem, the king constructs a mirror, places it on a tower and sits on his throne opposite it. While he himself remains hidden, his reflection is visible, and his subjects can safely gaze upon it. The parable hangs on the unusual signifying properties of the mirror and the peculiar ontological status of images. From one perspective, the image in the mirror is nothing other than the king himself, manifest in all his glory, and his lovelorn subjects can thereby satisfy their desire by gazing upon it. And yet from another perspective, the image is not 'the thing itself' but an iconic, imaginal representation that is necessarily other than the original. The image is thus simultaneously the king and not-the-king, and it is this peculiar mixture of revelation and concealment and identity and non-identity that grants the townsfolk a kind of proximity to their royal beloved while paradoxically maintaining a distance that protects both their lives and his transcendent incommensurability. By looking into the mirror, they see neither the king's face, nor the mirror, but a peculiarly signifying 'trace' (*neshan*).[24]

ʿAttar, in a homily preceding the parable, interprets it symbolically as an explanation of humans' inherent relationship to God: the mirror represents the heart, the organ of spiritual sight that God has mercifully created within us, and through which we are capable of envisaging and even travelling towards him just as the birds travel towards the Simorgh. But the story also serves as an apt illustration of allegory's peculiar mode of signification, through which the inaccessible is made accessible and the unrepresentable rendered concrete. God is utterly inapproachable and incomparable just like the beautiful king, who is described in the first line of the story as 'beyond likeness (*mesl*) and resemblance (*mesal*)'. The latter term's more technical meanings of 'example' and 'similitude', while not necessarily dominant, are also present. They endow the narrative with semiotic overtones and raise the question, at least implicitly, of how an entity that admits of no 'likeness' might ever be comprehended, let alone represented. The answer, according to this parable, is that while God cannot be glimpsed directly, he (or at least the attribute of his beatuy) can be accessed through a 'trace' that seems to function much like Ghazali's similitudes. Although ostensibly a visual reflection, this 'trace' is not a direct mimetic imitation – God, after all, transcends physical resemblance – but a kind of symbol through which he is made manifest in a sensible form. Through this iconic reflection, the townsfolk of 'Attar's parable can gaze on their otherwise inaccessible king, just as one can use allegorical similitudes of a transcendent God (or his attributes) to 'climb' towards his unreachable presence.[25]

Upwards and Inwards

The connection between allegorical interpretation and symbolic ascent is especially salient for a reading of the *Mosibat-nama*, a text whose central narrative conceit is a visionary journey through the cosmos. Its frame-tale, which recalls the Prophet's ascent to Heaven, features a sufi wayfarer (*salek*) who dialogues with personified entities from all realms of creation; allegory's power to grant access to higher ontological realms is thus concretised in the 'surface level' of its narrative. The *Mosibat-nama* is by no means unique in this regard. The plot of the journey, and in particular the upwards journey, was a fundamental narrative conceit in Arabic and Persian allegory and allegoresis, as it was in Greek and Latin. Ibn Sina, for example, provides an allegorical reading of Muhammad's ascent in his Persian *Me'raj-nama*, in which he interprets the Prophet's journey as a coded representation of his own metaphysical and psychological system. He also uses the topos of ascent to build his own allegories: his *Treatise of the Birds* narrates a flock of birds' flight over eight mountains in search of their king, and *Hayy ibn Yaqzan* recounts a symbolic geography that extends into the celestial spheres.[26] These prose philosophical allegories, and the tradition of visionary recitals that they inaugurated, were likely one source of inspiration for what became a distinct sub-genre of philosophical ascent poems in Persian. One of the earliest extant works in this poetic tradition is Sana'i's *Sayr al-'ebad*: its narrator recounts the process of his biological and psychological development before embarking on a metaphysical tour of the cosmos under the guidance of the Active Intellect, who, like Ibn Sina's Hayy, is personified as a youthful-seeming old man. In a more sufi vein, the *Mesbah al-arvah* of Bardasiri recounts the narrator's ascent through the various ranks of the soul towards annihilation in God. And in the *Rahiq al-tahqiq* of Marvrudi, a wise man questions a piece of paper as to why its face has been darkened with ink; it refers him to the ink, who refers him to the pen, all the way up through the chain of causality to God.[27] These poems all explore the structure of the phsyche and/or the cosmos through the topos of ascent.

In the *Mosibat-nama*, the wayfarer's ascent is motivated by the inherent pain of human existence and ontological separation from God. The narrative opens with a short description of gestation and the various stages of human life, all of which 'Attar metaphorically associates with suffering and deprivation.[28] To find some relief from this torment, the wayfarer sets out under the guidance of his spiritual guide (*pir*) on a cosmic journey, visiting forty beings that together represent the entirety of creation (Table 6.1). His journey begins with the archangels – Gabriel, Michael, Esra'fil and 'Azra'il – who are often associated with the hypostatic intelligences of Neoplatonic ontology. He supplicates each one in turn, extolling their virtues and power in a panegyric mode before begging them for help, but they all turn him away claiming that they too are suffering and can do nothing for him. After each encounter, the guide briefly explains each interlocutor's metaphysical role and symbolic associations and then narrates a series of embedded stories and homilies. The journey continues in this fashion following the path of Neoplatonic emanation: after the archangels, the wayfarer visits other metaphysically elevated entities of religious myth, such as the Throne and the Pen, before descending through the heavens and repeating the pattern with the fundamental elements – fire, air, water and earth – that comprise the sub-lunar world.

The wayfarer then turns upwards, ascending through the realms of compound being in order of increasing complexity and ontological rank. He visits the minerals, plants and animals, as well as the jinn, the Devil and an archetypal human being before encountering a series of prophets arranged in ascending chronological order: Adam, Noah, Abraham, Moses, David, Jesus and Muhammad.[29] The first six of these prophets are unable to cure the wayfarer's pain themselves, but they urge him onwards through their ranks and towards Muhammad. Their cognisance of their relative positions in the prophetic (and cosmic) hierarchy underscores Muhammad's role as the seal of the prophets.

As foretold by his forerunners, Muhammad is able to finally provide the wayfarer with some solid guidance. Although he cannot directly cure the wayfarer's pain, the Prophet explains that he must turn inwards and pass through five psychological faculties.[30] According to Muhammad, the wayfarer's journey will end once he reaches the soul (*jan*):

> You have five stages (*manzel*) in your being
> Truly a difficult route, full of swerves and curves.
> The first is sense, and its second is imagination;
> third is the intellect, the site of disputation.
> Its fourth station is the place of the heart,
> and the fifth is the soul (*jan*) – the route there is difficult.
>
> . . .
>
> So go now, and take the path of self;
> set out through the five valleys within.[31]

Following the path laid out by the Prophet, the wayfarer travels through sense, imagination, intellect and the heart before finally arriving at the 'ocean of the soul'.[32] He praises the soul in the highest terms; he eulogises it as the first created being, eternal, free from essence and attribute, and 'the breath of the merciful' *(dam-e rahman)*. In return, the ocean of the soul enjoins him to 'dive in' and lose himself in its depths. In 'Attar's striking image, the soul is a boundless, unitary ocean, but one which somehow has 'inlets' penetrating into individual beings.[33] It is at once the most 'interior' portion of the self and a supra-personal cosmological entity, encompassing and surpassing all other existents, including the archangels with whom the wayfarer began his journey. By submerging himself in its waters, the wayfarer renounces individual existence – 'he wash[es] his hands of self' – and attains proximity to God.[34] Similar to the birds' transformation at the conclusion to the *Conference of the Birds*,

Table 6.1 *The wayfarer's itinerary and the guide's discourses*

Interlocutor	*Topic*	*Interlocutor*	*Topic*
Gabriel	The name of God	Inanimates	Death's inevitability; seize the moment
Esra'fil	Bewilderment	Plants	Fools' impudence with God
Michael	Mercy and sustenance	Wild animals	Everything is from God
'Azra'il	Death	Birds	Contentment and spiritual fortune
Bearers of the Throne	Human superiority over angels	Tame animals	The carnal soul (*nafs*)
Throne	Compassion	The Devil	The Devil's relationship to God
Footstool	Justice (*'adl*); worldly power	Jinn	Fools' impudence excused
Tablet	Predestination	A human	God and the human soul
Pen	Sincerity in striving (*talab*)	Adam	Union
Paradise	Beatific vision	Noah	Pain and affliction
Hell	Condemnation of the world	Abraham	Intimacy (*khellat*) with God
Sky	Pain in striving	Moses	All-consuming love (*'eshq*)
Sun	Spiritual ambition (*hemmat*)	David	Loving friendship (*mavaddat*)
Moon	Weakness in love	Jesus	Kindness and mercy
Fire	Avarice	Muhammad	Spiritual poverty (*faqr*)
Wind	Temporality of the world	Sense	Multiplicity
Water	Impurity; the carnal soul (*nafs*)	Imagination	Love and union
Earth	Humility and forbearance	Intellect	Reason's limitations
Mountain	Seeking God in truth (*haqiqat*)	Heart	Heart as isthmus to the soul; love
Ocean	Moderation; effacement in love	Soul	Inward turn; effacement (*fana'*) in God

the wayfarer becomes the pinnacle of the metaphysical order, a pure servant of God through this effacement of the self:

> He found the two worlds to be a reflection of his soul,
> and he found his own soul to be greater than them.
> When he became sighted to the secret of his own soul,
> he was brought to life and became a servant of the Lord.

Now, after this, lies the true foundation of servanthood –
every breath, a hundred lives in life.[35]

It is at this point that ʿAttar tells us he can narrate no more; he has described the wayfarer's 'journey to God' but now begins the latter's 'journey in God', which he cannot reveal without divine consent.[36] The wayfarer's story ends here, and after some brief concluding material, including passages of poetic self-praise and self-criticism, as well as a proclamation of the virtues of silence, the poem comes to a close.

The wayfarer's journey is not a factual account of something that 'actually happened', at least not in a normal waking state. Rather, as ʿAttar makes clear in the poem's opening, its 'truth' is not apparent on its surface (*zaher*) but hidden in its depths (*baten*). If one considers only the former, the poem will appear 'crooked' and untruthful; once the latter is taken into account, its excellence appears:

If someone opines, based on appearances,
that these words run crooked like a bow,
He sees only their exoteric aspect (*zaher*);
in the esoteric aspect (*baten*), they are exceedingly excellent.
If the wayfarer speaks with the angels
and seeks out discourse with the earth and the sky,
or passes by the Throne and the Footstool,
or asks questions of this and that,
seeks assistance from the prophets,
listens to the happenings of the atoms,
that is all the 'language of state' (*zafan-e hal*),
none of it is the 'language of speech' (*zafan-e qal*).
In the 'language of speech' it's a lie (*kazb*), but
in the 'language of state' it's sincere (*sedq*) and excellent.
If you don't recognise the 'language of state',
just call it the 'language of thought'.
Because he speaks of state (*hal*) and not of speech (*qal*)
believe it, and don't say it's impossible.[37]

The poem's content is repeatedly characterised in this passage as an example of the 'language of state' (*zafan-e hal*) as opposed to 'language of speech' (*zafan-e qal*). In its most basic sense, the 'language of state' refers to the literary device of personification, the central rhetorical figure of debate poems (*monazera*) in which inanimate objects or animals imaginatively argue their relative merits.[38] Sometimes the term 'language of state' would be directly invoked to authorise these fictional dialogues. Although not a debate poem per se, the *Mosibat-nama* is a series of personifications, and 'Attar's insistence that it be understood as the 'language of state' is, on the one hand, an acknowledgement of its fictionality. At the same time, the 'language of state' is frequently associated with the revelation of deeper truths: the poet does not attribute just any speech to a mute entity but that which articulates some fundamental aspect of its 'state' (*hal*).[39] In some contexts, 'the language of state' refers not to a literary device at all but to the miraculous speech of inanimate objects perceptible only to the spiritual elite. Bayazid Bestami, for example, is rebuked by a dog for his concern over external ritual purity while ignoring the inner defilement of the self. And 'Ala al-Dowla Semnani, like 'Attar's wayfarer, conversed with personifications of celestial objects over the course of an ascent experience.[40] Similar to dreams and prophecy, this miraculous communication was theorised by Ghazali to operate on the level of the imagination, where it takes on an audible form perceptible to some while remaining imperceptible to others.[41] In 'Attar's opening defense, quoted above, all of these valences are simultaneously operative. In literary terms, the poem relies heavily on the device of personification, through which 'Attar gives voice to the fundamental contingency of all existence and the centrality of the soul, but the wayfarer also encounters these entities over the course of a visionary experience in which one might hear truthful speech from otherwise mute entities.

Taken as a whole, the visionary narrative of the wayfarer encodes an Islamicised Neoplatonic understanding of the cosmic order and humans' place within it. The soul links the macrocosm and individual microcosm, standing at the head of the former and the interior of the latter. In terms of its metaphysical rank, the soul is the first emanated being and thus contains and encompasses the rest of existence. It is the last step on the wayfarer's journey and the site of an ineffable proximity to God. At the same time, the soul is also 'inside' individual beings in a particularised form, whence they gain life and movement. It thus finds both metaphysical and psychological expression, serving as the isthmus between the cosmic macrocosm and the human microcosm. Salvation lies in an interior journey towards the soul as the deepest part of the self, which is also an upwards journey towards the soul as a transcendent, supra-personal entity that precedes all other existents. This is only possible, however, with the prophetic guidance of Muhammad. He not only provides the wayfarer with critical knowledge of the path to come, but he also offers a model for this inner ascent through his own journey into the heavens, which became a central myth in Islamic culture and a dominant paradigm for conceptualising mystical experience and spiritual wayfaring.[42] A number of sufi heroes, most famously Bestami, are said to have made their own ascents in imitation of the prophetic model, although their journeys were generally understood to be made in spirit, whereas the Prophet's was usually considered to be made in body.[43] As a cosmic journey, the *Mosibat-nama* recalls both the Prophet's *meʿraj* and the spiritual ascents of these later sufis, but the ascent topos is here reworked into an allegory for an 'inward turn' that is theoretically open to all human beings even if few undertake it and even fewer follow it to its end.

Beyond outlining this ideal course of spiritual progression and the metaphysical system that makes it possible, the poem also functions as a homiletic call to action. By narrating the wayfarer's journey, ʿAttar prods his readers to undertake an analogous inward turn of their own before it is too late. This purpose is made clear at multiple points throughout the poem, including the opening lines of the narrative of the wayfarer. After describing the pain and suffering inherent in every stage of human development and the terror and inevitability of death, ʿAttar addresses his readers directly and explains that the only cure is to activate their latent connection to the soul. This is a painful process, and the stakes could not be higher:

> Whoever is bound in this twisted situation
>   and has not recovered the soul dies into nothing.
> Until you find the far-seeing soul
>   how can you call yourself a human?
> A human is not a sperm drop of earth and water
>   A human is a holy secret and the pure soul.
> Why would a hundred worlds of angels in existence
>   prostrate themselves before a drop of sperm?

O you clump of dirt, doesn't the desire grip you
that this clump of dirt of yours would become pure soul?
But to find proximity with the soul from a drop of sperm
one must endure much pain without cure.
Confusion is the way out of this affair
'No-remedy' is the medicine for this pain.
Don't you see how far the road is
from its beginning as a sperm drop to this place?[44]

Human beings, by attaining to the soul, claim their proper position at the pinnacle of the metaphysical order, which explains why the angels bowed down to Adam. To fail in this, however, means to succumb to a purely material existence in which death is truly the end.

The *pir* exhorts the wayfarer in similar terms, and given the convergence of speakers characteristic of 'Attar's works, the reader is simultaneously the target of these exhortations. The hortatory lines quoted below, for example, follow an anecdote featuring Bestami in which he worries that his egotistical pride will prevent him from reaching pre-eternal proximity to God:

As long as your 'I-ness' and 'we-ness' remains,
you'll find no safe place to turn your face.
When you come out from 'I' and 'we' completely,
you'll be the two worlds in their totality.[45]

These sententious verses seem most likely to be spoken by the *pir* to the wayfarer as part of his interpretive, exhortative summary of the preceding anecdote's moral, and they also foreshadow the wayfarer's final transformation at the end of the narrative. At the same time, they blend with 'Attar's own homiletic speech to his readers, who are thereby urged to abandon their individual existence and recover their participation in the soul from which the whole universe emanates: then they, like the wayfarer, will find that they encompass the macrocosm within themselves. A final example, in which the interior nature of this journey is stressed, is found in the Prophet's address to the wayfarer during their visionary dialogue:

If you desire poverty and effacement,
and 'not' in the 'is' of God,

then become a shadow, lost in the sunlight;
become nothing – God knows the truth!
But your route to arrive at this station (*manzel*)
can only be through the interior of the heart.[46]

In all of these instances, the reader is called to turn inwards, just as the wayfarer does, and to thereby follow a trail blazed by the Prophet on his *meʿraj*.

Not only does the poem urge its readers towards this inward turn, but the act of reading itself constitutes the symbolic performance such an interior ascent. The performative, even ritual function of allegory dates back to the mode's origins in late antiquity, when Neoplatonic allegoresis was understood as a kind of literary theurgy that could manifest higher divinities in sensible form.[47] These ideas persisted in new forms in the Islamic period, as when Ghazali describes the lower world as a 'ladder' to the divine realm and similitudes as bridges between material forms and intelligible meanings. Against this intellectual background, the process of reading and interpreting allegory can easily take on the flavour of a ritual practice. Aaron Hughes, drawing on the work of Sarah Rappe, has suggested that Ibn Sina's *Hayy ibn Yaqzan* functioned as a 'mediation manual' guiding readers' imaginations upwards towards the celestial intelligences.[48] And Henry Corbin, in his work on Ismaʿilism, has observed that the interpretation of esoteric texts (*ta'wil*, which etymologically means 'to *cause to return*, to lead back') involves a simultaneous '*ta'wil* of the soul', a return of the interpreting subject to its celestial origins.[49]

The *Mosibat-nama*'s performative function is made especially clear in its introduction, where it is presented as a site for readers' re-enactment of the spiritual transformation that it depicts. The wayfarer traverses the cosmos before realising that the human microcosm precedes and contains the macrocosm, and he thus finds salvation internally within the soul. In a passage that closes the poem's prefatory material and directly precedes the beginning of the narrative (*aghaz-e ketab*), ʿAttar addresses his readers directly and invites them to undertake an analogous journey through the poem's literary representation of the cosmos:

Forty stages (*maqam*) will come before you,
and they will also come within the self.

When you have undertaken this retreat (*che[l]la*) on the way (*tariqat*),
then reunion with truth (*haqiqat*) will come.
When you search for yourself in forty stages,
you will be, in the end, everything.[50]

Read in isolation, the passage could be interpreted as a general exhortation to spiritual wayfaring. But given its position at the end of the preface, the coming forty chapters of the poem, and the indexical reference to '*this* retreat', its primary referent would seem to be the readers' upcoming textual encounter with the narrative of the wayfarer. The forty chapters of the poem are cast as 'stages' on the sufi path, and by moving through them, readers will, like the wayfarer, make a journey into the depths of the microcosm where they will be reunited with 'truth' and symbolically escape the clutches of death. In all likelihood, 'Attar's readers would have been well habituated to such anagogic modes of reading, and they would not have needed an explicit authorial declaration to appreciate the transformative potential of the text. For us, however, operating at a large historical remove, 'Attar's authorial statement is a powerful reminder that allegory was more than a way of communicating content; it was a performative act through which readers could insert themselves into a soteriological drama and ascend to an otherwise inaccessible realm.

Dream, Visions and Ritual Retreat

In the above-quoted passage, 'Attar not only characterises the readers' movement through the poem as an inward journey, but he also likens the text to a *chella*, the forty-day ritual retreat that serves as the setting for the wayfarer's quest. 'Attar was writing in the twelfth and thirteenth centuries when the practice of retreat was becoming increasingly institutionalised and playing a larger role in spiritual training, especially among the Kobraviya and Sohravardiya sufi orders. According to normative accounts of the practice, practitioners might witness spectral lights or visions over the course of the retreat, or even experience themselves ascending into the heavens. It is therefore an entirely plausible context for a visionary journey like the wayfarer's, and it testifies to the close connection between allegorical texts and visionary experience. Philosophical theories of the imagination had found wide currency among intellectuals by the twelfth century, including within sufi circles, and they were frequently used to theorise the epistemic status of dreams, visions and prophecy, as well as their amenability to symbolic hermeneutics.[51] The kind of symbolic signification found in literary allegories, however, was never explicitly theorised to the same degree. This is not because they were less important, but because they were so closely aligned with dreams and visions that no separate semiotics was needed. Indeed, the allegorical meaning-making of a literary text like the *Mosibat-nama* seems have been understood as an extension of the kind of meaning-making found in dreams and visions, and this elision is frequently observable within the allegorical narratives themselves.

This affinity between allegory and visions can be traced back to the beginnings of Neoplatonic allegoresis in late antiquity. Macrobius's commentary on Cicero's *Dream of Scipio*, for example, is a specimen of both allegorical interpretation and oneirocriticism.[52] In the Islamicate context, Ibn Sina's *Treatise of the Birds* is narrated as a first-person account of a visionary experience, and its narrator castigates those who would ascribe his words to a mere imbalance in the humors rather than accepting it as a veridical vision.[53] Likewise, Ibn Sina's *Meʿraj-nama* draws on a tradition according to which the Prophet's ascent took place in 'a state between sleeping and waking'.[54] (This stands in contrast to the more widespread view that it was a bodily journey.) In Sohravardi's *Avaz-e par-e Jebra'il*, the narrator recounts a visionary encounter he experienced as an adolescent after waking from a troubling dream at the break of dawn and moving from the women's quarters to the men's – a liminal state in more than one sense that was ripe for inspiration from the unseen.[55] The ascent recounted in the *Mesbah al-arvah* of Bardasiri, too, takes the form of a visionary initiation conducted at dawn after the performance of *samaʿ* and the drinking of wine.[56] And in the *Mosibat-nama*, the wayfarer's cosmic journey is explicitly framed as a visionary unveiling (*kashf*), a direct inspiration from the divine world:

> Since it is permitted to see anything in dreams,
> don't turn your head if someone sees something in unveiling (*kashf*)![57]

Coming on the heels of 'Attar's explanation of the 'language of state' and 'language of speech', this imperative offers yet another reason to refrain from dismissing the wayfarer's journey out of hand: like a dream, unveiling provides a glimpse of higher worlds that may not accord with the boundaries of normal experience as perceived by the outer senses, but which conveys a deeper truth.

Through their framing as dreams, visionary experiences and unveilings, these texts signal their amenability to a potentially exuberant hermeneutics while also laying claim to a specific kind of plausibility. Writers and storytellers in premodern Persian and Arabic frequently felt a need to explain how their narratives – even if overtly fictional – could plausibly refer to real-life events.[58] In the case of visionary allegories, which frequently include fantastic imagery, one obvious way to do this is by casting them as accounts of dreams or other visionary experiences. This does not mean that they recount specific dreams that someone actually witnessed. The *Treatise of the Birds*, for instance, has the feel of a literary construction; there is no indication its narrator is co-extensive with the historical Ibn Sina or anyone else. Likewise, the wayfarer and his cosmic journey in the *Mosibat-nama* seem to be entirely fictional. Nevertheless, the poem's framing as an unveiling, even a fictional one, still endows it with a certain plausibility, providing readers a way to think the wayfarer's journey *as if* it occurred in the world. It thereby justifies the narrative while simultaneously endowing it with the privileged halo of inspiration.

The wayfarer's vision is further situated as a product of the forty-day sufi retreat, or *chella*, which coalesced as a distinct, rule-based practice in Kobravi and Sohravardi circles around the time that ʿAttar was writing. Forty is a symbolically charged number with connotations of maturity and completeness, and the normative manuals of retreat produced during this period often cite the forty-day vigil God imposed on Moses (Quran 2:51) or the forty-day period that God allegedly kneaded Adam's clay to justify the practice.[59] Over the course of the retreat, practitioners would seclude themselves in a small room and perform a variety of ascetic activities, the most important of which was *zekr* – the repetition of a word or phrase silently or aloud in order to cleanse the heart and focus it on God. According to the manuals, extended *zekr* during seclusion could produce visionary unveilings: entities and meanings from the divine realm would descend and take on sensible form in the imagination, whence they could be perceived and interpreted for information about the subject's spiritual state.[60] For example, Najm al-Din Razi Daya writes that practitioners in retreat may behold visions of the angels, the Footstool or the Throne, which indicate that they are 'travelling through the angelic realm and acquiring praiseworthy attributes'.[61] Indeed, the visions witnessed during retreat were often conceptualised as forms of spiritual ascent. Ibn ʿArabi, for example, composed a stylised account of seclusion that, like the *Mosibat-nama*, involves a visionary journey through the various levels of the cosmos.[62] The Kobravi mystic ʿAziz al-Din Nasafi also posits a close connection between retreat and the 'ascent' (*ʿoruj*) of the sufis, and he writes that his own shaykh (presumably Saʿd al-Din Hammuya) travelled the heavens in spirit for thirteen days while his body remained in a catatonic state.[63] Practitioners might also witness visions originating from their own carnal souls – again invested with sensible form in the imagination – that indicate a lower spiritual state or signify specific vices. For instance, according to Daya, a vision of a snake indicates that rancour predominates in the soul, and a donkey, lust. If practitioners see themselves subjugating such animals, they will know they are overcoming those negative attributes.[64] Daya provides these and other interpretative pointers, but he, like most other writers on retreat, insists that ultimate hermeneutic authority rests with the practitioner's spiritual guide, who should regularly visit their disciples in seclusion to address difficulties, interpret spiritual unveilings and distinguish visions from the divine realm with those of psychic or even satanic origin.[65]

The practice of retreat outlined above serves as the implicit setting of the wayfarer's journey in the *Mosibat-nama*, as evinced by their numerous structural, terminological and practical parallels. Like the retreat, the wayfarer's experience also consists of forty distinct stages, and it involves a visionary unveiling (*kashf*) that takes the form of a cosmic ascent. Moreover, as ʿAttar explains while introducing the narrative and defending its truth, the wayfarer's *zekr* powers these visions:

> The travelling is done by the wayfarer's thought (*fekr*)
> A thought that is 'acquired' (*mostafad*) by his *zekr*.
> *Zekr* must be uttered to bring forth thought
> and hundreds of thousands of virgin meanings.
> A thought that comes from the delusion of the intellect
> is not from the unseen (*ghayb*) but from verbal transmission (*naql*).
> Intellectual thought is for the infidels
> Heart-thought is for the man of the way.

The wayfarer of thought, when he appears on stage,
comes not from the intellect, but from the heart.[66]

The wayfarer's visions are produced through the practice of *zekr*, by means of which he 'acquires' a visionary mode of thought that allows him to travel through the imaginal realm. 'Attar insists that this is not 'intellectual thought' but thought 'from the heart', a distinction that seems motivated by a desire to distance himself from the philosophical tradition that he was nonetheless deeply indebted to.[67] He further specifies that the wayfarer is threatened by satanic visions that might be mistaken for divine unveilings, another parallel with contemporary understandings of retreat:

Although there are satanic unveilings along the way,
There are also spiritual ones (*ruhani*) and those of God's dominion (*mal[a]kut*).
Taste and piety are needed, and passion for God,
to split the two paths in this affair.[68]

Given these interpretive difficulties, the wayfarer consults with his *pir* after each vision – just as Daya recommends – who explains its metaphysical significance and launches into a set of teaching stories and homilies on a related theme. The spiritual guide alone has the experience necessary to determine whether a particular vision is 'satanic' or belongs to 'God's dominion' and to interpret its true meaning.

The wayfarer's journey hews closely to Kobravi and Sohrawardi practices of institutionalised retreat, but forty-day periods of ascetic activity of a more general sort can also be found in 'Attar's narratives, and they too are associated with visions and profound spiritual transformations. For example, in the critical tale of Shaykh San'an, the disciples of the titular character devote themselves to forty days of prayer and fasting after abandoning their shaykh in Byzantium in the clutches of apostasy. On the fortieth day, the head disciple sees the Prophet in a vision (*kashf*), and the latter informs him that Shaykh San'an has returned to Islam and been cured of his disease.[69] Like the tale of Shaykh San'an, the previously discussed story of the jealous king also occupies a structurally key position in the *Conference of the Birds*, and it too features the transformative power of a forty-day period of ascetic practice. In that story, the king spends every night beneath the gallows from which he believes the executed body of his beloved hangs, all without eating or drinking. On the fortieth night, he sees the boy in a dream; upon waking he confesses his regret and describes the great pain he suffers, at which point his still-living beloved reveals himself.[70] The last anecdote narrated by the king in the *Elahi-nama* also features a kind of *chella*, but one drawn from the animal world. This short narrative explains the origins of musk, which it claims is produced by the musk deer when it abstains from eating for forty days and forty nights, contenting itself only with a few whiffs of pleasant flowers' scent. When this retreat is completed – *chella* is the Persian term used – the deer turns eastwards at dawn and inhales the morning air which mixes with its blood, producing musk at its navel. According to the subsequent homily, this transformation illustrates the power of spiritual alchemy: just as impure blood can be transformed into pure musk through that one inhalation (after forty days of ascetic preparation), so too can the clay of the body be transformed into pure soul through the light of God.[71]

These stories all demonstrate the transformative potential commonly associated with forty-day fasts, vigils and other forms of ascetic practice, and which was central to the spiritual work of the *Mosibat-nama*. Not only does the poem recount the *chella* undertaken by the wayfarer, but it also reduplicates the structures of ritual retreat in a textual form. As discussed in the previous section, 'Attar frames his readers' encounter with the text as an inward journey that, like the wayfarer's, precipitates a reunion with God. According to that same introductory passage, the readers' 'ascent' is also the performance of a 'retreat':

> Forty stages (*maqam*) will come before you,
> and they will also come within the self.
> When you have undertaken this retreat (*che[l]la*) on the way (*tariqat*),
> then reunion with truth (*haqiqat*) will come.[72]

'Attar here speaks directly to his audience, and the primary referent of 'this retreat' is not the setting of the wayfarer's journey, but the text itself: it is the metaphoric retreat through which readers can make their own turn towards the soul. This metaphor of book-as-*chella* is especially appropriate for the *Mosibat-nama*, not only because of its content, but because of its forty-fold, iterative structure. It consists of forty chapters that are all approximately the same length (around 150 distiches); the manuscript tradition labels each chapter with a number one through forty; and the opening line of each begins with the same formulaic phrase ('the wayfarer came . . .' [*salek amad* . . .]). Each chapter then follows the same pattern: the wayfarer encounters a cosmic interlocutor and begs for help, and after he is rebuffed by each in turn, the *pir* explains its significance and launches into a series of embedded stories and sermons. Like the *chella* that it depicts, the poem is thus composed of forty episodic units arranged in a strict sequential order, and by moving progressively through them from start to finish, readers can achieve 'reunion with truth', or so 'Attar suggests. The action narrated within the *Mosibat-nama* thus converges with the act of consuming the poem, and the wayfarer's retreat within the text is symbolically re-enacted by those who read it. It must be stressed that this conflation does not arise from narratorial illusion or the phenomenological immersivity characteristic of the modern novel. Rather, it results from formal, structural similarities between the text of the *Mosibat-nama* and the practice of ritual retreat, as well as Neoplatonic habits of thought in which analogical relationships point to deeper ontological connections. Just as the ritual *chella* involves a forty-day period of ascesis in the service of purifying the self, so too does the reader move through the forty chapters of the *Mosibat-nama* in the hopes of enacting spiritual reform and attaining an allegorical taste of proximity to God.

By framing the text as a *chella*, 'Attar calls attention to the act of reading as a durational, ritual activity; the sequential character of the poem is emphasised, as is the readers' movement through it. This sequentiality is further reinforced by the frame-tale, which organises the *Mosibat-nama*'s chapters into a strict hierarchy on the basis of the Neoplatonic path of descent and return, which is also mapped onto the sufi path. 'Attar's frame-tales, in addition to their other allegorical meanings, are accounts of spiritual wayfaring: the directional movement of the sufi towards God (or truth, *haqiqat*) along a path (*tariqat*) under the watchful eye of a spiritual guide. This path is composed of 'stages' (*maqam*), each one of which represents a specific virtue, psychological state or way of being. Although sufi theorists often disagree on the number of stages, their order and their specific meanings, there is almost unanimous agreement that they must be mastered sequentially.[73] Wayfarers must perfect each stage in turn before they can move on to the next. The seven valleys in the *Conference of the Birds* can easily be read as a set of sufi stages, and while many of the wayfarer's forty interlocutors cannot be so easily mapped onto specific virtues associated with mystical stations, his journey as whole represents the same kind of progressive, directional journey through a fixed hierarchy of discrete stopping points.[74] It is also carried out under the direction of a spiritual guide and ends – in so far as spiritual wayfaring can ever truly be said to end – with proximity to God. As was the case with the language of retreat, however, 'Attar applies the language of spiritual wayfaring in the above-quoted passage more directly to his imagined readers' progress through the text than to the wayfarer's journey through the heavens. 'Forty stages (*maqam*) will come before you,' he tells his audience, 'When you have undertaken this retreat (*che[l]la*) on the way (*tariqat*) / then reunion with truth (*haqiqat*) will come.' In addition to the performance of a metaphoric *chella*, an encounter with the *Mosibat-nama* is thus cast as a symbolic trodding of the sufi path, a progressive movement through forty stages towards reunion with God.

Premodern readers (and modern readers, for that matter) did not necessarily read the poem sequentially or completely – given the large numbers of anthologies and miscellanies that have been preserved, as well as the tendency towards parataxis, premodern Persian literary culture does not seem to have been overly attached to the idea of poems as inviolable, unitary works that must be consumed in their entirety. Nevertheless, with its progressive frame-tale and allegorical denouement, the *Mosibat-nama* lends itself to sequential reading in a way that other didactic *masnavis*, such as Sana'i's *Hadiqat al-hadiqa* and Rumi's *Masnavi-ye manavi*, do not. And by likening the poem to the sufi path and ritual retreat, 'Attar invites his readers to consume the forty-part text in its entirety as a vicarious ritual performance. Indeed, it is tempting to speculate that the *Mosibat-nama* might have even been read liturgically over the course of forty days, thereby mirroring the *chella* that it depicts. 'Attar advocates a similar practice of daily reading in his introduction to the *Tazkera*, where he quotes Yusof-e Hamadani's injunction that one ought to read eight pages of the saints' sayings every day in order to 'maintain spiritual health'.[75] He also adapts other sufi rituals into a textual form, as we have seen: the *Tazkera* is introduced as a collection of *verd*, or ritual invocations to be recited at specific hours, and the *Mokhtar-nama* was compiled as a storehouse of materials for *ta'ammol*, or sufi meditation.[76] It has been suggested that other forty-part texts, such as Nakhshabi's *Joz'iyat va Kolliyat*, may also have been designed for daily reading.[77] As tempting as this idea is, a lack of sources means it must remain in the realm of speculation. But no matter how the poem was historically consumed, its forty-fold structure still evokes the *chella* and the progressive nature of the sufi path, while its frame-tale endows its teachings with a clear sequential order. Whether consumed in its entirety over the course of forty days, or partially over a different period of time, readers are invited to approach the text as an organised regimen and to experience the act of reading as durational, disciplined activity aimed at spiritual transformation.

According to most authorities, the Prophet Muhammad made a *bodily* ascent to Heaven, while the sufi saints who followed him were limited to *spiritual* ones. In 'Attar's time, adepts in the Kobravi and Sohravardi orders might also have been subject to visionary experiences during ritual retreats that would have been interpreted through the paradigm of ascent. The *Mosibat-nama*, which 'Attar describes as 'a beautiful book for the elites (*khas[s]*) and the masses (*'am[m]*)', allows an even wider audience to undertake an *allegorical* ascent.[78] This might seem less dramatic than a bodily journey or visionary unveiling, but for 'Attar and his contemporaries it granted a mode of real, ontological access to higher entities nonetheless. In poems like the *Mosibat-nama*, specialised sufi rituals and rarified spiritual experiences were not only recounted in a stylised fashion, but transmuted into literary, textual forms that could be enacted by their readers: even those who would never perform the forty-day ritual retreat could make an analogous movement through the textual *chella* of the *Mosibat-nama* and thereby symbolically recover a pre-eternal proximity to God. Its allegorical frame-tale, however, is only part of the story. The frame-tale arranges the text into a hierarchy that maps onto the sufi way and the path of Neoplatonic return, but it is the embedded anecdotes and homilies that convey the poem's positive teachings at each 'stage' and do the hard work of prodding readers to move forward on the path, one step at a time. It is to these anecdotes – which, along with their accompanying homilies, form the engine of 'Attar's didacticism – that we now turn.

Notes

1. On 'Attar's attitudes towards philosophy, see 'Attar, *Mosibat-nama*, 156–7; Pourjavady, 'Naqd-e falsafi'; Taqi Purnamdarian, "Aql va falsafa az

nazargah-e 'Attar', in *Didar ba simorgh* (Tehran: Pazhuheshgah-e 'Olum-e Ensani va Motala'at-e Farhangi, 1374 [1995–6]). On allegory and Neoplatonism, see Peter T. Struck, 'Allegory and Ascent in Neoplatonism', in *The Cambridge Companion to Allegory*, ed. Rita Copeland and Peter T. Struck (Cambridge: Cambridge University Press, 2010).

2. See, inter alia, Jamal Elias, *Aisha's Cushion: Religious Art, Perception, and Practice in Islam* (Cambridge, MA: Harvard University Press, 2012), 198–235; Aaron W. Hughes, 'Imagining the Divine: Ghazali on Imagination, Dreams, and Dreaming', *Journal of the American Academy of Religion* 70, no. 1 (2002): 33–53; Fazlur Rahman, *Prophecy in Islam: Philosophy and Orthodoxy* (London: Allen & Unwin, 1958).
3. J. Stephen Russell, introduction to *Allegoresis: The Craft of Allegory in Medieval Literature*, ed. J. Stephen Russell (New York: Garland Publishing, 1988), xi.
4. Michael Chase, 'Some Observations on Pierre Hadot's Conception of Philosophy as a Way of Life', in *Philosophy as a Way of Life: Ancients and Moderns (Essays in Honor of Pierre Hadot)*, ed. Michael Chase et al. (Chichester: Wiley Blackwell, 2013), 283n3.
5. Rita Copland and Peter T. Struck, 'Introduction', in *The Cambridge Companion to Allegory*, ed. Rita Copland and Peter T. Struck (Cambridge: Cambridge University Press, 2010), 2.
6. Northrop Frye, 'Allegory', in *Princeton Encyclopaedia of Poetry and Poetics*, ed. Alex Preminger et al., enlarged ed. (London: Macmillan, 1974), 12.
7. Aaron W. Hughes, *The Texture of the Divine: Imagination in Medieval Islamic and Jewish Thought* (Bloomington: Indiana University Press, 2004), 37; Peter Heath, *Allegory and Philosophy in Avicenna (Ibn Sînâ): With a Translation of the Book of the Prophet Muhammad's Ascent to Heaven* (Philadelphia: University of Pennsylvania Press, 1992), 6–7.
8. 'Attar, *Divan-e 'Attar*, 109.
9. On the *mashal*, see David Stern, *Parables in Midrash* (Cambridge, MA: Harvard University Press, 1991).
10. 'Attar, *Mosibat-nama*, 236.
11. 'Attar, *Manteq al-tayr*, 425.
12. A similar distinction is frequently made in a certain strand of New Testament scholarship, in which terms like 'illustration', 'example' and 'allegory' are used for stories that illustrate some separable content, whereas 'metaphor' is valorised as a narrative whose more abstract teaching cannot be so easily detached from its specific literary enunciation. The heuristic is useful as long as it is not

allowed to resolve into too stark a binary or to smuggle in value judgements or metaphysical assumptions, as in the older Romantic denigration of mechanistic 'allegory' as opposed to the allegedly more organic and mysterious 'symbol'. See William Kirkwood, 'Parables as Metaphors and Examples', *Quarterly Journal of Speech* 71 (1985): 422–40; John Dominic Crossan, *In Parables: The Challenge of the Historical Jesus* (New York: Harper & Row, 1973), 6–22; Paul Ricoeur, 'Listening to the Parables of Jesus', *Criterion* 13 (1974): 18–22.

13. On the performative use of apophatic language, see especially Sells, *Mystical Languages of Unsaying*, 1–13.
14. 'Attar, *Manteq al-tayr*, 428, 435.
15. 'Attar, *Manteq al-tayr*, 428.
16. 'Attar, *Manteq al-tayr*, 429–35.
17. Davis, 'Journey as Paradigm', 179–81.
18. Abu Hamid Ghazali, *Mishkat al-anwar*, ed. Abu'l-'Ala 'Afifi (Cairo: al-Dar al-Qawmiyya li'l-Tiba'a wa'l-Nashr, 1964), 65–6. See also the translation by David Buchman, Abu Hamid Ghazali, *The Niche of Lights: A Parallel English-Arabic Text*, ed. and trans. David Buchman (Provo: Brigham Young University Press, 1998).
19. Ghazali, *Mishkat al-anwar*, 65.
20. Ghazali, *Mishkat al-anwar*, 67.
21. Ghazali, *Mishkat al-anwar*, 67, 69; Hughes, 'Imagining the Divine', 42–3.
22. See pp. 43–4. See also the parable of the Simorgh's feather (*Manteq al-tayr*, 265), discussed in O'Malley, 'Poetry and Pedagogy', 140–8.
23. 'Attar, *Manteq al-tayr*, 281–2.
24. 'Attar, *Manteq al-tayr*, 282.
25. Ghazali suggests that God himself cannot be made the subject of a similitude, but his attributes can. Ghazali, *Mishkat al-anwar*, 68; Hughes, 'Imagining the Divine', 42–3.
26. On Ibn Sina's allegories, see Corbin, *Visionary Recital*; Heath, *Allegory and Philosophy*; Zargar, *Polished Mirror*, 53–77; Hughes, *Texture of the Divine*.
27. On these, see De Bruijn, *Piety and Poetry*, 200–18; Nasrollah Pourjavady, introduction to *Rahiq al-tahqiq be enzemam-e ash'ar-e digar-e u,* by Fakhr al-Din Mobarak-Shah Marvrudi (Tehran: Markez-e Nashr-e Daneshgahi, 1381 [2002]), 13–56; Bo Utas, 'A Journey to the Other World according to the *Lantern of Spirits*', *Bulletin of the Asia Institute*, n.s., 4 (1990): 307–11.
28. 'Attar, *Mosibat-nama*, 160.
29. That the wayfarer encounters seven prophets is noteworthy in light of Landolt's

suggestion that 'Attar was connected to the Isma'ilis, who divided cosmic history into seven prophetic cycles. Most Isma'ilis, however, would not have included David as a 'speaking imam' at the head of one of those cycles. Instead, they would have looked forward to the coming of the Lord of the Resurrection (*qa'im al-qiyamat*) as the inaugurator of the seventh cycle at the end of time.

30. These five inner faculties recall the five 'human spirits' identified by Ghazali in the *Mishkat*: sensing, imagination, intellect, reflection and finally the prophetic spirit (76–7). In their number they also recall the five interior senses of Ibn Sina, although the latter have a more precisely defined role in his technical psychological system and are all ostensibly pre-rational in their activity.
31. 'Attar, *Mosibat-nama*, 398.
32. Sometimes this higher soul (as opposed to the carnal self, or *nafs*) is referred to as the *ruh*, sometimes as *jan* – sometimes even as *del* (heart). 'Attar is not particularly consistent with his terminology. Feuillebois-Pierunek, 'Mystical Quest and Oneness', 311–12.
33. 'Attar, *Mosibat-nama*, 438.
34. 'Attar, *Mosibat-nama*, 440.
35. 'Attar, *Mosibat-nama*, 446.
36. The distinction between the 'journey to God' and the 'journey in God' is also found in Kobravi sources. This is another indication of 'Attar's familiarity with Kobravi sufi discourse even if he does not seem to be formally connected to any known Kobravi teachers (Landolt, "Aṭṭār, Sufism, and Ismailism', 10).
37. 'Attar, *Mosibat-nama*, 158.
38. Nasrollah Pourjavady, *Zaban-e hal dar 'erfan va adabiyat-e parsi* (Tehran: Hermes, 1385 [2006–7]), 25–38.
39. Pourjavady, *Zaban-e hal*, 27–9.
40. 'Attar, *Tazkerat al-owleya*, 148–9; Pourjavady, *Zaban-e hal*, 28, 127–30, 339–49.
41. Pourjavady, *Zaban-e hal*, 129–30.
42. On the *me'raj* in sufism, see A. E. Affifi, 'The Story of the Prophet's Ascent (*Mi'rāj*) in Sufi Thought and Literature', *Islamic Quarterly: A Review of Islamic Culture* 2 (1955): 23–7; Nazeer al-Azma, 'Some Notes on the Impact of the Story of the *Mi'rāj* on Sufi Literature', *The Muslim World* 63, no. 2 (1973): 93–104. Regarding the development of the *me'raj* narrative and its later elaborations, see Christiane J. Gruber and Frederick Stephen Colby, eds., *The Prophet's Ascension: Cross-cultural Encounters with the Islamic* Mi'rāj *Tales* (Bloomington: Indiana University Press, 2010); Christiane J. Gruber, *The Ilkhanid Book of Ascension: A Persian-Sunni Prayer Manual* (New York: I. B. Tauris, 2010); Brooke Olson

Vuckovic, *Heavenly Journeys, Earthly Concerns: The Legacy of the* Miʿrāj *in the Formation of Islam* (New York: Routledge, 2005); David J. Halperin, '*Hekhalot* and *Miʿrāj*: Observations on the Heavenly Journey in Judaism and Islam', in *Death, Ecstasy, and Other Worldly Journeys*, ed. John J. Collins and Michael Fishbane (Albany, NY: SUNY Press, 1995).

43. The *locus classicus* for the bodily nature of the Prophet's journey versus the spiritual nature of the saints' is Hojviri, *Kashf al-mahjub*, 355. Some others claim, however, on the basis of a hadith from 'A'isha, that the Prophet's ascent was made only in spirit. Vuckovic, *Heavenly Journeys*, 79.
44. 'Attar, *Mosibat-nama*, 160.
45. 'Attar, *Mosibat-nama*, 402.
46. 'Attar, *Mosibat-nama*, 398.
47. Peter T. Struck, *Birth of the Symbol: Ancient Readers at the Limits of Their Texts* (Princeton: Princeton University Press, 2004), 228–53; Struck, 'Allegory and Ascent in Neoplatonism', 68.
48. Hughes, *Texture of the Divine*, 102–3.
49. Corbin, *Visionary Recital*, 28–35 (emphasis in original).
50. 'Attar, *Mosibat-nama*, 157.
51. On how the imagination clothes dreams, visions and prophetic revelation in sensible form, see Hughes, 'Imagining the Divine'; Rahman, *Prophecy in Islam*; Elias, *Aisha's Cushion*, 198–253. On visions and dream interpretation more broadly, see Marcia Hermansen, 'Dreams and Dreaming in Islam', in *Dreams: A Reader on Religious, Cultural, and Psychological Dimensions of Dreaming*, ed. Kelly Bulkeley (New York: Palgrave, 2002); Nile Green, 'The Religious and Cultural Roles of Dreams and Visions in Islam', *Journal of the Royal Asiatic Society* 13, no. 3 (2003): 287–313; Toufy Fahd, 'The Dream in Medieval Islamic Society', in *The Dream and Human Societies*, ed. G. E. von Grunebaum and Roger Caillois (Berkeley: University of California Press, 1966); Henry Corbin, 'The Visionary Dream in Islamic Spirituality', in *The Dream and Human Societies*, ed. G. E. von Grunebaum and Roger Caillois (Berkeley: University of California Press, 1966); Fazlur Rahman, 'Dream, Imagination, and *ʿĀlam al-mithāl*', in *The Dream and Human Societies*, ed. G. E. von Grunebaum and Roger Caillois (Berkeley: University of California Press, 1966).
52. Struck, 'Allegory and Ascent in Neoplatonism', 63–4.
53. Ibn Sina, *Traités mystiques d'Abou Alî al-Hosain b. Abdallah b. Sînâ ou d'Avicenne* (Leiden: Brill, 1889–91), 2:47–8.
54. Heath, *Allegory and Philosophy*, 125.

55. Sohravardi, *Mosannafat*, 3:209–10.
56. Utas, 'Journey to the Other World', 307.
57. 'Attar, *Mosibat-nama*, 158.
58. Drory, *Models and Contacts*, 11–47; Michael Cooperson, 'Probability, Plausibility, and "Spiritual Communication" in Classical Arabic Biography', in *On Fiction and* Adab *in Medieval Arabic Literature*, ed. Phillip F. Kennedy (Wiesbaden: Harrassowitz, 2005); Utas, 'Classical Persian Literature'.
59. On the number forty, see Schimmel and Endres, *The Mystery of Numbers*, 245–53. Normative accounts of retreat are preserved in Muhammad Isa Waley, "Aziz al-Din Nasafi on Spiritual Retreat', *Sufi* 17 (1993): 5–9; Daya, *Mersad al-'ebad*, 275–88; Abu Hafs 'Umar Suhrawardi, *'Awarif al-ma'arif* (Beirut: Dar al-Kitab al-'Arabi, 1983), 207–27; Gerhard Böwering, 'Kubra's Treatise on Spiritual Retreat, *Risāla fi'l-khalwa*', *Al-Abḥāth* 54 (2006): 7–34. See also Ohlander, *Sufism in an Age of Transition*, 220–2; Hamid Algar, '*Čella*. ii. In Sufism', in *Encyclopaedia Iranica*, posted 2020, https://doi.org/10.1163/2330-4804_EIRO_COM_7624.
60. Daya, *Mersad al-'ebad*, 283–4.
61. Daya, *Mersad al-'ebad*, 296.
62. Muhyi al-Din b. 'Arabi, *Risalat al-anwar*, ed. 'Abd al-Rahim Mardini (Damascus: Dar al-Mahabba, 2003). See also J. W. Morris, 'The Spiritual Ascension: Ibn 'Arabī and the *Mi'rāj*: Part 1', *Journal of the American Oriental Society* 107, no. 4 (1987): 629–52; J. W. Morris, 'The Spiritual Ascension: Ibn 'Arabī and the *Mi'rāj*: Part 2', *Journal of the American Oriental Society* 108, no. 1 (1988): 63–77.
63. Waley, "Aziz al-Din Nasafi on Spiritual Retreat', 9.
64. Daya, *Mersad al-'ebad*, 294–5.
65. Daya, *Mersad al-'ebad*, 231–2, 294–6; Suhrawardi, *'Awarif al-ma'arif*, 217; Jamal Elias, *The Throne Carrier of God: The Life and Thought of 'Alā' al-Dawla as-Simnānī* (Albany, NY: SUNY Press, 1995), 137; Waley, "Aziz al-Din Nasafi on Spiritual Retreat', 7.
66. 'Attar, *Mosibat-nama*, 159.
67. The term 'acquired' (*mostafad*) in the above quotation is especially interesting in this context. In Ibn Sina's psychology, the acquired intellect (*al-'aql al-mustafad*) refers to the state of a rational soul when it is actively engaged in intellection and unified with the Active Intellect, from which it acquires universals. 'Attar, by contrast, valorises thought that is 'acquired' through the practice of *zekr*, not ratiocination.

68. ʿAttar, *Mosibat-nama*, 158.
69. ʿAttar, *Manteq al-tayr*, 298.
70. ʿAttar, *Manteq al-tayr*, 433.
71. ʿAttar, *Elahi-nama*, 396–7.
72. ʿAttar, *Mosibat-nama*, 157.
73. See, for example, Hojviri, *Kashf al-mahjub*, 274.
74. Bürgel, ʿRepetitive Structures in ʿAṭṭārʾ, 200–1.
75. ʿAttar, *Tazkerat al-owleya*, 7.
76. ʿAttar, *Tazkerat al-owleya*, 7; ʿAttar, *Mokhtar-nama*, 71. See pp. 75–80 and 106–7.
77. Scott Kugel, *Sufis and Saints' Bodies: Mysticism, Corporeality, and Sacred Power in Islam* (Chapel Hill: University of North Carolina Press, 2007), 28.
78. ʿAttar, *Mosibat-nama*, 159.

7

Anecdotal Disruptions

An undercurrent of transgression ran (and continues to run) throughout the sufi tradition, even after it became a dominant, 'mainstream' form of piety over vast swaths of Islamic lands from the twelfth century onwards. Only a small minority of sufis directly engaged in antinomian behaviour, and most saw their piety as the culmination of 'orthodox' Islam. Still, even most 'sober' sufis who would never dream of violating the dictates of the religious law showed an affinity for discourse that inverts, destabilises or reinterprets religious valuations in counter-intuitive and seemingly radical ways to uncover higher forms of religiousity. This penchant for disruption is clearly visible in ʿAttar, who routinely subverts the religious expectations of what he casts as a rote, insincere Islam within the discursive world of his texts. For example, following Ahmad Ghazali and Hallaj, ʿAttar recasts the rebellious Satan – who refused to bow down before Adam as God commanded him – as an uncompromising monotheist and sincere lover of God.[1] ʿAttar was also a major practitioner of the *qalandariat* genre, in which the religious valences attached conventional signs of piety and impiety are inverted: the sufi cloak thus becomes a symbol of hypocrisy, while wine-drinking, gambling and the Christian cincture are celebrated as markers of a sincere religiosity beyond exoteric Islam.[2] The *qalandariyat*'s ethos of transgression is famously captured in one of ʿAttar's longest tales, that of Shaykh Sanʿan, in which the eponymous shaykh, an accomplished religious scholar, travels from Mecca to Byzantium after a disturbing dream. There he falls in love with a Christian girl, converts to Christianity and commits a variety of outrages against Islamic norms in the hopes of winning her affection. By the end of the story, Sanʿan converts back to Islam, but now that his faith has been refined in the crucible of love, it is purified from the dross of insincerity and self-attachment that had previously contaminated it.

'Attar's shorter anecdotes also participate in this transgressive ethos, and their conceptual inversions are frequently expressed through a specific narrative structure. As the anecdotes unfold, they seem to invite certain interpretive judgements only to suddenly subvert them and reframe the prior action's religious significance in dramatic ways.[3] To give but one example, the *Mosibat-nama* contains an anecdote about a Hindu 'travelled in the station of love', which, coming from 'Attar, would seem to point to a high spiritual state.[4] This Hindu encounters a group of pilgrims making the hajj, and when he learns they are off to 'God's house' he excitedly joins them, resolving to perform the pilgrimage in the fashion of a lover (*'asheq*). When he arrives at the Ka'ba, however, he is shocked to find it empty, and he asks the attendants where God is – why isn't he in his house? This would seem to be rank anthropomorphism, expected from a stereotyped Hindu but hardly appropriate for a Muslim, and he is rebuked by the attendants for his foolishness. The Hindu's subsequent despair, however, shows that his anthropomorphic misunderstanding is not incompatible with his status as a lover of God, but actually an expression of it: 'What good is his house without him!?' he exclaims, recalling the Arabic proverb beloved of sufis, *First the neighbour, then the house*. 'Either return me to my own home,' he continues, 'or give me the Lord of this house!' The Hindu is thus made a model for Muslim readers despite – or rather because of – his anthropomorphism, through which he performs his single-minded focus on God. This is a common pattern repeated throughout the *masnavi*s: puzzling, irreligious or foolish action is abruptly reframed in a way that not only renders it comprehensible but implies an inversion, redefinition or radical amplification of established religious values and concepts.

Through these sudden cognitive reframings, 'Attar explores the danger of rote religiosity and the transgressive demands of sincere religious practice. These themes are baked into a significant plurality – or even the majority – of his anecdotes through their shared narrative structure, and they thus serve as meta-themes in the *masnavi*s, overlaying the many other topics that they treat. 'Attar's anecdotes, as should be evident by now, illustrate a wide array of subjects: the dangers of the carnal soul, the love of material possessions, the inevitability of death, the transformative power of love, the nature of effacement (*fana'*), and so on. But no matter what an anecdote's primary message might be, 'Attar tends to illustrate it through narrative structures that invert or destabilise expectations. The story of the Hindu on the Hajj, for example, is part of a broader discussion of the virtue of *talab* (desirous seeking), but by making an infidel anthropomorphist an unexpected exemplar of this spiritual virtue, ʿAttar simultaneously raises a broader set of questions about sincerity and the ossification of religious praxis.

The present chapter shows how these conceptual reframings are calibrated to implicate readers as practitioners of a conventional, unthinking and ultimately insufficient Islam, and how they are thereby called to make a decisive turn to piety. It first examines the stasis–destabilisation–resolution pattern that structures these anecdotes, paying special attention to how sudden events abruptly reframe the prior narrated action. While the pious principles that ʿAttar illustrates in this way are not unique to him, and most readers would already be familiar with them to some extent, they are emplotted within the anecdotes as radical challenges to the status quo. To illustrate this in more detail, the second section delves into the *Conference of the Birds*' treatment of spiritual manliness, a central spiritual virtue that involves shades of generosity, sincerity, selflessness and single-minded commitment. These themes would not be new to readers with even a passing familiarity with Persian literary sufism – and ʿAttar himself treats them multiple times in his works – but over the course of the hoopoe's discourse on manliness, they are repeatedly illustrated as unexpected inversions of an imagined conventional Islam. Religious principles, such a structure suggests, can never be taken for granted, and religiosity is liable to stagnate and ossify if it is not periodically re-endowed with disruptive force. The chapter's third section then examines the humour found in many of these narrative reversals, which, structurally speaking, have much in common with a good joke. This is especially evident in ʿAttar's anecdotes of wise-fools, whose infelicitous reasoning and foolish utterances convey a hidden wisdom. In ʿAttar's hands, their humour serves didactic aims: by twisting language and logic, they defamiliarise religious assumptions and prompt a drastic reassessment of where 'wisdom' and 'insanity' actually lie.

As discussed in Chapter 1, ʿAttar's homilies imply a specific rhetorical relationship in which the poet's persona plays the part of teacher while the reader or listener is invited to adopt the positionality of a student at his feet. But, as we shall, the anecdotes also encode a version of this particular subject position through their very structure: they invite the audience to adopt seemingly conventional understandings and attitudes towards the narrated action, only to pull the rug out from under them with sudden reversals that reveal the insufficiency of those positions. Readers are thus thrust into the role of spiritual novices whose superficial understandings of piety must be disrupted, clearing a space for them to make a decisive turn to God again and again with each iteration of this pattern. While the frame-tales imply a progression towards God through an incremental series of ordered mystical stations, the anecdotes within them encourage a practice of continuous conversion: readers are repeatedly invited to make another definitive turn towards the sincere practice of Islam, stepping out onto the mystical path again, as if for the first time.

Sucker Punches, Donkey Farts and Other Unexpected Events

The sudden cognitive reframings of which ʿAttar was so fond are produced through a tripartite narrative pattern that, if not understood in too schematic a fashion, can be discerned in a large proportion of his narratives. It begins with a stasis, a recognised scene from daily life or literary discourse such as a study session in a mosque, a transaction in the bazaar or a drinking bout in a tavern, and which is usually associated with a specific set of conventional religious judgements and assessments, whether positive or negative. This scene, and the expected activities taking place within it, are then destabilised by an unexpected event that intrudes on the narrative. Sometimes this destabilisation is loosely foreshadowed, while other times it is completely unforeseen, but in either case it disrupts the stasis on both a narrative and cognitive level: the previous action cannot continue as it was, and prior understandings of the situation suggested by the narrative are no longer tenable either. In most of ʿAttar's anecdotes, the destabilisation is then resolved with an explanation that reinterprets the prior action and its religious significance, often in a way that is diametrically opposed to the original stasis.

A typical example of this narrative pattern, taken from the *Conference of the Birds*, features one Shaykh Abu Bakr Nayshaburi. Although we cannot identify this individual with any certainty, Shafiʿi-Kadkani suggests that ʿAttar refers here to Abu Bakr b. Hayyan Nayshaburi, one of the companions of Abu ʿUthman al-Hiri.[5] But whoever the historical referent of this character may be, he is portrayed as a successful spiritual leader and marked by the conventional trappings of the office:

Shaykh Abu Bakr Nayshaburi set out
from his *khanaqah*, accompanied with his followers (*moridan*).
He was mounted on his donkey, among his disciples (*ashabona*) . . .[6]

In these short opening lines, ʿAttar constructs a tableau of an august shaykh leaving his sufi lodge surrounded by his followers and disciples (*ashabona*). The latter term, borrowed from Arabic, includes a first-person plural possessive suffix and thus literally means 'our companions', but it is sometimes used in Persian as a simple noun. The use of an Arabism here – and one that includes a redundant, unnecessary grammatical structure at that – might also give a whiff of the shaykh's pretension, which will be revealed at the end of the anecdote. At this point, however, Abu Bakr appears to be a respected teacher much like any number of spiritual heroes whose feats are celebrated throughout the *masnavi*s, and he has the followers and lodge to prove it.

This initial stasis, however, is suddenly disrupted. Without warning, the shaykh's donkey lets lose a giant fart, the epitome of the unexpected (and unwelcome) event. The narration thus humorously descends from its description of the shaykh's procession to the mundane, bodily workings of his mount. Equally incongruous is the shaykh's reaction his donkey's flatus. He cries out, rends his garments and falls into a violent ecstatic state (*halat*) that might be expected at a *sama*ʿ session but hardly seems an appropriate response to this particular incident. Bouts of ecstasy were fraught performances, and sufis who engaged in such practices generally found it best to do so behind closed doors and not in public view. The shaykh's disciples are thus quite naturally puzzled and embarrassed: 'no one', writes ʿAttar, 'was pleased by this, not from among his disciples, nor among the others who saw it.'[7] That this particular bout of ecstasy was brought on by donkey flatulence renders it all the more strange and potentially damaging to the shaykh's reputation (and that of his followers). 'What', one observer asks with disbelief, 'could be here that would bring about such a state?' The observer's question gives voice to his companions' discomfort as well as the readers' confusion. Indeed, how are we to explain – and thereby resolve – this unexpected turn of events?

In response, the shaykh confesses that he had been vainly thinking of his great numbers of disciples clogging the road, such that he had even dared to compare himself to the great Bayazid Bestami. He had been further fantasising that tomorrow on the plain of resurrection he would be welcomed with great fanfare, just as he was then surrounded by devoted disciples, when the donkey suddenly broke wind. Understanding this as a divine rebuke of his spiritual vanity, he immediately fell into ecstatic lamentation. If those present think worse of him because of this odd ecstatic performance, so much the better, since his pride in people's recognition of his station was one of the failings that brought about this humorous rebuke in the first place. He sums up the lesson for his companions thusly: 'Whoever boasts falsely like this / The donkey gives him the answer; how much of this foolish posing?!' The symbols of spiritual authority with which the narrative had opened are now reframed as dangerous sources of pride that had nearly driven the shaykh off the path of piety had it not been for the fortuitous intervention of the donkey's fart.

Variations on this narrative pattern infuse the *masnavi*s. Sudden, unexpected and frequently humorous destabilisations provoke 'moments of awareness' in which the narrated situation is cast in an entirely new light.[8] It is not only characters in the anecdotes who are subject to these moments, but also 'Attar's audience, who must revise their previous understanding of the narrated situation. For example, in the *Asrar-nama*, a gambling Jew is revealed as a surprise exemplar of religious commitment. Through this sudden reversal, 'Attar shames Muslim readers while challenging them to do better:

I heard from a spiritual authority
    that a Jew once went into a tavern.
In a ruined corner of that wine house,
    the ruffians (*rendan*) had made their gambling den.
Two of them set to gambling
    and had filled their skirts with silver and gold.
The Jew came to gamble, and, all at once,
    lost all the dinars he had.
He had a garden and a home and lost both
    He didn't have anything left; he braced himself for poverty.
Since his hands were empty of gold and silver,
    in a moment, he gambled and lost an eye.
He had been stripped of all he had,
    so he staked an eye and became blind.

They said to him: 'Now that you are so deprived,
become a Muslim, and gamble away your faith.'
When the Jew heard this, lacking religion and full of anger,
he punched that Muslim right in the face,
saying: 'Do whatever ever you want,
but don't speak a word to me about my religion!'[9]

Gambling, of course, is legally prohibited for Muslims, so the Jew's gambling is emblematic of his distance from the true faith. The stakes he plays for become progressively more and more extreme – he gambles away his money, then his home and garden, before finally losing his eye to the dice. The stasis constructed here seems to be one of the Jew's depravity, at least in the eyes of Islamic legal norms. At the same time, gambling – in particular 'going all in' or 'staking it all' (*pak-bazi*) – can sometimes be construed as a spiritual virtue, especially in the context of the transgressive *qalandariyat*. This anecdote contains several terms associated with the *qalandariyat*, but the Jew himself does not present as a *qalandar* figure, who are usually lapsed Muslims who have renounced the hypocrisy of their prior religious practice. The Jew's gambling seems to be motivated more by foolishness, but it does end up proving his commitment in an unexpected manner. After forfeiting all his material goods and even a piece of his own body, he refuses to relinquish his Jewish faith, and he punches his Muslim interlocutor in the face at the very suggestion. Much like the donkey's fart, the punch seems to come out of nowhere, and it puts a surprising end to the narrative pattern of the Jew's increasingly extreme bets and losses. This sudden physical impact within the narrative precipitates an equally sudden cognitive shift: it demands that readers and listeners now revise their understanding of the Jew and his actions. His gambling had previously seemed to signal his impious distance from Islam – and it still does – but now it also proves the surprising strength of his religious commitment. Indeed, the more the Jew gambled – the more he sinned, in Mulism eyes – the more impressive his ultimate refusal to stake his Judaism turns out to be.

The elevation of the Jew to an exemplar of religious commitment implies a parallel indictment of 'Attar's addressee (assumed to be Muslim), who is now called on to learn a thing or two from this debauched non-Muslim. 'Attar makes this explicit in the subsequent interpretive homily, where he explains that if a Jew could behave like this, then the standard for Muslims must be unimaginably higher:

> When a Jew is like this in his Jewishness,
> I can only guess how the people of religion should be!
> He lost everything, up to his eye
> but never swerved in his religion.[10]

Muslim readers find the initial dismissal of the Jew as an irreligious gambler has boomeranged back onto them, an indictment of their lack commitment to the religion of Muhammad. The anecdote thereby inverts the assumed religious hierarchy of Jew and Muslim, and readers are invited to 'right' that inversion outside of the text by holding themselves to higher standards as is fitting of followers of the true faith.

Although the addressee is first criticised for falling short of the Jew, 'Attar soon shifts grears and draws an unexpected parallel between them. He accuses the former of wasting their life like the Jew in a gambling house – not just any gambling house, but the metaphorical gambling house of the world:

> O you who, in the gambling house of the world,
> have staked everything in just this way,
> once you lost your moon-like face,
> another time you lost your black locks.
> You lost your youth, and that arrow-like stature
> You have lost it all on this path and become old.
> Your illuminated heart and your bright eye
> were lost in ignorance in a corner of this rubbish-heap . . .
> Since the time has come, O man of delusions,
> turn away from this alley of ruins.[11]

The addressee has staked their youth and life in the pursuit of worldly pleasures, a frivolous enterprise in which the house always wins. But now that their moon-face and black locks have been lost, might not they, like the Jew, demonstrate their commitment? 'Attar thus ends with a hopeful call – perhaps the time has come to leave this gambling house altogether, and sever their entanglements with the world.

This is not the only anecdote in ʿAttar's oeuvre that features non-Muslims and other seemingly impious characters as spiritual exemplars. In one, a Zoroastrian who had built a bridge as a work of charity refuses to sell it to Sultan Mahmud and thereby give up his heavenly reward; he throws himself into the river rather than submit.[12] In another, a group of idolators immolate themselves, exemplifying sincere sacrifice on love's path.[13] We have already encountered the story of the Hindu on the Hajj. Other examples involve not religious minorities, but Muslims who would be judged as impious in other contexts, such as thieves and catamites. In one memorable anecdote, a 'catamite' (*mokhannas*) captured by the Byzantines proves more 'manly' than his two fellow prisoners, an ʿAlid and a *faqih*. Unlike them, he chooses death rather than convert to Christianity.[14]

Such anecdotes promote a weak form of tolerance: spiritual wisdom can be found in even unexpected places, so one must not judge non-Muslims or seemingly impious folk too harshly. At the same time, their didactic force derives from the fact that these inversions represent deviations from a normative state of Muslim religious superiority. The anecdote of the gambling Jew does not show Jews on the same level as Muslims. On the contrary, the religious inferiority of Jews is assumed, and if this particular Jew happened to display unexpected religious commitment, that ought to be a source of Muslims' shame. The anecdote inverts expected religious hierarchies not as a proclamation of equality, but as a didactic tool to motivate a recommitment to sufi Islam for an imagined Muslim readership for whom the unfavourable comparison to a Jew is assumed to sting.

Challenging to the Status Quo

In the above examples, the anecdotes were considered individually in isolation from their surroundings in the text. This is a legitimate approach that has been shared by many, both in the modern and premodern periods. As short narratives, the anecdotes are self-contained units that can be quite easily lifted out of the larger discursive structures in which they find themselves. Most anecdote-homily pairs are set off with independent titles in the manuscript tradition, which only encourages this feeling of separability. It seems safe to assume that premodern readers would frequently memorise anecdotes that interested them, summarising or quoting them as the situation permitted and deploying them as heuristic guide-posts for navigating life. They could also be adapted and creatively retold in new contexts: indeed, a number of anecdotes that appear first in ʿAttar or Sanaʾi and then later in different forms in Rumi or Jami were likely born of just such a process. Modern scholars, too, frequently analyse single anecdotes or a narrow range of anecdotes that speak directly to their research interests, although search engines, tables of contents and indexes have made this work much less reliant on memory than it was in the past.

At the same time, despite their modularity, ʿAttar's anecdotes also make meaning together as nodes in a wider 'network of inter-signification', as discussed in Chapter 1.[15] More specifically, they are clustered in thematic chapters in which each anecdote illustrates a particular aspect of the theme at hand, and where they are bound together with paratactic, homiletic transitions that expound and amplify their teachings. Because most readers will consume ʿAttar's *mansavi*s in line with these larger structures, they will be aware of the primary theme that any given anecdote will likely treat long before they read its first verse. The story of Abu Bakr Nayshburi and the Donkey's Fart, for example, is narrated by the hoopoe as part of his rebuke of a bird who believes that it has reached spiritual perfection, so the moral point of its climactic reversal – in which the trappings of the shaykh's spiritual authority are revealed to be dangerous sources of conceit – is not unanticipated. And even if a particular anecdote's moral point were not already hinted at by prior narratives or homiletic commentary, they generally illustrate well-known religious precepts that should be familiar to most readers. Nevertheless, these moral injunctions – despite their familiarity – are narrativised within the anecdotes as decisive breaks with the status quo. Even though the danger of spiritual conceit is a conventional topic in Persian literary sufism, it is illustrated within the Abu Bakr narrative as a surprise revelation that provokes a puzzling, ecstatic response that must be explained and which threatens to undermine the conventional signs of spiritual rank. Within each anecdote, well-worn principles of mystical piety are emplotted as unexpected challenges to ossified religiosity, and each chapter becomes a series of reversals in which its central theme is repeatedly defamiliarised and invested transgressive potential.

To examine this dynamic in more detail, let us turn to the *Conference of the Birds*' chapter on 'spiritual manliness' (*mardi*), a crucial concept for ʿAttar that combines notions of humility, altruism, generosity, sincerity and constancy.[16] It harkens back to the *fotovvat/javanmardi* ethics of the bazaar that was associated with the Malamatiya in Khorasan and later incorporated into sufism more broadly, and it also reflects a cultural habit of gendering spiritual success as male.[17] Like most thematic chapters in the *Conference of the Birds*, it begins when one of the birds poses a question: in this case, one of them confesses his inconstancy and 'effeminacy' (*mokhannas gowhari*) in spiritual matters. For ʿAttar and his contemporaries, a *mokhannas* was a mature male who allowed himself to be sexually penetrated by another man and thus occupied an unstable category between man and woman. As a spiritual *mokhannas*, this particular bird vacillates between sin and piety, 'flitting from branch to branch' and unable to consistently devote himself to the path. In response, the hoopoe reassures this bird that even if his carnal soul leads him astray from time to time, he can, with effort, develop a single-minded focus on God. He then launches into a series of three anecdotes that illustrate different facets of manliness – from humility and submission to love and single-minded devotion. These would not have been unfamiliar notions for ʿAttar's audience, and he invokes and elaborates on them in homiletic lines throughout section. Within the anecdotes themselves, however, he illustrates them as unexpected disruptions to the conventional spirituality that the reader is imagined to practice.

The first story centres on Shebli, a sufi hero who figures prominently in ʿAttar's oeuvre and was well known for his ecstatic utterances and odd antics.[18] One day Shebli disappeared from his usual Baghdad haunts and no one knew where he had gone; they searched for him everywhere, until someone eventually reported that he had been seen in a *mokhannas-khana* – likely a house of prostitution – where he was weeping and lamenting.[19] This is hardly where one would expect to find a religious man, even one known for puzzling behaviour like Shebli. A questioner, sensing that there must be more than meets the eye, asks Shebli to resolve the mystery: what could possibly have brought him, an enlightened 'seeker of secrets', to such a place? In response, Shebli characterises himself as *mokhannas* on the path of God; thus, he says, his rightful place is in the *mokhannas-khana*:

This is a debauched group;
    they are neither men nor women in the way of the world.

And I am like them, except in the way of religion –
neither a man nor a woman in religion; how much of this!
I am lost in my own lack of manly chivalry (*na-javamardi*),
and I am ashamed of my manliness (*mardi*).[20]

Shebli, of course, is the very definition of a 'man of the path', as ʿAttar calls the heroes of the sufi tradition. Yet he was so ashamed of his 'lack of manly chivalry' and undeserved reputation for 'manliness' that he took up residence in a *mokhannas-khana*, placing himself among those who are 'neither men nor women in the way of the world'. The narrative thus implies a drastic recalibration of the scale of spiritual achievement – if Shebli belongs in the *mokhannas-khana*, how about the rest of us? – and it simultaneously reveals true manliness to lie in the very disavowal of the same, a theme that ʿAttar amplifies in the subsequent homily:

Whoever has made his soul aware
has used his beard as a napkin on the path.
Like the true men, he has chosen abasement
He has scattered honour on the masters of the way.[21]

True men never boast of their status as such. Rather, they choose self-abasement, actively dismiss the outward signs of manly piety and banish any care for reputation from their hearts.

The dangers of spiritual conceit are a perennial topic in ʿAttar's poems and the Persian literary tradition more broadly. What makes this (and ʿAttar's other narratives) so intriguing, however, is that it takes the potentially trite injunction to be wary of spiritual self-satisfaction and concretises it in a way that demonstrates its heretofore unappreciated demands. To avoid the trap of conceit, Shebli rejects any claim to manliness by taking up residence in a brothel of catamites. His followers and associates are surprised to find him there, which only shows that they have failed to realise the true dangers of pride and the shocking actions needed to avoid to it. ʿAttar's audience is invited to participate in this surprise through the puzzled questioner, with whom they are encouraged to identify as targets of didactic address; the structure of the narrative, which casts Shebli's presence in the brothel as an unexpected event; and his paradoxical definition of manliness as the rejection of any claim to the same. In all of these ways, the admonishment to avoid spiritual self-regard is defamiliarised, invested with transgressive force and revealed as a radical challenge to the spiritual status quo.

The story of Shebli easily stands on its own, but within the *Conference of the Birds* it is immediately followed by a second narrative that effects another set of reversals. More specifically, it redefines manliness as a form of submission (*taslim*) while revealing the gap between this manly ideal and the 'effeminate' reality of most sufis. It recounts how two 'wearers of patched frocks' – ostensible dervishes – once brought a dispute before a judge. Instead of issuing a ruling, however, the judge excoriates them for their animosity and spiritual weakness. Bringing a legal claim, according to the judge, is antithetical to the spiritual ethos to which these so-called sufis pretend:

> The judge pulled them aside.
> He said: 'Sufis ought not to stir up conflict.
> You have taken your cloak of submission (*jama-ye taslim*),
> so why have you entered into this enmity (*khosumat*)?
> If you are people of conflict (*jang*) and rancour (*kin*),
> take these clothes (*lebas*) off at once!
> And if you are people of these cloaks (*jama*),
> then you have entered into enmity (*khosumat*) out of ignorance.
> I am a judge, and not a man of meaning,
> but I have shame before those cloaks (*moraqqa*ʿ)!
> For both of you wearing women's veils (*meqna*ʿ)
> would be better than wearing patched frocks (*moraqqa*ʿ) like this!'[22]

The rebuke opposes the 'submission' (*taslim*) proper of a sufi with 'enmity' (*khosumat*), 'treachery' (*jafa*), 'conflict' (*jang*) and 'rancour' (*kin*). In other contexts, submission and passivity might be considered more properly feminine traits, but here they are imagined as masculine spiritual attributes opposed to a 'feminine' tendency towards conflict. The *fotovvat* ethos absorbed into sufism celebrated generosity and altruism, especially among members of the same social group, an ideal that the two sufis in this anecdote have, through their rancour to each other, betrayed. But their antagonism is not only a violation of *fotovvat* ethics; it is also a sin against God. This becomes especially clear when the anecdote is considered in conjunction with the preceding homily, in which true servanthood (*bandagi*) to God is contrasted with the idolatrous 'pretension' (*da'va*) of religious practice motivated by the carnal soul:

> It's not possible, among either the elect or the masses,
> to attain a higher station than that of servanthood (*bandagi*).
> Perform servanthood (*bandegi kon*) and don't pursue pretension (*da'va*)!
> Become a man of God, don't seek glory from 'Uzza!
> When you have a hundred idols under your cloak (*dal[a]q*),
> how can you present yourself to the people as a sufi?
> O *mokhannas*, don't wear the clothes of men (*jama-ye mardan*)!
> Don't confuse yourself more than this![23]

Besides pretension and false boasting, *da'va* can also mean conflict and has the technical meaning of 'lawsuit' in Islamic legal procedure. By playfully conflating these meanings here, the would-be sufis' legal action is equated with idolatrous self-assertion and self-regard that violates the total submission to God's will expected of them.

Because the ideal of submission has been betrayed by those who pretend to embrace it, the signifiers of sufism have become detached from their intended meanings. The judge – a bearer of an exoteric Islam who is 'not a man of meaning' – proves himself more sensitive to the demands of manliness than the sufis before him; it is his court-room (*dar al-qaza*) and not the sufi lodge where manliness is actually understood. This inversion of the proper order of things is further exemplified in the passage's concern with clothing and its failure to signify. The patched frock (*moraqqa'*) is supposed to be a 'robe of submission', but idols are hidden beneath it; clothes are supposed to accord with gender, but 'effeminates' (*mokhannasan*) wear 'the robes of men'. The judge calls on the two hypocritical sufis who have come before him to remove their cloaks and don headscarfs (*meqna'*), which more accurately reflect their spiritual state. That those who claim to be 'men' would be better served by women's clothing testifies to sufism's alleged degradation, as well as the gap that has opened up between exterior markers of mystical piety and actual inner virtue.

The story of Shebli and the narrative of the litigious sufis explore different facets of manliness, but they both present their particular understandings of this virute as radical challenges to an imagined conventional Islam. In the first case, spiritual manliness is paradoxically and self-referentially redefined; in the second, it is revealed as submission to God that precludes animosity or rancour vis-à-vis one's fellow men. These notions of manliness would have already been familiar to most of ʿAttar's readers, at least in the abstract, but they are emplotted within the narratives as unexpected disruptions to stagnant religious valuations and assumptions: the true man places himself among the 'non-men' in the *mokhannas-khana*, and a judge must educate sufis on the meaning of their robes. This pattern holds through the final narrative of the chapter, which explores yet another manifestation of manliness – selfless devotion in love – that is similarly cast as an unanticipated challenge to insincere religiosity.

This particular narrative features a pauper who has fallen desperately in love with the king of Egypt. For any competent reader, this already suggests a specific allegorical mapping in which the king stands for God and the pauper for the human mystic. God is often represented as a king on the basis of his complete power over the universe; the beggar, on the other hand, is marked by impoverishment and impotence, and he represents human dependency and weakness vis-à-vis the divine. The figure of a beggar in love with the king is also a conventional literary trope with which ʿAttar's readers would doubtlessly be familiar.

When the king learns of the pauper's passion for him, he summons that 'misled lover' (*ʿasheq-e gomrah*) and delivers the following ultimatum:

> Since you are a lover of the sovereign,
> you now must choose between two options.
> Either commit to leave this city and this country,
> or, out of love for me, choose to lose your head!
> I've told you what's in store, now quickly,
> What will it be, death or exile?[24]

The king's displeasure, generically speaking, is expected. Falling in love with a social superior was an act of grave impropriety, and ʿAttar includes other stories in which members of low classes face execution for proclaiming their love of a prince or princess.[25] Confronted with this grim choice, the pauper chooses exile over death, since he was not, according to ʿAttar, 'a man of action' (*mard-e kar*). When the pauper begins to depart, however, the king suddenly orders his head to be struck off. A chamberlain seeks to make sense of this seemingly capricious reversal, and he asks the king to explain the mystery of his actions:

> A chamberlain said, 'he is innocent;
> why would the king order his destruction?'[26]

Indeed, the poor pauper agreed to exile – why, then, this brutal treatment?

In a long response to the enquiring chamberlain, the king explains the reason for his surprising order and sums up the moral point of the episode:

> Because he was no lover;
> he was not sincere (*sadeq*) in the path of loving me.
> If he really were a man of action (*mard-e kar*),
> certainly he would have chosen to have his head cut off,
> for whoever values his head more than his beloved
> is deficient in his loving.
> If he had chosen to lose his head,
> he would have risen to sovereign of a kingdom.
> (If he would have girded his loins in front of him,
> the Caesar of the World would have become his beggar.)
> But because he was a poser (*da'vi-dar*) in love,
> he certainly deserved his speedy decapitation.
> Whoever, in separation from me, minds his own head
> is a pretender (*modda'i*) and sullied.
> I've commanded this so those who lack illumination,
> might not boast so much of their false love for me.[27]

The choice of punishment offered to the pauper is revealed to not have been a real choice at all, but a test, and one that the pauper failed. By choosing exile over death, he demonstrated that his love was not sincere (*sadeq*) and he was not a 'man of action' (*mard-e kar*): he was a pretender (*modda'i*) and a poser (*da'vi-dar*) who made boats of his false love (*laf-e dorugh*).

Although the beggar's execution is sudden and unexpected, there were hints that all was not right. When he makes the choice of exile over death, 'Attar explains that the beggar was not a 'man of action' (*mard-e kar*), which suggests a moral failing; the same term is used by the king is his subsequent explanation.

At the beginning of the anecdote, the beggar is also called a 'misled lover' (*ʿasheq-e gomrah*), and while one might assume this refers to his misfortune of having been smitten by a king, it ultimately proves to be a comment on the wayward nature of his false love. Finally, the homiletic transition from the previous anecdote warns the reader against false boasts of love, an admonishment that, in retrospect, clearly foreshadows the beggar's decapitation:

> If you enter this field in pretension (*daʿva*),
> you will give up your head and lose your soul.
> Don't raise your head in so much pretension (*daʿva*)
> lest you perish in disgrace.[28]

These various threads, however, are only explicitly tied together when the king explains his actions to the surprised chamberlain, who, as the target of the former's didactic speech, also provides readers with a subject position from which to insert themselves into the drama of the text. The temporal rhythm of the narrative is thus one of an uneasy stasis marked by inklings that all may not be right, followed by a surprising destabilisation which is only fully resolved through the king's retrospective clarification of the incredibly high stakes of love.

The story of the King and the Insincere Lover, by virtue of its specific narrative structure, creates a situation in which the audience's surprise testifies to their failure to have appreciated love's demands: if they are shocked or confused by the king's execution of the beggar – as they are cued to be – then they have not understood ʿAttar's prior admonishment or gathered the hints that he has dropped, and thus have a long way to go on the spiritual path. Selfless commitment and constancy in love, like the other facets of manliness that ʿAttar explores here (humility, servanthood, submission, etc.), is not a novel understanding of the term, nor is it unique to him. Nevertheless, ʿAttar manages to emplot it as an unexpected challenge to those who would claim to love of God, and he thereby reveals the insincerity that has contaminated religious practice.

The Pleasures of Blasphemy and the Wisdom of Fools

Through these sudden disruptions and inversions, ʿAttar calls on his readers to make a radical turn towards a more sincere form of piety. But as anyone who has laughed at a well-constructed joke knows, abrupt cognitive reframings can also be exceedingly funny. It should come as no surprise, then, that many of ʿAttar's anecdotes are quite humorous. The 'moments of clarity' that they enact function much like punchlines; they not only reframe the prior narrative action in the service of a didactic lesson, but also provoke laughter. In a more general sense, the anecdotes' tendency to invert well-worn religious hierarchies provides a kind of titillation that, while operative in sufism's stylistics of transgression more broadly, is especially prominent in ʿAttar. Far from opposed to their religious message, humour and the pleasure of transgression are inextricably bound to the anecdotes' didactic work while simultaneously adding to their appeal.

One class of anecdotes in particular exemplifies the humour, titillation and didactic potential of unanticipated or infelicitous conceptual reframings: ʿAttar's narratives of wise-fools, whose oxymoronic name testifies to their disruptive potential.[29] These are liminal characters who inhabit graveyards, deserts, dumps and other areas on the periphery of human social geography. Some are driven to such marginal locations by abuse suffered at the hands of children or those agitated by their antics, while others consciously choose withdrawal on the basis of an exaggerated piety and disgust with human society. Often naked, they reject external markers of social status and instruments of bodily comfort. Their didacticism seems unintentional as they are generally unconcerned with those around them; they answer only when provoked and usually explain their actions as they pertain to themselves alone. In short, although necessarily a part of society, these wise-fools simultaneously resist its structures and its codes, and they are presented as unencumbered by human hierarchies and attachments. But precisely because they have withdrawn (or have been excluded) from the social realm, they remain uncontaminated by the threat of hypocrisy and self-aggrandisement that so troubled mystical thinkers and preachers.[30] They thus inhabit a privileged space from which to perceive the truth and destabilise ossified religiosity, not directly, but through uncanny hyperbole and humour that troubles 'normal' modes of discourse and calls the very categories of foolishness and wisdom into question.

Although individuals who conform to the wise-fool type are increasingly visible in the historical sources from the thirteenth century onwards, their existence as a literary topos can be documented centuries earlier.[31] Narratives of fools and their caustic speech were circulating from at least the early ʿAbbasid period, narrated by the likes of Jahiz (d. 868) and Ibn Abi'l-Dunya (d. 894), and the first surviving collection devoted exclusively to these characters was composed by one Hasan Naysaburi (d. 1015). The fools in Naysaburi's collection engage in all sorts of buffoonery, but their antics and utterances frequently demonstrate eloquence, keen wit and deep ascetic piety. Chief among them is Bohlul, a semi-legendary figure who, according to later reports, even dared to harangue the caliph Harun al-Rashid (d. 809) for his worldly attachments.[32] Almost two centuries after Naysaburi, Ibn al-Jawzi included notices on seventeen wise-fools, predominantly unnamed, in his hagiographical *Sifat al-safwa*; they appear as practitioners of a mystical piety and their madness is explained by their preoccupation with God or longing for him.[33] ʿAttar, for his part, was clearly fond of these characters, whom he portrays as so enraptured by love of God that they know not what they do, and who are thus permitted speech and actions that would be blasphemous for others. According to Foruzanfar, no less than 115 stories in ʿAttar's oeuvre feature fools, madmen or lunatics, and entire chapters are devoted to their antics in both the *Conference of the Birds* and the *Mosibat-nama*.[34]

Among the many transgressive behaviours of ʿAttar's fools, one of the most striking is their indictment of God: they loudly blame him for their pain and suffering in the world, accusing him of injustice or cruel indifference.[35] For instance, one anecdote in the *Mosibat-nama* tells of a starving fool in a lamentable state. A passer-by tries to console him: 'Don't cry,' he says, 'the Lord has suspended the dome of the sky without a single pillar; certainly he can provide you with daily bread, too.' (The creation of the sky without pillars is referenced in Quran 31:10, and it is frequently cited as an example of God's power.) The fool, however, is having none of it. 'I wish he would put up a hundred pillars!' he replies, 'and send me some bread without suffering! Bread needs eating and I need bread – what do I care for a sky without pillars?!'[36] In another example from the *Conference of the Birds*, we hear of a poor, barefoot fool dressed in rags. One day he catches sight of a troop of beautiful slaves outfitted with golden arms and jewels and mounted on handsome steeds. When the fool enquires who these beautiful beings belong to, he is told that they are the slaves of the governor of Khorasan. He immediately becomes distraught: 'Lord of the Throne', he calls out, 'learn from this governor how to treat your slaves!'[37] A temporal ruler is thus made the standard by which to judge God's generosity and his merit as provider – and the comparison is not to God's benefit.

These blaspheming fools are not presented as models for imitation, at least not directly. The pleasure of the narratives lies precisely in the fact that they invite readers to cross a line that most would not dare to violate 'in real life'. In a chapter devoted to wise-fools in the *Conference of the Birds*, 'Attar explains that they are permitted such indecorous accusations only because they are gripped by passion for God: 'If you are crazed by him,' writes 'Attar, 'speak boldly . . . but if you do not bear the leaves of this high branch, then don't perform boldness.'[38] Because these bold fools have lost their reason in love of God, they should not be judged for their outbursts: 'Restrain your tongues from their way / hold madmen and lovers to be excused.'[39] Besides their insanity and overwhelming love of God, 'Attar provides several other reasons why these fools are not culpable for their grave violations of propriety. They are likened to the intimate boon companions of a king who are permitted occasional moments of forthright speech that common soldiers and attendants are not.[40] Or they are like the women of Egypt, who, upon seeing Joseph, entered into an ecstatic state and cut their own hands without realising it; the fools are overcome by the divine and have lost their sense of self.[41] At multiple points 'Attar suggests that they are endowed with a deep sense of God's unity and his status as the ultimate cause of everything in the world: 'They hear everything from him, they say everything to him / They seek from him everything, and they seek everything through him.'[42] Similar sentiments are found in the *Mosibat-nama*:

> Intermediaries for this tribe have been lifted
>
> That's why their speech is most appropriate.
>
> They hear everything from him, and they say everything back, too,
>
> because they see nothing besides him that is not illusory.[43]

Some of 'Attar's excuses for these fools can come off as a little forced, but he never dismisses their accusations as the products of a crazed mind; rather, it is the impropriety of their utterances that he apologises for. The very characterisation of these fools as 'bold' (*gostakh*) suggests that they are performing a form of 'frank speech' that violates social norms but is fundamentally true.[44]

The transgressive appeal of these figures lies in the fact that their accusations against God, while unspeakable within the bounds a conventional believer–God relationship, are convincingly rooted in a very Islamic commitment to God's omnipotence and unity. Rather than attributing their blessings to God and absolving him of their misfortunes, these wise-fools see that everything – including the slings and arrows of outrageous fortune – come directly from God, and they therefore hold him personally responsible for their misery as the only true, non-metaphoric agent in the cosmos.

In addition to the transgression of religious norms, 'Attar's fools frequently blur the line between wisdom and madness by using category errors, hyper-literalism and other 'foolish' infelicities to articulate otherwise sound religious points.[45] For example, in the opening narrative of a chapter on death in the *Mosibat-nama*, a questioner confronts a deranged man who has taken up residence in a cemetery: 'Why are you sleeping away your whole life here?' he asks. 'Rise and come to the city, so that you might see countless people!'[46] The fool responds that he has spoken with one of the deceased, and he has dissuaded him from leaving the graveyard:

> 'This deceased one doesn't let me go,' he replied,
> '"Don't ever go!" – he says – "from this place,
> because if you go, your way will be really long,
> since you'll have to come all the way back here in the end!"'[47]

Besides the strangeness of receiving advice from a dead person, the fool approaches death's inevitability from an oddly practical perspective. He refuses to leave the graveyard not because he has devoted his life to prayer or conventional ascetic activities, but because a post-mortem 'return' to the graveyard would be a great bother. On the one hand, it seems to be laziness, not pious fear, that motivates him: given the certainty of his own death, he simply wants to spare himself the extra trip! At the same time, he appreciates the reality of death in a way his interlocutor does not, and he lives out the maxim to 'die before you die' in a quite literal fashion by taking up residence in a graveyard. The fool's answer is silly yet profound; he mocks life itself as a long walk to the graveyard that is not worth taking too seriously.

Another anecdote in the same chapter features Bohlul, the paradigmatic wise-fool who dominates Naysaburi's collection. According to this narrative, he was spotted one winter night drunk and barefoot, carrying his shoes in his hands. When asked what he was doing, Bohlul replied that he was headed to the graveyard where he heard a tyrant was buried:

> He replied: 'I'm hurrying towards the graveyard,
> because a tyrant lies there in torment.
> I'm going because his grave is full of flame;
> perhaps I'll get warm, since this cold is really unpleasant!'[48]

He begins by invoking the eschatological torment of a tyrant in hellfire and then finishes with a much more mundane concern: he wants to warm his feet. His mission, moreover, is clearly at odds with most people's experience of the world: hellfire does not physically fill the gravesites of those it torments, at least not in a manner perceptible to the living. But who is more foolish: Bohlul, who recognises the reality of eschatological torment, albeit a little too literally, or the allegedly reasonable people who live their lives without much thought of the afterlife, laughing at his apparent simple mindedness?

Both of these anecdotes are structured much like jokes. Their protagonists behave in a strange or unexpected fashion that is then explained according to a logic that is at best oddly practical (the first case) or infelicitous (the second), but which carries serious ethical consequences. It is partly this contrast between the fools' non-normative reasoning and their (at least partly) sound religious conclusions that makes these anecdotes so funny. And this humour is more than the sugar that helps the medicine go down, or a bit of levity that is extraneously added onto the didactic project: it is itself a didactic manoeuvre. The wise-fools may operate according to a hyper-literal, naive eschatology, or violate common-sense norms, but they also accept the reality of death and the afterlife and navigate the world with the certainty of its existence. These stories thus destabilise the binary between sane and insane, just as the label of 'wise-fool' would suggest. Their 'unreasonable' behaviours and utterances force readers to re-evaluate whether their own relationship to death is as 'reasonable' as they might assume, rendering these narratives both hilarious and deeply disturbing at the same time.[49]

Continuous Conversion

When ʿAttar turns to speak to his readers directly, he often addresses them as if they were complete neophytes, urging them to wake up and take that first step towards piety along the mystical path. We have already encountered a number of examples of this particular homiletic modality. 'Since the time has come, O man of delusions', he admonishes his addressee after the story of the gambling Jew, 'turn away from this alley of ruins.' In so far as readers are encouraged to identify with this addressee, they are figured as someone who has, up until now, wasted their life in the gambling house of the world, and they are thus called upon to make a definite break with the past and turn towards God. Similarly, prior to the parable of the King and the Insincere Lover, ʿAttar enjoins his readers to not 'raise your head in so much pretension / lest you perish in disgrace', implying that whatever spiritual progress they think they have made is, in fact, a vain and dangerous delusion of the carnal soul. Other times the addressee is figured as a sufi, but in name only: 'When you have a hundred idols under your cloak / how can you present yourself to the people as a sufi?' he asks. Through these addressees, readers – whatever their actual level of commitment to mystical piety may have been – are invited to play the role of those who have not yet made that definitive turn towards God, or at least have not done so in good faith; nevertheless, with ʿAttar's urging, they may be on the cusp of taking that momentous step.

This positionality is reinforced by the anecdotes, which repeatedly demonstrate the insufficiency of conventional religious judgements that they project onto the audience. The insane are thus shown to be more pious than the sane, and wiser too; spiritual exemplars perform manliness by denying it; the trappings of sufism are revealed as signs of hypocrisy and pride; and a Jew becomes a model for Muslim commitment. By bucking expectations and inverting initial judgements, the anecdotes destabilise seemingly natural categories and assumptions in the service of a reinvigorated piety. Well-worn mystical themes are emplotted as surprising revelations that unmask an imagined rote Islam, and ʿAttar implicates his audience for succumbing to this spiritual complacency by eliciting, and then overturning, seemingly common-sense assumptions and religious valuations.

These sudden narrative reversals and cognitive reframings recall a fundamental topos in sufi literature: the 'conversion' or 'repentance' (*towba*) that marks the first step on the sufi path. In a general sense, *towba* signifies a turning away from sin and a return to God, but in sufism it is further distinguished as the initial spiritual stage through which the novice embarks on a life of spiritual wayfaring.[50] As the hagiographical literature makes clear, conversion is usually imagined as a sudden, unforeseen event that brings about a decisive reorientation in religious outlook. One well-known example is that of Fozayl b. 'Eyaz, who, according to the hagiographical sources, lived a life of banditry until one day, when lying in wait for an approaching caravan, he heard his intended targets recite the Quranic verse 'Hasn't the time come for those who believe to humble their hearts before the remembrance of God?' (57:16).[51] He was so affected that he immediately gave up banditry and moved to Mecca. A variation of the same theme is at work in the account of Davud-e Ta'i, who allegedly converted to sufism after overhearing a few lines of verse on the impermanence of life.[52] Such experiences can mark an entry into other Islamic modalities besides the mystical, too. The famous Isma'ili poet and philosopher Naser-e Khosrow claims to have had a dream in which a mysterious figure rebuked him for drinking and commanded him to seek wisdom in the direction of the *qebla*. He was so shaken that, upon waking, he left Seljuk service in Marv, 'renounced worldly concerns', and set out on a multi-year journey to Cairo.[53] These accounts are doubtlessly unreliable in a positivist sense, but they demonstrate how conversion was popularly remembered, conceptualised and articulated: as a decisive existential turn to a new state of piety, brought on by the sudden destabilisation of previous values and assumptions. And as Naser-e Khosrow and Fozayl b. 'Eyaz show, the metaphorical 'return' of *towba* frequently involves an actual, physical journey as well.

Very few of 'Attar's anecdotes in the *masnavis* actually describe conversion to sufism per se. The specific modes of emplotment that 'Attar favours, however, do recall the temporal structure of conversion as it is imagined in the hagiographies, including his own prose *Tazkera*. Conversions to sufism are generally brought about by sudden, unexpected events that provoke drastic changes in religious outlook and life course, and 'Attar's anecdotes produce a very similar temporal pattern through their stasis–destabilisation–resolution structure. The donkey's fart, the Jew's punch, Shebli's surprising presence in the brothel, the king's order to execute the beggar – these are all presented as sudden, sometimes shocking disruptions of the status quo with far-reaching religious consequence. Like the poetic verses and Quranic lines overheard by Davud-e Ta'i and Fozayl b. ʿEyaz, they are abrupt intrusions into the narrative that call for a radical rethinking of religious practice. The donkey's fart is not just a silly bodily happening, but a reproach of spiritual vanity; the Jew's sucker punch displays high religious commitment; and the king's execution of the beggar demonstrates the unbearably high demands of love. All of these events are narrated as unexpected challenges to a complacent religiosity and demands for a decisive turn towards spiritual reform. They recall the temporal structure of hagiographical conversion narratives, but here ʿAttar's readers are made the ultimate targets of their disruptive call.

One of the noteworthy features of ʿAttar's anecdotes is that we almost never learn how the characters within the narratives react to these destabilisations and the conceptual realignments that they imply. In the story of the gambling Jew, how do the gamblers react after one of them is punched in the face? Do they give up their debauched lifestyle, moved by the Jew's commitment – or does a brawl break out in the gambling den? How do Shebli's companions respond to his confessions of spiritual effeminacy? Do the two litigious sufis realise their hypocrisy after their dressing-down from by the judge? Is the chamberlain satisfied with the king's explanation of why he had the beggar executed? We do not know whether these various teacher figures actually succeed in changing any minds within the worlds of their narration, or whether their addressees answer the call to turn towards a more sincere practice of Islam. But this is not their purpose. ʿAttar's readers are the true targets of their didactic interventions, as the shift to second-person imperative after these climatic moments makes clear. Indeed, it falls to the reader to answer the call and 'refigure', as Paul Ricoeur would put it, the narrative as a disruptive event in their own religious lives.[54]

Whatever affiliation and expertise specific readers may have with sufism – as advanced adepts, fresh novices or unaffiliated dabblers – the anecdotes invite them to play the role of someone whose conventional religiosity must be disrupted so that they can make a decisive turn towards a more sincere, reinvigorated form of piety. Unlike a formal conversion to sufism, however, the disruptive power of ʿAttar's anecdotes can be experienced again and again.

Indeed, over the course of a single reading of one of his *masnavis*, a reader will encounter dozens or even hundreds of anecdotes that perform this work, and ʿAttar urges his audience to read his *masnavis* multiple times, promising that they will find new benefits with each re-reading. They thus quickly learn that even the most basic spiritual principles cannot be taken for granted, and that almost any topic, in ʿAttar's hands, can be emplotted as indictment of religious complacency. The temporality of conversion – as a sudden call to a new way of life – is, in ʿAttar's *masnavis*, made into a continuous process. To read (or re-read) his *masnavis* is to step into an arena in which the radical turn to a deeper form of religious praxis never ends. Rote religiosity is not left behind once and for all, but must be repeatedly broken as one continuously re-orients oneself towards the truth.

Notes

1. Joseph Lumbard, *Aḥmad al-Ghazālī, Remembrance, and the Metaphysics of Love* (Albany, NY: SUNY Press, 2016), 109–12; Peter Awn, *Satan's Tragedy and Redemption: Iblīs in Sufi Psychology* (Leiden: Brill, 1983); Ritter, *Ocean of the Soul*, 548–67.
2. On the *qalandariyat*, see J. T. P. de Bruijn, 'The *Qalandariyyat* in Persian Mystical Poetry', in *The Legacy of Medieval Persian Sufism*, ed. Leonard Lewisohn (London: Khaniqahi Nimatullahi Publications, 1992); Miller, 'Poetics of the Sufi Carnival', 66–114; Ashk Dahlén, 'The Qalandar in the Persianate World: The Case of Fakhrod-din ʿArāqi', in *Holy Fools and Divine Madmen: Sacred Insanity through Ages and Cultures*, ed. Albrecht Berger and Sergey Ivanov (Neuried: Ars Una, 2018); Katherine Pratt Ewing and Ilona Gerbakher, 'The *Qalandariyya*: From the Mosque to the Ruin in Poetry, Place, and Practice', in *Routledge Handbook on Sufism*, ed. Lloyd Ridgeon (Abingdon: Routledge, 2020).
3. The general tendency of ʿAttar's anecdotes to invert the roles expected of their protagonists has been pointed out by Dick Davis in 'Sufism and Poetry', 286, and in the introduction to his and Afkham Darbanid's translation of the *Conference of the Birds*, 17–20. See also Claudia Yaghoobi, 'Against the Current: Farid al-Din ʿAttar's Diverse Voices', *Persian Literary Studies Journal* 1, no. 1 (2012): 87–109.
4. ʿAttar, *Mosibat-nama*, 289.
5. ʿAttar, *Manteq al-tayr*, 683n2933.
6. ʿAttar, *Manteq al-tayr*, 365.

7. ʿAttar, *Manteq al-tayr*, 365.
8. The term 'moment of awareness' was used in this context by Ghazzal Dabiri, 'When a Lion Is Chided by an Ant: Everyday Saints and the Making of Sufi Kings in ʿAttār's *Elāhi-nāma*', *Journal of Persianate Studies* 12, no. 1 (2019): 85–9.
9. ʿAttar, *Asrar-nama*, 200.
10. ʿAttar, *Asrar-nama*, 200.
11. ʿAttar, *Asrar-nama*, 200.
12. ʿAttar, *Elahi-nama*, 184–5.
13. ʿAttar, *Elahi-nama*, 197–8.
14. ʿAttar, *Elahi-nama*, 147.
15. See pp. 44–5. The term is Paul Ricoeur's, 'Listening to the Parables of Jesus', 20.
16. ʿAttar, *Manteq al-tayr*, 317–19.
17. Regarding the influence and development of *fotovvat* in sufism, see Lloyd Ridgeon, *Morals and Mysticism in Persian Sufism: A History of Sufi-Futuwwat in Iran* (Abingdon: Routledge, 2010); Muhammad Jafar Mahjub, 'Chivalry and Early Persian Sufism', in *Classical Persian Sufism: From Its Origins to Rumi*, ed. Leonard Lewisohn (London: Khaniqahi Nimatullahi Publications, 1993). On the Malamatiya, see p. 117.
18. Richard Gramlich, *Alte Vorbilder des Sufitums* (Wiesbaden: Harrassowitz, 1995), 1:513–665. Shebli features in a number of stories in ʿAttar's *masnavis*; for a list, see Ritter, *Ocean of the Soul*, 810. The chapter devoted to Shebli in ʿAttar's *Tazkera*, however, is likely spurious. See Esteʿlami, intro. to *Tazkerat al-owleya*, xxxvi–xxxvii.
19. Sirus Shamisa, *Shahed-bazi dar adabiyat-e farsi* (Tehran: Ferdows, 1381 [2002–3]), 93–4, 227–9.
20. ʿAttar, *Manteq al-tayr*, 317–18.
21. ʿAttar, *Manteq al-tayr*, 318.
22. ʿAttar, *Manteq al-tayr*, 318–19.
23. ʿAttar, *Manteq al-tayr*, 318.
24. ʿAttar, *Manteq al-tayr*, 319.
25. See, for example, the story of the dervish who fell in love with a princess and was executed, discussed in Chapter 4, p. 140 above.
26. ʿAttar, *Manteq al-tayr*, 319.
27. ʿAttar, *Manteq al-tayr*, 319.
28. ʿAttar, *Manteq al-tayr*, 318–19.
29. On the character of the wise-fool in general, see Michael W. Dols and Diana

Immisch, *Majnūn: The Madman in Medieval Islamic Society* (Oxford: Clarendon, 1992), 349–422; Ulrich Marzolph, '*'Uḳalā' al-madjānīn*', in *Encyclopaedia of Islam, Second Edition*, posted 2012, https://doi.org/10.1163/1573-3912_islam_SIM_8927. Regarding 'Attar's use of these figures in particular, see Nasrollah Pourjavady, 'Hekmat-e divanagan dar masnaviha-ye 'Attar', *Nashr-e danesh* 13, no. 1 (1371 [1992–3]): 2–16; Maryam Mosharraf, 'Shaluda-shakani-ye manteq-e vahshat dar asar-e 'Attar', in *'Attar-shenakht*, ed. Mohammad Reza Rashed Mohassel (Mashhad: Daneshgah-e Ferdowsi, 1385 [2006–7]); Kermani, *Terror of God*, 144–7, 163–7; Hellmut Ritter, 'Muslim Mystics' Strife with God', *Oriens* 5, no. 1 (1952): 1–15.

30. On the fools as models of sincerity and critics of hypocrisy, see especially Pourjavady, 'Divanagan'.
31. Historical individuals of this type are especially well documented in Syria and Egypt. See Josef Meri, *The Cult of Saints among Muslims and Jews in Medieval Syria* (Oxford: Oxford University Press, 2002), 91–2; Dols and Immisch, *Majnūn*, 403–22.
32. On Naysaburi and Bohlul, see Dols and Immisch, *Majnūn*, 356–9; Shereen El Ezabi, 'Al-Naysaburi's Wise Madmen: Introduction', *Alif: Journal of Comparative Poetics* 14 (1994): 192–205; Ulrich Marzolph, *Der weise Narr Buhlūl* (Wiesbaden: Deutsche Morgenländische Gesellschaft, 1983); Ulrich Marzolph, 'Buhlūl', in *Encyclopaedia of Islam, Three*, posted 2009, https://doi.org/10.1163/1573-3912_ei3_COM_23313.
33. Dols and Immisch, *Majnūn*, 375–9.
34. Foruzanfar, *Sharh-e ahval-e 'Attar*, 45; 'Attar, *Manteq al-tayr*, 356–60; 'Attar, *Mosibat-nama*, 306–13.
35. On the fool's accusations of God, see especially Ritter, 'Muslim Mystics' Strife with God'; Ritter, *Ocean of the Soul*, 165–87; Kermani, *Terror of God*.
36. 'Attar, *Mosibat-nama*, 312.
37. 'Attar, *Manteq al-tayr*, 357.
38. 'Attar, *Manteq al-tayr*, 358.
39. 'Attar, *Manteq al-tayr*, 360.
40. 'Attar, *Manteq al-tayr*, 356–7.
41. 'Attar, *Manteq al-tayr*, 358–9.
42. 'Attar, *Manteq al-tayr*, 359.
43. 'Attar, *Mosibat-nama*, 312.
44. The classic discussion of frank speech is found in Michel Foucault, *The Courage of the Truth (The Government of Self and Others II): Lectures at the Collège de*

France, 1983–1984, trans. Graham Burchell, ed. Frédéric Gros (New York: Palgrave Macmillian, 2011), 1–22.

45. Maryam Mosharraf has drawn attention to how these fools frustrate notions of reason's superiority, inverting the binary between sane and insane, 'Manteq-e vahshat'.
46. 'Attar, *Mosibat-nama*, 189.
47. 'Attar, *Mosibat-nama*, 189.
48. 'Attar, *Mosibat-nama*, 190.
49. Portions of this section were adapted from Austin O'Malley, 'Rhetoric, Narrative, and the Remembrance of Death in 'Aṭṭār's *Moṣibat-nāmeh*', *Iranian Studies* 51, no. 1 (2018): 34–6.
50. On *towba*, its etymology and its theological significance, see Atif Khalil, *Repentance and the Return to God:* Tawba *in Early Sufism* (Albany, NY: SUNY Press, 2019).
51. For Fozayl's repentance, see Hojviri, *Kashf al-mahjub*, 149–50. According to Qushayri, a woman whom Fozayl loved recited this verse from the Quran as he was climbing the wall to visit her surreptitiously, *al-Risala al-qushayriyya*, 47. 'Attar has attempted to combine the two narratives, *Tazkerat al-owleya*, 77.
52. 'Attar, *Tazkerat al-owleya*, 227.
53. Naser-e Khosrow, *Safar-nama*, ed. Mohammad Dabir Siaqi (Tehran: Zavvar, 1389 [2010]), 2.
54. Paul Ricoeur, *Time and Narrative*, trans. Kathleen Blamey and David Pellauer (Chicago: University of Chicago Press, 1984–8), 1:70–87.

Conclusion: Towards a Didactic Performativity

According to reader-response theorist Louise Rosenblatt, the 'poem' – by which she means any literary work, not necessarily just a poetic one – must not be confused with a 'text'. A text is a concrete set of signs in the world, whereas the poem is an 'event', a temporal unfolding produced through a particular reader's 'transaction' with a text.[1] A poem's significance – in a certain respect, its very existence – cannot be divorced from the act of reading. The poem-as-event, however, is necessarily more ephemeral than the text that it involves. Certainly, acts of reception can sometimes leave their marks on texts, especially in the materiality of the manuscript tradition. Among premodern Persian sources, instances of reading and performance are also depicted in certain genres, including hagiographies, biographical anthologies and other forms of anecdotal literature (whether accurately or not is another question). In most cases, however, a particular text cannot document or directly speak to its own reception, which it necessarily precedes. Still, texts can thematise reading and interpretation in a more general sense and recursively imagine their ideal reception, if not depict the actuality thereof; in this way, they might suggest certain modalities of engagement and perhaps even guide how actual readers approach them. Such themes infuse the work of 'Attar, who displays a thoroughgoing fascination with speech and its effects, including those of his own textualised discourse. His oeuvre is full of meta-poetic commentary and depictions of pedagogical relationships, didactic utterances and paraenetic speech situations. In this sense, his work is not only didactic, but meta-didactic: his poems call their readers to piety as they simultaneously meditate, in a reflexive fashion, on their own rhetorical function. Even though the experience of historical readers who encountered ʿAttar's poems largely eludes our grasp, we can still investigate how such encounters are recursively imagined within his texts, and how the structure of his poems imply particular reception stances to which his readers are thereby summoned.

Over the course of the previous seven chapters, *The Poetics of Spiritual Instruction* has examined how ʿAttar both performs didacticism and reflexively considers, sometimes more explicitly and sometimes less so, the purpose and conditions of his instructive work. By attending to his meta-poetic commentary and self-reflexive depictions of paraenetic speech events, an embedded poetics of didacticism has emerged that centres these poems' perlocutionary efficacy and spiritual function for mystically minded readers. From the perspective of this embedded poetics, ʿAttar's poems do much more than convey instructive content in an aesthetically pleasing form. To extend the speech-act terminology of J. L. Austin, they are performative utterances that 'do things' to their audiences, and those same audiences can also 'do things' with them: by enticing their readers to piety, these poems offer them a literary means of self-shaping and an opportunity for symbolic action within the imaginal realm. And by examining the poetics embedded in ʿAttar's oeuvre, we can recover this audience-directed performativity without being forced to forego literary studies' traditional focus on texts in favour of a historical analysis of their reception or an ethnography of reading practices.

ʿAttar's embedded poetics is not rigidly systematic, and poetry's performative action is conceptualised in several different ways throughout his oeuvre. Perhaps the most striking figure of its effective power, however, is the metaphorical notion of speech as medicine. From this vantage point – which is by no means limited to ʿAttar and can be found throughout the Persian didactic tradition and other intellectual discourses – speech not only communicates and provides aesthetic pleasure, but, like a medicine, heals, transforms and cures. It ontologically alters its recipients, bringing them to a state of spiritual health by strengthening the heart's physio-spiritual connection to God. ʿAttar suggests that speech, like a medicine, can even affect its recipients when they do not fully understand it. The medicinal metaphor thus implies a notion of poetic meaning that is not limited to a poem's propositional content or how that content is expressed, but extends to encompass the spiritual, affective, bodily and ontological changes that it produces in its recipients. This more expansive notion of meaning privileges speech's function within a human context: it is not only what a text *says* that counts, but what it *does* to its readers.

At the same time, readers and listeners are not passive subjects of the text's action: they are key participants in this process of meaning-making. Just as drugs must be taken according to particular regimens to be effective, so too must readers approach didactic poetry in specific ways to maximise its transformative effects. The audience thus actively participates in the unfolding didactic event, which, according to 'Attar's embedded poetics, takes on the character of a spiritual exercise, sometimes directly and sometimes in a more symbolic fashion, and in a manner conditioned by his works' particular textual forms. The *Tazkera*, as we have seen, is presented as a set of litanies (*verd*) that maintain spiritual health, which suggests a regular, disciplined reading process. The frame-tale *masnavi*s, by virtue of their narrative structure, lend themselves to a sequential mode of consumption that is likened to spiritual wayfaring along the sufi path, a visionary ascent to Heaven and the forty-day retreat; to read the *Mosibat-nama* is to symbolically enact these sufi ritual activities. In the case of the *Mokhtar-nama*, the work's arrangement facilitates the quick location of quatrains on particular themes that can then be memorised for contemplation (*ta'ammol*) in order to cultivate particular virtues or spiritual states. And the anecdotes within the *masnavi*s, through their narrative reversals, offer readers the opportunity to shock themselves out of religious complacency, clearing a space for them to recommit themselves to mystical piety, as if for the first time. In all of these cases, the textual encounter is cast as a ritualised, spiritual performance in terms drawn from contemporary sufi praxis, and which the recipient is invited to enact.

At the same time, the author – or, more properly, the author's persona – plays a critical role in the success of the didactic event. The efficacy of a didactic utterance in the premodern Persianate imagination is tied to the authority of its speaker, and didactic texts in the Persian tradition generally evoke the forms, settings and structures of oral pedagogical relationships in order to authorise their teachings. 'Attar takes this one step further with his innovative frame-tales, through which he constructs fictive paraenetic speech situations in which the textual content of his *masnavi*s is imaginatively delivered. He blurs the boundaries between narrative levels and elides the didactic speakers that inhabit them, rendering them avatars for his own instructive persona.

In these ways, ʿAttar seeks to transmute the conventions of oral pedagogical relationships into a literary, textual form and to thereby perform spiritual guidance through the written word.

This performative, recipient-centred poetics that emerges from ʿAttar's poems provides a window onto the workings of didacticism from an emic perspective that is often left out of the scholarly conversation. Didactic poetry, despite its prominence, was not systematically theorised in the Persian manuals on rhetoric or poetics, which tended to focus on Arabic-derived forms in the panegyric mode. They also privileged the evaluation of individual lines, generally with an eye to metaphor and other tropes: questions of narratology, which necessarily involve larger structures, are noticeably absent. This observation is not meant as an indictment – clearly, premodern Persian poets were more than capable of writing narrative and didactic verse, as were audiences of consuming it, and they apparently felt no need to systematise their understanding of how the didactic mode functioned. For us, however, attempting to reconstruct the habits of thought and poetic assumptions against which these poems made meaning at a large historical remove, the lack of a philosophical poetics of didacticism means that we must look elsewhere to understand its conceptual background. In this regard, a study of ʿAttar's embedded poetics proves immensely valuable, enriching our understanding of his work in particular and the tradition as a whole. Through these investigations, we can recover a robust, recipient-centred poetics that was never systematically delineated in the philosophical or rhetorical treatises, and only obliquely captured in the hagiographies and anecdotal literature, but which was central to the significance of sufi didactic verse.

This poetics of didacticism also serves as a useful corrective to widespread, modern assumptions about the tradition's complexity and poeticity (or lack thereof) that have coloured much of the scholarship. A tendency to question the poetic merits of didactic verse can be traced as far back to Aristotle, who wrote that didactic poetry was not properly poetry at all, but non-poetic discourse masquerading in poetic form. In the Persian context, where didactic poetry was a mainstay of the poetic tradition, its status as poetry does not seem to have been questioned in literary circles, but Aristotle's judgement was echoed by certain Islamicate philosophers: Ibn Rushd, for example, claimed that *Kalila and Demna* could not be considered poetry, even if composed in rhyme and metre, because it was fiction and thus inherently non-mimetic.[2] In the Romantic period, although poetry was thought to have much to teach, overtly instructive verse was dismissed for a different reason: namely, it was thought to subordinate the genius of the poet and the mystery of poetic experience to pre-existing ideas in a mechanistic fashion. This attitude has persisted into the twentieth and twenty-first centuries, where it is didacticism's alleged circumscription of the readers' interpretive freedom that garners the most objection. Didactic poetry, in this view, is a means to an end, a heavy-handed discourse that privileges predetermined ideational content at the expense of ambiguity and the aesthetic texture of its expression.

The notion of didactic poetry as separable content gussied up in rhyme and metre informs a significant proportion of the scholarly work on ʿAttar and other sufi poets. Their poems are often approached from a history of ideas perspective that attempts to extract, clarify and systematise their teachings. Understanding the theological, ethical and mystical systems that are reflected in ʿAttar's poems is a worthwhile endeavour, but this is not enough to explain their success or capture the full significance of the didactic project: most of the instructive points that ʿAttar makes are not, when separated from their particular expressions, particularly novel. On the other hand, some scholars have focused more on the poetic features of his works, or attempted to present a holistic treatment of their form together with their content. According to the didactic poetics embedded within them, however, ʿAttar's poems should not be reduced to their textual features, whether that be their teachings, their formal poetic characteristics or even the union of the two without considering how they interface with their audiences thereby.

And the encounter between text and audience, according to ʿAttar's metapoetic commentary, is a participatory event: the consumption of his texts is reflexively imagined as the symbolic performance of specific spiritual exercises, which testifies to how engagement with Persian literary texts had, by the thirteenth century, come to constitute a particular form of sufi praxis. Poetry had been used by mystically minded individuals in Khorasan since at least the eleventh century, when short verses, especially quatrains, were sung during *samaʿ* ceremonies and incorporated into homiletic performances. ʿAttar, however – following Sanaʾi – composed sufi-themed verse in the much longer *masnavi* form, and unlike the orally circulating, ad hoc verses that characterised earlier mystical poetry, his work is quite explicitly textual. 'Attar's poems, and the didactic texts of Persian literary sufism more generally, address a broad, variegated audience beyond the religious scholars and *khanaqah* dervishes among whom the prose and overwhelmingly Arabic-language sufi texts of previous centuries had circulated. In the case of 'Attar, the audience's encounter with these Persian literary texts is variously cast as an act of wayfaring, an ascent to Heaven or a process of continuous conversion (*towba*) towards God; the act of reading is thereby invested with ritual significance. Attar's poetry is 'sufi' not only in the sense that it deals with sufi themes and concerns, but also in its 'literarisation' and 'textualisation' of sufi rituals and social relationships. His texts, in addition to signalling the increasing intelligibility of sufi themes for a broad segment of the population, offer new ways for this variegated audience to 'do sufism' through literary practices of reading and interpretation. To read one of his didactic *masnavi*s, as 'Attar imagines it, is to willingly enter into a pedagogical relationship with a literary *pir*, under whose guidance movement through the narrative becomes a walking of the path. Far more than heavy-handed proclamations of separable ideational content, they are interactive sites of pedagogy and self-fashioning, through which readers symbolically enact spiritual progress in a literary mode.

Notes

1. Louise M. Rosenblatt, *The Reader, the Text, the Poem: The Transactional Theory of the Literary Work* (Carbondale: Southern Illinois University Press, 1978), 6–21.
2. Cantarino, *Arabic Poetics*, 186.

Bibliography

Abbott, Nabia. 'A Ninth-Century Fragment of the "Thousand Nights": New Light on the History of the *Arabian Nights*'. *Journal of Near Eastern Studies* 8, no. 3 (1949): 129–64.

Abuali, Eyad. 'al-Baghdādī, Majd al-Dīn'. In *Encyclopaedia of Islam, Three*. Article posted 2019. https://doi.org/10.1163/1573-3912_ei3_COM_25114.

Affifi, A. E. 'The Story of the Prophet's Ascent (*Mi'rāj*) in Sufi Thought and Literature'. *Islamic Quarterly: A Review of Islamic Culture* 2 (1955): 23–7.

Aflaki, Shams al-Din Ahmad. *Manaqeb al-'arefin*. Edited by Tahsin Yazıcı. 2 vols. Ankara: Türk Tarih Kurumu Basımevi, 1959–61. Reprint, Tehran: Donya-ye Ketab, 1382 [2003–4].

Al-e Davud, Sayyed Ali. 'A Review of the Treatises and Historical Documents in *Safīna-yi Tabrīz*'. In *The Treasury of Tabriz: The Great Ilkhanid Compendium*, edited by Ali Asghar Seyed-Gohrab and S. McGlinn, 79–89. West Lafayette, IN: Purdue University Press, 2007.

Algar, Hamid. '*Čella*. ii. In Sufism'. In *Ecyclopaedia Iranica*. Article posted 2020. https://doi.org/10.1163/2330-4804_EIRO_COM_7624.

Ali, Samer. *Arabic Literary Salons in the Islamic Middle Ages: Poetry, Public Performance, and the Presentation of the Past*. Notre Dame, IN: University of Notre Dame Press, 2010.

Anvar-Chenderoff, Leili. 'Le genre hagiographique à travers la *Tadhkirat al-awliā'* de Farīd al-Dīn 'Attār'. In *Saints orientaux*, edited by Denise Aigle, 39–53. Paris: De Boccard, 1995.

Askari, Nasrin. 'Élite Folktales: *Munes-nāma*, *Ketāb-e dāstān*, and Their Audiences'. *Journal of Persianate Studies* 12 (2019): 32–61.

'Attar, Farid al-Din. *Asrar-nama*. Edited by Mohammad Reza Shafi'i-Kadkani. 2nd ed. Tehran: Sokhan, 1388 [2009–10].

'Attar, Farid al-Din. *The Conference of the Birds*. Translated by Afkham Darbandi and Dick Davis. New York: Penguin, 1984.

ʿAttar, Farid al-Din. *The Conference of the Birds*. Translated by Sholeh Woplé. New York: W. W. Norton, 2017.

ʿAttar, Farid al-Din. *The Conference of the Birds, a Sufi Allegory, Being an Abridged Version of Farud-ud-din Attar's "Mantiq-ut-Tayr"*. Translated by Rustom Masani. London: Oxford University Press, 1924.

ʿAttar, Farid al-Din. *The Conference of the Birds, Mantiq ut-Tair: A Philosophical Religious Poem in Prose*. Translated by C. S. Nott. London: Routledge and K. Paul, 1961.

ʿAttar, Farid al-Din. *The Conference of the Birds: The Selected Sufi Poetry of Farid ud-Din Attar*. Translated by Raficq Abdulla. New York: Interlink, 2003.

ʿAttar, Farid al-Din. *Divan-e ʿAttar*. Edited by Taqi Tafazzoli. Tehran: Entesharat-e ʿElmi va Farhangi, 1386 [2007].

ʿAttar, Farid al-Din. *Elahi-nama*. Edited by Mohammad Reza Shafiʿi-Kadkani. 2nd ed. Tehran: Sokhan, 1388 [2009–10].

ʿAttar, Farid al-Din. *Manteq al-tayr*. Edited by Mohammad Reza Shafiʿi-Kadkani. 2nd ed. Tehran: Sokhan, 1387 [2008–9].

ʿAttar, Farid al-Din. *Manteq al-tayr*. Edited by Sayyed Sadeq Gowharin. Tehran: Bongah-e Tarjoma va Nashr-e Ketab, 1342 [1963–4].

ʿAttar, Farid al-Din. *Mantic uttaïr; ou, Le langage des oiseaux, poëme de philosophie religieuse*. Translated by Garcin de Tassy. Paris: Imprimerie Impériale, 1863.

ʿAttar, Farid al-Din. *Mokhtar-nama*. Edited by Mohammad Reza Shafiʿi-Kadkani. 2nd ed. Tehran: Sokhan, 1389 [2010–11].

ʿAttar, Farid al-Din. *Mosibat-nama*. Edited by Mohammad Reza Shafiʿi-Kadkani. 2nd ed. Tehran: Sokhan, 1388 [2009–10].

ʿAttar, Farid al-Din. *Mosibat-nama*. Edited by Nurani Vesal. Tehran: Zavvar, 2536 [1977–8].

ʿAttar, Farid al-Din. *The Speech of the Birds: Concerning Migration to the Real*. Translated by Peter Avery. Cambridge: The Islamic Texts Society, 1998.

ʿAttar, Farid al-Din. *Tazkerat al-owleya*. Edited by Mohammad Esteʿlami. Rev. ed. Tehran: Zavvar, 1383 [2004–5].

ʿAttar [attrib.], Farid al-Din. *Khosrow-nama*. Edited by Ahmad Sohayli-Khwansari. Tehran: Anjoman-e Asar-e Melli, 1339 [1961–2].

ʿAttarpur, Ardalan. *Eqteda be kofr: Pazhuheshi dar dastan-e Shaykh Sanʿan*. Tehran: An va Hama, 1382 [2003–4].

Austin, J. L. *How to Do Things with Words*. Edited by J. O. Urmson and Marina Sabisà. 2nd ed. Cambridge, MA: Harvard University Press, 1975.

Awn, Peter. *Satan's Tragedy and Redemption: Iblīs in Sufi Psychology*. Leiden: Brill, 1983.

al-Azma, Nazeer. 'Some Notes on the Impact of the Story of the *Mi'rāj* on Sufi Literature'. *The Muslim World* 63, no. 2 (1973): 93–104.

Baghdadi, Abu'l-Barakat. *al-Mu'tabar fi'l-hikma*. Edited by Muhammad 'Uthman. 2 vols. Cairo: Maktaba al-Thaqafa al-Diniyya, 2015.

Bal, Mieke. *Narratologie (Essais sur la signification narrative dans quatre romans modernes)*. Paris: Klincksieck, 1977.

Baldick, Julian. 'Persian *Ṣūfī* Poetry up to the Fifteenth Century'. In *History of Persian Literature: From the Beginning of the Islamic Period to the Present Day*, edited by G. Morrison, 113–32. Leiden: Brill, 1981.

Barthes, Roland. 'Death of the Author'. In *Image, Music, Text*, edited by Stephen Heath, 142–8. New York: Hill and Wang, 1977.

Bausani, Alessandro. 'Considerazioni sulla *Tadhkiratu 'l-Auliyā'* di 'Aṭṭār'. In *Colloquio italo-iraniano sul poeta mistico Fariduddin 'Aṭṭār (Roma, 24–25 Marzo 1977)*, 71–88. Rome: Accademia Nazionale dei Lincei, 1978.

Becker, C. H. 'Die Kanzel im Kultus des alten Islam'. In *Orientalische Studien: Theodor Nöldeke zum siebzigsten Geburtstag (2. März 1906)*, edited by Carl Bezold, 331–51. Gieszen: A. Töpelmann, 1906.

Becker, C. H. 'Ubi sunt qui ante nos in mundo fuere'. In *Aufsätze zur Kultur- und Sprachgeschichte*, 87–105. Breslau: M. & H. Marcus, 1916.

Beelaert, Anna Livia. *A Cure for the Grieving: Studies on the Poetry of the 12th-Century Persian Court Poet Khāqānī Širwānī*. Leiden: Nederlands Instituut Voor Het Nabije Oosten, 2000.

Berkey, Jonathan. *Popular Preaching and Religious Authority in the Medieval Islamic Near East*. Seattle: University of Washington Press, 2001.

Bonebakker, Seeger A. 'Some Medieval Views on Fantastic Stories'. *Quaderni di Studi Arabi* 10 (1992): 21–43.

Bosworth, Clifford Edmund. *The Medieval Islamic Underworld: The Banū Sāsān in Arabic Society and Literature*. 2 vols. Leiden: Brill, 1976.

Bosworth, Clifford Edmund. 'The Political and Dynastic History of the Iranian World (A.D. 1000–1217)'. In *The Saljuq and Mongol Periods*, edited by J. A. Boyle, 1–202. Vol. 5 of *The Cambridge History of Iran*. Cambridge: Cambridge University Press, 1968.

Böwering, Gerhard. '*Baqā' wa Fanā'*'. In *Encyclopaedia Iranica*. Article posted 2020. https://doi.org/10.1163/2330-4804_EIRO_COM_6606.

Böwering, Gerhard. 'Kubra's Treatise on Spiritual Retreat, *Risāla fi'l-khalwa*'. *Al-Abḥāth* 54 (2006): 7–34.

Boyce, Mary. 'Middle Persian Literature'. In *Iranistik: Literatur*, 31–66. Leiden: Brill, 1968.

Boyle, J. A. 'Popular Literature and Folklore in 'Aṭṭār's *Mathnavīs*'. In *Colloquio italo-iraniano sul poeta mistico Fariduddin 'Aṭṭār (Roma, 24–25 Marzo 1977)*, 56–70. Rome: Accademia Nazionale dei Lincei, 1977.

Boyle, J. A. 'The Religious *Mathnavīs* of Farīd al-Dīn 'Aṭṭār'. *Iran* 17 (1979): 9–14.

Brockelmann, C. and Ch. Pellat. '*Maḳāma*'. In *Encyclopaedia of Islam, Second Edition*. Article posted 2012. https://doi.org/10.1163/1573-3912_islam_COM_0634.

Browne, Edward. *A Literary History of Persia*. 4 vols. New York: C. Scribner's Sons, 1902–24.

Bulliet, Richard W. *The Patricians of Nishapur: A Study in Medieval Islamic Social History*. Cambridge, MA: Harvard University Press, 1972.

Bürgel, J. Christoph. *The Feather of Simurgh: The "Licit Magic" of the Arts in Medieval Islam*. New York: New York University Press, 1988.

Bürgel, J. Christoph. 'Some Remarks on Forms and Functions of Repetitive Structures in the Epic Poetry of 'Aṭṭār'. In *'Aṭṭār and the Persian Sufi Tradition: The Art of Spiritual Flight*, edited by Leonard Lewisohn and Christopher Shackle, 197–214. London: I. B. Tauris, 2006.

Burke, Kenneth. 'Literature as Equipment for Living'. In *The Philosophy of Literary Form: Studies in Symbolic Action*, 293–304. 2nd ed. Baton Rouge: Louisiana State University Press, 1967.

Cantarino, Vincente. *Arabic Poetics in the Golden Age*. Leiden: Brill, 1975.

Chabbi, Jacqueline. 'Remarques sur le développement historique des mouvements ascétiques et mystiques au Khurāsān'. *Studia Islamica* 46 (1977): 5–72.

Chalisova, N. 'Persian Rhetoric: *Elm-e badi'* and *elm-e bayân*'. In *General Introduction to Persian Literature*, edited by J. T. P. de Bruijn, 139–71. Vol. 1 of *A History of Persian Literature*, edited by Ehsan Yarshater. London: I. B. Tauris, 2009.

Chase, Michael. 'Some Observations on Pierre Hadot's Conception of Philosophy as a Way of Life'. In *Philosophy as a Way of Life: Ancients and Moderns (Essays in Honor of Pierre Hadot)*, edited by Michael Chase, Stephen R. L. Clark and Michael McGhee, 263–86. Chichester: Wiley Blackwell, 2013.

Clinton, Jerome. 'Esthetics by Implication: What Metaphors of Craft Tell Us about the "Unity" of the Persian *Qasida*'. *Edebiyat* 4, no. 1 (1979): 73–97.

Cohn, Dorrit. 'Metalepsis and *Mise en Abyme*'. Translated by Lewis S. Gleich. *Narrative* 20, no. 1 (2012): 105–14.

Cooperson, Michael. 'Probability, Plausibility, and "Spiritual Communication" in Classical Arabic Biography'. In *On Fiction and* Adab *in Medieval Arabic Literature*, edited by Phillip F. Kennedy, 69–83. Wiesbaden: Harrassowitz, 2005.

Copland, Rita and Peter T. Struck. 'Introduction'. In *The Cambridge Companion to Allegory*, edited by Rita Copland and Peter T. Struck, 1–11. Cambridge: Cambridge University Press, 2010.

Corbin, Henry. *Avicenna and the Visionary Recital.* Translated by Willard R. Trask. New York: Pantheon Books, 1960.

Corbin, Henry. 'Nasir-i Khusrau and Iranian Isma'ilism'. In *The Period from the Arab Invasion to the Saljuqs*, edited by R. N. Frye, 520–42. Vol. 4 of *The Cambridge History of Iran*. Cambridge: Cambridge University Press, 1975.

Corbin, Henry. 'The Visionary Dream in Islamic Spirituality'. In *The Dream and Human Societies*, edited by G. E. von Grunebaum and Roger Caillois, 381–408. Berkeley: University of California Press, 1966.

Cornell, Vincent J. *Realm of the Saint: Power and Authority in Moroccan Sufism.* Austin: University of Texas Press, 1998.

Cross, Cameron. 'The Poetics of Romantic Love in Vis & Rāmin'. PhD diss., University of Chicago, 2015.

Crossan, John Dominic. *In Parables: The Challenge of the Historical Jesus*. New York: Harper & Row, 1973.

Culler, Jonathan. *Theory of the Lyric.* Cambridge, MA: Harvard University Press, 2015.

Dabiri, Ghazzal. 'Reading 'Attār's *Elāhināma* as Sufi Practical Ethics: Between Genre, Reception, and Muslim and Christian Audiences'. *Journal of Persianate Studies* 11 (2018): 29–55.

Dabiri, Ghazzal. 'When a Lion Is Chided by an Ant: Everyday Saints and the Making of Sufi Kings in 'Attār's *Elāhi-nāma*'. *Journal of Persianate Studies* 12, no. 1 (2019): 62–102.

Dahlén, Ashk. 'The Qalandar in the Persianate World: The Case of Fakhrod-din 'Arāqi'. In *Holy Fools and Divine Madmen: Sacred Insanity through Ages and Cultures*, edited by Albrecht Berger and Sergey Ivanov, 125–53. Neuried: Ars Una, 2018.

Dällenbach, Lucien. *The Mirror in the Text*. Chicago: University of Chicago Press, 1989.

Dalzell, Alexander. *The Criticism of Didactic Poetry: Essays on Lucretius, Virgil, and Ovid*. Toronto: University of Toronto Press, 1996.

Daniel, Elton. 'The Rise and Development of Persian Historiography'. In *Persian Historiography*, edited by Charles Melville, 101–54. Vol. 10 of *A History of Persian Literature*, edited by Ehsan Yarshater. London: I. B. Tauris, 2012.

Davis, Dick. 'The Journey as Paradigm: Literal and Metaphorical Travel in 'Aṭṭār's *Manṭiq al-Ṭayr*'. *Edebiyat*, n.s., 4 (1993): 173–83.

Davis, Dick. 'Sufism and Poetry: A Marriage of Convenience?'. *Edebiyât: The Journal of Middle Eastern Literatures* 10, no. 2 (1999): 279–92.

Daya, Najm al-Din Razi. *Mersad al-'ebad*. Edited by Mohammad Amin Riahi. Tehran: Bongah-e Tarjoma va Nashr-e Ketab, 1391 [2012–13].

Daya, Najm al-Din Razi. *The Path of God's Bondsmen from Origin to Return*. Translated by Hamid Algar. Delmar, NY: Caravan Books, 1982.

De Bruijn, J. T. P. 'Chains of Gold: Jami's Defence of Poetry'. *Journal of Turkish Studies* 26, no. 1 (2002): 81–92.

De Bruijn, J. T. P. 'Comparative Notes on Sanā'ī and 'Aṭṭār'. In *Classical Persian Sufism: From Its Origins to Rumi*, edited by Leonard Lewisohn, 360–79. London: Khaniqahi Nimatullahi Publications, 1993.

De Bruijn, J. T. P. '*Mathnawī 2*. In Persian'. In *Encyclopaedia of Islam, Second Edition*. Article posted 2012. https://doi.org/10.1163/1573-3912_islam_COM_0709.

De Bruijn, J. T. P. *Of Piety and Poetry: The Interaction of Religion and Literature in the Life and Works of Ḥakīm Sanā'ī of Ghazna*. Leiden: Brill, 1983.

De Bruijn, J. T. P. *Persian Sufi Poetry: An Introduction to the Mystical Use of Classical Persian Poems*. Richmond: Curzon, 1997.

De Bruijn, J. T. P. 'The Preaching Poet: Three Homiletic Poems by Farīd al-Dīn 'Aṭṭār'. *Edebiyat: Journal of Middle Eastern Literatures* 9, no. 1 (1998): 85–101.

De Bruijn, J. T. P. 'The *Qalandariyyat* in Persian Mystical Poetry'. In *The Legacy of Medieval Persian Sufism*, edited by Leonard Lewisohn, 75–86. London: Khaniqahi Nimatullahi Publications, 1992.

De Bruijn, J. T. P. 'The Stories in Sanâ'î's *Faxri-nâme*'. In *Pand-o sokhan: Mélanges offerts à Charles-Henri de Fouchécour*, edited by Christophe Balaÿ, Claire Kappler and Živa Vesel, 79–93. Tehran: Institut français de recherche en Iran, 1995.

De Fouchécour, Ch.-H. *Moralia: Les notions morales dans la littérature persane du 3e/9e au 7e/13e siècle*. Paris: Recherche sur les civilisations, 1986.

De Jong, Irene. 'Metalepsis in Ancient Greek Literature'. In *Narratology and Interpretation: The Content of Narrative Form in Ancient Literature*, edited by Jonas Grethlein and Antonios Rengakos, 87–115. Berlin: De Gruyter, 2009.

De Menasce, Jean. 'Zoroastrian Pahlavī Writings'. In *The Seleucid, Parthian and Sasanid Periods*, edited by E. Yarshater, 1166–95. Vol. 3, pt. 2 of *The Cambridge History of Iran*. Cambridge: Cambridge University Press, 1983.

Denny, F. M. '*Tadjwīd*'. In *Encyclopaedia of Islam, Second Edition*. Article posted 2012. https://doi.org/10.1163/1573-3912_islam_COM_1145.

Denny, F. M. '*Wird*'. In *Encyclopaedia of Islam, Second Edition*. Article posted 2012. https://doi.org/10.1163/1573-3912_islam_SIM_7914.

Dols, Michael W. and Diana Immisch. *Majnūn: The Madman in Medieval Islamic Society*. Oxford: Clarendon, 1992.

Drory, Rina. *Models and Contacts: Arabic Literature and Its Impact on Medieval Jewish Culture*. Leiden: Brill, 2000.

Duff, David. *Romanticism and the Uses of Genre*. Oxford: Oxford University Press, 2009.

Ebn Monavvar, Mohammad. *Asrar al-towhid fi maqamat al-Shaykh Abi Saʿid*. Edited by Mohammad Reza Shafiʿi-Kadkani. 2 vols. Tehran: Agah, 1376 [1997].

El Ezabi, Shereen. 'Al-Naysaburi's Wise Madmen: Introduction'. *Alif: Journal of Comparative Poetics* 14 (1994): 192–205.

Elias, Jamal. *Aisha's Cushion: Religious Art, Perception, and Practice in Islam*. Cambridge, MA: Harvard University Press, 2012.

Elias, Jamal. *The Throne Carrier of God: The Life and Thought of ʿAlāʾ al-Dawla as-Simnānī*. Albany, NY: SUNY Press, 1995.

Elwell-Sutton, L. P. 'The "Rubāʿī" in Early Persian Literature'. In *The Period from the Arab Invasion to the Saljuqs*, edited by R. N. Frye, 633–57. Vol. 4 of *The Cambridge History of Iran*. Cambridge: Cambridge University Press, 1975.

Eqbal-Ashtiani, ʿAbbas. 'Jameʿ-e Maniʿi-ye Nayshabur'. *Mehr* 3, no. 11 (Farvardin 1315 [March–April 1936]): 1089–94.

Esteʿlami, Mohammad. Introduction to *Tazkerat al-owleya*, by Farid al-Din ʿAttar, xv–xli. Rev. ed. Tehran: Zavvar, 1383 [2004–5].

Ewing, Katherine Pratt and Ilona Gerbakher. 'The *Qalandariyya*: From the Mosque to the Ruin in Poetry, Place, and Practice'. In *Routledge Handbook on Sufism*, edited by Lloyd Ridgeon, 252–68. Abingdon: Routeldge, 2020.

Fahd, Toufy. 'The Dream in Medieval Islamic Society'. In *The Dream and Human Societies*, edited by G. E. von Grunebaum and Roger Caillois, 351–63. Berkeley: University of California Press, 1966.

Feuillebois-Pierunek, Eve. 'Mystical Quest and Oneness in the *Mukhtār-nāma* Attributed to Farīd al-Dīn ʿAṭṭār'. In *ʿAṭṭār and the Persian Sufi Tradition: The*

Art of Spiritual Flight, edited by Leonard Lewisohn and Christopher Shackle, 309–29. London: I. B. Tauris, 2006.

Flemming, Barbara. 'From Archetype to Oral Tradition: Editing Persian and Turkish Literary Texts'. *Manuscripts of the Middle East* 3 (1998): 7–11.

Foltz, Richard. 'Islam, Animals, and Vegetarianism'. In *The Encyclopedia of Religion and Nature*, edited by Bron R. Taylor and Jeffrey Kaplan, 2:873–75. London: Thoemmes Continuum, 2005.

Foruzanfar, Badiʿ al-Zaman. *Sharh-e ahval va naqd va tahlil-e asar-e Shaykh Farid al-Din Mohammad ʿAttar-e Nayshaburi*. Tehran: Chapkhana-ye Daneshgah, 1339 [1960–1]. Reprint, Tehran: Asim, 1389 [2010–11].

Foucault, Michel. *The Courage of the Truth (The Government of Self and Others II): Lectures at the Collège de France, 1983–1984*. Translated by Graham Burchell. Edited by Frédéric Gros. New York: Palgrave Macmillian, 2011.

Frye, Northrop. 'Allegory'. In *Princeton Encyclopaedia of Poetry and Poetics*, edited by Alex Preminger, Frank Warnke and O. B. Hardison Jr, 12–15. Enlarged ed. London: Macmillan, 1974.

Gacek, Adam. *Arabic Manuscripts: A Vademecum for Readers*. Leiden: Brill, 2009.

Gazorgahi, Mir Kamal al-Din Hosayn. *Majales al-ʿoshshaq*. Edited by Gholam Reza Tabataba'i-Majd. Tehran: Zarrin, 1375 [1996–7].

Genette, Gérard. *Narrative Discourse: An Essay in Method*. Translated by Jane E. Lewin. Ithaca, NY: Cornell University Press, 1980.

Gerd-Faramarzi, ʿAli Soltani. *Simorgh dar qalamrov-e farhang-e Iran*. Tehran: Mobtakeran, 1372 [1993–4].

Ghazali, Abu Hamid. *Ihya' ʿulum al-din*. 16 vols. Cairo: Lajnat Nashr al-Thaqafa al-Islamiyya, 1356–7 [1937–8].

Ghazali, Abu Hamid. *Kimia-ye saʿadat*. Edited by Ahmad Aram. 2 vols. Tehran: Ganjina, 1997.

Ghazali, Abu Hamid. *Mishkat al-anwar*. Edited by Abu'l-ʿAla ʿAfifi. Cairo: al-Dar al-Qawmiyya li'l-Tibaʿa wa'l-Nashr, 1964.

Ghazali, Abu Hamid. *The Niche of Lights: A Parallel English-Arabic Text*. Edited and translated by David Buchman. Provo: Brigham Young University Press, 1998.

Ghazali, Ahmad. *Majmuʿa-ye asar-e farsi-ye Ahmad-e Ghazali*. Edited by Ahmad Mojahed. Tehran: Daneshgah-e Tehran, 1979.

Giffen, Lois Anita. *Theory of Profane Love among the Arabs: The Development of the Genre*. New York: New York University Press, 1971.

Gramlich, Richard. *Alte Vorbilder des Sufitums*. 2 vols. Wiesbaden: Harrassowitz, 1995.

Green, Nile. 'The Religious and Cultural Roles of Dreams and Visions in Islam'. *Journal of the Royal Asiatic Society* 13, no. 3 (2003): 287–313.

Green, Nile. *Sufism: A Global History*. Chichester: Wiley-Blackwell, 2012.

Green, Nile. 'The Uses of Books in a Late Mughal *Takiyya*: Persianate Knowledge between Person and Paper'. *Modern Asian Studies* 44 (2010): 241–65.

Gruber, Christiane J. *The Ilkhanid Book of Ascension: A Persian-Sunni Prayer Manual*. New York: I. B. Tauris, 2010.

Gruber, Christiane J. and Frederick Stephen Colby, eds. *The Prophet's Ascension: Cross-cultural Encounters with the Islamic* Miʿrāj *Tales*. Bloomington: Indiana University Press, 2010.

Ha'eri, ʿAbdolhosayn. Introduction to *Safina-ye Tabriz: Chap-e ʿaksi az ru-ye noskha-ye khatti-ye Ketabkhana-ye Majles-e Shura-ye Eslami*, by Abu'l-Majd Mohammad b. Masʿud Tabrizi, v–viii. Tehran: Markez-e Nashr-e Daneshgahi, 1381 [2001–2].

Hafez, Shams al-Din Mohammad. *Divan*. Edited by Parviz Khanlari. Tehran: Entesharat-e Bonyad-e Farhang-e Iran, 1359 [1980–1].

Halperin, David J. '*Hekhalot* and *Miʿrāj*: Observations on the Heavenly Journey in Judaism and Islam'. In *Death, Ecstasy, and Other Worldly Journeys*, edited by John J. Collins and Michael Fishbane, 269–88. Albany, NY: SUNY Press, 1995.

Hamori, A. 'Ascetic Poetry (*Zuhdiyyāt*)'. In *Abbasid Belles Lettres*, edited by Julia Ashtiany, T. M. Johnstone, J. D. Latham and R. B. Serjeant, 265–74. Cambridge: Cambridge University Press, 1990.

Harb, Lara. *Arabic Poetics: Aesthetic Experience in Classical Arabic Literature*. Cambridge: Cambridge University Press, 2020.

Heath, Peter. *Allegory and Philosophy in Avicenna (Ibn Sînâ): With a Translation of the Book of the Prophet Muhammad's Ascent to Heaven*. Philadelphia: University of Pennsylvania Press, 1992.

Hermansen, Marcia. 'Dreams and Dreaming in Islam'. In *Dreams: A Reader on Religious, Cultural, and Psychological Dimensions of Dreaming*, edited by Kelly Bulkeley, 73–91. New York: Palgrave, 2002.

Hirschler, Konrad. *The Written Word in Medieval Arabic Lands: A Social and Cultural History of Reading Practices*. Edinburgh: Edinburgh University Press, 2012.

Hoffmann, Alexandra. 'Angry Men: On Emotions and Masculinities in Samarqandī's *Sindbād-nāmeh*'. *Narrative Culture* 7, no. 2 (2020): 145–64.

Hojviri, ʿAli b. ʿOsman. *Kashf al-mahjub*. Edited by Mahmud ʿAbedi. Tehran: Sorush, 1392 [2013–14].

Honigmann, E. and Clifford Edmund Bosworth. 'Nishapur'. In *Historic Cities of the Islamic World*, edited by Clifford Edmund Bosworth, 421–3. Leiden: Brill, 2007.

Hughes, Aaron W. *The Texture of the Divine: Imagination in Medieval Islamic and Jewish Thought*. Bloomington: Indiana University Press, 2004.

Hughes, Aaron W. 'Imagining the Divine: Ghazali on Imagination, Dreams, and Dreaming'. *Journal of the American Academy of Religion* 70, no. 1 (2002): 33–5.

Hunsberger, Alice C. *Nasir Khusraw: The Ruby of Badakhshan*. London: I. B. Tauris, 2000.

Hunsberger, Alice C. '"On the Steed of Speech": A Philosophical Poem by Nāṣir-i Khusraw'. In *Pearls of Persia: The Philosophical Poetry of Nāṣir-i Khusraw*, edited by Alice C. Hunsberger, 147–89. London: I. B. Tauris, 2012.

Hunsberger, Alice C., ed. *Pearls of Persia: The Philosophical Poetry of Nāṣir-i Khusraw*. London: I. B. Tauris, 2012.

Ibn 'Arabi, Muhyi al-Din. *Risalat al-anwar*. Edited by 'Abd al-Rahim Mardini. Damascus: Dar al-Mahabba, 2003.

Ibn al-Fuwati, Kamal al-Din. *Talkhis majma' al-adab fi mu'jam al-alqab*. Edited by Mustafa Jawad. 3 vols. Damascus: Wizarat al-Thaqafa wa'l-Irshad al-Qawmi, 1963–5.

Ibn al-Jawzi. *Kitab al-qussas wa'l-mudhakkirin*. Edited and translated by Merlin Swartz. Beirut: Dar el-Machreq, 1971.

Ibn al-Jawzi. *Ru'us al-qawarir*. Edited by Muhammad Nabil Sunbul. Tanta, Egypt: Dar al-Sahaba li'l-Turath, 1410 [1990].

Ibn Jubayr. *Rihlat Ibn Jubayr*. Beirut: Dar Sadir, 1964.

Ibn Jubayr. *The Travels of Ibn Jubayr*. Translated by R. J. C. Broadhurst. London: Jonathan Cape, 1952.

Ibn al-Nadim. *The Fihrist of al-Nadīm: A Critical Edition*. Edited by Ayman Fo'ād Sayyid. 4 vols. London: Al-Furqān Islamic Heritage Foundation, 2014.

Ibn Sina. *Traités mystiques d'Abou Alî al-Hosain b. Abdallah b. Sînâ ou d'Avicenne*. Edited by M. A. F. Mehren. 2 vols. Leiden: Brill, 1889–91.

Ibn Tufayl. *Hayy ibn Yaqzān: A Philosophical Tale*. Translated by Lenn Evan Goodman. Chicago: University of Chicago, 2009.

Ingenito, Domenico. *Beholding Beauty: Sa'di of Shiraz and the Aesthetics of Desire in Medieval Persian Poetry*. Leiden: Brill, 2021.

Irwin, Bonnie D. 'What's in a Frame? The Medieval Textualization of Traditional Storytelling'. *Oral Tradition* 10, no. 1 (1995): 27–53.

Iser, Wolfgang. *The Implied Reader: Patterns of Communication in Prose Fiction from Bunyan to Beckett*. Baltimore: Johns Hopkins University Press, 1974.

Ivanow, W. *Problems in Nasir-i Khusraw's Biography*. Bombay: The Ismaili Society, 1956.

Jami, 'Abd al-Rahman. *Nafahat al-ons men hazarat al-qods*. Edited by Mahmud 'Abedi. Tehran: Sokhan, 1394 [2015–16].

Jones, Linda. *The Power of Oratory in the Medieval Muslim World*. Cambridge: Cambridge University Press, 2012.

Jurjani, 'Abd al-Qahir. *Asrar al-balagha*. Edited by Hellmut Ritter. Istanbul: Istanbul Government Press, 1954.

Kanzog, Klaus. 'Rahmenerzählung'. In *Reallexikon der deutschen Literaturgeschichte*, edited by Paul Merker and Wolfgang Stammler, 321–43. 2nd ed. Berlin: W. de Gruyter, 1977.

Karamustafa, Ahmet T. 'Antinomian Sufis'. In *The Cambridge Companion to Sufism*, edited by Lloyd Ridgeon, 101–24. Cambridge: Cambridge University Press, 2014.

Karamustafa, Ahmet T. *Sufism: The Formative Period*. Berkeley: University of California Press, 2007.

Kennedy, Paul. *Abu Nuwas: A Genius of Poetry*. London: Oneworld, 2005.

Kennedy, Paul. '*Zuhdiyya*'. In *Encyclopaedia of Islam, Second Edition*. Article posted 2012. https://doi.org/10.1163/1573-3912_islam_COM_1392.

Kermani, Navid. *The Terror of God: Attar, Job and the Metaphysical Revolt*. Translated by Wieland Hoban. Cambridge: Polity Press, 2011.

Keshavarz, Fatemeh. 'Flight of the Birds: The Poetic Animating the Spiritual in 'Aṭṭār's *Manṭiq al-Ṭayr*'. In *'Aṭṭār and the Persian Sufi Tradition: The Art of Spiritual Flight*, edited by Leonard Lewisohn and Christopher Shackle, 112–34. London: I. B. Tauris, 2006.

Keshavarz, Fatemeh. *Reading Mystical Lyric: The Case of Jalal al-Din Rumi*. Columbia, SC: University of South Carolina Press, 1998.

Khalil, Atif. *Repentance and the Return to God:* Tawba *in Early Sufism*. Albany, NY: SUNY Press, 2019.

King, Anya. *Scent from the Garden of Paradise: Musk and the Medieval Islamic World*. Leiden: Brill, 2017.

Kirkwood, William. 'Parables as Metaphors and Examples'. *Quarterly Journal of Speech* 71 (1985): 422–40.

Knysh, Alexander D. *Islamic Mysticism: A Short History*. Leiden: Brill, 2000.

Konstan, David. 'Foreword: To the Reader'. In *Mega nepios: Il destinatario nell'epos didascalico*, edited by Alessandro Schiesaro, Phillip Mitsis and Jenny Strauss Clay, 11–22. Pisa: Giardini, 1993.

Kugel, Scott. *Sufis and Saints' Bodies: Mysticism, Corporeality, and Sacred Power in Islam*. Chapel Hill: University of North Carolina Press, 2007.

Landau, Justine. 'Naṣīr al-Dīn Ṭūsī and the Poetic Imagination in the Arabic and Persian Philosophical Tradition'. In *Metaphor and Imagery in Persian Poetry*, edited by Ali Asghar Seyed-Gohrab, 15–65. Leiden: Brill, 2012.

Landolt, Hermann. "Aṭṭār, Sufism, and Ismailism'. In *'Aṭṭār and the Persian Sufi Tradition: The Art of Spiritual Flight*, edited by Leonard Lewisohn and Christopher Shackle, 3–26. London: I. B. Tauris, 2006.

Lazard, Gilbert. 'Abū Šakūr Balḵī'. In *Encyclopaedia Iranica*. Article posted 2020. https://doi.org/10.1163/2330-4804_EIRO_COM_4686.

Lazard, Gilbert. *Les premiers poètes persans (IXe–Xe): Fragments rassemblés, édités et traduits*. 2 vols. Paris: Librairie d'Amérique et d'Orient, 1964.

Lazard, Gilbert. 'The Rise of the New Persian Language'. In *The Period from the Arab Invasion to the Seljuqs*, edited by R. N. Frye, 595–632. Vol. 4 of *The Cambridge History of Iran*. Cambridge: Cambridge University Press, 1975.

Leclercq, Jean. *The Love of Learning and the Desire for God: A Study of Monastic Culture*. Translated by Catherine Misrahi. New York: Fordham University Press, 1974.

Lewicka, Paulina B. *Food and Foodways of Medieval Cairenes*. Leiden: Brill, 2011.

Lewis, Franklin. 'Authorship, *Auctoritas*, and the Management of Literary Estates in Pre-modern Persian literature'. *Jerusalem Studies in Arabic and Islam* 45 (2018): 73–125.

Lewis, Franklin. 'The Modes of Literary Production: Remarks on the Composition, Revision and "Publication" of Persian Texts in the Medieval Period'. *Persica* 17 (2001): 69–83.

Lewis, Franklin. 'Reading, Writing, and Recitation: Sanā'i and the Origins of the Persian Ghazal'. PhD diss., University of Chicago, 1995.

Lewis, Franklin. *Rumi: Past and Present, East and West*. Oxford: Oneworld, 2008.

Lewis, Franklin. 'Sexual Occidentation: The Politics of Conversion, Christian-Love and Boy-Love in 'Aṭṭār'. *Iranian Studies* 42, no. 5 (2009): 693–723.

Lewis, Franklin. 'Solṭân Valad and the Political Order: Framing the Ethos and Praxis of Poetry in the Mevlevi Tradition after Rumi'. In *Persian Language, Literature and Culture: New Leaves, Fresh Looks*, edited by Kamran Talattof, 23–47. Abingdon: Routledge, 2015.

Lewis, Franklin. 'The Unbearable Lightness of Rhyming Meter: Jāmī's Confessions of a Versification Junkie'. Paper presented at A Worldwide Literature: Jami in the Dār al-Islām and Beyond, University of Chicago Paris Center, 14–15 March 2013.

Lewisohn, Leonard. 'Sufi Symbolism in the Persian Hermeneutic Tradition: Reconstructing the Pagoda of 'Aṭṭār's Esoteric Poetics'. In *'Aṭṭār and the Persian Sufi Tradition: The Art of Spiritual Flight*, edited by Leonard Lewisohn and Christopher Shackle, 255–308. London: I. B. Tauris, 2006.

Losensky, Paul. 'The Creative Compiler: The Art of Rewriting in 'Aṭṭār's *Taẕkirat al-awlīyā'*'. In *The Necklace of the Pleiades: Studies in Persian Literature Presented to Heshmat Moayyad on His 80th Birthday*, edited by Franklin Lewis and Sunil Sharma, 107–19. Leiden: Leiden University Press, 2010.

Losensky, Paul. 'Words and Deeds: Message and Structure in 'Aṭṭār's *Tadhkirat al-awliyā'*'. In *'Aṭṭār and the Persian Sufi Tradition: The Art of Spiritual Flight*, edited by Leonard Lewisohn and Christopher Shackle, 75–92. London: I. B. Tauris, 2006.

Lumbard, Alexis York and Demi. *The Conference of the Birds*. Bloomington, IN: Wisdom Tales, 2012.

Lumbard, Joseph. *Aḥmad al-Ghazālī, Remembrance, and the Metaphysics of Love*. Albany, NY: SUNY Press, 2016.

Macuch, Maria. 'Pahlavi Literature'. In *The Literature of Pre-Islamic Iran*, edited by Ronald E. Emmerick and Maria Macuch, 116–96. Companion vol. 1 to *A History of Persian Literature*, edited by Ehsan Yarshater. London: I. B. Tauris, 2009.

Madelung, Wilferd. 'Ethics in Islam'. In *Naṣīr al-Dīn Ṭūsī's Ethics: Between Philosophy, Shi'ism, and Sufism*, edited by Richard Hovannisian, 85–101. Malibu, CA: Undena Publications, 1995.

Mahdi, Muhsin. 'The Book and the Master as Poles of Cultural Change in Islam'. In *Islam and Cultural Change in the Middle Ages*, edited by Speros Vryonis, 3–15. Wiesbaden: Harrassowitz, 1975.

Mahjub, Muhammad Jafar. 'Chivalry and Early Persian Sufism'. In *Classical Persian Sufism: From Its Origins to Rumi*, edited by Leonard Lewisohn, 549–81. London: Khaniqahi Nimatullahi Publications, 1993.

Malamud, Margaret. 'Sufi Organizations and Structures of Authority in Medieval Nishapur'. *International Journal of Middle East Studies* 26, no. 3 (1994): 427–42.

Malina, Debra. *Breaking the Frame: Metalepsis and the Construction of the Subject*. Columbus: The Ohio State University Press, 2002.

Margoliouth, D. S. 'Abu'l-'Alā al-Ma'arri's Correspondence on Vegetarianism'. *Journal of the Royal Asiatic Society* (1902): 289–332.

Martin, James D. 'The Religious Beliefs of Abu'l-'Atāhiya according to *Zuhdīyāt*'. In *Transactions, Volume XXIII, 1969–1970*, edited by William McKane, 11–28. Glasgow: Glasgow University Oriental Society, 1972.

Marvrudi, Fakhr al-Din Mobarak-Shah. *Rahiq al-tahqiq be enzemam-e ash'ar-e digar-e u*. Edited by Nasrollah Pourjavady. Tehran: Markez-e Nashr-e Daneshgahi, 1381 [2002].

Marzolph, Ulrich. 'Buhlūl'. In *Enycylopaedia of Islam, Three*. Article posted 2009. https://doi.org/10.1163/1573-3912_ei3_COM_23313.

Marzolph, Ulrich. *Der weise Narr Buhlūl*. Wiesbaden: Deutsche Morgenländische Gesellschaft, 1983.

Marzolph, Ulrich. '*'Uḳalā' al-madjānīn*'. In *Encyclopaedia of Islam, Second Edition*. Article posted 2012. https://doi.org/10.1163/1573-3912_islam_SIM_8927.

Massé, H. and Cl. Haurt. '*Humā*'. In *Encyclopaedia of Islam, Second Edition*. Article posted 2012. https://doi.org/10.1163/1573-3912_islam_SIM_2947.

Matini, J. '*Āfarīn-nāma*'. In *Encyclopaedia Iranica*. Article posted 2020. https://doi.org/10.1163/2330-4804_EIRO_COM_4799.

McHale, Brian. *Postmodernist Fiction*. New York: Methuen, 1987.

Meier, Fritz. 'Khurāsān and the End of Classical Sufism'. In *Essays on Islamic Piety*, translated by John O'Kane and edited by Bernd Radtke, 189–219. Leiden: Brill, 1999.

Meier, Fritz. 'The Spiritual Man in the Persian Poet 'Aṭṭār'. *Papers from the Eranos Yearbooks* 4 (1954): 267–304.

Meisami, Julie Scott. 'The Ghazal as Fiction: Implied Speakers and Implied Audience in Hafiz's Ghazals'. In *Intoxication, Earthly and Heavenly: Seven Studies on the Poet Hafiz of Shiraz*, edited by Michael Glünz and J. Christoph Bürgel, 89–103. New York: Peter Lang, 1991.

Meisami, Julie Scott. 'Hafez v. Manuscripts of Hafez'. In *Encyclopaedia Iranica*. Article posted 2020. https://doi.org/10.1163/2330-4804_EIRO_COM_2596.

Meisami, Julie Scott. 'Nāṣir-i Khusraw: A Poet Lost in Thought?'. In *Pearls of Persia: The Philosophical Poetry of Nāṣir-i Khusraw*, edited by Alice C. Hunsberger, 223–55. London: I. B. Tauris, 2012.

Meisami, Julie Scott. *Structure and Meaning in Medieval Arabic and Persian Poetry: Orient Pearls*. London: RoutledgeCurzon, 2003.

Melchert, Christopher. 'Sufis and Competing Movements in Nishapur'. *Iran* 39 (2001): 237–47.

Melville, Charles. 'Ebn al-Fowaṭī, Kamāl-al-Dīn 'Abd-al-Razzāq'. In *Encyclopaedia*

Iranica. Article posted 2020. https://doi.org/10.1163/2330-4804_EIRO_COM_8686.

Meneghini, Daniela. '*Mokṯār-nāma*'. In *Encyclopaedia Iranica*. Article posted 2020. https://doi.org/10.1163/2330-4804_EIRO_COM_398.

Meri, Josef. *The Cult of Saints among Muslims and Jews in Medieval Syria*. Oxford: Oxford University Press, 2002.

Mikkelson, Jane. 'Flights of Imagination: Avicenna's Phoenix (*'Anqā*) and Bedil's Figuration for the Lyric Self'. *Journal of South Asian Intellectual History* 2 (2019): 28–72.

Mill, John Stuart. *Essays on Poetry*. Edited by F. Parvin Sharpless. Columbia, SC: University of South Carolina Press, 1976.

Miller, Matthew Thomas. 'Genre in Classical Persian Poetry'. In *Routledge Handbook of Persian Literature*, edited by Kamran Talattof. Abingdon: Routledge, forthcoming.

Miller, Matthew Thomas. 'Poetics of the Sufi Carnival: The "Rogue Lyrics" (*Qalandariyât*) of Sanâ'i, 'Attâr, and 'Erâqi'. PhD diss., Washington University in Saint Louis, 2016.

Mirafzali, Sayyed 'Ali. 'Aya Mokhtar-nama az 'Attar ast?'. *Nashr-e danesh* 17, no. 1 (1379 [2000]): 32–43.

Modarres-Razavi, Mohammad Taqi. *Ahval va asar-e Mohammad b. Mohammad b. al-Hasan al-Tusi molaqqab be Khwaja Nasir al-Din*. Tehran: Bonyad-e Farhang-e Iran, 1354 [1974–5].

Mojaddedi, J. A. *The Biographical Tradition in Sufism: The* Ṭabaqāt *Genre from al-Sulamī to Jāmī*. Richmond: Curzon, 2001.

Mojaddedi, J. A. 'The Ebb and Flow of "The Ocean inside a Jug": The Structure of Book One of Rūmī's *Mathnawī* Reconsidered'. *Journal of Sufi Studies* 3 (2014): 105–31.

Morris, J. W. 'The Spiritual Ascension: Ibn 'Arabī and the *Mi'rāj*: Part 1'. *Journal of the American Oriental Society* 107, no. 4 (1987): 629–52.

Morris, J. W. 'The Spiritual Ascension: Ibn 'Arabī and the *Mi'rāj*: Part 2'. *Journal of the American Oriental Society* 108, no. 1 (1988): 63–77.

Mosharraf, Maryam. 'Shaluda-shakani-ye manteq-e vahshat dar asar-e 'Attar'. In *'Attar-shenakht*, edited by Mohammad Reza Rashed Mohassel, 107–18. Mashhad: Daneshgah-e Ferdowsi, 1385 [2006–7].

Naser-e Khosrow. *Divan-e ash'ar-e Hakim Naser-e Khosrow*. Edited by Mahdi Mohaqqeq and Mojtaba Minovi. Tehran: McGill University, Center for Islamic Studies; Daneshgah-e Tehran, 1357 [1978–9].

Naser-e Khosrow. *Forty Poems from the 'Divan'*. Translated by Peter Lamborn Wilson and Gholam Reza Aavani. Tehran: Imperial Iranian Academy of Philosophy, 1977.

Naser-e Khosrow. *Safar-nama*. Edited by Mohammad Dabir Siaqi. Tehran: Zavvar, 1389 [2010].

Nasr, Seyyed Hossein. 'The Flight of the Birds to Union: Meditations upon "Aṭṭār's *Manṭiq al-ṭayr*"'. In *Islamic Art and Spirituality*, 98–113. Albany, NY: SUNY Press, 1987.

Nasr, Seyyed Hossein. 'Some Observations on the Place of 'Aṭṭār within the Sufi Tradition'. In *Colloquio italo-iraniano sul poeta mistico Fariduddin 'Aṭṭār (Roma, 24–25 Marzo 1977)*, 5–20. Rome: Accademia Nazionale dei Lincei, 1978.

Nezami-ye 'Aruzi. *Chahar maqala*. Edited by Mohammad Qazvini. Tehran: Eshraqi, 1368 [1989].

Nezami-ye Ganjavi. *Makhzan al-asrar: Matn-e 'elmi-enteqadi az ru-ye 14 nuskha-ye khatti*. Edited by Behruz Sarvatian. Tehran: Amir Kabir, 1387 [2008–9].

Nicholson, Reynold. Introduction to *The Mathnawí of Jalálu'ddín Rúmí*, by Jalal al-Din Rumi, 1:xiii–xviii. Cambridge: Gibb Memorial Trust, 2015.

Nussbaum, Martha. *The Therapy of Desire: Theory and Practice in Hellenistic Ethics*. Princeton: Princeton University Press, 1994.

Ohlander, Erik. *Sufism in an Age of Transition: 'Umar al-Suhrawardī and the Rise of the Islamic Mystical Brotherhoods*. Leiden: Brill, 2008.

O'Malley, Austin. 'Erotic Narratives and 'Attār's Refashioning of the Didactic *Masnavi*'. In *Routledge Handbook of Persian Literature*, edited by Kamran Talattof. Abingdon: Routledge, forthcoming.

O'Malley, Austin. 'From Blessed Lips: The Textualization of Abu Sa'id's Dicta and Deeds'. *Journal of Persianate Studies* 12, no. 1 (2019): 5–31.

O'Malley, Austin. 'Poetry and Pedagogy: The Homiletic Verse of Farid al-Din 'Aṭṭâr'. PhD diss., University of Chicago, 2017.

O'Malley, Austin. 'Rhetoric, Narrative, and the Remembrance of Death in 'Aṭṭār's *Moṣibat-nāmeh*'. *Iranian Studies* 51, no. 1 (2018): 23–46.

O'Malley, Austin. 'An Unexpected Romance: Reevaluating the Authorship of the *Khosrow-nāma*'. *Al-'Uṣūr al-Wusṭā: The Journal of Middle East Medievalists* 27 (2019): 201–32.

Omidsalar, Mahmoud. 'Charms'. In *Encyclopaedia Iranica*. Article posted 2020. https://doi.org/10.1163/2330-4804_EIRO_COM_7668.

Ong, Walter J. *Orality and Literacy: The Technologizing of the Word*. London: Routledge, 1991.

Ong, Walter J. 'The Writer's Audience Is Always a Fiction'. *PMLA* 90, no. 1 (1975): 9–21.

'Owfi, Mohammad. *Lobab al-albab*. Edited by Edward Browne. 2 vols. Leiden: Brill, 1903–6.

Paul, Jürgen. 'Hagiographic Literature'. In *Encyclopaedia Iranica*. Article posted 2020. https://doi.org/10.1163/2330-4804_EIRO_COM_2645.

Pedersen, Johannes. *The Arabic Book*. Translated by Geoffrey French. Princeton: Princeton University Press, 1984.

Pedersen, Johannes. 'The Criticism of the Islamic Preacher'. *Die Welt des Islam*, n.s., 2, no. 4 (1953): 215–31.

Pedersen, Johannes. 'The Islamic Preacher: *Wāʿiẓ, Mudhakkir, Qāṣṣ*'. In *Ignace Goldziher Memorial Volume*, edited by Samuel Löwinger and Joseph Somogyi, 1:226–51. Budapest: 1948.

Pellat, Ch. '*Ḳāṣṣ*'. In *Encyclopaedia of Islam, Second Edition*. Article posted 2012. https://doi.org/10.1163/1573-3912_islam_SIM_4002.

Pier, John. 'Metalepsis'. In *Living Handbook of Narratology*, edited by Peter Hühn, Jan Christoph Meister, John Pier and Wolf Schmid. Article updated 13 July 2016. www.lhn.uni-hamburg.de/article/metalepsis-revised-version-uploaded-13-july-2016.

Pifer, Michael. *Kindred Voices: A Literary History of Medieval Anatolia*. New Haven: Yale University Press, 2021.

Pifer, Michael. 'The Rose of Muḥammad, the Fragrance of Christ: Liminal Poetics in Medieval Anatolia'. *Medieval Encounters* 26 (2020): 258–320.

Pinault, David. *Story-Telling Techniques in the Arabian Nights*. Leiden: Brill, 1992.

Poe, Edgar Allen. *Critical Theory: The Major Documents*. Edited by Stuart Levine and Susan F. Levine. Urbana: University of Illinois Press, 2009.

Pourjavady, Nasrollah. 'Genres of Religious Literature'. In *General Introduction to Persian Literature*, edited by J. T. P. de Bruijn, 270–311. Vol. 1 of *A History of Persian Literature*, edited by Ehsan Yarshater. London: I. B. Tauris, 2009.

Pourjavady, Nasrollah. 'Hearing by Way of Seeing: *Zabān-e ḥāl* in Nāṣir-i Khusraw's Poetry and the Question of Authorship of the *Rawshanāʾī-nāma*'. In *Pearls of Persia: The Philosophical Poetry of Nāṣir-i Khusraw*, edited by Alice C. Hunsberger, 133–45. London: I. B. Tauris, 2012.

Pourjavady, Nasrollah. 'Hekmat-e divanagan dar masnaviha-ye 'Attar'. *Nashr-e danesh* 13, no. 1 (1371 [1992–3]): 2–16.

Pourjavady, Nasrollah. Introduction to *Rahiq al-tahqiq be enzemam-e ash'ar-e digar-e u*, by Fakhr al-Din Mobarak-Shah Marvrudi, 13–56. Tehran: Markez-e Nashr-e Daneshgahi, 1381 [2002].

Pourjavady, Nasrollah. 'Naqd-e falsafi-ye she'r az nazar-e 'Attar va 'Owfi'. *Ma'aref* 4, no. 3 (1366 [1987–8]): 3–18.

Pourjavady, Nasrollah. 'She'r-e hekmat: Nesbat-e she'r va shar' az nazar-e 'Attar'. *Ma'aref* 5, no. 2 (1367 [1988]): 3–56.

Pourjavady, Nasrollah. *Zaban-e hal dar 'erfan va adabiyat-e parsi*. Tehran: Hermes, 1385 [2006–7].

Purnamdarian, Taqi. "Aql va falsafa az nazargah-e 'Attar'. In *Didar ba simorgh*, 177–204. Tehran: Pazhuheshgah-e 'Olum-e Ensani va Motala'at-e Farhangi, 1374 [1995–6].

Purnamdarian, Taqi. "Attar va resalaha-ye 'erfani-ye Ebn Sina'. In *Didar ba simorgh*, 161–80. Tehran: Pazhuheshgah-e 'Olum-e Ensani va Motala'at-e Farhangi, 1374 [1995–6].

Purnamdarian, Taqi. 'Negahi be dastan-pardazi-ye 'Attar'. In *Didar ba simorgh*, 259–92. Tehran: Pazhuheshgah-e 'Olum-e Ensani va Motala'at-e Farhangi, 1374 [1995–6].

Purnamdarian, Taqi. 'Simorgh va Jebra'il'. In *Didar ba simorgh*, 73–97. Tehran: Pazhuheshgah-e 'Olum-e Ensani va Motala'at-e Farhangi, 1374 [1995–6].

Purnamdarian, Taqi. 'Tafsiri digar az dasatan-e Shaykh San'an'. In *Didar ba simorgh*, 249–71. Tehran: Pazhuheshgah-e 'Olum-e Ensani va Motala'at-e Farhangi, 1374 [1995–6].

Qazvini, Muhammad. Introduction to *Lobab al-albab*, by Mohammad 'Owfi, i–xxv. Leiden: Brill, 1906.

Qushayri, Abu'l-Qasim. *al-Risala al-qushayriyya*. Edited by 'Abd al-Halim Mahmud and Mahmud b. al-Sharif. 2 vols. Cairo: Dar al-Sha'b, 1989.

Qutbuddin, Tahera. 'Healing the Soul: Perspectives of Medieval Muslim Writers'. *Harvard Middle Eastern and Islamic Review* 2 (1995): 62–87.

Rahman, Fazlur. '*Baḳā' wa-Fanā'*'. In *Encyclopaedia of Islam, Second Edition*. Article posted 2012. https://doi.org/10.1163/1573-3912_islam_SIM_1083.

Rahman, Fazlur. 'Dream, Imagination, and *'Ālam al-mithāl*'. In *The Dream and Human Societies*, edited by G. E. von Grunebaum and Roger Caillois, 409–19. Berkeley: University of California Press, 1966.

Rahman, Fazlur. *Prophecy in Islam: Philosophy and Orthodoxy*. London: Allen & Unwin, 1958.

Ravān Farhādī, A. G. 'The *Hundred Grounds* of 'Abdullāh Anṣārī of Herāt (d. 448/1056): The Earliest Mnemonic Sufi Manual in Persian'. In *Classical Persian Sufism: From Its Origins to Rumi*, edited by Leonard Lewisohn, 381–99. London: Khaniqahi Nimatullahi Publications, 1993.

Reinert, B. "Aṭṭār, Farīd-al-Dīn'. In *Encyclopaedia Iranica*. Article posted 2020. https://doi.org/10.1163/2330-4804_EIRO_COM_6077.

Renard, John. *Friends of God: Islamic Images of Piety, Commitment, and Servanthood*. Berkeley: University of California Press, 2008.

Richter-Bernburg, Lutz. 'Hippocrates'. In *Encyclopaedia Iranica*. Article posted 2020. https://doi.org/10.1163/2330-4804_EIRO_COM_3097.

Ricoeur, Paul. 'Listening to the Parables of Jesus'. *Criterion* 13 (1974): 18–22.

Ricoeur, Paul. *Time and Narrative*. Translated by Kathleen Blamey and David Pellauer. 3 vols. Chicago: University of Chicago Press, 1984–8.

Ridgeon, Lloyd. *Morals and Mysticism in Persian Sufism: A History of Sufi-Futuwwat in Iran*. Abingdon: Routledge, 2010.

Ritter, Hellmut. "Aṭṭār'. In *Encyclopaedia of Islam, Second Edition*. Article posted 2012. https://doi.org/10.1163/1573-3912_islam_COM_0074.

Ritter, Hellmut. 'Muslim Mystics' Strife with God'. *Oriens* 5, no. 1 (1952): 1–15.

Ritter, Hellmut. *The Ocean of the Soul: Man, the World and God in the Stories of Farīd al-Dīn 'Aṭṭār*. Translated by John O'Kane. Edited by Bernd Radtke. Leiden: Brill, 2003.

Ritter, Hellmut. 'Philologika XI: Maulānā Ǧalāladdīn Rūmī und sein Kreis'. *Der Islam* 26 (1942): 221–49.

Ritter, Hellmut. 'Philologika XVI: Farīduddīn 'Aṭṭār IV'. *Oriens* 13/14 (1960–1): 195–239.

Rosenblatt, Louise M. *The Reader, the Text, the Poem: The Transactional Theory of the Literary Work*. Carbondale: Southern Illinois University Press, 1978.

Rubanovich, Julia. 'Metaphors of Authorship in Persian Prose'. *Middle Eastern Literatures* 12, no. 2 (2009): 127–35.

Rubanovich, Julia, ed. *Orality and Textuality in the Iranian World: Patterns of Interaction across the Centuries*. Leiden: Brill, 2015.

Rumi, Jalal al-Din. *Fihi ma fih va payvastha-ye no-yafta*. Edited by Towfiq Sobhani. Tehran: Parsa, 1388 [2009–10].

Rumi, Jalal al-Din. *Majales-e sab'a: Haft khetaba*. Edited by Towfiq Sobhani. Tehran: Kayhan, 1365 [1986].

Rumi, Jalal al-Din. *Masnavi*. Edited by Mohammad Este'lami. 7 vols. Tehran: Sokhan, 1393 [2014].

Russell, J. Stephen. Introduction to *Allegoresis: The Craft of Allegory in Medieval Literature*, edited by J. Stephen Russell, xi–xv. New York: Garland Publishing, 1988.

Rypka, Jan. *History of Iranian Literature*. Dordrecht: D. Reidel, 1968.

Sa'di. *Kolliyat-e Sa'di*. Edited by Mohammad 'Ali Forughi. Tehran: Amir Kabir, 1367 [1988–9].

Safa, Zabihollah. *Tarikh-i adabiyat dar Iran*. 5 vols. Tehran: Ferdowsi, 1371 [1992–3].

Safavi, Seyed Ghahreman and Simon Weightman. *Rūmī's Mystical Design: Reading the "Mathnawī," Book One*. Albany, NY: SUNY Press, 2009.

Safi, Omid. "Aṭṭār, Farīd al-Dīn'. In *Encyclopaedia of Islam, Three*. Article posted 2016. https://doi.org/10.1163/1573-3912_ei3_COM_23976.

Samarqandi, Dowlat-Shah. *Tazkerat al-sho'ara*. Edited by Fatema 'Alaqa. Tehran: Pazhuheshgah-e 'Olum-e Ensani va Motala'at-e Farhangi, 1385 [2006–7].

Sana'i, Majdud b. Adam. *Hadiqat al-haqiqa va shari'at al-tariqa (Fakhri-nama)*. Edited by Maryam Hosayni. Tehran: Nashr-e Daneshgahi, 1382 [2003–4].

San'atinia, Fatema. *Ma'akhez-e qesas va tamsil-e masnaviha-ye 'Attar-e Nayshaburi*. Tehran: Zavvar, 1369 [1990–1].

Schimmel, Annemarie. *Make a Shield from Wisdom: Selected Verses from Nāṣir-i Khusraw's 'Dīvān'*. London: The Institute of Ismaili Studies, 1993.

Schimmel, Annemarie. *A Two-Colored Brocade: The Imagery of Persian Poetry*. Chapel Hill: University of North Carolina Press, 1992.

Schimmel, Annemarie and Franz Carl Endres. *The Mystery of Numbers*. New York: Oxford University Press, 1993.

Schoeler, Gregor. 'Bashshār b. Burd, Abū'l-'Atāhiyah and Abū Nuwās'. In *Abbasid Belles Lettres*, edited by Julia Ashtiany, T. M. Johnstone, J. D. Latham and R. B. Serjeant, 275–99. Cambridge: Cambridge University Press, 1990.

Schoeler, Gregor. *The Genesis of Literature in Islam: From the Aural to the Read*. Translated by Shawkat M. Toorawa. Edinburgh: Edinburgh University Press, 2009.

Schoeler, Gregor. 'The Genres of Classical Arabic Poetry: Classifications of Poetic Themes and Poems by Pre-modern Critics and Redactors of *Dīwāns*'. *Quaderni di Studi Arabi* 5/6 (2010–11): 1–48.

Sells, Michael. *Mystical Languages of Unsaying*. Chicago: University of Chicago Press, 1994.

Seyed-Gohrab, Ali Asghar. 'Casing the Treasury: The *Safīna-yi Tabrīz* and Its Compiler'. In *The Treasury of Tabriz: The Great Ilkhanid Compendium*, edited by Ali Asghar Seyed-Gohrab and S. McGlinn, 15–42. West Lafayette, IN: Purdue University Press, 2007.

Seyed-Gohrab, Ali Asghar. 'The Flourishing of Persian Quatrains'. In *Persian Lyric Poetry in the Classical Era: Ghazals, Panegyrics, Quatrains*, edited by Ehsan

Yarshater, 488–568. Vol. 2 of *A History of Persian Literature*, edited by Ehsan Yarshater. London: I. B. Tauris, 2019.

Seyed-Gohrab, Ali Asghar. *Laylī and Majnūn: Love, Madness and Mystic Longing in Niẓāmī's Epic Romance*. Leiden: Brill, 2003.

Seyed-Gohrab, Ali Asghar and S. McGlinn, eds. *The Treasury of Tabriz: The Great Il-Khanid Compendium*. West Lafayette, IN: Purdue University Press, 2007.

Shabestari, Mahmud. *Majmu'a-ye asar-e Shaykh Mahmud Shabestari*. Edited by Samad Movahhed. Tehran: Tahuri, 1365 [1986–7].

Shackle, Christopher. 'Representations of ʿAṭṭār in the West and in the East: Translations of *Manṭiq al-ṭayr* and the Tale of Shaykh Ṣanʿān'. In *'Aṭṭār and the Persian Sufi Tradition: The Art of Spiritual Flight*, edited by Leonard Lewisohn and Christopher Shackle, 165–93. London: I. B. Tauris, 2006.

Shafiʿi-Kadkani, Mohammad Reza. Introduction to *Asrar al-towhid fi maqamat al-Shaykh Abi Sa'id*, by Mohammad b. Monavvar, v–ccxxxix. Tehran: Agah, 1389 [2010].

Shafiʿi-Kadkani, Mohammad Reza. Introduction to *Manteq al-tayr*, by Farid al-Din 'Attar, 17–230. 2nd ed. Tehran: Sokhan, 1387 [2008–9].

Shafiʿi-Kadkani, Mohammad Reza. Introduction to *Mokhtar-nama*, by Farid al-Din 'Attar, 11–66. 2nd ed. Tehran: Sokhan, 1389 [2010–11].

Shafiʿi-Kadkani, Mohammad Reza, ed. *Zabur-e parsi: Negahi be zendagi va ghazalha-ye 'Attar*. Tehran: Agah, 1378 [1999–2000].

Shahnavaz, S. '*Afyūn*'. In *Encyclopaedia Iranica*. Article posted 2020. https://doi.org/10.1163/2330-4804_EIRO_COM_4866.

Shaked, Shaul. '*Andarz* i. *Andarz* and *Andarz* Literature in Pre-Islamic Iran'. In *Encyclopaedia Iranica*. Article posted 2020. https://doi.org/10.1163/2330-4804_EIRO_COM_5432.

Shaked, Shaul. 'Specimens of Middle Persian Verse'. In *W. B. Henning Memorial Volume*, edited by Mary Boyce and Ilya Gershevitch, 395–405. London: Lund Humphries, 1970.

Shamisa, Sirus. *Sayr-e roba'i dar she'r-e farsi*. Tehran: Ashtiani, 1363 [1984].

Shamisa, Sirus. *Shahed-bazi dar adabiyat-e farsi*. Tehran: Ferdows, 1381 [2002–3].

Shams-e Qays. *al-Mo'jam fi ma'ayer ash'ar al-'ajam*. Edited by Mohammad Qazvini, Modarres-e Rezavi and Sirus Shamisa. Tehran: 'Elm, 1388 [2009–10].

Shelley, Percy. *Shelley's Poetry and Prose*. Edited by Donald H. Reiman and Neil Fraistat. 2nd ed. New York: Norton, 2002.

Shushtari, Sayyed Nurollah. *Majales al-mo'menin*. 2 vols. Tehran: Ketab-forushi-ye Eslamiya, 1365 [1986–7].

Silvers-Alario, Laury. 'The Teaching Relationship in Early Sufism: A Reassessment of Fritz Meier's Definition of the *Shaykh al-tarbiya* and the *Shaykh al-ta'līm*'. *The Muslim World* 93 (2003): 69–97.

Sís, Peter. *The Conference of the Birds*. New York: Penguin, 2011.

Sohravardi, Shehab al-Din Yahya. *Majmu'a-ye mosannafat-e Shaykh-e Eshraq*. Edited by Seyyed Hossein Nasr. Tehran: Anjoman-e Shahanshahi-ye Falsafa-ye Iran, 1976–77.

Stepien, Rafal. 'A Study in Sufi Poetics: The Case of 'Aṭṭār Nayshābūrī'. *Oriens* 41 (2013): 77–120.

Stern, David. *Parables in Midrash*. Cambridge, MA: Harvard University Press, 1991.

Stetkevych, Suzanne Pinckney. *The Mantle Odes: Arabic Praise Poems to the Prophet Muhammad*. Bloomington: Indiana University Press, 2010.

Stetkevych, Suzanne Pinckney. *The Poetics of Islamic Legitimacy: Myth, Gender, and Ceremony in the Classical Arabic Ode*. Bloomington: Indiana University Press, 2002.

Stewart, Devin. 'The *Maqāma*'. In *Arabic Literature in the Post-classical Period*, edited by Roger Allen and D. S. Richards, 145–58. Cambridge: Cambridge University Press, 2006.

Stock, Brian. *After Augustine: The Meditative Reader and the Text*. Philadelphia: University of Philadelphia Press, 2001.

Stone, Lucian. 'Blessed Perplexity: The Topos of *Ḥayrat* in Farīd al-Dīn 'Aṭṭār's *Manṭiq al-ṭayr*'. PhD diss., Southern Illinois University, 2005.

Stone, Lucian. '"Blessed Perplexity": The Topos of *Ḥayrat* in 'Aṭṭār's *Manṭiq al-Ṭayr*'. In *'Aṭṭār and the Persian Sufi Tradition: The Art of Spiritual Flight*, edited by Leonard Lewisohn and Christopher Shackle, 95–111. London: I. B. Tauris, 2006.

Struck, Peter T. 'Allegory and Ascent in Neoplatonism'. In *The Cambridge Companion to Allegory*, edited by Rita Copeland and Peter T. Struck, 57–70. Cambridge: Cambridge University Press, 2010.

Struck, Peter T. *Birth of the Symbol: Ancient Readers at the Limits of Their Texts*. Princeton: Princeton University Press, 2004.

Suhrawardi, Abu Hafs 'Umar. *'Awarif al-ma'arif*. Beirut: Dar al-Kitab al-'Arabi, 1983.

Sviri, Sara. 'Ḥakīm Tirmidhī and the Malāmatī Movement in Early Sufism'. In *Classical Persian Sufism: From Its Origins to Rumi*, edited by Leonard Lewisohn, 583–613. London: Khaniqahi Nimatullahi Publications, 1993.

Swartz, Merlin. 'Arabic Rhetoric and the Art of the Homily in Medieval Islam'. In

Religion and Culture in Medieval Islam, edited by Richard G. Hovannisian and Georges Sabagh, 36–65. Cambridge: Cambridge University Press, 1999.

Swartz, Merlin. 'The Rules of Popular Preaching in Twelfth-Century Baghdad, according to Ibn al-Jawzī'. In *Prédication et propagande au Moyen Age: Islam, Byzance, Occident*, edited by George Makdisi, Dominique Sourdel and Janine Sourdel-Thomine, 223–39. Paris: Presses universitaires de France, 1983.

Tabari, Mohammad b. Ayyub. *Tohfat al-ghara'eb*. Edited by Jalal Matini. Tehran: Ketabkhana, Muza, va Markez-e Asnad-e Majles-e Shura-ye Eslami, 1391 [2012–13].

Tabrizi, Abu'l-Majd Mohammad b. Mas'ud. *Safina-ye Tabriz: Chap-e 'aksi az ru-ye noskha-ye khatti-ye Ketabkhana-ye Majles-e Shura-ye Eslami*. Tehran: Markez-e Nashr-e Daneshgahi, 1381 [2001–2].

Tafazzoli, Ahmad. 'Andarz i Wehzād Farrox Pērōz, Containing a Pahlavi Poem in Praise of Wisdom'. *Studia Iranica* 1, no. 2 (1972): 207–17.

Talattof, Kamran. 'Nizāmī Ganjavi, the Wordsmith: The Concept of *Sakhun* in Classical Persian Poetry'. In *A Key to the Treasure of the Hakīm: Artistic and Humanistic Aspects of Nizāmī Ganjavī's 'Khamsa'*, edited by Johann-Christoph Bürgel and Christine van Ruymbeke, 211–44. Leiden: Leiden University Press, 2011.

Talmon-Heller, Daniella. *Islamic Piety in Medieval Syria: Mosques, Cemeteries and Sermons under the Zangids and Ayyūbids (1146–1260)*. Leiden: Brill, 2007.

Tawhidi, Abu Hayyan. *al-Imta' wa'l-mu'anasa*. Beirut: Dar al-Kutub al-'Ilmiyya, 1317 [1997].

Tha'labi, Abu Ishaq. *'Arā'is al-majālis fī qiṣaṣ al-anbiyā'; or, Lives of the Prophets*. Translated by William M. Brinner. Leiden: Brill, 2002.

Toohey, Peter. *Epic Lessons: An Introduction to Didactic Poetry*. London: Routledge, 1996.

Toorawa, Shawkat. *Ibn Abī Ṭāhir Ṭayfūr and Arabic Writerly Culture: A Ninth-Century Bookman in Baghdad*. London: RoutledgeCurzon, 2005.

Trilling, Lionel. *Sincerity and Authenticity*. Cambridge, MA: Harvard University Press, 1972.

Utas, Bo. 'Classical Persian Literature: Fiction, Didactics or Intuitive Truth?'. In *True Lies Worldwide: Fictionality in Global Contexts*, edited by Anders Cullhed and Lena Rydholm, 167–77. Berlin: De Gruyter, 2014.

Utas, Bo. 'A Journey to the Other World according to the *Lantern of Spirits*'. *Bulletin of the Asia Institute*, n.s., 4 (1990): 307–11.

Van Gelder, Geert Jan. 'Some Brave Attempts at Generic Classification'. In *Aspects of Genre and Type in Pre-modern Literary Cultures*, edited by Bert Roest and Herman Vanstiphout, 15–31. Groningen: Styx, 1999.

Van Gelder, Geert Jan. 'Traditional Literary Theory: The Arabic Background'. In *General Introduction to Persian Literature*, edited by J. T. P. de Bruijn, 123–38. Vol. 1 of *A History of Persian Literature*, edited by Ehsan Yarshater. London: I. B. Tauris, 2009.

Van Ruymbeke, Christine. *Kāshefi's "Anvār-e sohayli": Rewriting "Kalila and Dimna" in Timurid Herat*. Leiden: Brill, 2016.

Vuckovic, Brooke Olson. *Heavenly Journeys, Earthly Concerns: The Legacy of the* Miʿrāj *in the Formation of Islam*. New York: Routledge, 2005.

Wacks, David A. *Framing Iberia:* Maqāmāt *and Frametale Narratives in Medieval Spain*. Leiden: Brill, 2007.

Waley, Muhammad Isa. "Aziz al-Din Nasafi on Spiritual Retreat'. *Sufi* 17 (1993): 5–9.

Waley, Muhammad Isa. 'Contemplative Disciplines in Early Persian Sufism'. In *Classical Persian Sufism: From Its Origins to Rumi*, edited by Leonard Lewisohn, 497–548. London: Khaniqahi Nimatullahi Publications, 1999.

Waley, Muhammad Isa. 'Didactic Style and Self-criticism in 'Aṭṭār'. In *'Aṭṭār and the Persian Sufi Tradition: The Art of Spiritual Flight*, edited by Leonard Lewisohn and Christopher Shackle, 215–40. London: I. B. Tauris, 2006.

Weightman, Simon. 'Spiritual Progression in Books One and Two of the *Mathnawī*'. In *The Philosophy of Ecstasy: Rumi and the Sufi Tradition*, edited by Leonard Lewisohn, 269–79. Bloomington, IN: World Wisdom, 2014.

Wilcox, Andrew. 'The Dual Mystical Concepts of *Fanā'* and *Baqā'* in Early Sūfism'. *British Journal of Middle Eastern Studies* 38, no. 1 (2011): 95–118.

Williams, Alan. 'Open Heart Surgery: The Operation of Love in Rūmī's *Mathnawī*'. In *The Philosophy of Ecstasy: Rumi and the Sufi Tradition*, edited by Leonard Lewisohn, 199–227. Bloomington, IN: World Wisdom, 2014.

Wimsatt W. K., Jr and M. C. Beardsley. 'The Intentional Fallacy'. *The Sewanee Review* 54, no. 3 (1946): 468–88.

Wolf, Werner. 'Framing Borders in Frame Stories'. In *Framing Borders in Literature and Other Media*, edited by Werner Wolf and Walter Bernhart, 179–206. Amsterdam: Rodopi, 2006.

Yaghoobi, Claudia. 'Against the Current: Farid al-Din 'Attar's Diverse Voices'. *Persian Literary Studies Journal* 1, no. 1 (2012): 87–109.

Yaghoobi, Claudia. *Subjectivity in 'Aṭṭār, Persian Sufism, and European Mysticism*. West Lafayette, IN: Purdue University Press, 2017.

Yaghoobi, Claudia. 'Subjectivity in 'Attār's Shaykh of San'ān Story in *The Conference of the Birds*'. *CLCWeb: Comparative Literature and Culture* 16, no. 1 (2014): https://doi.org/10.7771/1481-4374.2425.

Zahiremami, Parisa. 'Sanā'ī's *Hadiqat al-Haqiqeh*: Between Narrative and Non-narrative'. *Iranian Studies* 54, no. 3–4 (2021): 485–519.

Zakeri, Mohsen. 'The *Rawshanā'ī-nāma* and the Older Iranian Cosmogony'. In *Pearls of Persia: The Philosophical Poetry of Nāṣir Khusraw*, edited by Alice C. Hunsberger, 103–16. London: I. B. Tauris, 2012.

Zakeri, Mohsen. 'Ṣāliḥ b. 'Abd al-Ḳuddūs'. In *Encyclopaedia of Islam, Second Edition*. Article posted 2012. https://doi.org/10.1163/1573-3912_islam_SIM_6537.

Zaman, Muhammad Qasim. '*Ahl al-ḥall wa-l-'aqd*'. In *Encyclopaedia of Islam, Three*. Article posted 2007. https://doi.org/10.1163/1573-3912_ei3_COM_0027.

Zargar, Cyrus Ali. *The Polished Mirror: Storytelling and the Pursuit of Virtue in Islamic Philosophy and Sufism*. London: Oneworld, 2017.

Zarrinkub, 'Abdolhosayn. *Ba karavan-e andisha: Maqalat va esharat dar zamina-ye andisha va akhlaq*. Tehran: Amir Kabir, 1363 [1984].

Index

Note: n indicates note, t indicates table, *italic* indicates figure